Education for Extinction

Education for Extinction

AMERICAN INDIANS AND THE
BOARDING SCHOOL EXPERIENCE,
1875–1928

David Wallace Adams

University Press of Kansas

For my parents
William Wallace Adams
and
Winona Marie Adams

Published by the University Press of Kansas (Lawrence, Kansas 66049), which was organized by the Kansas Board of Regents and is operated and funded by Emporia State University, Fort Hays State University, Kansas State University, Pittsburg State University, the
University of Kansas, and Wichita State University

Library of Congress Cataloging-in-Publication Data

Adams, David Wallace.
    Education for extinction : American Indians and the boarding
  school experience, 1875–1928 / David Wallace Adams.
      p.   cm.
    Includes bibliographical references and index.
    ISBN 0-7006-0735-8
    1. Indian youth—Education—United States.   2. Indian youth—
  Government policy—United States.   3. Indian youth—Cultural
  assimilation—United States.   4. Boarding schools—United States—
  History—19th century.   5. Boarding schools—United States—
  History—20th century.   6. Education and state—United States—
  History.   7. United States—Social policy.   8. United States—Race
  relations.   I. Title.
  E97.5.A35   1995
  371.97'97—dc20   95-7638

British Library Cataloguing in Publication Data is available.

Printed in the United States of America

10 9 8 7 6 5 4 3 2 1

The paper used in this publication meets the minimum requirements of the American
National Standard for Permanence of Paper for Printed Library Materials Z39.48–1984.

CONTENTS

ILLUSTRATIONS AND TABLES

Tables

Figures

Photographs

vii

PREFACE

In some respects the idea for this book originated some forty-five years ago. Growing up in southern California's "inland empire," or citrus ranch country, I frequently had occasion to be part of a family outing to the seacoast, a journey which took us through the community of Riverside. I still recall the keen sense of anticipation I felt when our 1941 pale green Pontiac sedan made the diagonal turn from Market Street onto Magnolia Avenue. Bordered by huge, stately palms and pungent-smelling eucalyptus and pepper trees, Magnolia would take us past Sherman Institute, the Indian school. In a few minutes it appeared, an impressive institution built in the mission revival architectural style characteristic of turn-of-the-century California. So Indians lived and went to school here. The idea fascinated me. And even though I rarely caught a glimpse of a "real" Indian, several questions came to mind. Why was this school located in Riverside, a community seemingly devoid of Indians? What was it like to be an Indian in such a school? Didn't they miss their parents? What happened when they got sick? Did they go to church? What in fact were they thinking and feeling? Our Pontiac sped on, the Spanish red-tiled roofs disappearing among the row of grey-green palms and eucalyptus. But the questions never went away. Finally, after nearly twenty years of research, I think I have some of the answers.

This study is the story of how policymakers sought to use the schoolhouse—specifically the boarding schools—as an instrument for acculturating Indian youth to "American" ways of thinking and living. The study has a three-tiered focus. On one level it is a study of policy formulation, how reformers and government officials came to look upon education as a central feature of the new Indian policy. Second, it offers a detailed analysis of how educational policy was translated into institutional practice, describing the entire process whereby Indian agents, school superintendents, teachers, and staff went about the business of "civilizing" Indian youth. Finally, it describes how students responded to these efforts, including the story of what happened when they returned to their reservation homes.

For several reasons this project turned out to be a much bigger undertaking than originally anticipated. For one thing, this study is comprehensive in scope. Although utilizing case studies to illustrate larger themes, this book is not about a single institution or Indian group. From the beginning I rejected this approach in the belief that the paucity of Indian source material required a much broader perspective if the larger patterns of student response were to be discerned. This assumption, it turns out, was well-founded. (The only schools specifically exempted from this study are those associated with the so-called "five civilized tribes," a story sufficiently unique as to require a separate investigation altogether, a project I leave to others.) Second, I clearly underestimated the amount of published scholarship having direct bearing on some particular aspect of my inquiry. In the course of my research I have had to explore such diverse subjects as cross-cultural gender roles, the function of rituals, the anthropology of sport, Native American spirituality, acculturation theory, Indian health issues, and the nature of "total institutions." Finally, there were those times when I faced the difficulty of making even superficial generalizations on subjects that I expected—mistakenly it turns out—to be fairly well-trod territory. I was surprised to discover, for instance, that even though historians have written voluminously on the background of teachers who went south to teach freedmen during the Reconstruction Era, not a single scholarly article exists on the background and experience of teachers, mostly women, who joined the Indian school service.

A word on voice. Or rather voices. I have written this book with a sort of double consciousness. On the one hand, I have attempted to lay bare the social and ideological outlook of those whites responsible for the creation of the boarding school system. Only when one understands reformers' assumptions and beliefs about the nature and fate of Indian America, I would argue, can one appreciate the full meaning of the educational programs they prescribed and designed. For this reason, in the early chapters especially, the words "civilization," "civilize," "savagism," and "savage" are widely used throughout the text, not because they offer an accurate description of the cultural dichotomies or processes involved but rather because they represent the deep-seated ethnocentric, if not racist, vision of policymakers. At the same time, this book seeks to describe in as realistic fashion as possible the nature and meaning of the boarding school experience from the Indian students' perspective. As any historian well knows, the problems involved in giving voice to Indians, a group for whom the documentary record is both sparse and unreliable, are legion. The additional challenge involved in representing the experience of a subgroup of this population, Indian children, seemed at times almost unsurmountable. Whether I have succeeded in this effort is for the reader to decide.

One thing is for certain: my childhood fascination with the Indian school, and by extension with all Indian schools, was justified. Established for the sole purpose of severing the child's cultural and psychological connection to his native heritage, this unique institution figured prominently in the federal government's desire to find a solution to the "Indian problem," a method of saving Indians by destroying them. Years later, when I would come to know and work with Native Americans, their stories confirmed what I had long suspected: attending boarding school had been one of the defining experiences of their lives. The story needs to be told.

In the process of researching and writing I have benefited from the aid and advice of numerous individuals and institutions. First, I owe an inestimable debt of gratitude to the archivists and librarians at the following institutions: the National Archives; the Smithsonian Institution; the Beinecke Rare Book and Manuscript Library, Yale University; Hampton University; Sherman Institute Museum; Phoenix Indian School; Haskell Indian Nations University; University of New Mexico; Indiana University; Arizona Historical Society; Elizabeth M. Watkins Community Museum, Lawrence, Kansas; and the Cleveland Public Library. I owe a special thanks to Cleveland State University, which has over the years generously supported my research efforts.

Numerous scholars and friends have offered criticism and encouragement along the way. I count among these Joseph Epes Brown, Shirley Engle, Edward B. McClelland, James D. Anderson, Francis Paul Prucha, Bernard Sheehan, Wilcomb E. Washburn, Norris Hundley, Floyd Adams, Marvin Pasch, Harrison J. Means, Margaret Gallagher, and Carol Takacs. Words cannot express my appreciation to William J. Reese, Patrick Miller, and Michael C. Coleman, all of whom gave generously of their time in reading portions of the manuscript.

Two individuals who deserve special attention are Linda Jackson and Maxine Paolucci for their undying patience in converting my original handwritten manuscript, through seemingly endless revisions, to typescript.

Finally, I owe the deepest debt of gratitude to my wife, Vicki, and our three children, Jason, Nathaniel, and Amanda, for allowing me to devote countless evenings, weekends, and summers to this project.

Prologue: 1882

For Herbert Welsh and Henry Pancoast, the journey from Philadelphia to Chicago had been ordinary enough, the railroad cars filled with middle-class passengers traveling from one great American city to another that was on the threshold of greatness. But the atmosphere on the westbound train out of Chicago was altogether different. Their traveling companions were now a much cruder lot—black-bearded westerners, gamblers, Iowa farmers, Norwegian and German immigrants. And then there was the endless space. Between Philadelphia and Chicago the landscape had been speckled with farms, churches, and schoolhouses. Now there were few signs of civilization.

"All day we pushed steadily into the level silence," Pancoast later wrote, "yet at sunset there was nothing to tell us we had advanced a foot. The only change was that from long, flat, treeless stretches to a more undulating country, where the mighty plain gathers itself in grassy swells, full of free, delicious curves and soft hollows." Now there was just the land. But someday there would be more. Much more. Meanwhile, "the earth seemed waiting, after the primeval fashion, for man to come in and possess it." And slowly, gradually, it was being possessed. The signs of civilization were already there—in the occasional cluster of immigrant shacks, the land offices, and the plows being unloaded at railroad junctions—and soon there would be farms, churches, and schools. Such was the nature of progress.

Finally, the puffing locomotive pulled into Chamberlain in Dakota Territory. Here, on the eastern bank of the Missouri River, both the railroad and white civilization came to an abrupt halt. But Welsh and Pancoast, both Philadelphia lawyers, were going still further west, "for on the other side of the fierce waters of the Missouri is another race and another order of things"—Sioux country. The decision to make the trip west had actually been Welsh's idea. As the nephew of William Welsh, a renowned Episcopalian minister and first chairman of the Board of Indian Commissioners, the younger Welsh had been invited by an old family friend, Bishop William Hare, to view conditions among the Sioux where Hare had labored for years as a missionary. No doubt Hare's motive was to enlist the younger Welsh in the work of Indian reform. If such was the Bishop's thinking, it was a stroke of brilliance, for both Welsh and Pancoast were affected deeply by what they saw and were immediately drawn to the cause.

Shortly after their return to Philadelphia, both travelers published detailed accounts of their four-week journey. Their separate renderings are instructive, not so much for what they reveal about life among the Sioux, but for what they reveal about the sensitivities, beliefs, and values of a new generation of reformers. Both Welsh and Pancoast portrayed Indian-white relations as being at a critical juncture. "The rush of Western settlement grows more and more; an enormous army pours continually into our Eastern seaports to spread itself over the West," Pancoast reported. Living a Stone Age existence, Indians could never withstand the never-ending onslaught of white settlement. Furthermore, the tide of progress could not be stopped. Hence, "We must either butcher them or civilize them, and what we do we must do quickly."

Both Welsh and Pancoast, of course, were horrified at the former prospect, and their journey had left them with the firm conviction that a reformed Indian policy was capable of transforming backward primitives into fully civilized members of the human race, fit candidates for American citizenship. According to Welsh, the Indian was "not a wild beast whose extermination is necessary to the safety of a higher order of creation, but a man for whom honor, purity, knowledge and love are not only within the range of possibility, but are qualities which already in numberless instances have been attained."

The two men had caught a glimpse of a new era in the mission schools at Yankton and Santee. After seeing the cultural offspring of Sitting Bull scratch their ABC's on slate tablets and ply newfound carpentry skills, the solution to the Indian question seemed close at hand. For Pancoast:

> Among all my remembrances of Dakota there is one that has for me a peculiar and serene beauty. The remembrance of one of those wonderful sunsets in an atmosphere of crystal clearness. . . . In front of a school-house, a ring of Indian children playing Jacob and Rachel. I can see now the free, unconscious grace of their motions, and hear the childish giggles and screams of laughter, and the funny little accent with which they shouted "Jakup" and "Rashel."
>
> I looked at these children and thought of the hideous record of unrighteous greed and bloody retaliation that makes up the sad story of their race, and of the lives that lay before them that they thought of so little. Yet to look at them is to hope. Mournful and oppressed as the condition of their race is, it may be that out of the darkness and the bondage "a little child shall lead them."[1]

PART ONE

Civilization

CHAPTER ONE

Reform

It would be difficult to imagine a hypothetical instance of cultural conflict more fundamental than that which occurred in the seventeenth century when European-Americans confronted Native American populations in the forests of New England and Virginia. In the next 200 years, as whites pushed further west, the same confrontation would occur again and again on successive frontiers. Cultural interaction and conflict are always subtle and complex processes but they are not always as devastatingly one-sided as in the case of Indians and whites. As the Iroquois, the Shawnee, and the Arapaho would eventually all discover, the white man's superior technology, hunger for land, and ethnocentrism seemingly knew no bounds. The white threat to Indians came in many forms: smallpox, missionaries, Conestoga wagons, barbed wire, and smoking locomotives. And in the end, it came in the form of schools.

In the 1790s, no question was more pressing for the new national government than that of deciding the future status of Indians. In the main, the policy issue could be reduced to this fact: Indians possessed the land, and whites wanted the land. In addressing this dilemma, the early architects of federal Indian policy never doubted that the vast wilderness stretching to the west would one day fall into white hands. It was not simply a matter of greed. On the contrary, the very survival of the republic demanded that Indians be dispossessed of the land. According to prevailing Lockean theory, only a society built upon the broad foundation of private property could guarantee public morality, political independence, and social stability. It followed that the fate of the republic was inextricably linked to an almost endless supply of free or cheap land; and if the nation possessed anything, it possessed an inexhaustible supply of land. Or rather, Indians possessed it. For early policymakers, then, a major priority was the creation of a mechanism and rationale for divesting Indians of their real estate. The matter was an especially delicate one, for although the divestiture of Indian land was essential to the extension of American ideals, that divestiture must also be ultimately justified by those same ideals. The problem was a difficult one.[1]

In the search for a resolution to this dilemma, policymakers were served well by long-standing images of Indians and their lifeways.[2] Basic to all perceptions was the conclusion that because Indian cultural patterns were vastly different from those of whites, Indians must be inferior. Whether discussing the Indians' worship of pagan gods, their simple tribal organization, or their dependency on wild game for subsistance, white observers found Indian society wanting. Indian life, it was argued, constituted a lower order of human society. In a word, Indians were savages because they lacked the very thing whites possessed—civilization. And since, by the law of historical progress and the doctrine of social evolution civilized ways were destined to triumph over savagism, Indians would ultimately confront a fateful choice: civilization or extinction. That the race would choose civilized ways or savage ways, there was little doubt. Wasn't civilization preferable to savagism? Wasn't life preferable to death?[3]

Viewing Indian-white relations in this context, policymakers were prepared to resolve the land question. Again, the answer lay in the Indians' civilization. Noting that the approach of white civilization always depleted the supply of wild game available to adjacent Indian populations, policymakers reasoned that red hunters would find it in their self-interest to take up sedentary agriculture. Moreover, once transformed into farmers, they would require less land, which would then be available to whites. In 1803, Jefferson observed that this ongoing process was in fact producing a "coincidence of interests" between the races. Indians, having land in abundance, needed civilization; whites possessed civilization but needed land. Upon this convenient conjoinment of greed and philanthropy an Indian policy slowly emerged.[4] In 1818, the House Committee on Indian Affairs urged Congress, "Put into the hands of their children the primer and the hoe, and they will naturally, in time, take hold of the plough; and, as their minds become enlightened and expand, the Bible will be their book, and they will grow up in habits of morality and industry, leave the chase to those whose minds are less cultivated, and become useful members of society." A year later Congress created the Civilization Fund, an annual appropriation of $10,000 to be administered by Thomas L. McKenny, the nation's first Superintendent of Indian Affairs.[5]

But the civilization program—an effort carried out mainly by missionary societies—proved unequal to the challenge at hand. Insufficient resources, the presence of land-hungry, Indian-hating frontiersmen who would rather lift Indian scalps than serve as guides and models of civilized living, and finally, the naive assumption that Indian students, once instructed in the ways of civilization, would readily shed their cultural skins for white ones all contributed to disappointing results.[6] These factors caused some observers to conclude what many had maintained all along: Indians might be incapable of transformation and thus were destined for extinction. For writers and artists there were endless metaphors and images to describe what was transpiring on the frontier: Indians—like the melting snow in the morning sunlight, like forest leaves withering in the chill air of autumn, like wild beasts retreating before the sound of the settler's axe—were a vanishing race. By the late 1820s political leadership was searching for a short-term policy that would simultaneously serve the demands of both empire and philanthropy. The result was Indian removal. Beyond the Mississippi, it was argued, Indians might for a time live according to their preferred customs, but more importantly, with the help of the government and missionaries, they would continue to make progress in learning the ways of civilization, unmolested now by the avarice of land-hungry whites.[7]

Unfortunately, demarcations intended to restrict Indian-white contact never lasted for long. In the 1840s Oregon land fever and dreams of California gold were sufficient motivations to prompt settlers, miners, and other frontier types to breach the Indian barrier. What began as a trickle soon became a flood, and the nomadic tribes of the Central Plains, whose fragile lifeways were enmeshed with the vast stretches of prairie grass and the great bison herds, found their way of life threatened as well. In 1851, 10,000 warriors, among them the Sioux, the Cheyenne, and the Arapaho, gathered in the West at Fort Laramie, signed a treaty by the same name, and agreed for the first time to live within specified boundaries. After the Civil War, the coming of the railroad, the telegraph, and a network of military forts further constricted the Indians' freedom of movement. Homesteaders, cattlemen, and sheepmen were close behind. Conflict was inevitable, and it came regularly in the form of thirty years of intermittent but bloody warfare. And then, as one tribe after another was crushed on the battlefield, after the great bison herds were all but exterminated, it was suddenly over. A new phase of Indian policy was slowly emerging—the reservation system. In 1871, Congress officially confirmed the altered status of Indians: they were now deemed to be wards of the government, a colonized people.[8]

These developments did not escape the notice and wrath of philanthropic observers who decried not so much the Indians' altered status as the often cruel and brutal manner in which it had been accomplished. Critics also focused on the mounting evidence that the Office of Indian Affairs, or as it was commonly known, the Indian Office or Indian Bureau—the division of the Department of the Interior charged with the administration of Indian affairs—was riddled with corruption from top to bottom. The result of these criticisms was the celebrated but short-lived Peace Policy announced by President Ulysses S. Grant in 1869. The Peace Policy was three-pronged: henceforth agency or reservation personnel would be appointed by church boards of the various religious denominations; federal support for educational programs would be expanded; and finally, the president would appoint a group of eminent philanthropists, a

Board of Indian Commissioners, whose responsibility it would be both to independently review and to jointly administer Indian policy with the Secretary of the Interior. But the new policy had scarcely gotten off the ground before it collapsed. Politicians, who coveted the Indian service with its growing number of field appointments as an endless source of patronage, and the Indian Office, which frowned on any attempt to reduce its control over the administration of Indian affairs, almost immediately began a campaign to frustrate and emasculate the power of the church boards to appoint agency officials. Similarly, the scope of the Board of Indian Commissioners' authority was shortly curtailed to that of issuing periodic advisory reports. All in all, little changed.[9]

By the early 1880s a chorus of voices from the pulpit, press, and Congress were again calling for a major overhaul of Indian policy. Several factors now aided the cause of reform. First, during the Peace Policy era the issue of Indian policy had competed for attention with the issues of Reconstruction; by the late 1870s this was no longer the case. Second, with Indians all but completely subjugated, talk of a military solution seemed increasingly inhumane to everyone except the most virulent Indian-hater. Meanwhile, one scandal after another continued to expose the entire Indian system as an ineffectual and graft-ridden bureaucracy. The image of the Indian agent, fraudulently lining his pockets while starving Indians feasted on diseased cattle and worm-infested flour, was now firmly fixed in the public mind. Still another factor was the tragic and heartrending accounts of Indian suffering in the West. Press stories about the attempt of a band of Poncas to reach their former home on the banks of the Missouri, the desperate and futile flight of the Northern Cheyenne from a hated reservation in Indian Territory, and the efforts of Chief Joseph and his band of Nez Percé to retain their home in the cherished Wallowa Valley were poignant reminders that the nation's Indian policy was based on shaky moral principles. Finally, reformers found a powerful spokesperson for their cause in Helen Hunt Jackson. In 1881, Jackson's *A Century of Dishonor: A Sketch of the United States Government's Dealings with Some of the Indian Tribes* recounted a hundred years of government deceit in Indian affairs and concluded that the nation's treatment of the red man constituted a dark and bloody stain on the nation's honor. Few were prepared to argue otherwise.[10]

By 1880, something approaching a consensus was emerging on the Indian question. Public discussions of the issue now increasingly concluded with the judgment that the government's treatment of its Indian wards had been unnecessarily shortsighted, harsh, and even cruel. It was time for a change. And not surprisingly, as discussion turned to the future, an old and familiar theme reasserted itself: Indians not only needed to be saved from the white man, they needed to be saved from themselves. In the beginning, it was remembered, Indians had been promised the gift of civilization in exchange for their land. Indian land, for the most part, was now white land. Indians, on the other hand, were still largely savages. It was time to redeem an old promise.

As reformers struggled to reorient Indian policy, tribal elders reflected on all that had taken place. So much had changed and it had happened so quickly. The land was gone. The buffalo were gone. The old ways were dying. There seemed to be no end to it. And what ordeals lay ahead? "I know that my race must change," said Joseph of the Nez Percé. "We can not hold our own with the white man as we are."[11] But how much change? Must hunters take up the plow? Must the sacred ways of the ancestors be thrown over for the black book of the missionary? And what of the children? Perhaps that was the most difficult question of all. What would become of the children? The answer was not long in coming.

THE NEW REFORMERS

Herbert Welsh and Henry Pancoast had scarcely returned from their sojourn among the Sioux in the fall of 1882 than they took up the cause of Indian reform. As Welsh later recalled, the journey had resulted in two firm conclusions: first, that Indians were capable of being assimilated into the mainstream of American life; and second, that the only barrier to achieving this objective was the lack of a sustained political will to do so. What was needed, the two men concurred, was a new organization devoted to molding political opinion along philanthropic lines. Toward this end, Welsh invited some thirty individuals of like persuasion to his Philadelphia home to consider the matter. The result was a new reform organization, the Indian Rights Association. The association, according to an early publication, sought "to secure the civilization of the two hundred and ninety thousand Indians of the United States (inclusive of the thirty thousand natives of Alaska), and to prepare the way for their absorption into the common life of our own people."[12]

For several reasons the Indian Rights Association soon established itself as the most influential force on the reform scene. First, there was the indefatigable energy and organizational abilities of Welsh, the association's director, whose capacity for speech-making and correspondence knew no bounds. Beyond this were the coordinated strategies adopted by the association to exert pressure on policymakers. Believing that the path to reform lay in galvanizing public opinion, the association, through its annual reports and special reports on selected issues, was soon turning out a steady stream of position statements on all aspects of Indian policy. A particularly unique feature of the association's work was that it periodically conducted investigations of conditions in the field. Whereas other reform organizations could speak with moral authority on the broad question of reform, the Indian Rights Association was able to address specific issues and events at the agency level of operations, often possessing facts more accurate than those available to the Indian Office. Finally, the association maximized its political influence by maintaining a full-time lobbyist in Washington. Over the years Charles C. Painter, Francis E. Leupp, and Samuel M. Brosius would serve in this post, patiently waiting in the outer office of the Commissioner of Indian Affairs or a congressman to press a point of interest.[13]

The Indian Rights Association, although the single most important reform body, was not the only one. In fact, by late 1883 it was only one of five such organizations dedicated to resolving the Indian problem along philanthropic lines. The oldest of these bodies, the Board of Indian Commissioners, was a holdover from the Peace Policy era. Although the board had been stripped of most of its powers by the mid-1870s, reduced to the ritual of issuing annual reports on the status of Indian affairs, it helped lay the groundwork for the new reform agenda. Thus, when reform fever reached a new high in the early 1880s, the Board of Indian Commissioners was well prepared to assume a place of significance in the philanthropic network.[14]

Two other reform organizations made their appearance in 1879. The Boston Indian Citizenship Association was the direct outgrowth of the public fury surrounding the forced removal of the much abused Poncas from their Dakota homeland. After launching a successful petition effort on behalf of the Poncas, the new association, led by Massachusetts Governor John D. Long, Helen Hunt Jackson, and U.S. Senator Henry L. Dawes, turned its attention to ways of achieving a long-term solution to the Indian question based upon the recognition of Indian treaty rights and citizenship. Although the Boston-based organization's influence was soon dwarfed by other reform bodies, it helped lay the groundwork for an emerging consensus. Meanwhile, the Women's National Indian Association was formed the same year when a small group of women began meeting in a Baptist church in Philadelphia to discuss reported white invasions of Indian land in the West. Thoroughly imbued with the spirit of evangelical Protestantism, the small gathering was slowly transformed into a national nondenominational women's organization devoted to the cause of Indian uplift and assimilation. Viewing Indian work as a field of activity particularly suited to "women's sphere," the association was soon supporting missionary efforts in the field, providing Christmas gifts for Indian schoolchildren, and stocking Indian school libraries with uplifting books. A special concern of the association was the education of Indian girls, who, as future mothers of their race, were perceived as being central to the long-term business of cultural transformation.[15]

When Welsh's Indian Rights Association made its appearance in early 1883, it numbered fourth in what was becoming an ever-expanding network of philanthropic organizations devoted to the Indian cause. As noted earlier, Welsh's organization, because of the sheer scope of its activity, would become the dominant reform body in the field. But even after its appearance, reformers realized that the network for reform remained incomplete. What was still needed was a public forum where reformers could come together for the purpose of translating the emerging consensus into concrete policy recommendations.

This need was met in 1883 with the appearance of the so-called Lake Mohonk Conference. The idea that reformers should come together for an annual meeting on the Indian question was the inspiration of Albert K. Smiley, a prominent Quaker philanthropist and a member of the Board of Indian Commissioners. As the owner of a luxurious New York resort on picturesque Lake Mohonk, Smiley decided to invite prominent philanthropists, government officials, missionaries, and even military figures to his plush hotel for several days of discussion and debate. Beginning in the fall of 1883, and continuing for over thirty years thereafter, these meetings would be attended faithfully by all those interested in the Indian question. Styling themselves as "friends of the Indian," participants engaged in freewheeling discussion and concluded their deliberations by passing resolutions calling for specific policy reforms. The annual proceedings of the conference were subsequently published and distributed to the press and Congress. Next to Welsh's Indian Rights Association, the Lake Mohonk Conference was the most influential force on the reform scene.[16]

When reformers gathered at Lake Mohonk, they had much more in common than their vision of Indian policy reform. Well educated and financially secure, almost to a person they came from the upper echelons of eastern society. Furthermore, while representing a number of religious denominations, they were almost universally guided by the tenets of evangelical Protestantism, never doubting for a moment that their effort to uplift Indians was a fulfillment of their Christian obligation to extend the blessings of Christianity to all peoples of the world.[17] Finally, they subscribed to a body of principles which, taken together, constituted the bedrock of mainstream American cultural outlook, what one historian has termed the Protestant-Republican ideology. As described by Carl F. Kaestle, core elements in this ideology included the following beliefs.

The sacredness and fragility of the republican polity (including ideas about individualism, liberty, and virtue); the importance of individual character in fostering social mobility; the central role of personal industry in defining rectitude and merit; the delineation of a highly respected but limited domestic role for women; the importance for character building of familial and social environment (within certain racial and ethnic limitations); the sanctity and social virtues of property; the equality and abundance of economic opportunity in the United States; the superiority of American Protestant culture; the grandeur of America's destiny; and the necessity of a determined public effort to unify America's polyglot population, chiefly through education.[18]

Philanthropic efforts to assimilate Indian peoples would be shaped in very fundamental ways by their adherence to these principles.

It was partly because reformers operated well within the ideological context of nineteenth-century America that they proved to be so successful. And this suggests another fundamental characteristic of the emerging consensus, namely, its pervasiveness. For although it is true that philanthropic organizations would provide much of the moral energy for the reform effort, it is also true that most of their views were readily accepted by policymakers and the public at large. To be sure, there would always be points of tension between reformers and the Indian Office, but on the broad aims of Indian policy there would be essential agreement. Moreover, the philanthropic consensus came to embrace much of the Indian service as well, from the Secretary of the Interior down to—although to a lesser extent—the agency employee in the field.

But to understand the basis for this consensus, it is not enough to know that the Indian problem cried out for solution, that reformers were well organized, or that they operated within the mainstream ideological tradition of American culture. In the end, this consensus was rooted in an idea, an idea almost deeper than ideology itself.

THE IDEA OF CIVILIZATION

The word was civilization. European and American societies were civilized; Indians, on the other hand, were savages. The idea functioned at several levels, or rather, served several purposes. On one level it operated as assumption; philanthropists simply assumed that because Indian ways differed from white ways, they must be less civilized. On another level, it served as a legitimizing rationale for the hegemonic relationship that had come to characterize Indian-white relations. In this connection, it served as a compelling justification for dispossessing Indians of their land. Finally, it was prescriptive. It told philanthropists what Indians must become, and as we shall see shortly, to what end they should be educated.

As we have already seen, the idea of civilization had always been an underlying assumption of the nations's Indian policy. Again, the basic idea was that all societies could be classified on a scale marking the various stages of man's evolution from savagism to civilization. Through historical and environmental circumstance—and some argued, by divine intent—America had managed to reach the uppermost stage in cultural development. Under the proper conditions, that is to say under white tutelage, Indians too might one day become as civilized as their white brothers. Indeed, the idea of civilization embodied within itself one of the most cherished ideas of the eighteenth and nineteenth centuries, the idea of progress. History, from this perspective, was largely the story of man's progressive evolution toward civilized perfection. This progression was both inevitable and desirable, for civilization, especially Christian civilization, gave expression to man's noblest sentiments. From all this it followed that just as savagism must give way to civilization, so Indian ways must give way to white ways. For some Americans it was simply in the natural order of things, one of those natural laws applied to the affairs of men. For others, it was a question of the nation fulfilling its divine mission. For most, it was a question of both.[19]

One only needed to look at the course of American expansion to see the scale of civilization, and its corollary, the doctrine of progress, vividly displayed. If the history of America was anything, it was the progressive triumph of civilization over savagism. As Jefferson observed in 1824:

> Let a philosophic observer commence a journey from the savages of the Rocky Mountains, eastwardly towards our sea-coast. These he would observe in the earliest stage of association living under no law but that of nature, subsisting and covering themselves with the flesh and the skins of beasts. He would next find those on our frontiers in the pastoral state, raising domestic animals to supply the defects of hunting. Then succeed our own semi-barbarous citizens, the pioneers of the advance of civilization, and so in his progress he would meet the gradual shades of improving man until he would reach his, as yet, most improved state in our seaport towns. This, in fact, is equivalent to a survey, in time, of the progress of man from the infancy of creation to the present day.[20]

As Roy Harvey Pearce has perceptively observed, for Jefferson and his contemporaries, the history of American civilization was seen as being a three-dimensional affair, "progressing from past to present, from east to west, from lower to higher."[21]

The idea of social evolution received authoritative verification in 1877 with the publication of Lewis Henry Morgan's *Ancient Society: Or Researches in the Lines of Human Progress from Savagery Through Barbarism to Civilization.* In this seminal work, Morgan set out to identify both the various stages in cultural evolution and those factors—institutional and ideational—that characterized each successive stage. Morgan calculated that there were seven "ethical periods" in all and that all peoples on the globe could be placed somewhere on this scale: lower savagery, middle savagery, upper savagery, lower barbarism, middle barbarism, upper barbarism, and civilization. Depending upon the particular tribal group, American Indian societies were classified as being at the level of either upper savagery, lower barbarism, or in a few instances, middle barbarism. In no instance had an Indian people ever achieved civilization. But it was inevitable that they would eventually do so. For as Morgan explained, each society had within itself the "germ" of progressive evolution. By the universal law of social progress, all peoples would someday join the ranks of the civilized.[22]

The reasons for the Indians' lowly position on Morgan's scale becomes clear when considering his requirements for civilized status. Under Morgan's scheme societies were ranked according to their level of technical and material development, their subsistence patterns, the complexity of their institutional arrangements, and finally, their "ideas, passions, and aspirations." Two evolutionary developments were of particular significance. The first of these was the monogamous nuclear family. This development was crucial because it contributed to firmly fixed ideas of familial responsibility, reflected a higher sense of moral understanding, and finally, established clearer lines for the inheritance of property. The second key development, and in many ways the linchpin to the wheel of progress, was the idea of property. Without the conception of private property a society's social, economic, and political institutions would be forever stunted. In Morgan's words, "Its dominance as a passion over all other passions marks the commencement of civilization." By this standard, and for that matter, by all others as well, Indians failed the test of civilization. But again, in time, all this could change.[23]

It is not clear how many reformers actually read Morgan's *Ancient Society,* but it is safe to say that the widespread publicity surrounding the book helped fortify the intellectual framework within which philanthropists operated. In any case, the idea of civilization pervaded reformers' thinking.[24] When William Torey Harris, U.S. Commissioner of Education, addressed the Lake Mohonk Conference, he placed the Indian problem in a context wholly familiar to his audience, After asking whether a member of Indian society was civilized, he answered:

No, he is at the tribal stage. He is at the patriarchal stage. Civilization below the patriarchal stage would not be above the brutes. Above that comes the village community, and many who believe in socialism would like to have us go back to that. Above the village community comes feudalism, wherein the individual is ground into subordination, so that division of labor can be established. No yellow race has passed through it. The black race has not passed through it except as it has come into the house of bondage. The nations of Europe and America have passed through it. It is a great thing to go through these stages.

As Harris went on to explain, attributes of civilization included a commitment to the values of individualism, industry, and private property; the acceptance of Christian doctrine and morality, including the "Christian ideal of the family"; the abandonment of loyalty to the tribal community for a higher identification with the state as an "independent citizen"; the willingness to become both a producer and consumer of material goods; and finally, an acceptance of the idea that man's conquest of nature constituted one of his noblest accomplishments.[25]

As a frame of reference, the idea of civilization pervaded not only the discussions at Lake Mohonk, but the entire Indian Bureau. Thus, when the agent to the Utes at White River Agency, Colorado, expressed his frustration at getting his Indians to adopt civilized pursuits, he noted, "Civilization has been reached by successive stages: first was the savage, clearly that of these Utes; next the pastoral, to which a few have now extended; next the barbaric; and finally the enlightened, scientific, and religious." For this agent there were apparently four rungs on the ladder to civilization. Most agents were either unable or chose not to spell out in detail the exact number of stages that Indians would have to pass through on their climb to civilization. For most, it was simply a case of trying to civilize savages. Thus, the agent to one of the Pueblo villages of New Mexico was moved to note, "To this indigenous race the conquests of civilization are unknown and the law of progress utterly void."[26]

Just as philanthropists in Jefferson's time had offered Indians a choice about their ultimate fate, so the new generation of policymakers did the same. Thus, Carl Schurz, former Commissioner of Indian Affairs, concluded in 1881 that Indians were confronted with "this stern alternative: extermination or civilization." In the same decade, Secretary of the Interior Lucius Q. Lamar pronounced that the "only alternative now presented to the American Indian race is speedy entrance into the pale of American civilization, or absolute extinction." Similarly, Commissioner of Indian Affairs Henry Price opined: "Savage and civilized life cannot live and prosper on the same ground. One of the two must die." Certainly, reformers hoped that Indians would choose assimilation over extinction. As Schurz observed, the idea "of exterminating a race, once the only occupant of the soil upon which so many millions of our own people have grown prosperous and happy, must be revolting to every American who is not devoid of all sentiments of justice and humanity."[27]

One way or another, the Indians' fate would be decided in the very near future, for time was quickly running out on savagism. Whereas Indians historically had been able to retreat before the moving line of civilization, the onrush of technology and white settlements had finally caught up with them. Great stretches of the prairie were now being churned by the settler's plow; the once-still prairie air was now alive with the hum of telegraph lines and the locomotive whistle; the rich grasslands, which had once fed vast buffalo herds, now supported the white man's thriving cattle industry. And what was the Indian to do in the face of this flowing tide of civilization? As Commissioner John Oberly noted, there was little he could do. The forests into which he had once run "whooping" had all but been felled. "The game on which he lived has disappeared. The war-path has been obliterated. He is hemmed in on all sides by white population." An Indian school superintendent in Kansas painted much the same scenario, "Gradually have their possessions dwindled, reservation after reservation disappearing before the invincible march of civilization, till now their domain is reckoned in acres instead of continents, and is bounded by surveyor's chains and links instead of oceans, gulfs, and lakes." And once again the conclusion, "The only alternative left is civilization or annihilation, absorption or extermination." Because time was clearly running out for the Indians, time was running out for reformers as well. Whereas earlier efforts to civilize the Indians were, in the words of Schurz, a "benevolent fancy," it now had "become an absolute necessity, if we mean to save them."[28]

And reformers remained optimistic that Indians could be saved. With public sentiment aroused, with philanthropic organizations working in concert with policymakers, there was still time to accomplish the Indians' absorption into American life. Philanthropists were also of one mind as to what was needed. The solution to the Indian problem lay in three areas: land, law, and education.

The land issue was linked to what reformers regarded as the biggest obstacle to Indian assimilation, the reservation system. The reservation was deplored for three reasons. First, it perpetuated the Indians' attachment to the tribal outlook and tribal institutions. Most notable in this regard was the high value placed on communal property holding and gift giving, traditions that reformers viewed as anathemas to the emergence of self-reliant individualism. Second, the reservation was inextricably linked to the rationing system, which, although well intentioned, had the practical result of instilling an attitude of dependency. Rather than relying on their own manhood for survival, Indians now saw the "Great Father" as the source of all their earthly needs. Finally, under the reservation system, Indians had little motivation to invest their labor in a farm that might be swept away in a new Indian removal program. As Welsh explained, "an Indian labors with no assurance whatsoever that he shall enjoy the scanty fruits of his toil, for no sooner has he abandoned the tent of roving day, and built himself a rude cabin of logs, and begun to gladden the ground about his dwelling with a little crop of corn, and wheat, and potatoes, than the greedy eye of some white neighbor spies his success, and Congress knows no peace until he is driven westward." For these reasons, Lyman Abbott pronounced, the reservation had to be "uprooted root, trunk, branch, and leaf, and a new system put in its place."[29]

The solution, reformers argued, lay in the allotment of Indian land in severalty. Allotment would smash the tribal connection, force Indians to work the land, and eventually bring an end to the rationing system. In 1887, Congress passed the General Allotment Act, more commonly referred to as the Dawes Act, named after its sponsor, the venerable senator from Massachusetts, Henry Dawes. Under the new legislation the president was authorized to identify selected reservations suitable for allotment, after which the following provisions were initiated. First, the reservation was surveyed and divided up among the Indians: 160 acres to each family head, 80 acres to single persons and orphans over eighteen years, and 40 acres to single persons under eighteen. Second, to protect allottees from avaricious whites, the actual deed to the allotment remained in the hands of the government for twenty-five years, during which time the land could not be sold or encumbered. Third, citizenship status was conferred upon all allottees whereupon they would become subject to the criminal and civil laws of the state or territory where they resided. Finally, after all tribal members had received an allotment, all surplus land might be sold to white settlers. The proceeds gained from these sales would be held by the government for the tribe's "education and civilization." Reformers viewed the Dawes Act as a major victory; in one bold stroke, it held out the possibility of smashing the tribal bond and setting Indians on the road to civilization.[30]

The second plank in the reformers' platform was to extend the rule and protection of the nation's legal system to Indians. The Dawes Act would facilitate this, but what about those Indians still caught in the backwaters of reservation life? To reformers, the answer was obvious: since laws and courts were civilizing influences, they must assume hegemony over tribal institutions. The creation of the reservation Indian police force in 1878 was a first step. As the system was set up, Indian policemen were selected from the ranks of cooperative tribesmen, given a badge of authority, and pledged to carry out the directives of the reservation agent, which ranged from supervising the distribution of annuity goods to arresting Indians charged with crimes. Another step was taken in 1883 when Congress provided for the creation of Indian courts to try cases involving minor crimes such as polygamy, theft, and participation in "heathenish" dances. Reformers won still another victory in 1885 when Congress extended the jurisdiction of U.S. courts over Indian reservations for major crimes such as murder, manslaughter, rape, and arson. Although these measures were important, reformers were constantly looking for new ways of bringing Indians under the civilizing influence of the white man's law. As Merrill Gates stated the issue, "The problem before us is, how shall we educate these men-children into that great conception of the reign of law, moral, civil, and political, to which they are now strangers?"[31]

The third area of reform was education.[32] Indians must be taught the knowledge, values, mores, and habits of Christian civilization. That reformers should turn to education as the third ingredient of policy reform is not surprising. Since the days of the common school movement, the schoolhouse had come to achieve almost mythological status. Reformers viewed it as a seedbed of republican virtues and democratic freedoms, a promulgator of individual opportunity and national prosperity, and an instrument for social progress and harmony. Moreover, because of the common school's alleged ability to assimilate, it was looked upon as an ideal instrument for absorbing those peoples and ideologies that stood in the path of the republic's millennial destiny.[33] Thus, the Board of Indian Commissioners would ask, "If the common school is the glory and boast of our American civilization, why not extend its blessings to the 50,000 benighted children of the red men of our country, that they may share its benefits and speedily emerge from the ignorance of centuries."[34]

The case for education was made on several levels. One of the strongest arguments was that the older generation of Indians was incapable of being civilized. As an agent to the Lakota mused: "It is a mere waste of time to attempt to teach the average adult Indian the ways of the white man. He can be tamed, and that is about all." The agent to the Shoshone concurred, reporting that the older Indians were making little progress toward civilization. "It is not in his mother's milk," he explained, "and as it was not born in the bone, it won't come out in the flesh." The only hope, he concluded was "in training the youth." Older Indians might be convinced to live on their allotments and to build houses, might be forced to obey the white man's law, and might even be prohibited from participating in their heathen ceremonies, the argument went, but in their hearts they remained attached to the old ways. They were likely, as Commissioner Leupp explained, to remain Indians of the "old school" until the grave, "but our main hope lies with the youthful generations who are still measurably plastic." The agent to the Utes observed in 1886:

It is food for thought to note the number of handsome, bright-eyed children here, typical little savages, arrayed in blankets, leggings, and gee-strings, their faces hideously painted, growing up in all the barbarism of their parents. A few years more, and they will be men and women, perhaps beyond redemption, for, under the most favorable circumstances, but little can be hoped from them after growth and matured, wedded and steeped in the vices of their fathers. It is rather the little children that must be taken in hand and cared for and nurtured, for from them must be realized the dream, if ever realized, of the philanthropist and of all good people, of that day to come when the Indian, a refined, cultured, educated being will assume the title of an American citizen, with all the rights, privileges, and aspirations of that favored individual.[35]

Another argument used by school advocates was that education would quicken the process of cultural evolution. Whereas white civilization had taken centuries to emerge to its present level, if Indian children could gain entrance to the common school, they would enter the struggle of life with roughly the same advantages as the children of their more civilized white neighbors. By means of the common school, Indians could, in effect, be catapulted directly from savagism to civilization, skipping all the intervening stages of social evolution in between. William T. Harris addressed this very issue at Lake Mohonk. After reviewing the stages in man's social evolution, Harris asked, "But shall we say to the tribal people that they shall not come to these higher things unless they pass through all the intermediate stages, or can we teach them directly these higher things, and save them from the slow process of the ages?" The latter course was fully possible, Harris explained. "Education has become a great potency in our hands, and we believe that we can now vicariously save them very much that the white race has had to go through." Commissioner of Indian Affairs Thomas J. Morgan had come to the same conclusion. "Time as an element in human progress is relative, not absolute," he explained. Where Indians were concerned, "a good school may thus bridge over for them the dreary chasm of a thousand years of tedious evolution." Thus, schools could not only civilize, they could civilize in record time.[36]

Finally, the case for education was also made on economic grounds. This line of argument took several forms. First, educating Indians promised to relieve the government of the responsibility of feeding and clothing them. Schooling, if it promised to do anything, promised to prepare Indians for economic self-sufficiency.[37] Another argument was that it was less expensive to educate Indians than to kill them. Carl Schurz, for instance, estimated that it cost nearly a million dollars to kill an Indian in warfare, whereas it cost only $1,200 to give an Indian child eight years of schooling. Similarly, Secretary of the Interior Henry Teller calculated that over a ten-year period the annual cost of both waging war on Indians and providing protection for frontier communities was in excess of $22 million, nearly four times what it would cost to educate 30,000 children for a year.[38] A final version of the economic argument was a throwback to Jefferson's idea that Indian ignorance of civilization retarded both white settlement and national prosperity. According to Commissioner Morgan:

> A wild Indian requires a thousand acres to roam over, while an intelligent man will find a comfortable support for his family on a very small tract. When the rising generation of Indians have become civilized and have learned how to utilize the land they live on, a vast domain now useless can be thrown open to settlement and become the seat of great farms, happy homes, thriving towns and cities, and vast mining and commercial industries. Barbarism is costly, wasteful and extravagant. Intelligence promotes thrift and increases prosperity.[39]

Again, education made economic sense.

In constructing their rationale for education, philanthropists stressed still another point, namely, that the success of the two other planks of their platform—allotment and law—were ultimately dependent on schooling for Indians. This was the point that Charles Painter stressed when he announced at Lake Mohonk that the passage of the Dawes Act, although necessary, had also created a "crises" in Indian affairs. As Painter explained, under the terms of the Allotment Act the Indian was "about to be thrown into the seething activities of our complex civilization and take his chances in free competition with other races." In their current untutored state, Painter warned, Indians would never be able to survive that competition without the help of the "schoolmaster." A year later, Lyman Abbott expressed similar concerns. After acknowledging the importance of land, law, and education to the Indians' transformation, Abbott declared education to be "by far the most important problem of the three." John Oberly even argued that philanthropic measures should be sequenced in a particular order. "I would first teach the Indian how to work," Oberly began, "then I would teach him our ideas of the rights of property, and give him lands in severalty; then I would abolish the reservation system, and then make the Indian a citizen and enfranchise him."[40] Education was not only important to the Indians' transformation, it was fundamental.

And so, the "friends of the Indian" turned to schools as a solution to the

Indian problem. Education would give Indians the knowledge and skills necessary for survival in a civilized world. As Commissioner of Indian Affairs William Jones explained, "To educate the Indian in the ways of civilized life, . . . is to preserve him from extinction, not as an Indian, but as a human being."[41] It mattered little that Indians might not find the terms entirely satisfactory. Indeed, that was part of the problem; as savages, Indians were incapable of determining what was in their own best interests. In time, reformers reasoned, they would come to accept the wisdom of their philanthropic benefactors.

AIMS OF EDUCATION

Convinced that schools were the ultimate solution to the Indian problem, policymakers turned next to the question of educational aims. Once again, the idea of civilization provided the context for the discussion. If the problem with Indians was that they were savages, then what Indian children needed was a civilized education. As one observer of Indian affairs pointed out, "The kind of education they are in need of is one that will habituate them to the customs and advantages of a civilized life, . . . and at the same time cause them to look with feelings of repugnance on their native state."[42]

The first priority was to provide the Indian child with the rudiments of an academic education, including the ability to read, write, and speak the English language. The "talking paper" of the white man had always impressed Indians as one of their subjugator's most powerful weapons. As philanthropists saw the issue, the Indians were essentially correct in this perception, since a fundamental difference between civilization and savagism was the former's reliance on the written word and the printed page as a means of recording and preserving the accumulated wisdom of the race. As the Superintendent of Indian Schools observed in 1887, an Indian's "inability to speak another language than his own renders his companionship with civilized man impossible." But reformers not only wanted to civilize Indians, they wished to acculturate them to American life and institutions. As Commissioner of Indian Affairs John D. C. Atkins pointed out in 1887, "This language, which is good enough for a white man and a black man, ought to be good enough for the red man."[43]

Beyond language instruction, Indian schools should introduce the child to the civilized branches of knowledge—arithmetic, science, history, and the arts—not with the idea that he would master these areas, but that he might "catch at least a glimpse of the civilized world through books." If the more inquiring student chose to move beyond a superficial introduction to these subjects, so much the better. In the meantime, even an elementary acquaintance held out the promise of liberating the child from the mind-dulling weight of tribal tradition, opening up instead the possibility of discovering the "self-directing power of thought."[44]

Second, Indians needed to be individualized. In many ways, the issue of individualization went to the very heart of the Indian question. In the philanthropic mind Indians were savages mainly because tribal life placed a higher value on the tribal community than individual interests. Never was this more true than in the economic realm. Tribal society had somehow gotten matters all wrong; rather than operating on the progressive principle that the whole of society stood to benefit when the individual's acquisitive instincts were given their full play, tribal life was rooted in the idea that the welfare of the community depended upon the individual curbing material desires. Whereas a Protestant American measured an individual's worth by his capacity to accumulate wealth, an Indian did so by what he gave away. This, combined with Indians' aversion to labor and disdain for private property, went a long way toward explaining their backwardness. As Merrill Gates noted: "There is an utter barbarism in which property has almost no existence. The tribal organization tends to retain men in such barbarism. It is a great step gained when you awaken in an Indian the desire for the acquisition of property of his own, by his own honest labor."[45]

Education should facilitate individualization in two ways. First, it should teach young Indians how to work.[46] More specifically, it could teach them a host of practical skills and trades that would prepare them for the changed realities of their existence. This meant, in the words of one educator, teaching "the Indian boy to till the soil, shove the plane, strike the anvil, and drive the peg, and the Indian girl to do the work of the good and skillful housewife." A school superintendent among the Sioux agreed, noting that "the theory of cramming the Indian youth with text-book knowledge alone has been and always will be a failure. The best education for the aborigines of our country is that which inspires them to become producers instead of remaining consumers." Thus, "a string of text-books piled up in the storehouses high enough to surround a reservation if laid side by side will never educate a being with centuries of laziness instilled in the race." It followed that the sound of the hammer, the swing of the ax, and the rhythm of the bucksaw were just as fundamental, perhaps more so, than the "meaningless jargon of textbook makers."[47]

But teaching Indians how to work was not enough. In the end, they must be inculcated with the values and beliefs of possessive individualism. They must come to respect the importance of private property, they must internalize the ideal of self-reliance, and they must come to realize that the accumulation of personal wealth is a moral obligation.[48] Thus, Superintendent of Indian Schools John Oberly argued in 1888 that a major objective of Indian schools was to wean the student from "the degrading communism of the tribal-reservation system" and to imbue him "with the exalting egotism of American civilization, so that he will say 'I' instead of 'We,' and 'This is mine,' instead of 'This is ours.' " According to Merrill Gates:

> We need to *awaken in him wants.* In his dull savagery he must be touched by the wings of the divine angel of discontent. Then he begins to look forward, to reach out. The desire for property of his own may become an intense educating force. The wish for a home of his own awakens him to new efforts. Discontent with the tepee and the starving rations of the Indian camp in winter is needed to get the Indian out of the blanket and into trousers,—and trousers with a pocket in them, and with a *pocket that aches to be filled with dollars!*

Similarly, Senator Dawes argued that the primary obligation of policymakers was to take the Indian "by the hand and set him upon his feet, and teach him to stand alone first, then to walk, then to dig, then to plant, then to hoe, then to gather, and then to keep." For Dawes, the last step was the single most important stage in the process of individualization.[49]

The third aim of Indian education was Christianization. Because the philanthropic movement drew its moral energy from the reformers' quest to create a Protestant America and because their ethnocentrism caused them to look upon native religious practices as primitive and barbaric remnants of a precivilized existence, it is not surprising that the Indians' religious conversion should surface as a major educational objective. As one Indian educator noted, "A really civilized people cannot be found in the world except where the Bible has been sent and the gospel taught; hence, we believe that the Indians must have, as an essential part of their education, Christian training." It was not simply that philanthropists wished to snatch the Indians' souls from a hellish fate; their commitment to Christianization was also rooted in the assumption that civilization, as the highest stage of man's social evolution, was only possible when erected upon a firm foundation of Christian morality. It was not a simple matter of happenstance, they argued, that American civilization was also a Christian society. As William T. Harris told his audience at Lake Mohonk, Christianity was not merely a religion, but an "ideal of life penetrating the whole social structure."[50] Thus, it was not enough for Indians to abandon their childish faith in kachina gods, medicine bundles, and spirit guides, and then profess allegiance to the white man's God. On the contrary, embracing Christianity meant embracing an entire ethical code which included, among other things, the principle that an individual was responsible for both his economic and spiritual self.

The fourth aim of Indian schooling was citizenship training. As the Commissioner of Indian Affairs said in 1890, "The general purpose of the Government is the preparation of Indian youth for assimilation into the national life by such a course of training as will prepare them for the duties and privileges of American citizenship." Toward this end, Indian youth needed to be taught the fundamental principles of democratic government, the institutional and political structure of American society, the rights of citizens under the Constitution, and the role and sanctity of law in a democratic society.[51] Beyond this, education for citizenship involved the delicate business of engendering a deep devotion to the nation and its flag. The Indian student would have to study American history and in the process come to internalize the national myths that were central to it, including the idea that the westward sweep of the American empire, that is to say the dispossession of Indian land, was clearly justifiable. In this connection, the Indian student must be taught the terms upon which Indian and white societies had confronted one another—savagism versus civilization—and that the only hope for the race's survival was for it to join the march of historical progress. Granted, all this called for an artful use of schooling as an instrument for furthering the process of white political and ideological hegemony, but philanthropists were convinced they could pull it off.

These constituted the main ends of Indian schooling. All in all, the Indian child was to be totally transformed, all vestiges of his former self eradicated. As Superintendent of Indian Schools John Riley expressed it, the Indian child was "a prickly thorn that must be made to bear roses; he is a twig bent out of the perpendicular, and he must be straightened so that the tree will stand erect, inclining in no way; he is a vessel of bronze that must be made bright by constant rubbing."[52] It was a noble undertaking to be sure, one worthy of philanthropic effort.

AN ARMY OF SCHOOLTEACHERS

When President Andrew Jackson, in his Second Annual Message, December 6, 1830, turned to the question of Indian policy, he uttered a chilling rebuke to those critics who found him unsympathetic to the Indian's plight.

> Humanity has often wept over the fate of the aborigines of this country, and philanthropy has been long busily employed in devising means to avert it, but its progress has never for a moment been arrested, and one by one have many powerful tribes disappeared from the earth. To follow to the tombs the last of his race and to tread on

the graves of extinct nations excite melancholy reflections. But true philanthropy reconciles the mind to those vicissitudes as it does to the extinction of one generation to make room for another. Philanthropy could not wish to see this continent restored to the condition in which it was found by our forefathers. What good man would prefer a country covered with forests and ranged by a few thousand savages to our extensive Republic, studded with cities, towns, and prosperous farms, embellished with all the improvements which art can devise or industry execute, occupied by more than 12,000,000 happy people, and filled with all the blessings of liberty, civilization and religion?[53]

If Jackson's comments reflected his insensitivity to the Indian's plight, they also made an important point: philanthropists, like Jackson, preferred civilization to savagism. Indeed, they wanted it both ways: they would save Indians from extinction but they would do it by civilizing them.

In this, of course, they would fail miserably. The lure of cheap land, the frontiersman's image of Indians being scarcely superior to the beasts they hunted, and the mythological underpinnings of westward expansion all served to cast an air of unreality over philanthropic rhetoric. The cruel fact was that as whites conquered the continent, Indians were left behind to suffer the pitiful existence of reservation life. Clearly the time had arrived, reformers argued, to fulfill an old promise. Now that whites had taken the land, it was time to instruct Indians in the ways of civilization.

The connection between education and the idea of civilized progress received dramatic visual treatment in 1872 in a painting by John Gast. Issued a year later as a chromolithograph under the title "American Progress," and now accompanied by a short explanatory text, this popular print constituted a vivid rendering of American civilization's sweep across the continent. Center stage in the print is given to Columbia, a virtual "goddess of progress," who floats westward over the American landscape. Behind her on the eastern seaboard are depictions of the advanced technology and commercial empire—civilization. Directly below her at mid-continent are the symbols of an advancing civilization, the frontiersmen and yeomen farmers who will tame the wilderness and plow the prairies. As for the goddess, close examination reveals that her forehead is decorated by a star, which, the text explains, is the "star of empire." With one hand she stretches westward the telegraph wire, a powerful symbol of advancing technology and national unity. With the other she clutches a large volume to her bosom. It is only when an observer turns to the left of the print, to the expanse of territory still beyond the reach of Columbia's

"American Progress." Chromolithograph issued by George Crofutt, 1873. (Courtesy of the Library of Congress)

influence, that one sees the triumph of American progress is not without its tragic dimension. Here, the Indians are depicted as the pathetic remnants of a vanishing race retreating before the rush of civilization. As the text explains, they are fleeing "from 'Progress,' and towards the blue waters of the Pacific." All they can do is "turn their despairing faces . . . as they flee from the presence of, the wondrous vision. 'The Star' is *too much for them.*"[54]

Ten years later, "American Progress" was still a vivid expression of the meaning of the American experience, a visual rendering of an essentially moral tale: the triumph of Christian civilization over a savage land and people. But now reformers would have altered the print in one significant respect. The Indian need not vanish from the face of the earth. The answer was in the book that Columbia clutched to her breast, as upon inspection, the book contains the inscription "common school." If the fleeing Indians would but accept the gift of the book, if Columbia would but offer it to them, they might be civilized and thus saved from extinction.

And so it was time to build schools, and Congress built them. In 1877, Congress began appropriating funds expressly for the purpose of Indian education. The figures tell the story: 1877, $20,000; 1880, $75,000; 1885,

$992,800; 1890, $1,364,568; 1895, $2,060,695; and 1900, $2,936,080. The figures on school enrollment are also revealing: 1877, 3,598; 1880, 4,651; 1885, 8,143; 1890, 12,232; 1895, 18,188; and 1900, 21,568. A related measure is the percentage of Indian school-age population actually provided for. Whereas the Indian Office estimated in 1884 that only one-fourth of Indian children were provided for, by 1890 the figure had grown to half, by 1920 70 percent, and by 1926 nearly 83 percent.[55]

The war against Indians had now entered a new phase. Conquering a continent and its aboriginal peoples had been a bloody business, and for a Christian people, not without moral discomfort. Now the war against savagism would be waged in gentler fashion. The next Indian war would be ideological and psychological, and it would be waged against children. Thus, Merrill Gates, president of the Lake Mohonk Conference, declared in 1891 that "the time for fighting the Indian tribes is passed." What was needed now was an "army of Christian school-teachers."

> That is the army that is going to win the victory. We are going to conquer barbarism, but we are going to do it by getting at the barbarism one by one. We are going to do it by the conquest of the individual man, woman, and child which leads to the truest civilization. We are going to conquer the Indians by a standing army of school-teachers, armed with ideas, winning victories by industrial training, and by the gospel of love and the gospel of work.[56]

It all seemed so simple. "Cannot civilization civilize?" former commissioner of Indian affairs, George E. Ellis, asked in 1882.[57] He, like other reformers, believed that it could. The answer lay in education.

CHAPTER TWO

Models

It was one thing to conclude that schools were the solution to the Indian problem and quite another to determine the manner in which Indian children should be schooled. For at least a decade policymakers focused their attention on a single question: how much institutional hegemony was it necessary to establish over the child to accomplish his transformation? Although the issue would never be completely resolved to the satisfaction of all, by the end of the 1880s an answer had emerged. The path to this resolution, or rather compromise, can be traced by analyzing policymakers' successive enthusiasm for three institutions—the reservation day school, the reservation boarding school, and the off-reservation boarding school.

The most elemental approach was the reservation day school. Located on the outskirts of Indian villages, day schools served as the educational outposts of civilization. By the 1860s, forty-eight such schools were in existence. The theory behind this approach was that in the early morning hours children would pour forth from the nearby Indian camp and at day's end return to their homes wiser in the ways of white civilization. The education received was clearly at the primary level. Most attention was given to language instruction, where in the initial stages the teacher was urged to forego the textbook for the slate and the blackboard. Eventually, reading lessons, recitations, writing, and spelling found their way into the schoolroom. In addition to language instruction and a smattering of elementary arithmetic, the day school teacher was also obligated to introduce the child to the concept of industrial training. For boys this usually meant exposing them to the world of hammers and saws and frequently included the opportunity to work in a small garden. For girls it meant working with needles and thimbles and helping in the preparation of noon meals and cleaning. Interspersed with academic and industrial training, the day school curriculum also provided for lighter activities such as singing and calisthenics, the former offering a perfect opportunity to introduce the Christian message in the form of hymns.[1]

The day school approach offered several distinct advantages. First, it was relatively inexpensive to operate. Second, it seemed to engender the least opposition from parents. As we shall see later, neither tribal elders nor parents looked favorably upon the idea of having young children forcibly removed and sent off to boarding school, sometimes a great distance from the village camp. Finally, the day school held out the possibility that the child might become a daily messenger of civilized ways to his parents. In time, the argument went, parents might come to appreciate the fact that their child was acquiring valuable and useful knowledge from the white schoolteacher, knowledge from which they as well might benefit. What day school advocates hoped for, then, was a reversal of the traditional educational configuration in the parent-child relationship; the Indian parent, it was said, would come to sit at the feet of his wiser offspring.

In spite of these claims, policymakers soon became disenchanted with the day school model because it suffered from one overwhelming defect: by itself, it simply was not an effective instrument of assimilation. The major drawback of the day school concept stemmed from what was thought to be its major asset, namely, its proximity to the tribal community. Efforts to raise up the child during school hours, it was argued, were obliterated at night by the realities of camp life. "It must be manifest to all practical minds," one agent observed in 1878, "that to place these wild children under a teacher's care but four or five hours a day, and permit them to spend the other nineteen in the filth and degradation of the village, makes the attempt to educate and civilize them a mere farce." In 1879, another agent made a special effort to describe the conditions to which his day school students returned at night, an environment in which children "sit in the dirt and live in the dirt in many instances with an apology for clothing; their persons covered with the dust about them and literally plastered upon them." The worst of it was that the natives seemed "content and happy; happy in their degradation and filthiness; seemingly content to remain as they are with little ambition to change for the better." In such an environment, a day school was next to useless.[2]

The problem was exacerbated when Indian parents were adamantly opposed to all white education whatsoever, a situation that resulted in chronic absenteeism and runaways. Thus, the agent to the Sac and Fox reported in 1882 that the boarding school was having some success.

> But in regard to the day school, it has been out of the power of the teacher to do much on account of the parents of the children refusing to let them attend the school. Every effort has been made to induce them but to no purpose; the children run away as soon as the teacher shows them a book. The Indians scare the children by telling them if they attend school they will be taken from their home and made soldiers. The Indians have a prejudice against schools. I have labored hard to do away with it, but it takes a good deal of time to overcome their objection.

An agent to the Sioux came directly to the point: "I regard all expenditures on . . . day schools in this tribe as a waste."[3]

By the late 1870s most policymakers freely acknowledged that the day school was of limited value as a mechanism for weaning young Indians from their native ways. Secretary of the Interior Carl Schurz reported to Congress in 1879, "It is the experience of the department that mere day schools, however well conducted, do not withdraw the children sufficiently from the influences, habits, and traditions of their home life, and produce for this reason but a . . . limited effect."[4] This problem, the need to insulate the child from tribal influence during the civilization process, contributed to the rise of a second model of Indian schooling, the reservation boarding school.

THE RESERVATION BOARDING SCHOOL

By the late 1870s, the reservation boarding school had emerged as the most promising method of educating Indians. Boarding schools were usually located at agency headquarters and were under the direct supervision of the agent. Day-to-day supervision of the school fell to the school superintendent, whose staff included one or more teachers and at least one matron, an industrial teacher, a cook, a seamstress, and a laundress. The curriculum was divided into four primary grades and an equal number of "advanced" grades. Half the school day was devoted to English and basic academic subjects, half to industrial training. In the latter regard, boys worked on the school farm, tried their hand at stock raising—horses, cattle, and sheep—and acquired skills such as blacksmithing, carpentry, and harness-making. Girls, on the other hand, were to be "systematically trained in every branch of housekeeping." As the Indian Office explained, its industrial work schools were expected to be as self-sustaining as possible, "not only because Government resources should be as wisely and carefully utilized as private resources would be, but also because thrift and economy are among the most valuable lessons which can be taught Indians." Again, a dose of moral training rounded out the curriculum.[5]

The chief advantage of the boarding school was that it established greater institutional control over the children's lives, with students being kept in school eight to nine months out of the year. Only during the summer vacation period, and in some instances the Christmas holidays, were students allowed to return to their homes. In any case, sustained confinement was now deemed to be the key element in the civilization process. As the Superintendent of Indian Schools noted in 1885:

> These schools strip from the unwashed person of the Indian boy the
> unwashed blanket, and, after instructing him in what to him are the

mysteries of personal cleanliness, clothe him with the clean garments of civilized men and teach him how to wear them. They give him information concerning a bed and teach him how to use it; teach him how to sit on a chair, how to use knife and fork, how to eat at a table, and what to eat. While he is learning these things, he is also learning to read and write, and, at the same time, is being taught how to work, how to earn a living.[6]

In citing the advantages of the boarding school, observers frequently mentioned a characteristic that was originally ascribed to the day school, the potential for serving as an uplifting influence on parents. Their reasoning went as follows: even though the boarding school removed the child from the camp for extended periods of time, that removal was not absolute; by occasionally visiting the school or by observing his child's progress during the summer months, the parent would hopefully become a friend of the school and the civilization it represented.[7] Thus, in 1885 the Superintendent of Indian Schools observed, "The reservation boarding school may be made a great civilizer of Indian children, and at the same time be used to reflect some of the light of civilization into the Indian camp."[8]

But such optimism was not universal. Indeed, although some agents and policymakers would continue to sing the praises of the reservation boarding school, this approach, like the day school before it, fell under heavy criticism. And oddly enough, the point of criticism was a familiar one: failure to exert sufficient influence over the children's minds. Even in the more controlled environment of the boarding school, the children still were not sufficiently removed from the degrading influence of tribal life.

The most dramatic manifestation of this was the phenomenon of relapse, the tendency of the children to slough off newly acquired civilized habits in favor of tribal ones. This, of course, had occurred nightly in the case of the day school. Now it occurred during vacation periods, especially in the summer months. Thus, the agent to the Wichita observed in 1879 that it was surprising "how soon they seem to forget all they have been taught, after they return to camp." The report from Osage Agency was much the same, the agent commenting that the children "lose in a few weeks what they will gain in months." Moreover, the parents "are persistent in their claims for their children, and there seems no way at present to avoid the annual vacation." As for the Mescalero Apache, "They go back at once to the savage mode of life, and a few weeks is sufficient to obliterate every vestige, so far as casual observation goes, of the teacher's long and patient labor." Even Christmas vacation could set back the school's work. One school superintendent reported that students left the school healthy but returned with severe colds and contagious diseases, their bodies covered by "vermin—body lice, head lice, bed bugs." And predictably there was the complaint that children had slipped back into their old habits, with some experiencing the most dramatic form of relapse of all: "Several of our pupils did not return at all during the rest of year."[9]

But the influence of the tribal community on the children was not limited to vacation periods. Some agents complained of the constant efforts of Indian parents to visit their children at school. Although some looked upon such visits as a welcome opportunity for garnering tribal support for the civilization program, others clearly came to view such visits as a positive nuisance and disruptive to the schools's smooth operation. The problem was that any contact whatsoever awakened in the children a natural longing for camp life. The situation was particularly troublesome when the school was located at agency headquarters where Indians regularly gathered to draw rations, conduct business, or exchange gossip. Although schools were usually fenced, and the children kept from wandering at random around the school grounds, it is clear from agency reports that school workers were clearly unable to prohibit all communication between the children and the outside world. Thus, the agent to the Ute Indians complained of the fact the children "are so intimately connected with the tribe, even when they are at school, that they know nothing . . . except what their superstitious parents tell them." Similarly, another agent concluded that his boarding school would never be a success while located at the agency "where the children's parents and friends can visit them everyday."[10]

Part of the problem with allowing such interaction, agents discovered, was that parents often took the opportunity to overtly subvert the efforts of the school. The agent at one reservation claimed, "Members of the tribe daily visit the school to its detriment in many ways, notably in retarding English speaking by the pupils, in persuading the children to run away, or to refrain from performing their alloted work, and in giving notice of the time of dances and their whereabouts to the pupils." Dances were a particular problem. "A dance is announced a week in advance," came word from another agency, "and at once you see the young mind reveling in the thought until study and all thoughts of books are driven out and nothing but Indian remains, and weeks pass before the scholars get back to their regular work."[11]

It took very little, it seems, for students to become infected with a prolonged bout of homesickness. For those students who had already internalized the rhythm and pulse of native society, including the tribe's ceremonial calendar, the sight of smoke on the morning horizon or the faint sounds of ceremonial chants at night were sufficient to trigger emotions

Pine Ridge Indian Boarding School, ca. 1891. The proximity of Indian settlements was one of the major arguments against reservation schools. (Courtesy of the Library of Congress)

and longings uniquely Indian. Francis La Flesche, who attended a missionary boarding school in the mid 1860s, would always remember the morning that students watched from a second-story dormitory window as their nearby Omaha relatives broke camp for an extended buffalo hunt. "It was a wonderful sight to us," he later recalled, "the long procession, the winding trail, like a great serpent of varied and brilliant colors. . . . It was nearly noon when the end of the line went out of sight." The sight had a profound impact on the school's operation. "We slowly . . . ate our noonday meal without speaking. There seemed to be a general depression among the remaining pupils at the school. A silence pervaded all the surroundings which made each boy wish to retire from the other and to be alone."[12]

And then there was ration day, those times designated weekly or bimonthly, when Indians gathered at the agency to receive their allotments of flour, sugar, and coffee. It was on just such occasions that the agent and school superintendent were pestered with requests to visit the children and inspect the school. Moreover, the students' knowledge that friends and relatives were gathered nearby, telling stories and exchanging gossip, also had a detrimental effect on their studies. "This school is unfortunately located," came word from the agent to the Crow. "Being at the agency, the coming of the 'camp' every week for rations has a demoralizing effect on the pupils, practically undoing in one day all the good of six days' teaching."[13]

More than one observer commented on the unhealthy effect of issue day on the boarding school. And their most stinging comments were reserved for the issuance of beef "on the hoof." One of the most vivid descriptions of this affair was written by J. B. Harrison in a report for the Indian Rights Association. Harrison's report illustrates the sorts of scenes that reformers conjured up in their minds when they spoke of the debilitating influence of reservation life.

> The gate opens and a gigantic steer leaps out, frightened and wild-eyed. He trots uncertainly down the lane of horsemen. The dogs fly at him, and he sets off in a gallop. Two Indians gallop after him, and everybody looks that way. But by this time another is out, and soon half a dozen are racing away in different directions, each closely followed by two or three mounted Indians. . . . Five or six of the cattle go off together, with a dozen men pressing behind and at the side of the fleeing group. A horseman fires, and steer drops, so suddenly, head first, that he turns a complete somersault, and the pony just behind, unable to stop, repeats the movement, tumbling over the prostrate beast, and dismounts his rider. Some of the cattle are, at first, only slightly wounded, other are cripples so that they cannot run, but several shots are required to dispatch them. Now and then one turns in fury upon his pursuers, and the ponies swerve aside to avoid his charge. . . . The dying animals lie all about the plain. Some struggle long, getting up and falling again, and the Indians wait warily till it seems safe to approach, for a mortally wounded beast will sometimes make a plunge at his tormentor. . . .
>
> As the carcasses all about the plain are opened the work of the Indian women begins. They attend to the "fifth quarter" of the beef, the entrails. They remind me of the witches in "Macbeth." As we drive out homeward, threading our way between the bloody groups around the flayed and dismembered beasts, many Indians are already beginning their feast. They are seated on the ground, eating the raw, blood hot liver. . . . It is a brutal and brutalizing spectacle.[14]

What Harrison found remarkable was that on the following day, while visiting the agency boarding school, the principal informed him that he intended to let the students witness the entire spectacle the next time around. The question may be asked, why would schoolchildren be permitted to attend what was an obvious, if pathetic, reenactment of the tribe's more glorious buffalo hunting days? Perhaps it was a reward for good behavior. Perhaps it was a recognition that the day's events made any efforts at schoolwork sheer pretense, since the children's attention was hopelessly diverted. Or perhaps it was a practical means of discouraging runaways, the recognition that to prohibit students from attending the spectacle was simply inviting trouble. Indeed, at one school we are told that the girls "would run away on the morning of beef issue, and search would invariably find them in a canyon nearby, where the squaws were slaughtering the beeves. There the children satiated themselves on the raw entrails." On such days, the account continues, it was "a common sight to see Indians, young boys and girls, and even babies, in arms, sitting under the shade of the Agent's office, tearing with their teeth, and eating liver and intestines smoking from natural heat." As despicable as agents might find such scenes, it appears that a number of them found it easier to open the school gates to the bloody spectacle. Jim Whitewolf, a Kiowa-Apache, recalls in his memoirs, "Friday was ration day, and they always let us go."[15]

Reservation officials were beleaguered with problems as they sought to eradicate all attachment to tribal ways. The result was that some agents began to search for ways to further isolate the school from any contamination from Indian life. One solution was to recommend that the school vacation periods be eliminated. "I am satisfied an Indian school should be kept in session the whole year," concluded one agent, "in order that the children may be kept away from the savage influences which they encounter when they return to camp during the annual vacation."[16] Another approach was to move the school away from agency headquarters, where interaction between parents and pupils could be more closely regulated and where agency affairs would be less inclined to spill over into the school.[17] A third strategy, and a less expensive one, was to erect more definable physical barriers between the school and the agency. Thus, one agent proposed, "There should be a board fence 12 feet high, enclosing a space 200 by 300 yards around the school buildings." Similarly, an agent in the Southwest informed Washington that he was having an eight-foot adobe wall built around the school. This, he hoped, would entirely separate the schoolchildren "from all outside influence and contact with the tribe, which is positively necessary in order to teach them morality."[18]

Although such measures would no doubt improve the situation, a growing number of policymakers were reaching the conclusion that the reservation boarding school approach was fundamentally flawed. Relocating school buildings, erecting higher fences, and abolishing vacation would never succeed in entirely eliminating the insidious influences of reservation life. Savagery, it seemed, was in the air. Like a mysterious, invisible vapor, it seeped into the classrooms and dormitories, clouding and intoxicating the minds of the children within. How could even the most dedicated teacher, it was asked, compete with the real and imagined dramas unfolding just beyond the school fence and in the surrounding hills? If Indian children were to be thoroughly civilized, it was reasoned, a more radical solution was called for. "On the reservation no school can be so conducted as to remove the children from the influence of the idle and vicious who are everywhere present," concluded one agent. "Only by removing them beyond the reach of this influence can they be benefited by the teaching of the schoolmaster."[19] In uttering these words, P. P. Wilcox, the agent to the San Carlos Apache, was offering his support for still a third model of Indian education, the off-reservation boarding school.

A SCHOOL FOR TEACHING CIVILIZATION

On a spring day in 1875, before the first rays of the sun had cleared the surrounding hills, Fort Sill, Indian Territory, was already buzzing with activity. When preparations were complete, seventy-two Indian warriors, all in leg irons, shuffled to the awaiting army wagons. Ordered to sit with their backs to the sides of the wagon, a long chain was slipped through each prisoner's legs so that the Indians were shackled both to one another and to the wagon. Meanwhile, a throng of Indians had gathered to witness the departure of the captives, the women succumbing to an eerie wailing as if mourning a beloved one killed on the battlefield. It was a familiar sound to soldiers who had served on the frontier any length of time and it only added to the tension, a tension fed by rumors that a dramatic rescue might be attempted. As it turned out, the plot, if there had ever been one, never materialized. And so, the train of wagons, under heavy military guard, left the fort and passed through the throng without incident, beginning a journey of several days to the railroad, where the Indians were to be boarded on a special train and taken to Fort Leavenworth, Kansas.[20]

Except for Lone Wolf, a Kiowa chief who had once accompanied a delegation to Washington to see the "Great Father," riding in the "iron horse" was an altogether novel and unnerving experience. Lt. Richard Henry Pratt, the officer in charge of the operation, later recalled, "As the train started, the prisoners were at first greatly interested, but as it increased in speed beyond anything they had ever experienced, it was plain that some of them were not a little disturbed, and these at first pulled their blankets over their heads and quit looking out." One prisoner, Bear's Heart, was convinced that Pratt was planning to execute him. As the train rolled along, he later recalled, "all the time I think by and by he will kill me." Upon reaching Leavenworth, Bear's Heart and the other prisoners were again thrown into the guardhouse. What the Indians' long-term fate might be, they could scarcely imagine.[21]

The seventy-two prisoners were a mixed lot, composed of thirty-four

Fort Sill prisoners being loaded into wagons, 1875, as drawn by Bear's Heart. (Courtesy of the Beinecke Rare Book and Manuscript Library, Yale University)

Cheyenne, two Arapaho, twenty-seven Kiowa, nine Comanche, and one Caddo. Although several older Cheyenne and Kiowa chiefs were among the group, most were young warriors in their twenties and mid-thirties. Nearly all were charged by the army with a host of crimes committed during the so-called Red River War of 1874.[22] More a series of skirmishes than an outright war, the conflict was precipitated by the refusal of the Southern Plains Indians to accept the terms of recent treaties confining them to reservation life. With the depletion of the southern buffalo herds, the invasion of the white settlers, and the failure of Congress to live up to treaty obligations, Kiowa, Cheyenne, and Comanche warriors struck out in fury, determined to make one last stand against white incursion and to settle some old scores in the process. Cruel and bloody acts of violence followed, many of them directed against the innocent and unsuspecting.[23]

Once the offenders were locked up at Fort Sill, the army began the tedious process of gathering evidence and charging the prisoners with their crimes. The final list ranged from theft and rape to murder. The problem was what to do next. Originally, the intent was to try them before a military commission, but this plan ran afoul of a ruling by the attorney general that a military trial would be illegal because a state of war could not technically exist between "a nation and its wards." On the other hand, a civilian trial was out of the question for the simple reason that frontier sentiment against Indians rendered a fair trial impossible. The solution, an arbitrary one to be sure, was to imprison the group at old Fort Marion in St. Augustine, Florida. Originally named Castillo de San Marcos, the fortress had been constructed by the Spanish in the late seventeenth century as a bastion against naval attack. Now, its great stone walls would be put to a different use.[24]

While the prisoners were under lock and key at Fort Leavenworth, Pratt received notice that he was to oversee the exile of the Indians to St. Augustine and then supervise their incarceration. The lieutenant was not disappointed at his new assignment. Quite the contrary, he had requested it. Pratt had spent most of his youth in Logansport, Indiana, where life had been pleasant until the age of thirteen when his father's unexpected death suddenly thrust adult responsibilities on young Pratt's shoulders. Forced to leave school to support the family, he worked as a printer's helper, a rail spitter, and a tinsmith, In April 1861, only eight days after the attack on Fort Sumter, Pratt joined an Indiana cavalry unit to fight for the Union. When the war was over he returned to Logansport, married, and went into the hardware business. But the ex-soldier soon discovered that he was temperamentally ill-suited to running a hardware store; he was bored and missed military life. So in March 1867, he joined the regular army and was commissioned a second lieutenant in the Tenth United States Cavalry, an all-Negro unit except for the officers, who were white. The Tenth was being sent west to keep the peace and to fight Indians. One of Pratt's first responsibilities was to take charge of a group of Cherokee scouts attached to the unit. This was Pratt's first experience with Indians. He soon learned that the scouts assigned to him were not only experienced soldiers but had acquired a smattering of education in Cherokee schools. Pratt would spend eight years in the West, keeping the peace and fighting Indians. During these years Pratt, like the "humanitarian generals" of his day, came to the conclusion that there was only one way for the Indians to survive the onslaught of progress: they would have to be swallowed up in the rushing tide of American life and institutions. That was the only solution.[25]

Transporting the prisoners from Fort Leavenworth to Florida turned out to be no easy matter. First, there was the problem of the large crowds. Before the train pulled into the larger stopovers—St. Louis, Louisville, Nashville, Atlanta, Jacksonville—the press would circulate stories about the route of the train and its unique cargo. The result was clamoring crowds that pressed around the cars hoping to get a glimpse of the "savages" within. And then there were the two casualties. Approaching Nashville, one of the Cheyenne leaders, Lean Bear, produced a small penknife and in an attempt to commit suicide, stabbed himself several times in the chest and neck. Presumed dead, the body was taken off the train for burial at Nashville. (Only later was it learned that he was still very much alive.

Several weeks later, he was sent to St. Augustine.) About the death of another Cheyenne, Gray Beard, there was little doubt. Throughout the ordeal Gray Beard had grown more despondent than the rest, unable to reconcile himself to the confinement and exile in store for him. Somewhere near the Georgia-Florida state line, late at night, Gray Beard managed to slip through one of the windows and jumped from the moving train. The escape was immediately discovered, the train slammed to a halt, and guards were soon picking their way through the surrounding forest with lanterns and rifles. When Gray Beard jumped from behind a palmetto to cross the tracks, he was ordered to stop. He didn't and a guard shot him, the bullet passing through his chest. Still alive but bleeding profusely, he was loaded onto the rear of the last car. His old friend Manimic, a war chief, was brought back to comfort him. As Gray Beard lay dying, the prisoner-train rumbled deeper into Florida. The Indians finally arrived in St. Augustine on May 21, 1875.[26]

Pratt's orders were vague; he was instructed to oversee the incarceration of the Indians. Indeed, if he had interpreted his orders narrowly, the Fort Marion affair might have simply become an interesting but minor incident in the story of Indian-white relations. But such was not the case. Shortly after the train's arrival at St. Augustine, Pratt was struck with an idea that would not go away. Entirely free of any direct supervision by superiors, he decided to carry out a bold experiment: he would turn his prison into a school for teaching civilization to the Indians.

But first he took stock of the situation. Security would not be a problem. With the exception of a small side door, the only entrance from the walled fort was through two immense pitch-pine doors that opened to a large drawbridge spread across a moat surrounding that part of the fort not facing the open sea. The design of the fort was simple and functional: a large open court surrounded on all sides by casemates and a small chapel. Although a terreplein, or platform, existed on the upper level of the outer wall, thereby giving one a view of both the open sea and St. Augustine, it could easily be sealed off. The casemates, which would serve as the prisoners' living quarters, were windowless on the outside wall, with only small air vents near the ceiling, while on the inside walls small iron-grated windows permitted a view of the court. Immediately sensing that the damp and poorly ventilated cells would create health problems for Indians used to the open prairie, Pratt ordered that the dirt floors be covered with wooden planks and that beds be constructed. Under heavy guard and still in leg irons, the Indians settled in.[27]

There were problems almost immediately. The humidity and summer heat began to take effect, and in the first few weeks several of the Indians died. These factors exacted a heavy psychological toll on the prisoners, and most fell into a state of "depression and hopelessness." In response

Group of Indian prisoners at Fort Marion at time of arrival, 1875. (Courtesy of the Beinecke Rare Book and Manuscript Library, Yale University)

Pratt began to make changes. First, the leg irons were removed and the prisoners were allowed to move more freely. Next he arranged to have their long hair cut off and issued them discarded army uniforms. The transition to uniforms didn't go easily. Preferring traditional Indian leggings to the white man's trousers, several prisoners cut off the pant legs at the hip, throwing away the upper half of the trousers. After a stern lecture, the prisoners were not only wearing their uniforms properly but folding their trousers along crease lines and conscientiously polishing their brass buttons and shoes. A particularly risky step on Pratt's part was when he decided that the white guards should be removed and an Indian company be organized to patrol the prison. The plan worked brilliantly. Slowly but deliberately, Fort Marion began to take on all the attributes of a military camp, with smart-looking officers barking out commands and carefully drilled soldiers marching in perfect timing. Meanwhile, Pratt was meeting with the Indians every evening to lecture them on what they must do to survive as a people, that is, embrace the white man's civilization. Indeed, if his prisoners would play the role of obedient children, Pratt was more than willing to play the role of the stern but benevolent father and raise them up from savagery. Somewhat traumatized by the prison ordeal, some began to listen.[28]

With obedience came freedom, and prison life gradually became more bearable as Pratt made a concerted effort to introduce the Indians to the world beyond the prison. At first this effort took the form of an occasional camping expedition to a nearby island. On such occasions the prisoners fished, swam, dug for oysters, and competed in foot races on the long stretches of sandy beach. One day Pratt arranged for them to hunt what the Indians called "water buffalo," meaning sharks. At Pratt's urging, a local fisherman devised a method whereby sharks in the harbor were enticed to take chunks of meat dangled on a hook from a rowboat, the baited hooks connected to lines that extended to the beach where the Indians held on for dear life. When a shark took the bait, a tug of war immediately ensued. According to Pratt, "It was a great sport for the twenty or more Indians who whooped and tugged and pulled until the shark surrendered." "Sometimes," he continued, "when they were pulling their hardest the shark would turn suddenly and dash toward shore and the crowd all fall down and before they could get up the shark was going the other way." In the end, they landed five, one weighing almost 1,200 pounds.[29]

Along with recreation, Pratt made an effort to integrate his prisoners into the social and economic life of St. Augustine. The Indians, although initially feared by some, were an object of great curiosity. Pratt made the most of this fact by inviting citizens to visit the prison, and soon he was issuing passes to selected prisoners to leave the prison. In time, the prisoners, usually in pairs, could be seen walking from shop to shop on the streets of St. Augustine. Blurring the demarcation between the prisoners and the wider community was a conscious reflection of Pratt's belief that in order for his prison-school to be successful, the Indians must understand firsthand the white man's way of living. Also fundamental was a need to instill in the Indians the work ethic—but where to begin? The solution came in the unlikely form of sea beans or seeds, which covered the shores around St. Augustine. Once polished and strung on necklaces, these beans were a major sales item for local curio dealers. Upon learning that dealers were willing to pay ten cents for the polishing of a single bean, Pratt secured a contract for his Indians. Within a few months they had polished 16,000 beans, for an income of $1,600. Soon the Indians were making canes and bows and arrows, painting scenes of traditional Indian life, and receiving the full sales amount when the items were sold. In the matter of a year or so the Indians were being hired out as laborers— to pick oranges, work as baggage men at the railroad depot, clear land, care for horses, and milk cows for local farmers. To awaken the spirit of economic individualism, Pratt kept individual savings accounts for each of the prisoners, and the prisoners could use the money they had earned to make an array of purchases in St. Augustine.[30]

The ultimate success of Pratt's experiment depended upon his ability to teach the Indians the white man's language. What he required were volunteer teachers sympathetic to his aims, and as it turned out, there would be no problems in attracting them. The first to come to his aid, Sarah Mather, was a retired teacher living in St. Augustine. Educated at Mt. Holyoke, and a former director of a girls boarding school, Mather was a teacher of extraordinary ability and zeal. The idea of teaching Pratt's prisoners, strangers to civilization and God, appealed mightily to her Christian and philanthropic sensibilities. With Mather's enlistment to the cause, others followed. In the summer of 1876, Pratt could report to General Sheridan: "I have a two-hour school daily with an average of fifty pupils, divided into four classes, with a good teacher for each. The teachers work from the purest and best motives of Christian charity and, as a consequence, successfully." With four casemates now serving as classrooms, Fort Marion's famed warriors now struggled with the ABC's, and soon, with words and entire sentences.[31]

With words came ideas. When the opportunity afforded itself, Miss Mather and her assistants lectured their pupils on various aspects of the white man's civilization, especially the ideals and values that served the basis for that civilization. In time, the discussion turned to religion. The words "cat" and "dog" gave way to "Bible" and "God," and the stone walls of the prison school were soon resonating with recitations of the Lord's Prayer and the melodies of Christian hymns. All of this reinforced the religious instruction that was already going on, for by now Pratt was regularly holding weekly prayer meetings in the prisons. After gaining the cooperation of local pastors, he began urging the prisoners to attend local church services. The message came from all directions.[32]

In the meantime, Episcopal Bishop Henry Benjamin Whipple arrived on the scene. Whipple, a renowned missionary among the Sioux, happened to be wintering in St. Augustine in 1876 and when hearing of Pratt's experiment was immediately drawn to the prison. "I was never more touched than when I entered this school," Whipple would soon write. "Here were men who had committed murder upon helpless women and children sitting like docile children at the feet of women learning to read. Their faces have changed. They have all lost that look of savage hate, and the light of a new life is dawning on their hearts." Over the course of several weeks, Whipple paid regular visits to the prison, preaching simple sermons about the Christian God and his son who died on the cross. The Indians especially liked the Bible stories: "They seemed to hang upon my words as if I were a messenger of life from heaven."[33] Was there a mass conversion to Christianity by the prisoners? Probably not, but some of the Indians appear to have discarded their native beliefs for the so-called "Jesus book." The testament of Soaring Eagle, a twenty-six-year-old Cheyenne warrior, certainly has the ring of authenticity:

> It is good to go to church. When I was at my home, I did not know about church. When I was at my home, I did not wear good clothes. My hair was long. I know now to spell and read a little, and will know more. When I go home, I hope to sit down and sing God's hymns. . . . At home, I did not know who Jesus was, I loved to hunt, shoot, and sleep on Sundays like other days, but the Bible God's book has told me it was wrong. I now look up to Jesus who has been so good to me and pray to him to forgive all my past sins and make me his child.[34]

To all who visited the fort, it appeared that Pratt, the stern Christian soldier, had wrought a near miracle. The Indians had arrived as savages; now they were decent Christian men walking the path of civilization. Slowly, the word spread through philanthropic circles. Among those who assisted in the process was Harriet Beecher Stowe, then a resident of St. Augustine. Visiting the prison in April 1877 and astonished by Pratt's success, Stowe drew upon her old abolitionist fervor and described in two articles for *The Christian Crisis* what she had seen. She had heard stories, she wrote, about how the Indians had arrived, looking like bloodthirsty warriors. Thus, upon entering the prison she was immediately struck by the altered appearance of the prisoners: "We found now no savages." Sitting in on a classroom, she observed, "there were among these pupils seated, docile and eager, with books in hand, men who had seen the foremost in battle and bloodshed. Now there was plainly to be seen among them the eager joy which comes from the use of a new set of faculties." Stowe lavished praise on the Indians' neatness, discipline, and industriousness. The most moving scene was a prayer meeting when the prisoners were led in mournful, wailing prayer by old Chief Manimic, a virtual "cry unto God." Was there not an immense lesson in all of this?

> Is not here an opening for Christian enterprise? We have tried fighting and killing the Indians, and gained little by it. We have tried feeding them as paupers in their savage state, and the result has been dishonest contractors, and invitation and provocation to war. Suppose we try education? . . . Might not the money now constantly spent on armies, forts, and frontiers be better invested in educating young men who shall return and teach their people to live like civilized beings?[35]

As visitors came and went, Pratt struggled with his superiors over the question of the prisoners' fate. From the very beginning he had divided the Indians into two groups: the older ones, who were generally charged with more serious offenses and, by virtue of age, were less amenable to schooling, and the younger ones, who were making more rapid progress and repeatedly expressed a desire to learn more of civilized ways. As early as June 1875, Pratt recommended that some of the more notorious prisoners be transferred to a penitentiary where they could be taught a trade. The request was denied. In March 1876 he proposed that some of the brighter and younger Indians be sent to an agricultural or trade school to continue their education. Again the request was denied. A year later, Pratt again expressed the view that no further purpose could be served by imprisoning the older Indians and they should be released. As for the younger prisoners, he was still recommending further education.[36]

In the spring of 1878, Pratt received word that the prisoners could be released and that neither the Indian Office nor the army had any opposition to the younger prisoners receiving further education. Earlier on, Pratt had asked the younger men how many wanted to remain in the East for further education. Twenty-two had stepped forward. Now, with the government having removed all objections, two problems still needed to be solved. The first was that of financing the Indians' education. As it turned out, this was to be the least of Pratt's worries. One by one, individuals who had witnessed firsthand the Indians' progress stepped forward to assume the financial burden, in some instances volunteering to sponsor the entire education of one or more students. What Pratt could not get in the form of larger gifts he received in the form of small donations collected at benefits in St. Augustine. The second problem proved to be more difficult: finding an institution that would accept twenty-two Indians. Pratt appealed to several state agricultural colleges, but all were hesitant to take in the former warriors. Indeed, for a while it appeared that further schooling was out of the question. Although four were to be taken in by an Episcopal clergyman in New York, and another by Dr. and Mrs. Horace Curuthers of Tarrytown, for the remaining seventeen, prospects appeared bleak. Finally, word came from Hampton, Virginia, that Samuel Chapman Armstrong, founder and principal of Hampton Normal and Industrial Institute, would take the seventeen Indians.[37]

Armstrong's unique background explains his decision. Born in 1839 on the island of Maui, he spent the first twenty years of his life in the Sandwich Islands under the tutelage and influence of his New England–bred father, Richard Armstrong, who labored as a missionary to the dark-skinned native islanders. In 1860, the younger Armstrong left Hawaii to attend Williams College. Graduating from Williams in 1862, he was immediately swept up in the storm of the Civil War and joined the Union cause as an abolitionist. Following the war, Armstrong learned that a normal school was to be established for blacks at Hampton, partly funded by the American Missionary Association (AMA), and he immediately volunteered to assume the principalship. In April 1868, Hampton Institute opened its doors with fifteen students. In two years, partly because of Armstrong's remarkable skill for fund-raising, Hampton was largely independent of AMA support and fully under Armstrong's control. Charismatic and strong-willed, Armstrong shaped the Hampton program along lines that were fully consistent with his conception of black educational needs in the postbellum South. According to Armstrong, blacks had emerged from slavery culturally and morally inferior to whites and only under the benevolent tutelage of whites could they hope to make genuine racial progress. The solution lay in a Hampton-style education, an education that combined cultural uplift with moral and manual training, or as Armstrong was fond of saying, an education that encompassed "the head, the heart, and the hand."[38]

It is plainly evident that Armstrong's invitation to Pratt's Indians was in keeping with his previous work.[39] And it is also clear that he was more than a little nervous about his decision. Several teachers and trustees were openly skeptical about extending the school's work to Indians, and there also was the problem of getting black students to accept them. One evening when students were assembled for prayer, Armstrong announced that the Indians were coming. After a persuasive appeal for acceptance and understanding, which ended with the words, "Freely ye have received, freely give," he asked for seventeen volunteers who would each take charge of one of the Indians. Although the students had responded favorably to the general idea of inviting the Indians, the request for volunteers met with strong silence. Exasperated, Armstrong pressed on. "Why is this? Is no one here man enough to do for another race what has so freely been done for his?" At this point the truth came out. Rising, one student responded: "We want to but we're scared—we're afraid they might scalp us." To this, Armstrong explained, there was nothing to fear, and after another appeal he finally got what he wanted. One by one, they stood up: "I'll take one, General." In the end, all seventeen were accounted for.[40]

In spite of Armstrong's public assurances that the Indians were now tame, he was privately worried. "There might be some difficulty in case of bad Indians," he wrote to Pratt in late January. "We send negroes home as a severe punishment; what would be done with an objectional Indian?" By March, however, he was making light of the situation. In a letter to Robert C. Ogden, a prominent Hampton trustee, he observed that although the Indians were once "terrible cutthroats," they were now "said to be tamed." And then in a crude attempt at humor he added, "Now and then they will try to scalp a darky but their war hatchets won't make much impression on him."[41] In any case, the Indians were coming.

Meanwhile, the Fort Marion prisoners were preparing for their departure. The older prisoners, it was decided, would accompany the latter group as far as Hampton and then leave for the West. Pratt, it was agreed, would help the seventeen students get settled in their new home. For Tsait-Kope-ta, one of the five who would be going to New York, leaving Pratt was not easy. One of Pratt's prize Kiowa pupils, he had come to look upon Pratt as a father, almost a savior. Before leaving for the north, he wrote the captain a letter.

> A long time I have not written to you. Now I want to tell you something. I cannot speak good yet. I can read some and understand a good deal, but I cannot talk much. White man's talk is very hard. I try, maybe in a few years I can talk good. Long time ago when you first began to teach us, you showed us a card and asked us what that was. It was A.B.C., but I did not know anything about it. I only laughed in my heart. By and by I think yes! He wants to show us the road. . . . You talked a good deal. I could not listen good nor understand. In one year I heard a little, and something I began to know of what you said. Again in one more year I understood a heap. Again in one more year I knew almost all your talk. And now I can write a letter like a white man, and when I open a book I can read a good deal of it. I am surprised and glad. I think, once it was not so—once all of us Indians knew nothing. Now I am a white man—I think. Now I know that good white men live a good life—no steal, no lie, no hurt anything— no kill, kind to all. By and by I hope I will be the same.

It had been a long, difficult journey, the young Kiowa continued.

> I am very happy now—very glad, some of my friends, old men and young are going home. Capt. Pratt may be you glad—I don't know. I think so. Maybe I shall go to school—I shall not forget you—I love you Capt. Pratt. I shall keep you—always I am glad to think of you. You have done so much for me. You have given me everything— clothes, pants, coat . . . all. You have talked to me just the same as to a child and told me what to do and I have done it just the same as one of your little girls would. Capt. Pratt you have planted seed just as men do corn, or potatoes or anything, among us young men, and maybe it will be just the same with us as the seed—some will turn out good, and other, good for nothing.
>
> Sometime Capt. Pratt I hope you will write to me. Your friend.
>
> Tsait-Kope-ta[42]

On April 13, 1978, sixty-two Indians descended on the campus of

Hampton. Within a few weeks, the *Southern Workman* observed, "The experiment is an experiment, and all that can be claimed at this early stage is that it is working smoothly so far."[43] Smoothly, indeed. Armstrong was so impressed with the Indians that he was soon entertaining suggestions that Hampton expand its Indian enrollment.[44] When Congress appropriated funds for the purpose of educating Indian children in "special schools," the prospect was all the more attractive. In August, Armstrong received word from Washington that Hampton could enroll fifty more Indians—this time girls as well as boys—and that Pratt could stay on to oversee the project. By the end of August, Pratt was canvassing Indian agencies for students in the Dakotas and Nebraska. Meanwhile, Armstrong was making preparations for his burgeoning Indian program; a new building, the Wigwam, was being constructed for the boys, and material was being purchased for uniforms.[45]

It was at this point that Armstrong and Pratt came up with an ingenious public relations scheme that both would utilize in the coming years with the utmost effect—the use of photographs to illustrate the conditions of Indians both "before" and "after" their institutionalization. Thus, on the eve of Pratt's departure for Nebraska, Armstrong wrote him: "We wish a variety of photographs of the Indians. Be sure and have them bring their wild barbarous things. This will show whence we started." Armstrong advised Pratt that if he liked, he could have the photographs taken in the West whereupon Hampton would purchase the negatives, but one way or another, the students must be photographed in their native state. Pratt, who had already seen the publicity value of photographs while at St. Augustine, understood perfectly. From the West he wired Armstrong that the photographs would have to be taken at Hampton. "The argument will be all the better. '*Condition on arrival at Hampton.*'"[46] In the fall of 1878, Pratt returned to Hampton with his quota of Indians—Sioux, Gros Ventre, Mandan, and Arikara. Photographs were immediately taken.

Meanwhile, Pratt was restless. His growing uneasiness stemmed in part from the fact that whereas in St. Augustine he had answered only to himself, at Hampton he was merely an assistant to Armstrong. The two men apparently got along well together, but Pratt was not temperamentally suited to being second in command. Also, he and Armstrong had slightly divergent views on how the education of the Indians ought to proceed. Although they were in agreement in the main—that the path to Indian civilization was through a combination of academic and industrial training—there were differences. "I told the General," Pratt recalls in his memoirs, "my dissatisfaction with systems to educate the Negro and Indian in exclusively race schools and especially with educating the two races together." At Hampton, Pratt had concluded, the Indians would be largely isolated from the surrounding white community, thus eliminating one of the factors that had been so crucial to his success at St. Augustine. Pratt was also convinced that Indians would suffer from their association with blacks, not because blacks would prove a degrading influence, but simply because white prejudice against blacks would inevitably spill over toward Indians. For these reasons, Pratt would rather go back to his regiment than remain at Hampton.[47]

About this time Pratt noted in a newspaper that Congress had recently passed an army appropriation bill providing for "the detail of an army officer not above the rank of captain with reference to Indian Education," an obvious reference to his work at Hampton. With Armstrong's blessing, he left for Washington to lobby for his own school. After a round of meetings with the secretary of interior, the commissioner of Indian affairs, the secretary of war, and several influential congressmen, Pratt was authorized to recruit 125 students for a new Indian school. As for the school's location, he was invited to inspect some unused military barracks at Carlisle, Pennsylvania. Pratt investigated the site and concluded that with a few changes, they would do just fine.[48]

Pratt immediately set about the business of recruiting a small staff. Once again, Miss Mather, now back in St. Augustine, agreed to join him and oversee the Indian girls. Pratt, who possessed a talent for surrounding himself with dedicated and efficient teachers, soon had the required staff. By September 1879, he and Mather were searching for students in the Dakotas, concentrating their attention on the Sioux at the Pine Ridge and Rosebud agencies. Pratt had wanted to return to Indian Territory where he was known among the Indians, but Commissioner Ezra Hayt insisted that he take a number of recruits from the Sioux to whom the Indian Office wanted to introduce the "school idea." At Rosebud, Pratt had a particularly difficult time convincing the Sioux chiefs to turn over their children. But the strong-willed Pratt was relentless, hammering away over and over again at the idea that the Indians' only defense against the white man was to learn his language and ways. Finally, Chiefs Spotted Tail, White Thunder, Milk, and Two Strike agreed to hand over a number of children. At Pine Ridge, it went a little easier, and altogether, Pratt left Sioux country with sixty boys and twenty-four girls. A return trip to Indian Territory, where Pratt had sent two Hampton boys as advance agents, resulted in additional recruits, thirty-eight boys and fourteen girls. Meanwhile, Pratt had arranged for eleven of his original prisoner-students from Ft. Marion to be sent up from Hampton. On November 1, 1879, Carlisle Indian School officially opened.[49]

In a repetition of what had occurred at St. Augustine and Hampton, a parade of visitors descended on the campus to witness the miracle that Pratt was performing. As Pratt's photographs so dramatically illustrated, the Indians had arrived in a pitifully heathen state, clad in filthy blankets and moccasins, their bodies and long hair ornamented with all variety of shabby trinkets. As reported by the *New York Daily Tribune,* the new recruits were as foreign "to the ways of civilization as so many freshly captured wolves."[50] But as they marched and drilled in their new uniforms, as they stumbled over the rocky paths of the printed page, as they mastered the new weapons required for the struggle ahead of them—the hammer, saw, and carpenter's plane—they seemed to have about them the semblance of civilized men and women. Indeed, after just three and a half months of Carlisle's existence, a visiting delegation composed of Commissioner Schurz and members of the House Committee on Indian Affairs and the Board of Indian Commissioners concluded that the change wrought in the Indians was nothing less than "astonishing."[51]

How did the students feel about the ordeal they were undergoing? On October 6, 1880, one year to the day that the contingent of Sioux had arrived from Rosebud and Pine Ridge, Pratt brought the school together for an anniversary ceremony. In his usual straightforward manner, he asked students the question: Should the work at Carlisle be carried forward? According to one account, "Every hand went up in favor of continuing it, and some of the boys even stood up and held up both hands." One of the teachers then read a poem she had composed especially for the occasion, putting into rhyme what she presumed the Indians were feeling but could not express in their new language. "Anniversary Day, 1880" asked the question:

> Are we the same boys
> Who, with trinkets and toys,
> Moccasins, blankets, and paint,
> And a costume most quaint,
> On the 6th of October,
> The long journey over,
> Came to this friendly roof,
> One year ago?

The answer:

> Yes, we are the very same
> Who to these good Barracks came,
> Where kindly friends a welcome gave us,
> Did all they could to teach, and save us,
> From idle habits, and bad ways.
> And carry us safely through the maze
> Of reading, writing, and of talking

Richard Henry Pratt, superintendent of Carlisle Indian School, with three students, ca. 1880. (Courtesy of the Smithsonian Institution)

And even have improved our walking;
This we learn at dress-parade,
Where, like soldiers, we are made
To face, and march, and counter-march,
While the Band under the arch
    Of the stand . . .
With their bugles and coronets, cymbals and drum,
Play old "A.B.C."—then with double-quick run
    To our quarters we go,
And you hardly would know
We're the very same boys,
Who, on the 6th of October,
The long journey over,
Came to this friendly roof,
    One year ago.[52]

PRATT'S VISION

In establishing Carlisle, Pratt created the prototype for yet a third approach to Indian schooling, the off-reservation boarding school. As the tenacious and outspoken headmaster of Carlisle for the next twenty-five years, he would remain the singlemost important figure on the Indian educational scene. For that reason, his views demand further exploration, and in doing so, it is important to remember the singularity of conviction with which they were advanced. Indeed, Pratt's uncompromising nature and his tendency to adhere to absolutes were central to his being. Having fought and lived among Indians and having engineered the St. Augustine experiment, Pratt was fully convinced that he understood Indians and their needs better than most, and he had nothing but disdain for those who criticized his methods. This single-mindedness, coupled with a tendency to vent his spleen against those who saw matters differently, would in time produce two altogether contradictory assessments of his character. Some clearly regarded him as a righteous warrior on behalf of Indian welfare; others would come to see him as a bellicose and arrogant zealot. He had a particular talent for rankling his superiors. Eventually, they tired of him and he was dismissed. In the meantime, he was a formidable campaigner for his ideas.[53]

Pratt liked Indians, but he had little use for Indian cultures. Believing that Indian ways were in every way inferior to those of whites, he never questioned the proposition that civilization must eventually triumph over savagery, but this did not require the extinction of the race. As he once pointed out, his position differed slightly from the popular slogan in the

West that held that the "only good Indian is a dead one." Instead, Pratt subscribed to the principle, "Kill the Indian in him and save the man." The solution to the Indian problem lay in the rapid assimilation of the race into American life. As to how this might be done, he was certain he had discovered the means—schools. But it was not schools per se that mattered; only off-reservation schools located in civilized communities were capable of accomplishing the task ahead. Schools on the reservation, at least by themselves, could never succeed.[54]

The basis for the Indian's inferiority, therefore, was cultural, not racial. Pratt was adamant on this point. The difference between a savage and a civilized man could be explained by environment.

> It is a great mistake to think that the Indian is born an inevitable savage. He is born a blank, like the rest of us. Left in the surroundings of savagery, he grows to possess a savage language, superstition, and life. We, left in the surroundings of civilization, grow to possess a civilized language, life, and purpose. Transfer the infant white to the savage surroundings, he will grow to possess a savage language, superstition and habit. Transfer the savage-born infant to the surroundings of civilization, and he will grow to possess a civilized language and habit.[55]

Environment was everything. On one occasion, Pratt illustrated this point by telling the story of one of Carlisle's first recruits, a sixteen-year-old "light-complexioned" boy collected at Rosebud Agency. "He came in blanket, leggings and moccasins," Pratt recalled. "His hair was long and matted. He was as dirty and as much covered with vermin as any in the party. He spoke no word of English, but could speak the Sioux language with as much fluency as the others." The boy's parents, he explained, were both white. While crossing the plains, the party had been attacked by the Sioux. The father was killed, and the pregnant mother was taken captive and had eventually married among the Sioux. Meanwhile the baby was raised as a "white Indian." But when he came to Carlisle he was Sioux through and through. In fact, Pratt explained, the boy's teachers found that, although possessing a good mind, "he learned English with less readiness and made slower progress than many of the Indian boys who came with the same party and under like circumstances." This was just one illustration of a larger truth, Pratt told his audience. "There is no resistless clog placed upon us by birth. We are not born with language, nor are we born with ideas of either civilization or savagery." The white child was potentially a savage, just as the Indian child was potentially civilized.[56]

Given the importance of environment, Pratt was unbending in his criticism of all those forces that perpetuated tribal cohesion and identity. The heart of the problem was the so-called Indian system. With its herding and massing of Indians on reservations, with its endless gifts of food and clothing, with its paternalistic governance of all things having to do with Indians, the Indian system only served to prolong the tribal relation. "We make our greatest mistake in feeding our civilization to the Indians instead of feeding the Indians to our civilization," he observed. The present reservation system worked at "colonizing" Indians, whereas Carlisle worked at "individualizing" them. Again, the answer to the question of how to solve the Indian problem lay in immersing the Indians into the mainstream of American life. "The boy learns to swim by going into the water; the Indian will become civilized by mixing with civilization."[57]

Given his assimilationist stance, one might expect to find Pratt an ardent supporter of land allotment. Although endorsing it as one mechanism for undermining tribalism, he was disturbed by the tendency of some to view it as an all-encompassing solution to the Indian problem. Pratt was skeptical of the Dawes Act for two reasons. First, he was adamant on the point that education should proceed land allotment and citizenship, not follow it. Second, Pratt was convinced that allotment, although it might succeed at breaking up reservations as political entities, would continue to perpetuate Indian communities. The allottee was "still chained to the locality and neighborhood in which the commune before prevailed, and for that very reason the influence of the commune and the old system will continue."[58] As for Pratt's solution to the land issue: "I would blow the reservations to pieces. I would not give Indians an acre of land. When he strikes bottom, he will get up."[59]

It was precisely because Pratt favored the rapid and absolute assimilation of the Indians that he was so critical of reservation schools. Reservation schools, he maintained, were still Indian schools, surrounded and ultimately engulfed by the conditions of reservation life. The reservation school said to the Indian child: "You are Indians, and must remain Indians. You are not of the nation, and cannot become of the nation. We do not want you to become of the nation." It said this not so much in words as in practice. In the reservation school, civilization could only be presented to the children as a theoretical concept; they could not experience it firsthand. In such schools, Pratt argued, Indian children could never be prepared for competition with "the more skillful, aggressive, and productive race"—the white man. If Indian children were to be assimilated, they must be gotten into the "swim of American citizenship. They must feel the touch of it day after day, until they become saturated with the spirit of it, and thus become equal to it."[60]

This was what Carlisle proposed to do, remove children from the isolating, tribalizing influence of the reservation and immerse them in a totally civilized environment. The question arises here: Wasn't Carlisle, by virtue of the fact that it was an exclusively Indian school, also segregating Indian youth from the "experience" of civilization? Not so, claimed Pratt. The ultimate rationale for the off-reservation school lay in its capacity to integrate students into the civilized community beyond the school's walls through the so-called outing system. The idea for the outing system had come from Pratt's experience in St. Augustine with integrating his prisoners into the economic life of the city. Pratt had long ago concluded that this aspect of the St. Augustine system had been vital to his success. During the first year of Carlisle's operation, Pratt initiated the idea anew, the first summer distributing eighteen students among Pennsylvania farm families. In a few years, the outing experience had become a central component in the school's program. Living among white families, Pratt asserted, the Indian student rapidly mastered the English language, internalized the habits of industriousness, and generally speaking, acquired the everyday habits of civilized living. Although at first student outings were only for the duration of the summer, Pratt was soon placing students for a year at a time, thus enabling them to attend the public schools in their families' respective communities.[61] Indeed, public schools were the ideal. But Pratt cautioned that it would be a waste of time to educate Indians in *Indian* public schools in the West. Again, this would only result in more segregation. The ideal solution—Pratt's fantasy—was to scatter the entire population of Indian children across the nation, with some 70,000 white families each taking in one Indian child.[62] That, of course, would be the ultimate outing system, the ultimate solution to the dilemma of how to assimilate Indians. But as things stood, the off-reservation boarding school offered the most effective alternative.

Was Pratt opposed to all reservation schools? Not really. As a practical matter he came to accept the fact that the reservation boarding school would always constitute an element in the emerging Indian school system. The important thing was not to overestimate their capacity to assimilate. At Lake Mohonk he told his audience that the reservation boarding school was like a "hot-bed." "It may give the seeds a start," he said, "but it cannot grow cabbages."[63] Pratt conceived of Indian schooling as an open-ended affair. And although he would have preferred that all Indian children experience civilization firsthand, he recognized that many would not. The important thing was not to place any limitations on Indian students' aspirations.

I believe in Indian schools at the agencies. I believe in mission schools at the agencies. But I believe in them only as the merest stepping-stones, the small beginnings that will start to a reaching after better things. We must have schools away from the Indian reservations, plenty of them; but these should be only tentative, additional stepping-stones, higher in the scale than the agency schools, but still far below the top. Our Indian children must be educated into the capacity and the courage to go out from these school[s], from *all these schools* into our schools and into our life.[64]

The Carlisle slogan would always be: "To civilize the Indian, get him into civilization. To keep him civilized, let him stay."[65]

Meanwhile, the savage in the Indian must be obliterated. Pratt never forgot that in his crusade to assimilate Indians, he was waging a kind of war. In April 1880, when Pratt's request that another officer from his regiment be detailed to Carlisle to assist him in his work received a negative response from General William T. Sherman with the comment that army officers better served their country in their regiments, a furious Pratt protested directly to President Rutherford B. Hayes: "*I am at this time, 'fighting' a greater number of 'the enemies of civilization,' than the whole of my regiment put together, and I know further that I am fighting them with a thousand times more hopes of success.*" He continued:

Here a Lieutenant struggles to evolve order out of the chaos of fourteen different Indian languages! Civilization out of savagery! Industry and thrift out of laziness! Education out of ignorance! Cleanliness out of filth! And is forced to educate the courage of his own instructors to the work, and see that all the interests of his Govt. and the Indian as well are properly protected and served.[66]

War was indeed hell.

THE RISE OF OFF-RESERVATION SCHOOLS

Reports of Pratt's and Armstrong's successes at civilizing Indians were welcome news to policymakers. Indeed, Carlisle was scarcely under way when Secretary of the Interior Carl Schurz announced that another off-reservation school would soon open, this time in the far west—Oregon.[67] Others were to follow. Meanwhile, support for Pratt's ideas also came from agents in the field. Having observed firsthand the detrimental influence of reservation life on agency schools, a number had come to the same conclusion as Pratt: Indian children would have to be removed from the reservation environment altogether if they were going to be effectively assimilated. Thus, in 1881, after an agent at Crow Creek Agency confessed that his boarding school had produced meager results and the day schools had proven to be a "total failure," he added, "The only practical educational measure thus far adopted for Indian children is the establishment of the schools at Carlisle and Hampton."[68] Although such comments were common, it should be noted that agents were not of one mind on the question. Early on, especially after the first trickle of students began to return from distant schools, a number of agents expressed grave concerns over the wisdom and practicality of educating students so far away from their homes. But initially there was sufficient support at the agency level to reinforce policymakers' early enthusiasm for off-reservation schools.[69]

Reform organizations also lent support. In fact, for several years, philanthropists looked upon Pratt as a sort of Moses for the Indians. He had demonstrated what Christian reformers so passionately believed: the Indians' deficiencies were to be explained by environment, not race, and education was the path to their transformation and citizenship. Because of Pratt, Herbert Welsh proclaimed at Mohonk, "We need no longer ask the question, Can the Indian be civilized?" As for Merrill Gates, he had seen the photographs.

> The years of contact with ideas and with civilized men and Christian women so transform them that their faces shine with a wholly new light, for they have indeed "communed with God." They came children; they return young men and young women; yet they look younger in the face than when they came to us. The prematurely aged look of hopeless heathenism has given way to that dew of eternal youth which makes the difference between the savage and the man who lives in the thoughts of an eternal future.[70]

The Christian reformers were an important factor in the expansion of the Carlisle idea. As a group, however, they were less adamant on the point of whether all children should have an off-reservation experience. It was a generalized faith in education, rather than a commitment to any one institutional form, that shaped most philanthropic thinking. Still, most were convinced that the day school by itself could never make over the Indian children and that some form of boarding school experience was necessary. Meanwhile, they perceived the off-reservation school as playing a central part in the assimilation effort.

In 1884, four more off-reservation schools were opened at Chilocco, Oklahoma; Genoa, Nebraska; Albuquerque, New Mexico; and Lawrence, Kansas. By 1902, the number of such schools had risen to a high of twenty-five (see Table 2.1). What is noteworthy about this list is that all schools subsequent to Carlisle were built in the West. Pratt had called for locating off-reservation schools in fully civilized white communities, locations where Indian students might observe civilization in its most advanced state, where white prejudice against Indians was almost nonexis-

Table 2.1. Location and Opening Date for Off-Reservation Boarding Schools

Location of School	Date of Opening
Carlisle, Pennsylvania	1879
Chemawa, Oregon (Salem)	1880
Chilocco, Oklahoma	1884
Genoa, Nebraska	1884
Albuquerque, New Mexico	1884
Lawrence, Kansas	1884
Grand Junction, Colorado	1886
Santa Fe, New Mexico	1890
Fort Mojave, Arizona	1890
Carson, Nevada	1890
Pierre, South Dakota	1891
Phoenix, Arizona	1891
Fort Lewis, Colorado	1892
Fort Shaw, Montana	1892
Flandreau, South Dakota	1893
Pipestone, Minnesota	1893
Mount Pleasant, Michigan	1893
Tomah, Wisconsin	1893
Wittenberg, Wisconsin	1895
Greenville, California	1895
Morris, Minnesota	1897
Chamberlain, South Dakota	1898
Fort Bidwell, California	1898
Rapid City, South Dakota	1898
Riverside, California	1902

Source: Annual Report of the Commissioner of Indian Affairs, 1905, 41.
Note: The school at Riverside, California, was a replacement for a boarding school at Perris, California, which was opened in 1893.

tent, and where the psychological pull of reservation life on students would be minimized. Policymakers saw matters differently.

Several factors explain this development. First, there was the issue of expense; the costs involved in transporting thousands of Indian children over such long distances were perceived to be prohibitive.[71] Second, many policymakers took exception to the idea that the Indian children should be totally cut off from all association with their geographical and familial origins. Supporters of this position were in a sense arguing for the best of both worlds; Indian children should be schooled at a distance from the reservation, but not so far away that they would lose all understanding and appreciation for the conditions to which they must someday return. Thus, the school superintendent at Albuquerque declared in 1885 his preference for off-reservation schools, where "the parents may often visit their children, and thus grow accustomed to their improvement, and

Table 2.2. Indian Schools and Average Attendance, 1877–1900

	Boarding Schools		Day Schools		Total	
	Number	Attendance	Number	Attendance	Number	Attendance
1877	48		102		150	3,598
1880	60		109		169	4,651
1885	114	6,201	86	1,942	200	8,143
1890	140	9,865	106	2,367	246	12,232
1895	157	15,061	125	3,127	282	18,188
1900	153	17,708	154	3,860	307	21,568

Source: Annual Report of the Commissioner of Indian Affairs, 1909, 89.

so that the children may spend each year a long vacation at their homes."[72] Although such proposals were never universally adopted, the fact remains that in some off-reservation schools, parental visitations and student vacations, if not encouraged, were at least permitted. Finally, there were political motivations for establishing such schools in the West. The fact was not lost on boosters of growing frontier communities that establishing a sizable federal institution in the nearby vicinity could have a beneficial impact on the local economy. A large Indian school would be a source of employment for local residents, would purchase many supplies on the open market, and through the school's outing plan might supply a cheap source of labor for local farmers, ranchers, and businessmen. Thus, when the *Arizona Republican* in 1890 calculated the advantages of establishing an off-reservation school in Phoenix, it noted that such an institution would add an additional $50,000 annually to the city's economy and that "in a few years our lands, now being so extensively planted with fruit trees and vines, would give employment to many of the pupils."[73] Politics, as well as philanthropy, contributed to the rise and location of off-reservation schools.

Although policymakers differed on such matters as how far and for how long the Indian children should be removed from their native environment, by the mid-1880s they were clearly committed to the idea that some sort of boarding school experience was essential (see Table 2.2). Attendance figures are revealing in this regard. Although attendance at day schools grew slightly through the 1880s and 1890s, boarding school attendance rose at an enormous rate. By 1900, of the 21,568 students in school, nearly 18,000 were attending either an off-reservation or reservation boarding school. And although not shown here, it is also noteworthy that as Congress continued to build off-reservation schools through the 1890s, a continually greater proportion of boarding school attendance can be attributed to off-reservation schools. By 1900, over a third of boarding school students were in such schools. Once more, this percentage would continue to rise, until by the late 1920s, nearly half of boarding school enrollments were in off-reservation schools.[74] The figures on attendance are all the more striking when considering the fact that by the 1890s most of those attending day schools and many of those attending reservation boarding schools would eventually graduate to the next level of schooling. Thus, a high percentage of Indian children in the late nineteenth century were destined to have a boarding school experience.

Slowly at first, and then with ever-increasing momentum, the idea was gaining force that Indian children needed to be removed from their tribal homes for the assimilationist promise of education to be realized. Only by attending boarding school, policymakers were now convinced, could savage institutions, outlooks, and sympathies be rendered extinct. Only by attending boarding school could Indian youth, stripped bare of their tribal heritage, take to heart the inspiring lessons of white civilization. The educational solution to the Indian problem truly appeared to be at hand.

CHAPTER THREE

System

With the rapid growth of schools, philanthropists next turned to the difficult business of forging a genuine "system" of Indian education. Speaking at Lake Mohonk in 1885, Superintendent of Indian Schools John Oberly could only describe the present organization of Indian schools as a "Topsy system." Like the famous literary character, the Indian school system "never had a father; it never had a mother; it never was born; it 'just growed.'" Two years later, J. B. Harrison of the Indian Rights Association complained, "There is, as yet, no coherent or comprehensive system or plan for the education of the Indians under government supervision. It does not appear, indeed, that anybody has thought of the necessity of such a system."[1]

As things stood there was little systematic relationship between the day school, the reservation boarding school, and the off-reservation school. Nor was there any standardized policy prescribing the manner in which students were to be recruited and sorted among the three types of institutions, nor any consistency in how agents interpreted and carried out government policy, or for that matter, any assurance that policies were being carried out at all. Questions abounded. Was school attendance to be compulsory? If so, how should it be enforced? Upon what basis should employees for the Indian schools be selected, or perhaps more importantly, who should select them? How should the lines of authority be drawn between agents and reservation boarding school superintendents? These were just a few of the issues demanding attention. One thing was certain: for schools to become effective civilizing machines, policies and procedures would have to be routinized, responsibilities specified, and activities monitored.

The call for systemization was also prompted by the sheer size of the educational program. As already described, the 1880s and 1890's witnessed a dramatic growth in both school enrollments and school construction. Not surprisingly, these developments were paralleled by a similar increase in the number of workers employed in Indian school service. Table 3.1 is revealing in this regard. Between 1877 and 1897 the number of employees in the educational division of the Indian service grew from 114 to an astonishing 1,936. Perhaps just as significant is that over the

Table 3.1. Number of Indian Field Service Employees, 1877–1897

	Agents and Clerks	Education	Law and Order	Medical	Other	Total
1877	98	114	9	41	461	723
1879	115	139	295	54	854	1,457
1881	128	238	824	60	852	2,102
1883	121	267	633	53	569	1,643
1885	111	403	639	59	680	1,892
1887	117	708	695	66	641	2,227
1889	117	708	795	65	654	2,339
1891	126	1,088	930	77	696	2,917
1893	128	1,326	937	78	650	3,119
1895	139	1,736	958	79	734	3,646
1897	141	1,936	954	86	800	3,917

Source: Adapted from Paul Henry Stuart, "The U.S. Office of Indian Affairs, 1865–1900: The Institutionalization of a Formal Organization" (Ph.D. dissertation, University of Wisconsin, 1978), 279.

same period the number of school employees came to comprise an increasing percentage of the Indian service work force. Although the school force accounted for only about 16 percent of the total Indian service in 1877, by 1897 the figure was close to 50 percent. Not surprisingly, as the number of school employees continued to rise, more and more consideration was given to how their selection and supervision might be more routinely standardized.

What reformers wanted to create was a smooth-running and efficient system of Indian education. The Indian Bureau, widely known for its corruption and incompetence, would have to be restructured from top to bottom. In the end, power and control would need to be more centralized, lines of responsibility more clearly demarcated, bureaucratic procedures more routinized, and personnel selection removed from the influence of politicians. In this chapter I discuss the reformers' efforts to create a "one best system" of Indian education.[2]

TRANSFORMING THE BUREAUCRACY

No individual did more to systematize the Indian Office than Thomas J. Morgan, commissioner of Indian affairs from 1889 to 1893. Morgan's background and views were ideally suited to carry out the business of reform. Before coming to the commissionership, he had distinguished himself as a union officer in the Civil War, been ordained a Baptist minister, taught theology at Baptist Union Theological Seminary in Chicago, served as principal of several state normal schools, and along the way, wrote a book on pedagogy. The archtype Protestant reformer, Morgan's views on the Indian question were wholly congruent with those who gathered at Lake Mohonk. To wit, Indians were culturally inferior to whites, but with proper tutelage were fully capable of being assimilated into mainstream American life. It was Morgan's grand objective to translate this vision into administrative practice, and step by step the pieces began to fall into place.[3]

The first issue to be resolved was that of bringing the day school, the reservation boarding school, and the off-reservation school into some sort of systematic relationship. What Morgan envisioned was a three-tiered system in which the two lower institutions became feeders for the level directly above them. Spread across the three institutions, the curriculum was to be divided into four levels: day school, primary school, grammar school, and high school. (In fact, Morgan paid little attention to the day school, since it was nonexistent in many Indian communities.) The primary school curriculum was to be largely the responsibility of the reservation boarding school, and the grammar school curriculum that of most off-reservation schools. The high school curriculum should be offered at only a few select off-reservation schools; in the early years, at Carlisle, Haskell, and Chemawa. As conceived, the primary curriculum was designed for six years, the grammar school curriculum for five, and the high school curriculum for another five. Morgan's long-term objective was to bring the emerging Indian school system into closer alignment with the nation's public school system. As Morgan put it, "An Indian high school should be substantially what any other high school should be."[4]

All of this required that the curriculum be standardized.[5] Morgan took the first step in this direction in 1890 when he issued a course of study for Indian schools, complete with an official list of textbooks. Focusing on the primary grades, the new outline of studies placed a heavy emphasis on language skills, academic subject matter, and moral training, but also gave considerable attention to industrial training. Interestingly, the new course of study deviated from Morgan's original plan in that the primary curriculum, originally considered to be equivalent to six years of white schooling, was now spread over an eight-year span for Indian schools. Morgan explained the two-year disparity by noting that Indian schools had the added responsibilities of teaching English as a "foreign tongue" and of introducing pupils to the idea of industrial training. In 1891, Morgan announced that the new curriculum was being adopted throughout the system and was proving instrumental in "bringing the various schools gradually more and more into harmonious relations."[6] The 1890 course of study would be just the first of several to be issued in the next forty years.[7]

It is important to emphasize that during the period examined in this study the Indian school system never did come to approximate Morgan's ideal. As late as 1913, Commissioner of Indian Affairs Cato Sells admitted to the fact that even the better off-reservation schools only provided academic education equivalent to the eighth or ninth grades. The exceptions to this were a few schools such as Carlisle, Haskell, and Santa Fe, which, after 1894, offered normal and commercial courses of study beyond the basic eight-year program. Indeed, it was not until the late 1920s that several off-reservation institutions attained the status of full-fledged high schools.[8] It is also important to remember that a distinction must be made between the curriculum offered and the actual number of pupils completing it. As extraordinary as it may seem, it was not until 1889 that Pratt was able to present fourteen diplomas to students completing the Carlisle grammar school program. By 1899, after some 3,800 students had attended Carlisle, only 209 had actually graduated.[9] After the turn of the century, the number of graduates at Carlisle and other selected schools would climb significantly, but the vast majority of Indian pupils during the period of this study never attained anything much above a primary education. Although Morgan's grand scheme was not to be realized for many years to come, at least the curriculum was being increasingly standardized.

A second issue to be decided was whether school attendance should be made compulsory.[10] There was virtually unanimous agreement on this question for the simple reason that it went to the very heart of the philanthropic consensus, namely, that the Indian's surest path out of savagery was the education of their children. It necessarily followed that as greater numbers of children were enrolled in schools, the general uplift of the race would proceed. "We cannot civilize ten," Superintendent of Indian Schools John Oberly remarked in 1885, "and then trust the force of their example to civilize ninety other Indian boys. The savagery of the ninety will obliterate the civilization of the ten." Morgan agreed, compulsion must be at the very heart of the philanthropic program.[11]

The net result of this line of thinking were two important pieces of legislation. On March 3, 1891, Congress authorized the Commissioner of Indian Affairs "to make and enforce by proper means such rules and regulations as will secure the attendance of Indian children of suitable age and health at schools established and maintained for their benefit." Two years later Congress addressed the issue of enforcement again, this time authorizing the Indian Office to "withhold rations, clothing and other annuities from Indian parents or guardians who refuse or neglect to send and keep their children of proper school age in some school a reasonable portion of each year."[12] Although Congress ducked the question of using force, it was generally accepted that agents were justified in using agency police to gain parental compliance.

Since the question of school enrollment was directly linked to the availability of facilities, it can be argued that these measures were largely symbolic. It would be well into the twentieth century before anything approaching compulsory education would become a fact of life for all Indian children.[13] On the other hand, the legislation did lend legal authority to the Indian Office's efforts to enforce attendance at those schools where space existed. Moreover, endorsement of the principle of compulsory attendance presented reformers with a standard against which to measure future congressional action, or inaction, as the case might be.[14]

A third problem area requiring systematic resolution was the matter of how students were recruited for and sorted between the various schools. At the reservation boarding school the issue was relatively simple. Although agents would often be at wits' end in their efforts to fill their schools, at least their responsibilities in this regard were fairly well defined. When persuasion failed, they were expected to bring pressure to bear until the school was filled. The situation was altogether different when it came to filling the off-reservation schools. Since superintendents of these schools had no direct authority on reservations, they were forced to devise their own means to gain recruits. Their motivation to do so was not simply philanthropic but economic, the annual funding of all Indian schools being based on the number of students in attendance.

In theory, schools on the reservation were to transfer their most advanced students to off-reservation ones. Some agents understood this clearly and appear to have made an honest attempt to use the schools under their jurisdiction as feeders for distant ones. The head of a boarding school in Indian Territory, for instance, reported in 1881 that he made a conscious effort to send his better students on to Carlisle. "It gives us pleasure," he claimed, "to send them and then go back and take others by the hand and help them over the same road the others had trodden." But for those not converted to the idea of off-reservation schooling, or those resentful of having the cream of Indian youth skimmed off their school rosters, there were numerous ways of undermining recruitment efforts. Indeed, at one point Commissioner Morgan was willing to admit that "good material has been parted with reluctantly, and [the] attempt has even been made to use the non-reservation school as a means of getting rid of the poor material with which the reservation school was encumbered." From the very beginning, then, superintendents of off-reservation schools were forced to rely on direct recruiting at the agency. In fact, by the early 1890s the competition for students was so stiff at some agencies that representatives of the local missionary boarding school, the government reservation boarding school, and one or two off-reservation schools could be found working the field simultaneously.[15]

A more efficient method of selecting and sorting was clearly called for, and in the coming years the Indian Office moved to create one. Three interconnected trends emerged. First, the general principle was established that only older students with previous training should be enrolled in off-reservation schools. Progress was slow, however, because in some regions, notably the Southwest, few reservation schools existed. In 1902, for example, the Indian Office reported that in some regions five- and six-year-old children were still attending schools off the reservation. Not until 1909 did Washington inform superintendents of off-reservation schools that from reservation schools they should only accept transferees fourteen years and older.[16] Second, the canvassing activities of off-reservation schools were increasingly restricted. In 1896 superintendents of these schools were informed that henceforth they must limit their direct recruiting to specific districts assigned by Washington. In 1908, the Indian Office went even further, announcing that thereafter "no collecting agent shall canvass any territory in the interests of a nonreservation school."[17] Third, Indian agents and reservation school superintendents were periodically and severely lectured about their responsibilities with regard to transferring students to off-reservation schools.[18] In other words, a system of selection and transfer was slowly falling into place—on the surface at least. Meanwhile, the off-reservation school superintendent was forced to devise strategies to maintain a thriving institution. Most were able to do so, in part because the increasing number of regulations and guidelines were filled with loopholes and also because Washington could not object to what it did not know.

One thing that superintendents and Indian agents could not do after 1893 was send an Indian child to an off-reservation school without the "full consent" of his parents. In making this announcement, the Indian Office was in essence saying that although education was compulsory, it was not compulsory beyond the boundaries of the reservation. Reformers were generally divided on the question. In defense of the new policy, Commissioner of Indian Affairs Daniel Browning maintained that "even ignorant and superstitious parents have rights, and their parental feelings are entitled to consideration." Browning may have simply adopted the new position anticipating that Congress would soon mandate it, which it did the following year.[19]

In the realm of financing, the fourth area in which reformers sought to establish greater systemization, their efforts again met with limited success. Funding for Indian schools came from essentially three sources: those appropriations provided for by treaty agreements; accumulations of funds in the Treasury resulting from the sale of Indian lands; and annual congressional appropriations. Whatever the source, boarding schools were generally funded at the annual rate of $167 per student.[20] A particularly troublesome question had to do with the eligibility for public money of so-called contract schools, primarily sectarian institutions that had contracted with the government to educate Indians. The movement to cut off congressional support for contract schools was fueled by several considerations: the argument that such funding was in violation of the principle of the separation of church and state; the belief that missionaries were more interested in converting Indians to a particular faith than promoting their wholesale civilization; but especially by the fact that Catholics were capturing an increasing percentage of contract funds. (In 1889, out of a total appropriation of $530,905 to mission schools, Catholic schools received $347,672.) Hence, throughout the 1890s Congress progressively whittled away its support until all such funding ended completely in 1900.[21] One school that avoided the congressional ax was Hampton Institute. Although originally founded by the American Missionary Society, Hampton, under Armstrong's leadership, nominally had become a nonsectarian school and therefore was able to wrest from Congress a special annual appropriation until 1912, when it too was finally denied continued support.

The fifth item on the reform agenda called for purging the Indian system of partisan politics. What reformers hoped to accomplish here was the elimination of the coveted spoils system, where political connections and party affiliation often took precedence over merit in gaining a post in the Indian service. According to the Indian Rights Association, too many politicians had come to view the reservation as nothing more than "a green pasture where their political herds might comfortably browse and fatten." The ideal of efficiency required both competence and continuity in the Indian Office's operations, not a recurrent shuffling of unqualified personnel each time a new political party come to power. The solution lay in civil service.[22]

Much of the focus was on reforming the reservation system. At particular issue was the role and position of the Indian agent. Traditionally a spoils appointment, the agent's overall responsibility was to set the Indians under his charge on the path to civilization and citizenship. His educational responsibilities included that of overseeing the school program, maintaining school enrollments, and fostering a high moral atmosphere in the conduct of agency and school affairs. For these reasons alone, his general competence, dedication, and moral character were fundamental to the school's success. Beyond this, at various times the Indian Office permitted agents to select their subordinates, including such positions as superintendent, teacher, farmer, matron, seamstress, laundress, and any other employees. When nepotism and political considerations took preference over competence, as they so often seemed to, the effects on the school program could be disastrous.[23] Superintendent of Indian Schools Daniel Dorchester included in his annual report this description of an all too typical scenario:

A new agent arrives at the agency. Very soon he shows a dislike for the superintendent of the school, for the matron and some of the teachers. He leaves no stone unturned to make their positions uncomfortable. An earnest, faithful, Christian young lady teacher is vilified and crowded out, to make room for a favorite who has no fitness for teaching or desire to benefit the pupils, but who can occupy the place and draw the salary. Often employees are removed to make place for persons of the agent's liking. Gradually the influence of the superintendent is crippled, and he finds himself presiding over an insubordinate corps of employees and the insubordination countenanced by the agent. After a time an industrial teacher is appointed who is dissolute, profane, and drunken. . . . The superintendent interposes for the protection of the boys, but finds himself the victim of a conspiracy to involve him in insurmountable difficulties by the foulest means, as a pretext for his dismissal. He has the love and respect of the pupils, but must be driven out that the agent may put at the head of the school one who will be his tool. The faithful superintendent steps aside, and the advent of his successor ushers in more immoral practices, for the corrupt regimen is now fully in the ascendancy.[24]

The first tentative steps in the direction of reform were taken by Superintendent of Indian Schools John Oberly, who informed agents in 1886: "No changes should be made on political grounds. Qualifications for the work to be done, and not affiliation with a political party, must govern in the employment of school employees." But such announcements did little to alter actual operations in the field. When Oberly, a friend to the reform cause, was appointed as Commissioner of Indian Affairs in 1888, he pressed for the extension of civil service to the Indian service but to no avail. The election of Benjamin Harrison to the presidency, and the subsequent appointment of Morgan as the new commissioner in 1889, brought renewed hope to reformers that the spoils system might be thrown over.[25] Indeed, in April 1891, President Harrison announced that the positions of school superintendent, assistant superintendent, teachers, matrons, and physicians were to receive civil service classification. Five years later clerks, industrial teachers, carpenters, cooks, laundresses, seamstresses, and disciplinarians also came under the civil service umbrella. Under the new guidelines the Civil Service Commission sent the names of three qualified persons for a given post to the Commissioner of Indian Affairs, who made the final appointment.[26]

What reformers really wanted was the elimination of the agent's position altogether and the transfer of all agency responsibilities to the school superintendent. In 1893, Congress took a step in this direction and authorized the Commissioner of Indian Affairs to abolish any agent's position deemed appropriate. Reformers cheered this development and in the coming years pressed the Indian Office for an aggressive application of the policy. The final victory came under the Roosevelt administration. As a civil service commissioner in the 1890s, Roosevelt had been an early advocate of the application of civil service regulations to the Indian service. With the appointment of Francis Leupp, Washington agent of the Indian Rights Association, to the commissioner's post in 1905, the conditions were in place for the triumph of civil service principles. By 1908 the position of Indian agent was abolished.[27]

The sixth administrative reform was to create an apparatus for managing and monitoring the burgeoning educational bureaucracy. At the heart of this effort was the Indian Office's formalization of an ever-expanding body of rules and procedures designed to standardize administrative procedures and lines of authority in the field. Until the Indian Bureau's operations were regularized and routinized, reformers argued, the efficiency ideal would remain an illusion. Thus, throughout the 1890s, the Indian Office was constantly updating and refining its *Rules for Indian School Service.*[28] Indeed, it might be argued that this slim volume constituted the essential glue that held the educational bureaucracy together. It proved to be especially important to agents and school personnel in the field, who were frequently thrown into a frantic search for some official guide about how to proceed when conflicts arose or a novel problem demanded immediate action.

Specifying rules and regulations for field operations helped, but it accomplished little if the lines of authority were not clearly delineated at the top of the organization. One of the principal issues was defining the scope of authority of the Superintendent of Indian Schools. Early on, reformers had made it clear that the emerging educational bureaucracy should be an autonomous unit in the Indian Office, managed by an "eminent educator" free of political ties. In 1882, Congress authorized the creation of the position "school inspector"; within three years this post had evolved into the Superintendent of Indian Schools. Before the extension of civil service rules, reformers pressed for giving the superintendent the responsibility for appointing and dismissing all employees connected with the Indian school service. Only briefly in the 1880s, however, was such authority granted. In fact, in 1889 Congress specifically stripped the superintendent of the authority to make appointments, leaving the office no real authority other than to inspect Indian schools and to make recommendations for their improvement to his superiors.[29]

Over the years, reformers struggled to increase the superintendent's authority, largely without success.[30] Still, the office played a significant role in standardizing administrative practice and supervising school operations. To assist him in these matters he was allowed a small number of district supervisors. Throughout the 1880s and 1890s the number fluctuated, depending upon congressional priorities. William Hailmann appears to have regarded it as a major breakthrough in 1897 when his office was allowed to expand the number of supervisors from three to five. But it is difficult to imagine that Hailmann or others who followed him were actually convinced that such a small number could effectively oversee the vast network of schools. Furthermore, the system was only as effective as the quality of the persons appointed. And since the position of supervisor for many years remained outside the domain of civil service, political considerations often held sway in selection. Indeed, in a letter to Welsh, a frustrated Hailmann privately complained at one point that his staff recommendations were being regularly overridden in favor of spoils. The result was that the supervisors appointed possessed "no visible fitness" for the work at hand.[31]

Another mechanism for monitoring field operations was the so-called Indian inspection system. Since 1873, when President Ulysses S. Grant appointed the first inspectors to investigate agency operations, the inspection system had become a fundamental component in the administration of Indian affairs. Appointed for four-year terms, inspectors were expected to periodically visit agencies to ascertain the competency and honesty of field staff in their implementation of Indian Office policies. As educational work assumed an increasing proportion of the Indian Office's responsibilities, more attention was given to schools.[32] It also frequently happened that a school would be singled out for a "special" investigation. Special investigations might be triggered by anything from a local newspaper's charge that an agent was mishandling agency affairs to a teacher's charge that the superintendent was addicted to "demon rum."

The inspection report was at the core of the inspection system. Written in the field, the reports were sent directly to the Secretary of the Interior, who in turn sent them on to the commissioner's office. If action was called for, the commissioner either dismissed, reprimanded, or transferred the employee to another location. Frequently, the latter occurred. Unless the inspector had been able to ascertain flagrant incompetence or wrongdoing, it was often difficult to fix blame. This was especially so since many investigations amounted to little more than charges and countercharges, often of dubious veracity, by agency personnel who had developed an intense dislike for one another. In such instances, it was easier for Washington to follow the line of least bureaucratic resistance and arrange a transfer.

The final monitorial position in the Indian Office was that of the "special agent." Appointed first in 1880, special agents seldom numbered more than two or three and reported to the Commissioner of Indian Affairs. Their primary function was to carry out especially sensitive assignments for the Indian Office. In point of fact, they functioned in much the same way as inspectors and occasionally were called upon to investigate schools caught up in crises situations.[33]

By the mid 1890s, a true "system" of education was emerging. In addition to standardizing the curriculum, systematizing procedures for enrolling and sorting students, and extending civil service to the Indian service, reformers were creating a more centralized, hierarchical, and self-monitoring bureaucratic structure. An organizational chart of the Office of Indian Affairs at the end of Morgan's term as commissioner reveals several characteristics. (see Figure 3.1). First, one sees an increasingly centralized organization with greater appointment and supervisory authority being vested in the commissioner. Second, the power of the agents is weakened, mainly by the extension of civil service classification to key agency and school personnel. Finally, through a combination of inspectors, Indian school supervisors, and special agents, a system for monitoring field operations is in place. To be sure, the emerging system seen here was not ideal, but it was a beginning.

Meanwhile, the wheels of the large Indian bureaucracy turned. And in the process, policies and regulations found expression in human actions across the Indian Office's far-flung empire. Agents rounded up children, school superintendents searched for fresh recruits, teachers preached the gospel of civilization, and inspectors and supervisors reported their observations. And through it all, the Indian Office tried to stay on top of things, including the growing mountain of reports flowing into Washington. All of which raises questions: How clearly did the actual operation of the system come to approximate reformers' expectations? How did the Indian Bureau function on the outer reaches of the Indian frontier—for instance, Duck Valley, Nevada?

SHOWDOWN AT DUCK VALLEY

Straddling the Nevada-Idaho border at an elevation of 6,000 feet, the Duck Valley Reservation, or Western Shoshone Agency, is mostly rocky and mountainous country. The exception is Duck Valley itself, which slopes to the Owyhee River, whose waters sweep across the reservation, cutting a northern path to the great Snake River. In 1899, the Duck Valley

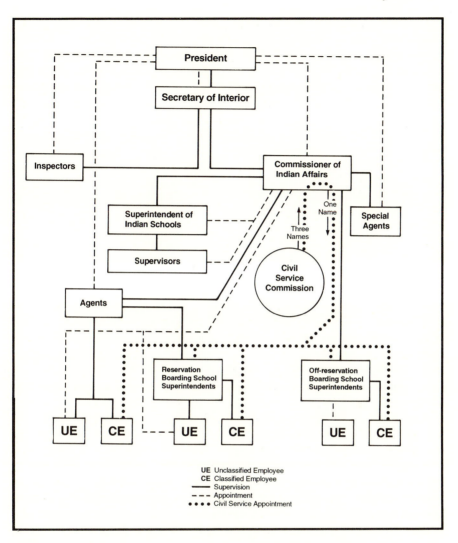

Figure 3.1. Organization of the Office of Indian Affairs, 1892.

Reservation was home to 296 Western Shoshone and 276 Northern Paiute. Two years before, agent William Hargrove described the two tribes as a "simple, kind, and gentle people" and, significantly, favorably disposed to government schools. Of the reservation's 124 school-age population, 58 were enrolled at the boarding school, which was filled to capacity. Agent Hargrove was convinced he might easily enroll up to 80 students if the necessary facilities existed. Meanwhile, parents had willingly sent 13 students off the reservation for schooling.[34]

Then disaster struck. On April 17, 1899, two warring factions of agency employees—the followers of the school superintendent Anna Egan, and those of the agent, John Mayhugh—resorted to pistols to settle some unresolvable differences. Staff factionalism was common in the field but seldom did it reach catastrophic proportions. When news of the episode reached Washington, Commissioner William Jones quickly recognized that the situation required a full investigation. But the wheels of bureaucracy turned slowly. Not until June 7, almost two months after the explosion, did Inspector Andrew J. Duncan arrive on the scene to begin the tedious process of collecting written testimony from participants and eye witnesses. From Duncan's report and other documents it is possible to reconstruct the events surrounding the Duck Valley shoot-out.[35]

Anna C. Egan—Irish, Catholic, red-headed—was in her mid-thirties when she arrived at Western Shoshone Agency on December 23, 1898. Before coming to Duck Valley, Egan had spent a number of years in the Indian school service as a teacher, notably at Santa Fe, New Mexico, and Keams Canyon, Arizona. In his report Inspector Duncan describes her as "bright, intelligent, energetic," and then goes on to comment that she was "endowed with considerable temper, well liked by her friends and disliked very energetically by her enemies." The inspector was not the only one to comment that Egan had a short fuse. Agent Mayhugh characterized her as a woman of "most violent temper and tongue."

John Mayhugh was sixty-five years old and fully comfortable in his role as Indian agent. A long-time resident of Nevada, Mayhugh had served in the same post in the 1880s before his reappointment in 1898. Mayhugh, like Egan, is described as intelligent and of good character but also "somewhat impulsive and evidently aggressive." From Mayhugh's agency reports, it is also clear that he was disdainful of recent reforms limiting the agent's authority to make appointments and dismissals and deemed the civil service system to be a disaster: "How so many disqualified persons pass a favorable examination is a mystery to the country and an imposition on the service."[36] Within the confines of the "new order," however, it must be said that Mayhugh had fully exercised his authority, and to his own financial benefit. At the time of Egan's arrival, both the agent's wife and his daughter were employed, Mrs. Mayhugh as acting clerk and Stella Mayhugh as acting matron at the school. Meanwhile, the position of school superintendent was being temporarily filled by Charles Mayers, the agency farmer and a close friend of the agent's.

Egan and Mayhugh offer distinctly different accounts of their first encounter. Egan testified that when she arrived at the agency she received a "cold, curt reception" from Mayhugh "with a refusal to acknowledge me as superintendent of the school until personally notified by the Indian Office." This version indicates that Mayhugh virtually ignored Egan for five full days until he saw fit to acknowledge her authority. Mayhugh's account is somewhat different. "The day after her arrival," he testified, "I visited her office to show her over the premises, show her the hay stacks, stables, cattle . . . and other livestock and everything else appertaining to the school industrial work."

Egan and Mayhugh clearly got off on the wrong foot. And although the ensuing feud can be explained in part by the conflicting and overlapping spheres of authority granted to agents and superintendents, it also appears to have been partially fueled by Superintendent Egan's suspicion, probably correct, that Mayhugh, as a nineteenth-century male on the Nevada frontier, expected her to passively accept his overall authority. If such was the case, it was a terrible miscalculation on Mayhugh's part. In any event, from Egan's statements it is clear that she found the agent's general demeanor to be overbearing and paternalistic, traits entirely repugnant to her belief that she was fully capable of discharging her new responsibilities. According to the agent, not more than twenty minutes after her arrival she announced "that she intended to have full and complete control and authority" over the school and that "for the first time in her life she was placed in full power and she knew how to use it."

In the coming months Western Shoshone Agency rapidly split into two camps. On one side were the Mayhughs and Charles Mayers, the agency farmer. On the other, were Egan and her supporters. Among these can be counted Mary Rodgers, who arrived in late January to replace Stella Mayhugh as matron, John Brown the industrial teacher, and most significantly, the agency physician, Dr. A. P. Merriweather and his wife. Merriweather, who had transferred from Pima Agency and arrived at Duck Valley a month or so before Egan, had developed an almost instant dislike for the Mayhughs. Thus, when the Egan-Mayhugh split came, the doctor naturally gravitated to Egan's side.

Disagreement over Mayhugh's role in the investigation of a small fire at the school and the proper procedure for the agent's disbursement of school supplies were the first incidents of conflict. Within weeks both superintendent and agent were firing letters off to Washington, each complaining of the other's performance. According to Egan, Mayhugh was an "insolent and overbearing" bully, constantly interferring with her stipulated responsibilities. In a letter to Commissioner Jones dated January 30, 1899, Mayhugh charged that Egan was uncommonly cruel in her punishment of the children, was unable to manage the Indian boys, knew nothing about managing the school farm, and perhaps most importantly, was impudent and disrespectful toward the agent, refusing to acknowledge his legitimate authority.[37]

Late in February, Mayhugh received a response. Commissioner Jones began by stating that Egan had also been in correspondence with him and he was of the decided opinion that Mayhugh was not rendering to Egan "that courtesy and helpful assistance which every agent should render the superintendent of the school. While it is true," Jones continued, "that you are the official head of the reservation and are held responsible for the general conduct of affairs, your interference in the school is unwarranted and must be stopped." After this wrist slapping, Jones added: "Miss Egan is also expected to render you proper deference and to obey all legitimate orders. She is responsible to this office through you for the success of the school and I shall hold her to a strict account of her position."[38]

Mayhugh was furious and immediately wrote a seventeen-page defense of his position. The charge of interference in the school, he protested, was simply not true. In his investigation of the five he had simply carried out his responsibility as agent to protect and maintain agency property. The hard truth of the matter was that Egan was unfit for the position of superintendent. The school's stock was being mismanaged; hay had been allowed to rot in the fields, and proper precautions to prevent fire still were not being taken. "I say right here she is incompetent for any line of work except that of teacher." There was really no need for a superintendent anyway; why not turn the school over to the agent?

> I learned from practical experience of 64 days when there was no superintendent here, that the school could be managed very readily by the agent or rather by his directions without any detriment whatever to the school or agency and during that period the discipline of the school was first class and there was no friction. The progress of the children was excellent not only in the school room but in other industrial work, they were happy and contented, peace and harmony prevailed. Now the discontentment of the children . . . is apparent.

Why, Mayhugh asked, had the commissioner been corresponding with Egan to begin with? Did the commissioner know that Egan was circulating the commissioner's letters among her supporters? "Mr. Commissioner is not this humiliating and degrading to an agent, is it not creating insubordination and disrespect of the school and agency employees toward the agent?" Finally, "why should I be reprimanded for this woman's shortcomings and her insolence?"

Meanwhile, Mayhugh had secretly taken steps to undermine Egan's position. Suspecting that Egan might have a reputation in the Indian service as a troublemaker, Mayhugh wrote Col. Thomas Jones, superintendent of Cheyenne Boarding School at Darlington, Oklahoma. Jones had been superintendent of Santa Fe Boarding School in the early 1890s when Anna Egan had served as the primary teacher. Jones's response verified Mayhugh's suspicions: "I do know her probably better than any man in this country and unhesitatingly state that she is the most corrupt woman and the most dangerous I ever knew." Jones's advice to Mayhugh:

You can not be too careful to watch this woman as she has the most wonderful capacity of getting other women under her influence, but I never saw anyone yield to authority as she will if you assert yours. She is an arrant coward with all her boasting. The mistake I made was in treating her as if she was a lady.

Mayhugh now put Jones's letter to use by passing it around the agency. Egan later recounted how one morning Charles Mayers, the school farmer and "a tool and a spy in the agent's hand," strolled into the school kitchen and, with an air of "I told you so," showed the letter to the school cook. On a different occasion another employee of the school, Miss Walker, was called to the agent's house, where Mrs. Mayhugh and her daughter "read her this letter and warned her against me, stating positively that I was an immoral woman and had an evil influence over other women. She was told never to let me touch her wrist as I had hypnotic powers that brought people whom I touched in this way under my evil influence." According to Egan, the same story was being told to the Indians. All this was part of a larger campaign:

Stories of all kinds about my character were put in free circulation by the Mayhughs, Mrs. Mayhugh in particular. I had positive proof that the Indians were, from the first, being prejudiced against me. Every means at the Mayhugh's command was used to break into my control over the pupils. The clerk . . . heard Mrs. Mayhugh tell the children not to mind anything "that little red headed, Irish paddy" said.

But Egan was determined to stick it out.

By the end of March, the quarter mile between the school and the agency amounted to a buffer zone separating two warring camps. Occasional contact took place with regard to requisitioning supplies, but for the most part Egan and Mayhugh kept their distance from one another. The relative calm, however, was soon to be shattered. Ironically, the spark that ignited the showdown that followed did not come from Mayhugh or Egan, but from the Indians.

On Friday, April 14, several headmen and the three members of the Indian court—Charlie Wines, Frank Smith, and Captain Sam—reported to

agent Mayhugh that they wished to hold court regarding a problem at the
school. The issue, they explained, had to do with the immoral influence
of two "bad" girls on the rest of the students. The two individuals in
question were Kitty Blaine, the school's mess cook, and Essie Valley, a student. The next day, Mayhugh sent a note up to the school instructing superintendent Egan to "immediately" send the individuals in question and
several other witnesses down to the agency in order that the court might
cross-examine them. Egan, instantly sensitive to the fact that the court
was treading on her terrain, accompanied the summoned group to the
agent's office. Intending to sit in on the proceedings, she was informed by
Mayhugh that the Indians wished to conduct their business in private.

There is no written record of the two-hour proceedings, but from statements later made to Inspector Duncan it is possible to get the gist of the
charges brought against Blaine and Valley. The clearest indication comes
from Charlie Wines, one of the three judges; "One Sunday my girl told
me she saw Essie Valley with a school boy at the ice house doing bad
things, and also under the step outside the front of the kitchen, and all the
Indian mothers who had girls and young boys at the school did not like it,
and felt bad about it." As for Kitty Blaine, the cook, she was also a "bad
woman." According to Wines, one of the agency policeman "saw her at
night in Frank Smith's stable with Alford Jack—she had the larger school
boys around her at the mess kitchen and the Indians did not like [it]." In
any event, the council was in agreement that the two young women
would have to go and after the meeting told Agent Mayhugh of their decision. They also explained that the parents felt deeply about the issue. If
Valley and Blaine were not removed, the parents would take their children out of the school. "Our children are good and we want to keep them
good."[39]

Mayhugh, who later states that the two individuals on trial were in fact
guilty of "scandalous" behavior and no doubt reacting as well to the
judges' announcement that there would be a mass exodus of students
from the school if the court's judgment was not carried out, accepted
their decision. Besides, the court was being most reasonable; upon removal of Essie Valley, the Indians promised a replacement from the
camps. But one problem remained; would Miss Egan accept the court's
judgment?

On the following morning, Sunday, one of the judges paid the school a
visit. His garbled testimony follows:

I Charley Wines went to the school house this Sunday morning to see
my children. Miss Egan she wants to see me. She talk about what we
judges settle about children yesterday. I told him [her] I am the first
man that send my little girls to school on this reservation. Other Indi-

ans keep their children and the mammas cry. That is the reason why I wanted to see my children good, and have no bad children in school to learn them bad things. My own children were good. We have never have this trouble before Essie Valley come. . . . I say if that girl don't go away, maybe all the schoolchildren run away. You can't help that. If you believe me what judges say, take Essie Valley and then we keep all our school children in school. I tell her we settled it yesterday.

In Egan's account of the meeting, she explained to Wines in no uncertain terms that the Indian court had overstepped its authority; only the superintendent, and then only with the permission of the Commissioner of Indian Affairs, could remove a student from school. At this point, according to Egan, Wines became irate and had to be "calmed down" by Doctor Merriweather, who happened to be in the office at the time. It also should be noted that Egan was apparently convinced that the charges against the two young women were groundless. In her statement to Inspector Duncan she observed, "I know that no such conduct as these two girls are accused of could go on in my school and I not to be aware of it, and I am not aware of it."[40]

That afternoon Egan tried to drum up support among the Indians. Evidence for this comes from the statements of George Washington, one of the agency policeman, and his wife, Sallie. Policeman Washington, it turns out, sided with Mayhugh and had little use for Superintendent Egan. He later testified:

I say that we have no trouble about school until Miss Egan came here. I hear her talk bad about the Agent. She says agent will be soon out. She tell me she got a big friend at Washington and Mr. Mayhugh soon go away. . . . We all like our agent. He is a good man. He never shoot or fight or talk curse words. I know him 25 years and never see him have pistol or gun. . . . Woman superintendent no good. She no fix fence all down. Man superintendent better.

But Egan was apparently unaware of Washington's low regard for her. So late Sunday afternoon, she walked the short distance from the school to the Washington's cabin to talk with Sallie Washington. In the words of policeman Washington, the superintendent made his wife a proposal: "Why don't you come up and help the Doctor and me. Maybe so, by and by, Doctor agent and all my Indian friends get places." Doctor Merriweather as the next agent? If Egan's scenario was designed to win support to her side, it was ill-chosen. For although Merriweather was conscientious in his attendance to schoolchildren, he appears not to have been particularly popular across the reservation. George Washington would later make this clear to Inspector Duncan: "Dr. Merriweather never go around and see sick Indians. Captain Henry he now sick in canyon with broke rib and Doctor no go see him. My wife no well. He no care. He never go camp see Indians. All Indians never like him. He never feel our hands, only look at us quick, then go." In any event, Sallie Washington walked with Egan back to the school where, sitting on the porch, Egan tried to win her over. Sallie Washington's brief statement provides an indication of Egan's disposition on the eve of the Duck Valley shootout. At one point in the conversation, Sallie claimed, "she show me a cartridge belt under her dress. She talk sad about agent, said no like agent." Anna C. Egan, it seems, was prepared to go to the limit.

On the next day, Monday, April 17, Long John, captain of the agency policemen, would earn his pittance of a salary. Shortly after reporting for duty, agent Mayhugh informed him that the two women were to be taken from the school that day, and that Long John's daughter, who was not in school, should be offered up as a replacement for Essie Valley. The first order of business was for the captain to select five other policemen, proceed to the school, and then return to the agency with Valley and Blaine in hand.

Egan saw them coming. Her first act was to place Kittie Blaine in the superintendent's office for safekeeping. By the time Long John arrived, Egan had also secured her revolver. According to the captain, when he announced that he had come for the girl, Egan angrily ordered him back to the agency, saying: "You no come into this house again. Next time you come, I kill you." (Egan later explained that she was furious at the "cowardliness" of Mayhugh's act—"to send five great and strong men to overpower one poor little woman.") By now, Egan had a coterie of followers about the school: Dr. Merriweather, Miss Rodgers, and John Brown. Frank Smith, a former employee, also had returned to the school to offer his support. Long John reported all of this to the agent. Meanwhile, Indians were beginning to gather around the school, in part out of concern for the welfare of their children, in part to witness the unfolding drama.

Mayhugh now tried a slightly different tack. He sent Long John back up to the school with a note for the superintendent: "You are hereby directed by me as United States Indian Agent to deliver up peaceably to my Chief of Police one Essie Valley an Indian girl, as I desire to remove her from the school for the present. By doing this, you will save further trouble." Interestingly, Mayhugh makes no mention of Kittie Blaine whatsoever. If this was an effort to compromise, it failed. Egan ordered the captain off the premises and once again threatened to shoot him if he persisted in his attempt to interfere with her school. Other notes followed: one from Mayhugh to Merriweather, requesting him to stay out of the matter; another to Frank Smith, ordering him to leave the school grounds, as he was no longer employed there. Both failed in their purpose. (Egan fumed, "Thank heaven, there were a couple *men* at Western Shoshone that day.)

Egan and company were now prepared for the worst. And they soon had reason to believe that the situation might turn ugly. In a second-story window Egan's followers had mounted a large telescope to observe events below at the agency. Just before noon, Mrs. Merriweather, who was keeping watch, excitedly called Egan to look through the telescope. What Egan observed—or at least thought she observed—was the agent's wife handing out pistols: "I did so, and distinctly saw Mrs. Mayhugh hand two revolvers to Indian policeman. . . . From time to time that morning we could see her passing amongst the Indians talking excitedly, and no doubt inciting them to riot. Otherwise, why should she arm them?"

Meanwhile, the agent had come face to face with the realization that he would have to confront Egan himself. After sending a message to Egan that he wished to meet with her at the school, he asked his friend Charles Mayers to accompany him to the school. Mayers agreed but first excused himself, whereupon he walked to his house and secured an unloaded, broken revolver, commenting to his wife, "I can not hurt anybody with it, you know, but maybe I can scare someone with it, if they show pistols to us." Mayhugh, unarmed, and Mayers, with his broken pistol, then mounted and pointed their horses toward the school. The policemen stayed behind.

Approaching the school, Mayhugh noticed that Dr. Merriweather was moving among several "young bucks," talking to them in whispers, and the agent "asked the young fellows: 'What are you doing up here on the grounds this morning?' They did not reply." Mayers was now convinced that he and Mayhugh had ridden into a trap. On the school porch, which was several feet above the ground, were Mrs. Merriweather, armed with a two-foot club, and Miss Rodgers. Still on his horse, Mayhugh now asked Rodgers to fetch the superintendent in order that he might speak to her.

Egan, all the while, had been positioned at an upstairs window, where she had observed Mayhugh and Mayers ride into the schoolyard. "As they rode up under my window," she later related, "I distinctly saw the butt end of a revolver in Mayers' hip pocket." Thus, Egan once again secured her own pistol before stepping out on the porch with Dr. Merriweather to confront Mayhugh. Egan later testified:

When I went out, I asked, addressing agent Mayhugh, "Do you wish to see me?" He replied, "Yes, I want to know if you are ready to given up those two bad girls?" I emphatically replied "No sir." He then asked what it was I had in my right hand? I, in answer, raised my revolver and showed it to him, saying, "That, do you see it?" and then added, "Now I want you to go back where you came from, you old, white livered coward," and I meant every word I said. I then raised my left hand and showed him some letters that I had received from the Hon. Commissioner, reminding him that he had told the Indians that I was only lying. . . . I then turned to Mayers and said, "And you Mayers, you have dared to take my reputation into your hands" and before I could get farther he said with a sneer, "Have I?" and reached for his hip pocket. At this instant the revolver which was hanging at my right side was snatched from me.

Events now moved swiftly. Merriweather, who had grabbed Egan's pistol, immediately fired a shot in the direction of Mayers, the bullet grazing his abdomen. Reeling in the saddle, Mayers was still struggling to retrieve his own pistol. Meanwhile, at the sound of the pistol shot, Mayhugh's horse jumped in front of Mayers's horse, thereby placing the agent in the direct line of fire. The doctor fired a second shot, which although apparently also intended for Mayers, came dangerously close to striking Mayhugh.[41]

In the midst of this confusion, Frank Carson jumped Mayers in an effort to wrestle the pistol from him. He apparently was successful for one schoolboy later testified, "Frank Carson point pistol at the agent's head, pistol snap and then he [Carson] run in school house quick." (If nothing else, this verifies the fact that Mayers's pistol was worthless.) At about this point Long Johns's policemen, who had been on guard at the agency for any sign of trouble, galloped onto the scene. After firing a shot over the heads of those on the porch, more as a defensive measure than anything else, the police shielded Mayhugh's and Mayers's retreat to the agency. A fourth and final shot was fired from the school porch, probably by the industrial teacher, John Brown, but with no effect. Making his retreat to the agency, Mayhugh heard shouts from the school, "Look at the cowards run."

Back at the agency, Mayers headed for his house, where his wife inspected his wound, which amounted to nothing more than a scratch. Mayhugh, distraught and dizzy, collapsed in bed. Up on the hill, Egan and company celebrated their victory. As for the Indians, enough was enough. In a matter of hours, Shoshone and Piaute pupils were back in the camps. (In the coming weeks, when the school was back in session, no less than three attempts would be made by students to set the school on fire.)[42]

Such were the complicated circumstances and events surrounding the Duck Valley shoot-out. After sifting through the testimony, Inspector Duncan entered his judgment on the matter. There was little doubt in the inspector's mind that both Egan and Merriweather, on the one hand, and Mayhugh, on the other, had violated regulations. As for Mayhugh, he had no authority either to directly discipline or discharge employees at the school or to remove students from the school without concurrence from the superintendent; the agent was clearly not appreciative of the enlarged authority given to school superintendents. Beyond this, he had conducted himself in a dictatorial manner toward Egan and her staff; he had improperly dug up gossip about Egan's history at other posts; and finally, he should have consulted the commissioner's office rather than attempting to remove Essie Valley.

As for Egan and her associates, they had committed an act of reckless insubordination when they resorted to force. Although it was true that Mayhugh had shown his own reckless disregard for Indian service rules, Egan had committed a more serious breach by ignoring that provision of the regulations which "provided for the settlement of emergencies or difficulties between the agent and any employee." The rule provided that:

> The agent shall not require of the superintendent of a school under his charge anything inconsistent with his position. He shall give direction in regard to the duties of school employees and other school matters through the superintendent, and all his orders and directions must be obeyed, subject, however, on appeal, to the approval of the Commissioner of Indian Affairs.[43]

The bottom line of the matter, according to Duncan, was that Egan should have turned Essie Valley over to the agent (even though he had no authority to demand her), after which the superintendent was free to appeal the case to Washington.

Using this line of reasoning—shaky at best—Duncan recommended that Egan and Merriweather be requested to resign from the service, that Matron Rodgers be transferred to another location, and that Mayhugh be reprimanded but not dismissed. As it turned out, the commissioner's office, perhaps feeling the heat of the Indian Rights Association, which got wind of the episode, chose another solution. In the spirit of reform, Western Shoshone Agency was converted into a superintendency. As for the principal players in the drama at Duck Valley—Mayhugh, Egan, and Merriweather—all moved on to greener pastures.

What does the episode at Duck Valley reveal about the "one best system" for the Indians? For one thing, it is a revealing look at how the Indian Bureau's educational program functioned, or failed to, in an administrative structure still midway in its evolution toward a more centralized, civil service–governed organization. Personalities aside, one of the underlying causes of the conflict was that both Mayhugh and Egan had some responsibility for the school's operation. Indeed, situations like that at Duck Valley provided reformers with just the sort of ammunition they needed to press for the total elimination of the agency system, something they eventually got. The incident also illustrates the peculiar nature of the Indian Office bureaucracy, an administrative structure at once centralized in its organization yet geographically decentralized in its vital functions. On the bureaucratic frontier, where administrative personnel were forced to make decisions on a daily basis without guidance from Washington, it is not surprising that field operations often took on a life of their own, independent of bureaucratic intent. Reformers, however, chose to ignore this troubling aspect of the Indian "one best system," choosing instead to place their faith in the vision of a spoils-free benevolent bureaucracy efficiently carrying out its humanitarian mission—lifting Indian children out of savagism. And at the very center of that vision was the schoolteacher.

TEACHERS AND THE INDIAN SCHOOL SERVICE

Policymakers were always cognizant of the fact that the success of their efforts ultimately depended on the Indian Bureau's ability to attract and retain a core of devoted teachers. It was for this reason that reformers concentrated so much effort on purging the Indian school service of politics through the extension of civil service regulations, which raises some related questions: What was the makeup of the Indian Bureau's teaching force? Where did they come from? Why did they join in the first place? How long did they stay? and finally, Why did they leave?[44]

The average teacher appears to have been a single woman in her late twenties. Between 1892 and 1900, out of 550 teachers, assistant teachers, and kindergartners appointed under civil service rules, some 312, a modest majority, were women. A dramatic shift was taking place, however, and by 1900 the Indian Office reported that of the 347 teachers employed, 286 were women.[45]

It is not surprising that such was the case. By the middle of the nineteenth century, teaching was pretty much defined as women's work. Part of the reason was economic; it was simply less expensive to hire young women who taught a few years before marriage than it was to pay a respectable wage to males who chose teaching as a lifelong enterprise. But there was a deeper reason as well. Teaching children was rapidly becoming associated with prevailing definitions of "woman's sphere." According to the cultural outlook of the day, although women were mentally and physically inferior to men, they were genuinely superior in their natural roles as purveyors of culture and moral virtue. Because of their natural gifts in working with children, their proper place was in the home, and by extension, in the classroom. Moreover, as the nation marched westward to the Pacific, it was women's "high calling" to protestanize, republican-

Table 3.2. Number of Male and Female Applicants to Indian School Service Who Passed Civil Service Teacher Examination in 1892, 1894, 1895, and 1900, by Region

	Northeast	South	Midwest	Plains	Far West	Total
1892	5	5	24	14	3	51
1894	9	10	40	45	16	120
1895	12	19	62	65	19	177
1900	12	9	61	27	14	123

Source: Compiled from *Ninth Annual Report of the U.S. Civil Service Commission*, 1892, 118–19; *Eleventh Annual Report of the U.S. Civil Service Commission*, 1894, 168; *Twelfth Annual Report of the U.S. Civil Service Commission*, 1895, 40; and *Seventeenth Annual Report of the U.S. Civil Service Commission*, 1900, 360–61.
Note: Northeast: Conn., Del., Maine, Mass., N.H., N.J., N.Y., Pa., R.I., and Vt.; South: Ark., D.C., Fla., Ga., Ky., La., Md., Miss., N.C., S.C., Tenn., Va., and W.Va.; Midwest: Ill., Ind., Iowa, Mich., Minn., Mo., Ohio, and Wis.; Plains: Kans., Nebr., N.Dak., Okla., S.Dak., and Tex.; Far West: Ariz., Calif., Colo., Idaho, Mont., Nev., N.Mex., Oreg., Utah, Wash., and Wyo.

ize, and generally educate the progeny of rough-hewn settlers who had crossed the boundaries of civilization into lands, until recently, peopled by savages. Thus, the one room schoolhouse, with the proverbial school-marm standing in the doorway as a symbol of literacy and civilization, was one of the first landmarks of a western community.[46]

It would be fundamentally wrong, however, to assume that the Indian service drew most of its teachers from the oldest areas of settlement, New England and the Atlantic seaboard (see Table 3.2). On the contrary, throughout the 1890s civil service records for those years available indicate that the vast majority of applicants came from the regions of the Midwest, the Plains, and the Far West. This pattern is confirmed when examining the states from which superintendents and teachers received their appointments. In 1892, for instance, when the Indian Office employed some 418 superintendents and teachers, the various regions contributed the following numbers: Northeast, 40; South, 11; Midwest, 76; Plains, 181; and Far West, 110. The three states making the single highest contributions were Kansas with 63, Nebraska with 46, and South Dakota with 35. Thus the great majority of teachers drawn to the Indian service came not from the region most directly associated with Indian reform, the Northeast, but from those areas closer to the Indian frontier.[47]

A fascinating picture of teacher characteristics is gained by looking at the employee composition at a single institution over a twenty-year period—Santa Fe Boarding School (see Table 3.3). Out of sixty-nine teachers employed between 1891 and 1911, fifty-seven were women, and forty-five of this group were single. Moreover, the average age of both male and female teachers was approximately thirty years. (Quite possibly, for many of these teachers, Santa

Table 3.3. Gender, Age, Marital Status, and Region of Residence of Santa Fe Boarding School Teachers, 1891–1911

	Marital Status			Region of Residence				
	Single	Married	Average Age	New England	South	Midwest	Plains	Far West
Female	45	12	30.8	4	5	24	10	11
Male	3	9	30.3	0	1	7	1	2

Source: "Register of Employees, 1891–1917," Santa Fe Indian School, entry 51, OIA, Denver Branch.
Note: The figures do not include temporary teachers, and in a few instances, records do not indicate state residence.

Fe was not their first position in the school service. Salary aside, many teachers regarded landing a position in an off-reservation school in an "urban" area as a decided step up from an assignment on a remote reservation where living conditions were less attractive.) Once again, the same trend emerges as to the teachers' geographical origins, with the great majority coming from the Midwest, the Plains, and the Far West regions.

Why did women teachers join the Indian school service? Some no doubt were motivated by the same sentiments that moved reformers generally, a sense of Christian responsibility to save a vanishing race from extinction. For those women who embraced the ideology of domesticity, including its basic tenet that women were the moral guardians and purveyors of Christian civilization, one can only imagine the emotions stirred up by reformers' heartbreaking depictions of benighted Indian children whose only salvation lay in educational uplift. Like Commissioner Morgan, they may have imagined Indian children crying out:

> We are like leaves driven by the tempest, like sheep without a shepherd, like vessels at sea with no sails or rudder, like buffaloes fleeing before the destructive prairie fire, like chickens in the presence of the hawk, and there is no longer any land of refuge to which we can fly. We are surrounded on every side by the resistless tide of population; a tide we cannot withstand nor escape nor compete with. Our only hope is in your civilization, which we cannot adopt unless you give us your Bible, your spelling book, your plow and your ax. Grant us these and teach us how to use them, and then we shall be like you.[48]

Simply put, by joining the Indian service the idealistic teacher could make a difference in the great moral drama unfolding on the frontier. Surely this was women's work: to lift Indian children out of savagery, to save a race from extinction.

Others seem to have been motivated by economic and career consider-ations.[49] Such factors clearly came into play in the case of Estelle Aubrey Brown, who has provided one of the few autobiographical accounts of life in the Indian service. Born to "Scotch-Puritan" parents in rural New York, Brown began her teaching career at the tender age of sixteen in a one-room schoolhouse. Conscious of her age and inexperience in a class where many of her students were as old as she was, she recalls, "My skirts were down, my hair up, and no nonsense." It wasn't easy going. "Every-body in my schoolroom owned a jackknife and possessed the urge to re-lieve the building's barren surfaces with his own conception of phallic symbols." While teaching in this environment four to five months of the year, for which she received $24 a month, Brown managed to save suffi-cient funds to finance her own further education at a nearby academy. But prospects appeared to be limited until she came upon information that kindergartners were needed in the Indian service. Within two weeks of passing the required civil service examination, she received a telegram from the Indian Bureau offering her a position at the Crow Creek Indian School, South Dakota, at a salary of $600 per annum. Brown immediately accepted and admits that she was completely ignorant of Indians. Indeed, she was genuinely horrified when her father informed her of the back-ground of her future pupils: "South Dakota. That will be the Sioux Indi-ans. Sioux. They're the ones that butchered Custer and his men."[50]

The Indian school service also held out the promise of greater indepen-dence and autonomy, an escape from the time-honored expectations that came with being a woman in nineteenth-century America. It is clearly evi-dent, for instance, that Estelle Brown found the prevailing notions of "woman's sphere" in rural New York to be patently unbearable. "I early came to resent the hamlet's smug assumptions that women were not really members of the human race but merely appendages to it, to be wagged by men." Brown continues: "I wanted to do my own wag-ging. . . . I wanted a purse of my own." But the options available to a sin-gle woman were few. Brown bitterly recollects:

If a girl failed to get a husband, she could teach at rural school—if she could spell. She could be a country dressmaker—if she could sew. Failing these, she could be a burden, for which no qualifications were necessary. But she could not be employed in the office of a businessman or profes-sional man. The facade of a bank would have lifted up its pillars in horror at the idea of a woman passing through it for the purpose of making a liv-ing. For a girl, life in the hamlet was a dreary business that made even the threat of Indian atrocities in distant lands seem preferable.[51]

Finally, there was the sheer adventure of it all. For Flora Gregg Iliff the impetus to join the Indian service came during a teachers' institute in Oklahoma Territory. During one of the enrichment sessions, the speaker had talked at length about the lifeways of a remote Indian people in Arizona Territory, at one point pleading, "The Havasupai—the People of the Blue Water—need you." The longer the speaker talked, Iliff recalls, the more she could feel excitement rising in her. "It was 1900 and I was young and unwilling to weigh consequences. Adventure? Danger? Life was waiting to be lived!" After passing the required civil service examination, Iliff received notice of an opening at a school on the Walapai reservation. Although not her first choice, she accepted it and began making plans for her departure. There were the usual second thoughts. Had she done the right thing? Could her mother manage without her? Perhaps it was absurd, "a young woman who had travelled little, setting out to civilize Indians." But the decision had been made. After making the painful farewells, she boarded the westbound train on a chilly October morning.

> As the train gathered speed I thought of a trip I had made ten years before, in a covered wagon, from our old home in Kansas to my father's claim in Oklahoma Territory. He had stopped his team in that bright new land of opportunity at an Indian burial ground, and the entire family had scrambled to gaze in awe at lines stretched from the tops of poles to stakes in the ground. On the lines, like a family wash put out to dry, hung human scalps. The long, silky hair of white women and the short, crisp hair of white men lifted and rippled in the breeze that blew across the prairie.

But even in her childhood, Iliff recalls, she had always sensed there was another side to the story. This was an opportunity to "hear at last the Indians' version of the long and bitter struggle between the white men and the red men for possession of the land." Yes, she had made the correct decision. "I was born with a thirst for adventure; this teaching position would be an adventure in a new field of service."[52]

Typically, the decision to join the Indian service was probably based on the coalescence of several motivations. There was nothing contradictory in seeking to simultaneously satisfy humanitarian impulses, feminist yearnings, the need for financial security, and the restless curiosity sparked by the vision of unseen territories.[53] For Gertrude Golden, who joined in 1901, several of these considerations were operating.

> I was tired of it all. Although I was not longing for adventure especially, I did crave a change of scenery. Teaching in the country and village schools of Monroe, Michigan, was all right as far as it went, but

it was too limiting, too monotonous a life. This added to low pay and hard work, had created a situation from which I wanted to escape.

And escape she did. After taking the civil service examination she was offered an appointment in eastern Oregon. Golden immediately accepted it. "I was elated," she remembers. "Here was everything: a salary twice what I was getting, with the promise of an increase; a chance to study human types in which I had always been interested; an opportunity to travel and see something of the country." Once more, Golden seems to have never regretted her decision and spent some fifteen years in the Indian service.[54]

Most didn't stay so long. In fact, one of the nagging problems facing the Indian Office was that of maintaining a stable teaching force. The problem of teacher turnover manifested itself in two ways. First, there was the simple fact of attrition, school administrators and teachers alike leaving the Indian service altogether. Although the introduction of the civil service system improved the situation slightly, it hardly put the issue to rest. In 1897 the Indian Office released figures showing that by 1896, over two-thirds of the teachers and three-quarters of the superintendents employed in 1892 had left the service.[55] Second, there was the great frequency with which employees transferred from school to school. Sometimes the request for a transfer originated with the teacher, the opportunity to move up the salary ladder by accepting an assignment with more responsibility. As often as not, however, an unpleasant location or employee factionalism was sufficient cause to prompt teachers to make lateral transfers. Teachers also could be transferred at the recommendation of agents, superintendents, and inspectors. In any case, Gertrude Golden may be close to the truth when she asserts that the Indian school service was largely composed of "employees going, employees coming; transfers by request, transfers by somebody's orders."[56]

Why such turnover? For one thing, living conditions were often primitive. Many an enthusiastic teacher would arrive at her appointed designation, only to find that her new accommodations were scarcely more civilized that those of Indians living in the hills. Minnie Jenkins recalls that her adobe living quarters at Blue Canyon, Arizona, were little better than a cave, the chief furnishings consisting of an iron cot, an old bureau, a chair, and an overturned crate upon which set a tin water basin and pitcher. Another teacher remembered her stay at Shawnee Boarding School chiefly by the bedbugs. "They had really taken over, they were in curtains, door facings, everywhere. . . . Another trouble was the drinking water. I had always drunk a lot of water but here the water was hauled in barrels, and the very sight of it sickened me." J. B. Harrison, in a report to the Indian Rights Association in 1887, made special note of the fact that at many schools teachers were forced to use filthy, foul-smelling outbuildings and then added: "As many of the teachers are young women from the Eastern States, with as much refinement and delicacy as are possessed by those who remain in their Eastern houses, these conditions and surroundings are inexpressibly revolting." Thirty years later, poor housing was still cited as one of the chief causes for the "restlessness" of the teaching force.[57]

The work was also terribly exhausting. In addition to spending a fatiguing day in the classroom, teachers were frequently expected to conduct an evening study hour, supervise student chores, chaperone Saturday evening social events, and conduct Sunday school classes. Expectations were particularly severe at reservation schools, where there were fewer employees among which to apportion the same number of obligations and where staff vacancies caused additional responsibilities to be assigned. Employees were forewarned by the Indian Office that "long hours of service are required, and that every employee must be willing to work night or day if special emergencies arise; and that the duties of an employee do not end at a given hour, but may be continued indefinitely." And such was the reality. Minnie Jenkins describes how on separate occasions at Blue Canyon she played nurse for fourteen hours a day when the school was struck by a pneumonia epidemic, saved the school's flour stores from a flash flood, and in the role of seamstress cut and sewed some fifty student uniforms. Although many young women joined the Indian service anticipating new challenges, probably few realized the extent to which their new vocation would test the limits of their physical and emotional endurance. On the verge of collapse, some sought escape.[58]

Others suffered from the heart-wrenching pain that came from being cut off from family, friends, and community. For Jenkins the link with her Virginia home came in the form of occasional packages sent from her mother and friends. During one particularly desperate period time at Blue Canyon, she and her roommate, the school cook, kept their spirits up by apportioning out bits of fruitcake that had arrived so stone-hard that the pieces had to be sawed off and boiled in an empty tomato can. Another civilized delicacy was a jar of olives. Twice a day the two women would allow themselves one olive each, and when the supply was gone, they sparingly rationed out the remaining juice at the rate of three teaspoons a day. A more durable source of comfort, but also one which produced homesickness, was a rose-petal pillow sent by her mother.

> I went by my room to . . . get a handkerchief. On opening the door, a powerful odor of roses greeted me from the rose-petal pillow behind my flowered curtain. A sudden wave of homesickness swept over me, with the pillow recalling as it did the rose hedge in Mother's flower garden. I could see the hedge in full bloom with the dew on

the cabbage roses in the early morning. I could smell the violets, lilies, and jasmine. What a sharp contrast to my present surroundings with only the smell of desert dust and sage brush!

Holidays were an especially difficult time. Estelle Brown recalls that "resentment was keen" at Crow Creek as Christmas approached. "Any real cheer had to be supplied from our own spiritual resources, which were difficult to keep replenished." And Jenkins remembers that the employees at Blue Canyon made a genuine spectacle of themselves during a school Thanksgiving Day program that was scheduled to close with the employees singing "Home Sweet Home." All went well for the first verse. "But when we came to the refrain: Home, ho-home, sweet, sw-e-et home, in spite of all our efforts at self-control, we began to weep."[59]

And then there was the bureaucratic authority that regulated their lives. There is genuine irony here. Although one of the motives for joining the Indian service was that it offered the opportunity to break through traditional definitions of "woman's sphere," many teachers soon came to realize that life in the Indian service was anything but liberating. Gertrude Golden, for instance, refers to the first superintendent under whom she served, as "her august majesty," the "reigning sovereign of the first absolute monarchy under which I had the misfortune to live." She continues: "I was not long at the school before I learned that this tiny absolute monarchy contained all the elements that make up authoritarian rule everywhere undesirable. Fear, hypocrisy, intrigue and sycophancy held sway while sincerity and straight-forwardness were generally missing."[60]

The Indian school service was full of figures such as "her august majesty," who were capable of making life unbearable. What was particularly exasperating was that there was little an employee could do to alter the situation. Indian Office regulations forbade teachers from circumventing their superiors and communicating directly to Washington, although it is clear that this frequently happened. Occasionally, a sympathetic inspector might listen to an employee's complaints, but all experienced employees knew that inspectors were easily manipulated by those above. Moreover, an unsuccessful attempt at filing a complaint was more likely than not to result in a critical evaluation. The bureaucratic facts of life were brought home to Golden when, during a visit by Superintendent of Indian Schools Estelle Reel, Golden hinted at employee dissatisfaction with their tyrannical superintendent. Reel responded: "Miss Golden, absolute, unquestioning obedience to superior officers is necessary in the Indian service. If Commissioner Jones should order me to *black his boots,* I should do so immediately." The ground rules were now clear. "So that was that," writes Golden. "At last I had found out from someone who knew. There was no redress of wrongs in the Indian service. In a contest

Table 3.4. Indian School Service Employees by Rank and Sex in 1900

	Superintendent and Assistant Superintendent	Principal	Teacher	Assistant Teacher
Male	91	19	33	9
Female	8	29	232	25

Source: Annual Report of the Commissioner of Indian Affairs, 1900, 703–41.

the superior officer always won, and the lesser was demoted or discharged. So the only thing to do was to accept what came one's way or resign."[61]

Another rude awakening for women who looked to the Indian service for opportunities for career mobility was the stark reality that it was largely a male-governed bureacracy (see Table 3.4). To be sure, the picture wasn't entirely bleak. Women teachers willing to invest years in the Indian service were clearly able to advance to the level of principal, and in a few instances, even to that of superintendent. But for the most part, this last rung on the bureaucratic ladder was beyond their grasp. Ironically, the reform movement to convert agencies to superintendencies, which resulted in the shift of greater responsibilities to the shoulders of the school superintendent, only exacerbated the situation.

Staff factionalism was also a cause for turnover.[62] Sometimes the discord was the outgrowth of a power struggle between the school superintendent and the reservation agent; sometimes its origins were rooted in the favoritism shown by the superintendent toward particular employees; sometimes it resulted from the perception of one group that another group was not pulling its weight. Often however, it stemmed from the simple fact that employees, as complete strangers, were thrown together at a distant post where the only source of social engagement was one another's company. Under such circumstances, minor irritants could easily blossom into deep resentments. Thus, Jenkins tells us that at Blue Canyon, the agent's wife, who was also the dispenser of the mail, "would study the postmarks on the letters, and often ask us outright whom we wrote to at such and such a place." At Fort Yuma, Golden recalls that a minor crisis arose when the school cook was accused of putting two extra strawberries into Golden's dessert. Brown recalls how a superintendent of modest intelligence became irritated over a matron's gift for stimulating conversation, prompting him to post the following misspelled notice: "EMPLOYEES ARE FORBID TO TALK AT TABLE ABOUT THINGS THAT DO NOT INTEREST OTHER PEOPLE. YOU MAY BE GRATE DEEL SMARTER THAT OTHER PEOPLE BUT AFTER THIS KEEP YOUR OPINIONS TO YOURSELF."[63]

Still another reason for employee dissatisfaction was the oppressive regulation of employees' personal and social life, especially that of women. In part, the strict social atmosphere stemmed from the expectation that women teachers, as missionaries of Christian civilization, should serve as Victorian role models for Indian girls. But this explanation must be placed in the larger context of nineteenth-century mores governing middle-class male-female social intercourse. Generally speaking, Victorian society went to great pains to structure the circumstances under which single women engaged the opposite sex in company.[64] As women in increasing numbers left the household to earn a living, these traditional mechanisms of control were seriously undermined. "One of the most radical aspects of women's entry into the federal work place," writes Cindy Sondik Aron, "was that it brought middle-class women into contact with strange men without the protection of male family members or the benefits of well-observed and respected codes of behavior." If this was a problem for civil service employees generally, one can imagine the heightened concern for the welfare of the Indian Office's women employees stationed at remote posts.[65]

The Indian Office's response was to fall back to the first line of defense: women employees should be held to the strictest standards of decorum and respectability. The implementation of this policy, which was reinforced by gossip as much as by anything else, meant that women teachers' social life was abnormally dull. "In no other way of American life are women so brazenly deprived of the right to privacy," remembers Estelle Brown. Brown no doubt sums up the attitude of many women employees when she recounts her response to a question asked by a handsome young gentleman who happened to be visiting her agency. In reply to his question, "What do you people do here evenings?" Brown answered: "We ossify."[66]

On the other hand, some women were driven from the Indian service by male employees who made crude sexual advances. The logical recourse to such harassment was to appeal to the Indian Office for an investigation. Failing to get the Indian Office to pay attention, teachers sometimes appealed to the Indian Rights Association. In 1895, for example, Herbert Welsh received a long letter from a teacher at Sacaton Agency, Arizona, protesting the antics of the school superintendent. In addition to being "insulting, overbearing and tyrannical to the other employees," on one occasion, he advanced the insulting proposition that she spend the weekend with him in a nearby town where "we would have a *gay time*." Or this letter from a teacher in Nevada:

I had been here but a short time when the familiar conduct of the Superintendent toward myself and other lady employees made me think he was an immoral man, and I conducted myself in such a way that he would find no chance for such repulsive conduct. However, when he was under the influence of intoxicating liquor, there was no way of avoiding him. On the afternoon of March 4th, he called me to his house and, pretending illness asked me to do something to relieve the pain in his head. His wife was not at home. I obeyed. When I went to place a wet cloth on his head, he caught hold of me and with the most disgusting language, would have assaulted me, but I got loose from him and ran from the room. When I resented such treatment he became incensed and threatened my dismissal and accused me of improper conduct with the Indian boys.[67]

Shortly thereafter, she was in fact dismissed.

Ironically, it was an inspector's sexual advances that ultimately drove Estelle Brown from the service in 1918. The incident occurred while Brown was at Phoenix Indian School. The offender's name is never given; Brown simply refers to him as "Inspector X." While driving into Phoenix one Sunday morning to attend church, Brown spotted the inspector, whom she had met earlier at breakfast, and offered him a ride into town, which he happily accepted.

Inspector X began at once to tell me in great detail of his current love affair with a friend of his wife, an affair he had reluctantly interrupted to accept this appointment. He said he was reconciled to accepting it only because it gave him opportunity to learn at first hand the sexual attractions of Indian girls. He hoped to find some girls at our schools who had learned to do something besides knit. He commented truthfully and disparagingly on the large number of widows and old maids at Phoenix, a kind of game too old to attract his favorable attentions. And doubtless he believed he was paying me the highest possible compliment when he found me worthy of the bestowal of his attentions and his roving hands began exploring the situation. I drove for one block with my left hand, using the other to fend him off. Any woman who has found herself in this situation knows that one defensive feminine hand is inadequate against two offensive male paws. I stopped at a crossing and, lying, told him I had to turn there to reach the church. He got out reluctantly, using my leg for leverage.[68]

Brown reported the incident to the school superintendent, who in turn reported it to Washington. The Indian Office, however, failed to act on the charges. Instead, Inspector X would eventually gain his revenge by having Brown dismissed from the service. Her crime? The Indian Office reported that Brown, who had once been hospitalized with a severe illness, had actually had an abortion.[69]

Beyond the reasons for turnover already cited, three others should be briefly mentioned. First, many teachers must have been disappointed to discover that Indian pupils were often less than appreciative of the government's effort to save them from their cultural selves. Second, many teachers discovered early on that they were neither temperamentally suited nor sufficiently trained to teach Indians. As one school official explained, teachers who "seem to imagine that they are 'specially called' . . . by some mysterious providence to teach the Indians" often were surprised by the actual reality of the enterprise. An Indian child's "home life and training, his language, his habits of thought, his surroundings, his interests, his ambitions, his motives to action, his accumulation of ideas, are all new and strange and often incomprehensible to such a teacher." All too often teachers simply packed their bags in midyear and departed. And finally, one wonders how many teachers, after seeing the Indian system at close hand, came to doubt the entire operation. Estelle Brown, for instance, writes near the end of her narrative: "I entered the Service believing implicitly in the Bureau's wise and honorable aims. Disillusionment came slowly. . . . I saw sick, hungry, and overworked children. And I did nothing. I was cowardly and acquiescent." Presumably, others came to the realization earlier and got out.[70]

In the end, as the anonymously written poem "The Pessimistic and Optimistic Indian School Employee" explains, those who joined the Indian service eventually were of one of two minds: For the optimist,

> To the service I came and I'm glad of the same;
>   I find it a pleasure in life
> To be able to go and learn how to know
>   These people where peace is now rife.
>
> I can travel for less and can eat at the mess
>   And that saves a nice little sum.
> 'Tis a good place to be and it satisfies me;
>   So I'm glad to the service I've come.

For the pessimist, on the other hand,

> What does it matter if I go away?
>   Nobody cares for me; no one will say
> "What shall we do without him or her?"
>   I'm going to try to get a transfer.

> I can't do my work so that it will please;
>   It seems that complaining never will cease.
> I'm so weary of this same hum-drum,
>   I wish to the service I had never come.[71]

Reformers, of course, had hoped for more. They had hoped to create a genuine "system" of Indian education, a bureaucracy that was both benevolent and efficient, and one staffed with dedicated missionaries of American civilization. To be sure, many of those who entered the Indian service, and some who stayed, lived up to reformers' expectations. Many others, however, did not. Still, policymakers had a legitimate basis for hoping that the business of civilization could be carried out. They had succeeded in constructing a vast bureaucratic machine, and although not perfect in all respects, it was surely capable of civilizing savages.

PART TWO

Education

CHAPTER FOUR

Institution

The boarding school, whether on or off the reservation, was the institutional manifestation of the government's determination to completely restructure the Indians' minds and personalities. To understand how it functioned in this regard one must attempt to understand how Indian students actually came to know and experience it. And this effort must necessarily begin at that point in time when Indian youths left behind the familiar world of tribal ways for the unfamiliar world of the white man's school. For philanthropists, of course, the journey of Indian children to boarding school was that first step out of the darkness of savagery into the light of civilization. For most Indian youths it meant something entirely different. In any event, the day they left for boarding school could never be forgotten.

For a young Lakota Sioux named Ota Kte, or Plenty Kill—later named Luther Standing Bear—the idea of attending the white man's school first presented itself in the fall of 1879, when he and a friend noticed a crowd gathering around one of the agency buildings at Rosebud. Curious, the two boys approached the building and peered through a window. The room was mostly filled with Sioux, but there were also a few whites among them.

> When they saw us peeping in at the window, they motioned for us to come inside. But we hesitated. Then they held out some sticks of candy. At this, we ran away some little distance, where we stopped to talk over this strange proceeding. We wondered whether we had better go back again to see what the white people really wanted. They had offered us candy—and that was a big temptation. So we went back and peeped in at the window again. This time the interpreter came to the door and coaxed us inside. He was a half-breed named Charles Tackett. We called him Ikubansuka, or Long Chin. We came inside very slowly, a step at a time, all the time wondering what it meant.[1]

From Long Chin, Plenty Kill learned that the whites had come to collect children for a school in the East (the man in charge of the white party was Captain Pratt, recruiting his first volunteers for Carlisle). If Plenty Kill wanted to go to the white man's school, Long Chin explained, he must bring his father, Standing Bear, to the agency to enter his son's name in the ledger. Plenty Kill was both suspicious and intrigued with the proposal. After giving the matter some thought, however, he decided he wanted to go with the captain. As for his reasons, he later recalled:

> When I had reached young manhood the warpath for the Lakota was a thing of the past. The hunter had disappeared with the buffalo, the war scout had lost his calling, and the warrior had taken his shield to the mountain-top and given it back to the elements. The victory songs were sung only in the memory of the braves. So I could not prove that I was a brave and would fight to protect my home and land. I could only meet the challenge as life's events came to me. When I went East to Carlisle School, I thought I was going there to die; . . . I could think of white people wanting little Lakota children for no other reason than to kill them, but I thought here is my chance to prove that I can die bravely. So I went East to show my father and my people that I was brave and willing to die for them.[2]

The next day, Plenty Kill, the other recruits, and a number of parents left for the Missouri, where the final parting would take place as the children boarded a steamer to take them south. The final farewell was emotional. The children had no sooner boarded the steamer than both parents and children began to sob. "It was a sad scene," Plenty Kill recalls. "I did not see my father or stepmother cry, so I did not shed any tears. I just stood over in a corner of the room we were in and watched the others all crying as if their hearts would break."[3]

The next day, the steamer pulled into shore whereupon the recruits were directed to a "long row of little houses standing on long pieces of iron which stretched away as far as we could see." Each house had a little stairway. Instructed to climb up into the "little houses," the Indians found them to be lined with cushioned seats.

> I took one of these seats, but presently changed to another. I must have changed my seat four or five times before I quieted down. We admired the beautiful room and the soft seats very much. While we were discussing the situation, suddenly the whole house started to move away with us. We boys were in one house and the girls in another. We expected something terrible would happen. We held our blankets between our teeth, because our hands were both busy hanging to the seats, so frightened were we.

As the locomotive picked up speed, Plenty Kill noticed the line of telegraph poles passing by. "It seemed to me that the poles almost hit the windows, so I changed my seat to the other side."[4]

When the train pulled into Sioux City, Iowa, the Indians were informed that they would be taken from the train to one of the city's restaurants. Not knowing what to expect, some of the older boys placed feathers in their hair and painted their faces. Just three years after the Custer debacle, this act further excited a crowd of spectators who were on hand to see firsthand the sons and daughters of Sitting Bull's Sioux. Indeed, as Pratt ushered the Indians through the mob of onlookers, they heard frightening imitations of the Sioux war whoop. "We did not like this," recalls Plenty Kill, "and some of the children were naturally very much frightened. I remember how I tried to crowd into the protecting midst of the jostling boys and girls." Once in the restaurant, the Indians noticed a crowd of whites pressing their faces against the window. Too upset to eat, the Indians scooped up the food in their blankets and took it back to the train.[5]

By the next day, the "iron road" had taken them as far as "Smoky City," or Chicago. "Here we saw so many people and such big houses that we began to open our eyes in astonishment. The big boys said, 'The white people are like ants; they are all over—everywhere.'" Since the layover in Chicago was a long one, the Indians were placed in a large waiting room where they entertained themselves by dancing. Back on the train, "the big boys began to tell us little fellows that the white people were taking us to the place where the sun rises, where they would dump us over the edge of the earth, as we had been taught that the earth was flat, with four corners, and when we came to the edge, we would fall over." On the second night out of Chicago the anxiety was at fever pitch.

> Now the full moon was rising, and we were traveling toward it. The big boys were singing brave songs, expecting to be killed any minute. We all looked at the moon, and it was in front of us, but we felt that we were getting too close to it for comfort. We were very tired, and the little fellows dozed off. Presently the big boys woke everybody. They said they had made a discovery. We were told to look out the window and see what had happened while we were dozing. We did so, and the moon was now behind us! Apparently we had passed the place where the moon rose![6]

After a journey of several days, the train finally arrived at Carlisle, Pennsylvania. A two-mile walk brought the travel-weary recruits to the great gate that served as the entrance to the Carlisle barracks. Plenty Kill would later lay claim to a very special distinction: "I was the first Indian boy to step inside the Carlisle Indian school grounds."[7]

Such is Plenty Kill's remembrance. It is, of course, just one story. How others experienced the journey depended on several factors. Younger children, for instance, must have felt the pain of being separated from family and community more severely than older ones. Those coerced into attending school were surely more bitter than those who went voluntarily and with their parent's blessing. Children who had attended a day school, which constituted a sort of intermediate introduction to white schooling, must have found it easier than those taken directly from the camp. Moreover, it must have been much more difficult for the first generation of children, who had no idea of what lay ahead, than it was for later recruits, who had the benefit of learning from returned students what to expect. Finally, because different tribes had been exposed to white ways with varying intensity, it stands to reason that those children coming from cultures where there had been sustained contact with whites would find both the idea and necessity of schooling more comprehensible than those to whom the school was the first taste of white civilization.

But regardless of these differing circumstances, leaving for boarding school was almost always a painful affair, as evidenced by an account left by Hoke Denetsosie, a Navajo, who, at the age of six, was carted off to a reservation boarding school in 1926. In this instance the departure occurred after an all-night ceremony of ritualistic praying and singing, an apparent effort by parents to protect their children against any evil that might lie ahead.

> Early in the morning, after we had eaten, the police assembled us near . . . two old black Model "T" Fords. They started to warm up the cars, and the machines just shook all over. Altogether there were 14 boys and girls, all taller than I was. Some of the parents gathered around talking to their kids. Some were weeping. There was a wave of sadness all around. All of us wore our hair long, tied into bundles behind our necks. Just before we climbed into the cars some of the girls' parents got shears, and cut off the hair bundles and kept them. As we moved out everyone wept again, and we all waved good-bye; then we were on our way.[8]

THE ASSAULT ON CULTURAL IDENTITY

From the policymakers' point of view, the civilization process required a twofold assault on Indian children's identity. On the one hand, the school needed to strip away all outward signs of the children's identification with tribal life, that is to say, their savage ways. On the other, the children needed to be instructed in the ideas, values, and behaviors of white civilization. These processes—the tearing down of the old selves and the building of new ones—could, of course, be carried out simultaneously. As the savage selves gave way, so the civilized selves would emerge. As a "total institution," the boarding school was designed to systematically carry out this mission.[9]

For boys the stripping away process began when the school sheared off their long hair. Shortly after arriving at Carlisle, Luther Standing Bear noticed "some white men come inside the school grounds carrying big chairs." The interpreter informed the boys that the men had come to cut their hair. While sitting in class Standing Bear noticed that one by one the boys were being quietly removed: first, Ya Slo; then, Whistler. Each returned looking strange in his short hair. When it came to Standing Bear's turn, he comments that "it hurt my feelings to such an extent that the tears came into my eyes." All the short-cropped Sioux boys felt strange. "We still had our Indian clothes, but were all 'bald-headed.' None of us slept well that night; we felt so queer. I wanted to feel my head all the time."[10]

The short-hair policy was rooted in two considerations. First, it made it easier to control the problem of head lice. Head lice were by no means universal among recruits, but a general policy of short hair made dealing with the problem much simpler. Frank Mitchell, a Navajo, recalls that after bathing and having his hair cut, a "blue ointment" was immediately applied "to kill the bugs." After this, "they checked our heads every now and then and would give us treatments. They kept us clean by bathing us every so often. And of course, finally, they got rid of all of those scabs and sores."[11]

But the reason for short haircuts went deeper than cleanliness. At the heart of the policy was the belief that the children's long hair was symbolic of savagism; removing it was central to the new identification with civilization. It is interesting that Standing Bear rejects the idea that cleanliness was the primary reason for the short-hair policy: "The fact is that we were to be transformed, and short hair being the mark of gentility with the white man, he put upon us the mark." This motivation can clearly be seen in an incident recalled in a letter from S. M. McCowan to a former student at Fort Mohave Boarding School. McCowan, who had been superintendent of the institution, recalled:

I can remember when I first took you into the Ft. Mojave school and what a time I had in cutting your hair for the first time. I can see now all the old Mojave women standing around crying, while you covered your long hair with your arms and told me that I wouldn't dare to cut that hair off, but the hair was cut in spite of all your efforts and the direful predictions of the Mojave women. I compelled you to have

your hair cut off, not because of any objections to the long hair in itself, but merely because the long hair was a symbol of savagery.[12]

The haircutting exercise, in addition to being a traumatic experience,
could also spark deep resentment and occasionally even resistance. Commissioner Morgan made note of this fact after witnessing a haircutting session involving Hopi boys. "The boys had beautiful, glossy, black, long
straight hair," reports Morgan, "but unfortunately it did not bear close examination, and when they had submitted their hair to the scissors and
their locks were thrown into the fire there was, . . . a great destruction of
the innocents." Morgan went on to confess that a number of school superintendents were having difficulty keeping older boys in school, in part
because of their aversion to losing their hair.[13]

Perhaps the most serious rebellion occurred at the opening of Pine
Ridge Boarding School. Anticipating that the Sioux would not take kindly
to having their braids cut off, the plan of operation was for each child to
be called individually into a room where a teacher and a matron, supplied
with a pair of scissors, would carry out the hair removal beyond the view
of the anxious onlookers who were outside pressing against shade-drawn
windows. But just as the first child was seated, a breeze swept aside the
window shades, revealing the horrible sight of the matron about to slice
off a long braid. According to one account:

> Like a war whoop rang out the cry: *"Pahin Kaksa, Pahin Kaksa!"*
> The enclosure rang with alarm, it invaded every room in the building
> and floated out on the prairie. No warning of fire or flood or tornado
> or hurricane, not even the approach of an enemy could have more ef-
> fectively emptied the building as well as the grounds of the new
> school as did the ominous cry. "They are cutting the hair!" Through
> doors and windows the children flew, down the steps, through the
> gates and over fences in a mad flight toward the Indian villages, fol-
> lowed by the mob of bucks and squaws as though all were pursued
> by a bad spirit. They had been suspicious of the school from the be-
> ginning; now they knew it was intended to bring disgrace upon
> them.[14]

According to Luther Standing Bear, a revolt against Pratt's haircutting
order by Carlisle's first recruits nearly occurred as well. On the evening after the boys were informed that their hair must be cut, they held a secret
"council." Standing Bear remembers Robert American Horse proclaiming, "If I am to learn the ways of the white people, I can do it just as well
with my hair on." Almost to a person, the assembled boys shouted
"Hau," signifying their agreement. But this resolve weakened the next

day as, one by one, they were summoned to the barber's chair. The question remained whether any of the boys would actually make a stand.[15]

Pratt knew nothing about any of this. Instead, thinking that all was going smoothly with the barbers, he left for a scheduled trip to Indian Territory, leaving the school under Mrs. Pratt's charge. It was after his departure that one of the older boys steadfastly refused to have his braids removed. Wishing to avoid an incident, Mrs. Pratt sent the barbers away, declaring that the fate of the one holdout would be resolved upon her husband's return. Late that night, however, Mrs. Pratt and the white staff were awakened suddenly by a general commotion. The long-haired recalcitrant had undergone a change of heart. Securing a knife, he had walked out on the parade ground to publicly cut off his braids. Since by Sioux tradition the cutting off of hair was always associated with mourning, the boy's dramatic act spontaneously evoked a characteristic response from those in the barracks. Boys and girls alike now filled the night air with a shrill wailing that was both eerie and not a little unsettling to the staff. Mrs. Pratt feared that the nearby residents of Carlisle might be aroused, provoking even a worse situation. Finally, however, order was restored.[16]

The second step in the civilization process called for changing the students' dress. It made little difference whether students arrived wearing elegant buckskin or threadbare trade blankets; shortly after their arrival, their traditional clothing was exchanged for the standard school uniform. Indian service regulations held that each boy should be provided with two plain suits, with an extra pair of trousers, and each girl with three dresses. In some instances, boys also received a Sunday suit of better quality. The annual clothing ration also included the necessary underwear, nightclothes, and finally, boots.[17]

In spite of such standards, considerable variability in the quality of clothing existed among schools. Generally speaking, students at off-reservation schools were better provided for, in part because such schools were showcases for the government's Indian policy. Another factor was that these schools possessed large sewing and tailoring classes, where capable students were expected to turn out sufficient uniforms and dresses to meet the school's needs. A number of schools—Carlisle, Haskell, Genoa, Phoenix, and others—were well-known for their handsome and smart-looking dress. At Carlisle, for instance, the shoulders of the boys' dark blue uniforms were decorated with red braid, with student officers sporting red stripes as well. Carlisle girls, meanwhile, had their dark blue cloaks lined in bright red. In 1893, the superintendent of the boarding school at Albuquerque reported that since the Indian girls had recently taken to comparing their own dress with the pervading style of white girls, they had been allowed to adorn their school dresses with a few ruffles and a bit of lace. This change, it was noted, had "made a vast differ-

Navajo student Tom Torlino as he appeared at the time of his arrival at Carlisle, ca. 1880. (Courtesy of the Smithsonian Institution)

Navajo student Tom Torlino as he appeared three years after his arrival at Carlisle. (Courtesy of the Smithsonian Institution)

Sioux boys in their Carlisle uniforms, ca. 1880. (Bureau of Indian Affairs photo no. 75-1P-1-12 in the National Archives)

ence in the general feeling among the girls, who are much more willing and cheerful."[18]

The situation was decidedly different at remote reservation schools. Students often had to make do with tattered clothes, oversized boots, and beaten hats, while an overworked seamstress patched, mended, and prayed daily for a new clothing allotment. "Wearing mended clothes may implant habits of economy and be of some practical value," one agent complained in 1897, "but the wearing of crownless, brimless, and otherwise illshapen hats, and the continued wear of boots and shoes long after

As this group photograph of young women at the Fort Yuma School illustrates, the prescribed dress for female students ca. 1900 was sometimes attentive to the demands of both institutional uniformity and Victorian femininity. (Courtesy of the Arizona Historical Society Library)

they have served their purpose, lessens the wearer's self-respect, lowers the school in his estimation, and in short, creates a formidable barrier to the attainment of the end and aim of education." Sometimes, students gave up a finer quality of clothing than what they received in return. One Hopi boy, for instance, recalls being separated from a "beautiful new blanket with colored stripes" that his grandfather had specially woven for him in exchange for the standard school issue—in this case, a blue shirt, mustard-colored pants, and heavy shoes. As for the fate of the blanket, "I saw it later, in the possession of the wife of the superintendent."[19]

Students reacted differently to this aspect of their transformation. According to one school official: "A school uniform is a great cross to Indian pupils. One Indian never likes to appear like any other." Besides going against the grain of Indian youngsters' individuality, some articles of white clothing were resented simply because they were uncomfortable. Stiff boots and woolen underwear were clearly in this class. And of course many students must have seen the emphasis on uniform dress for what it was: yet another aspect of the school's design to turn Indians into carbon copies of their white overseers. Still, it appears that this aspect of the transformation process was less traumatic than the haircutting policy. Indeed, some appear to have experienced a certain excitement in dressing up like whites, even though, as we see below, the occasion was sometimes marked by a good deal of confusion.

> How proud we were with clothes that had pockets and boots that squeaked! We walked the floor nearly all that night. Many of the boys even went to bed with their clothes all on. But in the morning, the boys who had taken off their pants had a most terrible time. They did not know whether they were to button up in front or behind. Some of the boys said the open part went in front; others said, 'No, it goes at the back.' There is where the boys who had kept all their clothes on came in handy to look at. They showed the others that the pants buttoned up in front and not at the back. So here we learned something again.[20]

Yet another assault on tribal identity came in the form of new names. The policy of renaming students was motivated by several concerns. First, many students arrived at school with names the teachers could neither pronounce nor memorize. Most teachers had little patience with such names as Ain-dus-gwon, John Sang-way-way, Wah-sah-yah, Min-o-ke-shig, and Mah-je-ke-shig. As one Indian Office official observed at a national educational conference, "a teacher would be at a disadvantage in trying to be either affectionate or disciplinary with an eight-syllabled girl like Sah-gah-ge-way-gah-bow-e-quay." Second, some students had names that, once translated, were perceived to be ridiculous and occasionally humiliating—such as Mary Swollen Face, Nancy Kills-a-Hundred, Sam Slow-Fly, John Bad-Gum, Ada Parts-His-Hair, and Lizzie-Looks-Twice.[21]

Finally, renaming students was part of a conscious government policy to give Indians surnames. As Indians became property owners and thoroughly imbued with the values of possessive individualism, it would be virtually impossible to fix lines of inheritance if, for example, the son of Red Hawk went by the name Spotted Horse. "When Indians became citizens of the United States under the allotment act," Commissioner Morgan informed agents and school superintendents, "the inheritance of property will be governed by the laws of the respective states, and it will cause needless confusion and, doubtless, considerable ultimate loss to the Indians if no attempt is made to have the different members of a family known by the same family name on the records and by general reputation." For this reason, Indian Office employees in the field were instructed to move forward with the renaming process. The work proceeded slowly, and although most of the responsibility fell to the Indian agent, school officials also played a vital role, particularly in the early years.[22]

The renaming process followed several patterns. One pattern was to use the original untranslated Indian name, although sometimes in shortened form, as a surname. When practical, this was the preferred policy of the Indian Office. In a circular issued in 1890, Commissioner Morgan admitted that in many instances "the Indian name is difficult to pronounce and to remember," but then went on to say that "in many other cases the Indian word is as short and as euphonious as the English word that is substituted." Fourteen years later, an Indian Office official reiterated the point by saying: "Let the Indian keep both his personal and race identity . . . for the sake of his property it is necessary that he adopt our system of family names, but that is no reason why we should ruthlessly thrust upon him our English names when his own will answer just as well, even better. We want to educate the Indian—lead him on, not stamp him out."[23] By this liberal policy, if it may be termed as such, a Kiowa man with the name of Richard Sitahpetale or a Navajo woman called Ruth Chesehesbega could make their way in civilized society as easily as a Richard Smith or a Ruth Miller.

Another pattern was to use the translated Indian name as a surname. Under this system a Robert Redhawk or a William Swiftriver would do nicely. But such translations were not always workable. As noted earlier, some Indian names, once translated, appeared to be ridiculous and even uncouth, others were too long, and many simply could not be translated without losing their original meaning. As Alice Fletcher pointed out, the translated Dakota name Young-Man-Afraid-of-His-Horses conveyed little of the meaning behind the original, which actually meant "the young man whose valor is such that even the sight of his horses brings fear to his enemies." In such instances, if the Dakota original was short and pronounceable, it should be retained. Otherwise, it should be abandoned.[24]

A third pattern was to give children completely new names. At this point, agents and superintendents were presented with several options. One approach, recommended by John Wesley Powell, was to select from the tribal vocabulary names for geographical forms and animal life with which Indians could readily identify. For instance, the Sioux word for Roanhorse might be received with greater enthusiasm than Miller or Erickson. Another option was simply to randomly bestow common American names such as Smith, Brown, and Clark. Still another method, and one practiced for many years with conscious intent, was to rename students after famous historical figures. Harriet Patrick Gilstrap tells us that when her father, the agent at Sac and Fox Agency, gave the Indians

NUMBER	INDIAN NAME.	ENGLISH NAME.
17	*Ai - la*	*Preston Louck*
18	*Kuti - qui - ah - a - mah*	*Walter Scott*
19	*Su - wah - ki - ka*	*Paul Jones*
20	*Ni - ta - mai*	*Roger Sherman*
21	*Ku - ka - tci*	*Albert Gallatin*
22	*Si - long - ji*	*Gussie Lee*
23	*Ma - ku - ai*	*Michael Angelo*
24	*Ah - say - no*	*Perry Douglass*

This detail from the 1889 roster at Keams Canyon Boarding School, an institution enrolling mainly Hopi, illustrates one pattern for renaming—assigning names of prominent historical figures. (Courtesy of the National Archives)

new names, "first came the names of the presidents, then the vice-presidents, then prominent people of the day."[25]

But the Indian Office increasingly frowned on such ridiculous changes, and some schools made a conscious effort to retain at least a modicum of the Indian name. Thus, Hampton Institute was critical of the fact that two of its new transfer students had arrived with the names Julius Caesar and Henry Ward Beecher. Such names were nonsensical, declared the *Southern Workman*. A more humane approach was the Hampton method. When a boy arrived at the school with the name Hehakaavita (Yellow Elk), an inquiry about the boy's father's name evoked the response "Good Wood." Hence, the boy's new name became Thomas Goodwood. On another occasion, the son of an old chief, Medicine Bull, was given the new name of Samuel M. Bull. Such alterations, Hampton held, met the necessity of assigning a new name yet recognized the individuality, if not the heritage, of the student. Besides, renaming alone would not civilize savages: "Old Sitting Bull would be nonetheless a savage were he to take to himself the most honorable name we know . . . George S. Bull Washington."[26]

Whatever process superintendents used in bestowing new names, the fact remains that it constituted a grave assault on Indian identity. This is true for two reasons. First, as George A. Pettit has made clear in his landmark study *Primitive Education in North America,* traditional Indian names and the naming process itself were fundamentally connected to the process of cultural transmission and served a variety of educational purposes: as a stimulus to self-improvement, as a reward for a special achievement, and finally, as a means of transferring the traits of a revered relative or tribal figure to a member of a new generation. Because some Indian youth were sometimes given a series of names in the course of their development, and since the giving of names was frequently ritualized in elaborate ceremony, tribal naming practices were clearly central to the perpetuation of cultural outlook.[27] Second, as already discussed, a major justification for changing names was the argument that assigning surnames was an essential step in transforming Indians into self-reliant property owners. Thus, the renaming process was pregnant with cultural significance.

It is difficult to judge how students actually experienced the renaming process or what meanings they ascribed to it, but three instances from Carlisle are suggestive. Luther Standing Bear recalls that after a few days at Carlisle the interpreter announced: "Do you see all these marks on the blackboard? Well, each word is a white man's name. They are going to give each one of you one of these names by which you will hereafter be known." The first boy stepped forward and with a long pointer touched one of the names, which was written on a piece of tape and attached to the back of his shirt.

> When my turn came, I took the pointer and acted as if I were about to touch an enemy. Soon we all had the names of white men sewed on our backs. When we went to school, we knew enough to take our proper places in the class, but that was all. When the teacher called the roll, no one answered his name. Then she would walk around and look at the back of the boys' shirts. When she had the right name located, she made the boy stand up and say "Present." She kept this up for about a week before we knew what the sound of our new names was.[28]

Another boy at Carlisle was given the name "Conrad."

Dear Captain Pratt:

> I am going to tell you something about my name. Captain Pratt, I would like to have a new name because some of the girls call me Cornbread and some call me Cornrat, so I do not like that name, so I want you to give me a new name. Now this is all I want to say.

Conrad[29]

Jason Betzinez, an Apache youth from Geronimo's band, was more fortunate. Shortly after arriving at Carlisle,

> Miss Low selected for me the name of Jason. She said that Jason was
> some man who hunted the golden fleece but never found it. I
> thought that was too bad but it didn't mean anything to me at that
> time so I accepted the name. In the intervening years I believe that
> the story of Jason and his search for the golden fleece has set a pat-
> tern for my life.[30]

In this instance the name "Jason" served the same instructional function
that many tribal names had served in traditional Indian life; it gave meaning and guidance to his life. The object of Betzinez's search and that of the
famous mythological figure were, of course, altogether different. The Jason of Greek lore sought the golden fleece; Jason, an Apache thrown into
the strange world of the white man, would seek something far more precious, his very identity. Still, the Carlisle Apache's new name could serve
as a metaphor for his life, and for that matter, for countless other Indians
as well.

ADJUSTMENTS TO NEW SURROUNDINGS

Meanwhile, students were adjusting to their new physical surroundings.
Since the overriding purpose of the boarding school was to bring about
the student's civilization, it logically followed that the physical environment should approximate a civilized atmosphere as closely as possible. At
the very least, physical facilities should be of firm structure, should be
large enough to house the students enrolled, and should reflect a mindful
consideration for sanitation and hygiene. This was the ideal. Unfortunately, it was not always achieved. In 1882, Indian Commissioner Price
lectured Congress, "Children who shiver in rooms ceiled with canvas,
who dodge the muddy drops trickling throughout worn-out dirt roofs,
who are crowded in ill-ventilated dormitories, who recite in a single
school-room, three classes at a time, and who have no suitable sitting-
rooms nor bathrooms, are not likely to be attracted to or make rapid advancement in education and civilization." According to Price, the Indian
Bureau was currently forced to use facilities "which long ago should have
been condemned as unserveable and even unsafe."[31]

In the next decade living conditions improved markedly, especially at
off-reservation schools. Touring several schools in 1892, Special Indian
Agent Merial A. Dorchester found that the best ones provided each girl
with a single bed, washstand, towel, bowl and pitcher, and brush and

comb. Some dormitories had sliding curtains between the beds, "making a retired place for each girl, which helps her on the line of modesty." Others were divided into small rooms where the girls "are taught how to arrange and beautify them in a pretty and hygienic manner." Superintendent of Indian Schools William Hailmann also stressed the progress being made when he addressed the Lake Mohonk Conference in 1897. In school after school, he explained, the kerosene lamp was giving way to the electric light, the wood stove to steam heat, the bathtub to the "needle bath." At remote reservation schools, however, such renovations were slow in coming. Just a year after Hailmann's optimistic assessment, Commissioner William Jones admitted that too many schools suffered from a "deplorable deficiency" in providing Indian youth with acceptable living facilities.[32]

Adjusting to a new physical environment also meant adjusting to new conceptions of space and architecture.[33] The boarding school, the new recruits quickly learned, was a world of lines, corners, and squares. Rectangular dormitories and dining rooms and square classrooms were filled with beds, tables, and desks—all carefully arranged in straight rows. Whites, Indians surmised, largely conceived of space in linear terms. This was no mean observation, especially for students who came from cultures where definitions of space and the meanings assigned to it were radically different. For Lakota students, for instance, the essential touchstones of cultural reality—the sky, the sun, the moon, the tepee, the sundance lodge, and the "sacred hoop"—were all circular phenomena. Thus, an old Lakota, Black Elk, would tell John Neihardt in 1931: "You will notice that everything the Indian does is in a circle. Everything that they do is the power from the sacred hoop." But now, Black Elk would lament, his people were living in houses. "It is a square. It is not the way we should live. . . . Everything is now too square. The sacred hoop is vanishing among the people. . . . We are vanishing in this box."[34] Although the circle held less symbolic significance in other cultures than it did for the Sioux, the larger point should not be missed: conceptions of space are not neutral.

The same could be said for the layout of school grounds. "Our sense of place—of space—is largely determined by the manner in which we see ourselves in relation to nature," writes Jamake Highwater. In the landscaping of school grounds, Indian students received another lesson on white civilization's attitude toward space and nature. In his annual report in 1898, Commissioner William Jones informed superintendents that in order to impress upon the minds of Indian youths a new conception of "order," "system," and "the beautiful," they should attempt to reconstruct "unsightly banks and rugged hillsides so as to make them more pleasing to the eye." Elsewhere, superintendents were instructed, "The grounds

At boarding school, Indians and nature were made to conform with white concepts of order, space, and beauty as evidenced in this scene at Phoenix Indian School, ca. 1900. (Bureau of Indian Affairs photo no. 75-PA-1-2 in the National Archives)

around the buildings must receive proper attention, insofar that agreeable designs in landscaping be improvised, diversified with flowers, shrubs, and trees and swarded areas, producing pleasing and attractive surroundings." In other words, weeds, cactus, and earth must give way to manicured lawns, pruned trees, and contoured gardens. The lesson in all this was clear: nature existed to serve man's ends. In the interest of symmetry and order, the wild must be tamed, just as the Indian must be civilized.[35]

Adjusting to the white man's food—and the lack of it—was another challenge. According to official policy as stated in 1890, "Good and healthful provisions must be supplied in abundance; and they must be well cooked and properly placed on the table." Moreover, schools were urged to offer a varied menu and to use the school farm and dairy to furnish the necessary amount of fruits, vegetables, and dairy products. Although coffee and tea could be served on occasion, milk was deemed preferable. In those instances where school farms produced great amounts of fresh produce and where dairy, stock raising, and poultry departments were going concerns, the stipulated standards were met. One Navajo boy who attended the school at Fort Defiance recalls: "When I entered school there was plenty to eat there, more food than I used to get at home. . . . So I was happy about that; I was willing to go to school if they were going to feed me like that."[36]

But most would remember this aspect of boarding school life with considerable bitterness. Sometimes this displeasure stemmed from being forced to abandon traditional foods for those of the white man. Others complained about the way the food was cooked. Perhaps the most serious complaint was that they left the table half-starved. A Klamath Indian, who was detailed as a meat cutter at his boarding school, recalls that the best cuts went to the employees, while the children got only the necks and ribs. He remembers, "I learned to steal at school to keep from going hungry." Don Talayesva, a Hopi, vividly recalls his first meal at Keams Canyon Boarding School. It was a hearty breakfast consisting of coffee, oatmeal, fried bacon and potatoes, and syrup. Not a bad breakfast by white standards perhaps, but Talayesva found the bacon to be too salty and the oatmeal too "sloppy." Lunch was worse.

> We went to the dining room and ate bread and a thing called hash, which I did not like. It contained different kinds of food mixed together; some were good and some were bad, but the bad outdid the good. We also had prunes, rice, and tea. I had never tasted tea. The smell of it made me feel so sick that I thought I would vomit. We ate our supper but it did not satisfy me. I thought I would never like hash.

Helen Sekaquaptewa, who attended the same school, recalls: "I was always hungry and wanted to cry because I didn't get enough food. They didn't give second helpings, and I thought I would just starve. You can't go to sleep when you are hungry."[37]

Were Indian children underfed? The evidence seems to suggest that conditions varied greatly from school to school. But there is little doubt that great numbers suffered from undernourishment. From the very beginning, Pratt found the school service per capita food allowance inadequate and managed to have Carlisle put on army rations, a unique distinction that the school enjoyed during its entire existence. Estelle Brown says that she was at her first post only a week when she realized that the children were undernourished. "I did not know that for sixteen years I was to see other children systematically underfed." Describing her experience at another school she comments, "I knew these girls were consistently overworked, knew that they were always hungry. Simply, they did not get enough to eat. We all knew it; most of us resented it, were powerless—or too cowardly—to try to do anything about it."[38]

So students endured it as best they could. Some resorted to stealing, a risky enterprise. Others were occasionally the beneficiary of a small gift of Indian food brought by a relative on a visit to the agency. One Sioux girl who attended boarding school in the early 1920s recalls: "There was a place called the trunk room. That's where we kept our steamer trunks. They were filled with dried foods like *papa* and *wasna* because our parents thought that the white people wouldn't feed us right." After school,

"Ready for Dinner." Crow Agency Boarding School, ca. 1900. (Bureau of Indian Affairs photo no. 75-EXE-CROW-8B in the National Archives)

she relates "we would get the keys to our trunks from the matrons. And we'd go down and open our trunks and eat the Indian food." But in the main, students were dependent upon the often inadequate school ration, causing the girls at one school to compose the jingle: "Too much government gravy / Make me lazy."[39]

As students soon learned, they were not only expected to eat new foods but to eat them in a special manner. In short, they must acquire the food rites of civilized society. Enter the world of knives, forks, spoons, tablecloths, and napkins. In the finer schools, tin plates and cups would eventually give way to glassware and white china. Thus equipped, the school dining room became a classroom for instructing Indians in the rudiments of middle-class table manners. Frank Mitchell recalls:

> One of the problems we faced . . . was that we did not know how to eat at a table. We had to be told how to use the knife, fork and spoons. And when we started eating, we were so used to eating with our fingers that we wanted to do it that way at school, and we had to be taught. Although we had things there to eat with, like a fork, we had never used them at home, so we did not know what they were or how to use them; so we always wanted to stick our fingers in our

food. Of course, it took some time before we got used to how we were to conduct ourselves with these different things.[40]

Food not only had to be eaten in a certain manner but it had to be eaten at precise intervals in the day, which typified another distinctive feature of boarding school life—the relentless regimentation. As every new recruit soon discovered, nearly every aspect of his day-to-day existence—eating, sleeping, working, learning, praying—would be rigidly scheduled, the hours of the day intermittently punctuated by a seemingly endless number of bugles and bells demanding this or that response. As one school official observed, the Indian "knew he was coming to a land of laws, but his imagination could never conceive of such a multiplicity of rules as he now finds thrown about them; bells seem to be ringing all the time, and the best he can do is to follow his friendly leader." Follow his "friendly leader" is exactly what Jim Whitewolf did on his first day of boarding school.

> Logan was still with me. He told me that when the first bell rang, we would go to eat. He said that when we got down there he would tell me what to do. The second bell had rung and we were going to dinner. We all lined up according to height. Logan told me to watch the others who had been there some time already. Some fellow there gave a command that I didn't understand, and I saw all the others were standing there at attention with their arms at their sides. Then this fellow said something else and we all turned. This fellow would hit a bell he was carrying and we were supposed to march in time to it. I didn't know at the time what it was for. My legs just wouldn't do it so I started walking. When we got to the eating place, there were long tables there in rows. . . . When we got to a certain table he told me to just stand there. There was a lady there in charge who had a little bell and, when she hit it, everybody sat down. . . . I watched the others and did what they did. After we sat down they rang the bell again and everybody had his head bowed. . . . The bell rang again and we started eating.[41]

As Whitewolf's narrative suggests, the boarding school environment was patently militaristic. This was especially the case at off-reservation schools, where students organized into army units and drilled in elaborate marching routines. On special celebrations, when marching students shouldered rifles, brass bugles gleamed in the sunlight, drums pounded out marching rhythms, and school banners flapped in the breeze, the military atmosphere was only enhanced. No aspect of school life left a more profound impression on students. One Hopi who attended an off-reservation school at the turn of the century remembers that it was like "a school for Army or soldiering." "Every morning," he recalls, "we were rolled out of bed and the biggest part of the time we would have to line up and put guns in our hands." In broken English a former student at Albuquerque recalls:

> We would be in the school, but part of the time we can practice something else. That was being soldiers with the gun. Line up with it different ways, learn how to handle gun, like we being soldiers. This was sure hard thing for me to do. The most hard thing was to do this early in the morning early while it was cold; hands cold on the guns. We got more than one captain to take care of these soldiers. Then we boys made a lot of mistakes when we doing that. Sometimes we don't take the right step like they wanted us to. The ones that don't know how to do, the captain would go up to this boy and take him by the shoulders and shake him and tell him to do like the way he was told to do. The ones that are making a lot of mistakes, they can be punished for it.

While learning to march, one student at Chilocco acquired a lifelong nickname—Dizzy. Years later he would recall: "I remember, many times [the] company commander saying 'You dizzy bastard, get in step!' And it kind of stuck with me."[42]

Although spared the burden of bearing rifles, girls were subjected to the same drill routines. In fact, for Anna Moore Shaw, who attended Phoenix Indian School, the cadence of military marching was so internalized that it was hard to walk in a normal manner.

> At first the marching seemed so hard to learn, but once we had mastered the knack, we couldn't break the habit. Sometimes on our once-a-month visit to town, a talking machine would be blasting band music outside a store to attract customers. Then we girls would go into our act; try as hard as we could, we just couldn't get out of step. It was impossible! We'd try to take long strides to break the rhythm, but soon we would fall back into step again. How embarrassing it was![43]

Why were schools organized like military training camps? Part of the answer lies in the sheer organizational problems created by having to house, feed, teach, and, most significantly, control several hundred "uncivilized" youths. Good health, neatness, politeness, the ability to concentrate, self-confidence, and patriotism were also attributed to military regimen. The superintendent of Haskell even reported in 1886 that by or-

Students at Sherman Institute, one of the Indian Bureau's showcase schools, performing their marching routines, ca. 1910. (Courtesy of Harvey Oster)

ganizing the school into a battalion of five companies, he had managed to break up persisting tribal associations; forcing students to sleep in dormitories and to sit in the mess hall by their assigned companies required them to converse in English.[44]

But there were deeper reasons for the military atmosphere, reasons related to policymakers' perceptions of the "wildness" of Indian children. Indian children, it was argued, were products of cultures almost entirely devoid of order, discipline, and self-constraint, all prized values in white civilization. It was a well-known fact, according to Commissioner Morgan, that Indian parents "generally exercise very little control over their children and allow them the utmost freedom." Part of the problem, policymakers surmised, stemmed from Indians' unfamiliarity with the white man's clock and once exposed to it, their general disdain for it. From a less ethnocentric perspective, anthropologist Bernard Fontana has made a similar observation, namely, that Indian and white societies have historically subscribed to different conceptions of time. Whereas white society has increasingly become governed by "clock time," Indians have traditionally been oriented to "natural time." "In devising a mechanical means of arbitrarily segmenting the day into regularly spaced units," writes Fontana, white society has "made an artifact of time. . . . Our notion of time and our methods of time-keeping are the very underpinnings of our entire industrial system." Indians, on the other hand, have traditionally lived out their lives in accordance with natural phenomena. Fontana makes an important point. The cultural and psychological distance separating the two orientations was immense, as this Arapaho remembrance makes clear:

> It was a long time before we knew what the figures on the face of a clock meant, or why people looked at them before they ate their meals or started off to church. We had to learn that clocks had something to do with the hours and minutes that the white people mentioned so often. Hours, minutes, and seconds were such small divisions of time that we had never thought of them. When the sun rose, when it was high in the sky, and when it set were all the divisions of the day that we had ever found necessary when we followed the old Arapaho road. When we went on the hunting trip or to a sun dance, we counted time by sleeps.[45]

Until the students' concept of natural time was supplanted by that of clock time, school authorities reasoned, it would be next to impossible to develop in them an appreciation for the importance of promptness and punctuality, key values in civilized life. "Make the most of time," one school newspaper exhorted. "You have no right to waste your own time; still less, then, the time of others. Be punctual in the performance of all your duties." By constantly marching and drilling, the clocklike, mechanical movements on the drill field would hopefully carry over to other areas of student behavior. As students internalized the measured units of the clock, so too would they come to discipline and regulate their bodies and lives. "Be punctual to the minute. Even a little beforehand is preferable to being behind time. Such a habit . . . no doubt will mean a great deal to you in the after life"—that is, life after boarding school.[46]

Part of being civilized, the logic went, was being able to follow orders in a hierarchical organization, and what better training than that gained on the drill field? Thus, when Secretary of the Interior Richard Ballinger spoke to Phoenix Indian students in 1909, he referred to the school's military organization to make his major point: "We have got to become men and women and we have got to take our place in line in life, just as you take your places in the ranks of your companies. You have got to march through this world; the world expects you to do something, not simply to play and not simply to have pleasure." Or as students at one school were reminded:

> Obedience is the great foundation law of all life. It is the common fundamental law of all organization, in nature, in military, naval, com-

mercial, political, and domestic circles. Obedience is the great essential to securing the purpose of life. Disobedience means disaster. The first disastrous act of disobedience brought ruin to humanity and that ruin is still going on. "The first duty of a soldier is obedience" is a truth forced upon all soldiers the moment they enter upon the military life. The same applies to school life. The moment a student is instructed to do a certain thing, no matter how small or how great, immediate action on his part is a duty and should be a pleasure. . . . What your teachers tell you to do you should do without question. Obedience means marching right on whether you feel like it or not.[47]

THE ROLE OF DISCIPLINE

The military atmosphere of schools was reinforced by a stern discipline policy, and central to that policy was the threat of corporal punishment. In this connection, it should be emphasized that often there was very little congruence between actual school practice and official Indian Office policy. By 1890, the official position of the government was that corporal punishment should be resorted to "only in cases of grave violation of rules" and even then it was to be administered or supervised by the superintendent. For students twelve years and older, however, who were "guilty of persistently using profane or obscene language; of lewd conduct; stubborn insubordination; lying; fighting; wanton destruction of property; theft, or similar misbehavior"—in other words, just about everything—superintendents were permitted to inflict corporal punishment and even to imprison students in the guardhouse. But even then, no "unusual or cruel or degrading punishment" was to be exercised.[48]

More and more, the Indian Office began to emphasize "moral influence" as the most effective means of enforcing discipline. In 1891 the Superintendent of Indian Schools even argued that the "element of perversity" was not as prevalent in Indian children as white children. Many of the discipline problems with Indians, he asserted, stemmed from simple misunderstandings, the inability of students to comprehend and respond to commands given in a language still foreign to them. Teachers must be patient.

But a year later Commissioner Morgan was not so sure. Although in favor of exhausting "moral measures" and light punishments before resorting to severer ones, he emphasized that the boarding schools were full of Indians who "are naturally brutish and whose training has developed their anima and left their higher nature underdeveloped . . . and can be reached apparently in no other way than by corporal punishment, confinement, deprivation of privileges, or restriction of diet." Still, by 1896 the Indian Office was able to announce that corporal punishment was "steadily yielding along the line to more thoughtful and humane methods of discipline." In 1898 the *Rules for the Indian School Service* stipulated, "In no case shall the school employees resort to abusive language, ridicule, corporal punishment, or any other cruel or degrading measures."[49]

So much for official policy. In reality, many agents and superintendents continued to apply the strap. One Hopi woman who attended boarding school after the turn of the century recalls, "Corporal punishment was given as a matter of course; whipping with a harness strap was administered in an upstairs room to the most unruly. One held the culprit while another administered the strap." One Navajo woman would never forget the punishment she and some other girls received for leaving the school to pick apples in a nearby canyon. That evening the matron lined up the girls in the dormitory. "She told us to pull our blankets down and lie on our stomachs. She had a wide strap in her hand. She began whipping us one by one, and we screamed with agony." A former student at Fort Sill, Oklahoma, recalls: "Generally, the officers in charge of the companies gave the whippings. They either used a board or a belt. They had what they called a 'belt-line'; everybody took off their belts and they ran the student right down through the company."[50]

Eastern reformers generally abhorred such punishments and the Indian Rights Association made a point of exposing the contradiction between official policy and actual practice. The association's most effective technique was to independently investigate and publicize instances of outrageous cruelty. In 1903, it found a notable example in the person of George Harvey, superintendent of Pawnee Indian School. The target of two Indian Office investigations besides the association's own independent inquiry, Harvey was charged with a number of infractions. All paled, however, beside his inhuman treatment of an Indian girl who had a "slight difficulty" with the school laundress. As related in the association's annual report:

> Virginia Weeks, the pupil in question, was an orphan of the Pawnee Tribe, about eighteen years of age, of rather fragile body, she being consumptive. The girl's testimony was that in punishment for the offense the superintendent took her to his private office and locked the door so that no one could witness the chastisement; that he beat her with a yard stick, throwing her to the floor and jerking her about; finally took her to the laundry where the offense was committed, demanding that she apologize to the employee with whom she had the difficulty. This she refused to do, and the superintendent then took her to the barn, where he could not be seen, and beat her with a strap about five feet long, which he held by the loose ends in his hand so

that the doubled portion could be applied to her body. After beating her with the strap for some time, he again asked if she was willing to apologize. Still refusing, the superintendent continued the whipping until he beat her into submission, whereupon he returned to the laundry and she repeated after him the words of apology demanded.[51]

Harvey was eventually forced from the Indian service, but the association continued to call attention to other instances of blatant brutality. In 1912, it told of a thirteen-year-old boy who was held, handcuffed, and almost beaten into "insensibility" with a strap. The result was that "the boy collapsed, lay on the floor almost helpless, and that, after sixteen days, twenty-six cruel scars remained upon his body, and eleven upon his right arm." Two years later, it was reported that at the Walker River Agency School in Nevada, the superintendent, unable to identify which one of ten girls had stolen a can of baking powder, decided to punish the entire group. "The superintendent ordered these girls, who were between thirteen and eighteen years of age, stripped of clothing to the waist, and each was flogged with a buggy whip on the naked body." With charges, of course, came investigations. Investigations, in turn, resulted in resignations, transfers, and dismissal. Meanwhile, Indian children continued to be whipped.[52]

Corporal punishment was just one way of disciplining students. Although placing students in a school "jail" or "guardhouse" was officially discouraged in the late 1890s, this also remained a standard form of punishment.[53] Actually, school officials employed a variety of techniques to keep students in line. Boys might be forced to march back and forth for long periods in the school yard in girls' clothing. Girls, on the other hand, were directed to hold their arms out at length for achingly long periods, to cut the school grass with scissors, or to wear a sign saying, "I ran away." For minor infractions in the classroom, teachers resorted to time-worn techniques for maintaining control: palm slapping, standing in the corner, and the dunce cap. Disobedience could also result in being assigned to extra chores like scrubbing the floors or cleaning up the school grounds.[54] One woman who attended a boarding school in Oklahoma recalls that students who spoke Kiowa were made to brush their teeth with harsh lye soap. "The kids would end up with the whole inside of their mouth raw." At Albuquerque, the punishment for speaking Indian was a meal of bread and water.[55]

It must be said that many conscientious employees went out of their way to avoid corporal punishment. As early as 1886, an agent in Nevada claimed that he didn't believe in whipping and prided himself for being able to reason with his Indian students. If all else failed, he resorted to a reprimand before the entire school. This was particularly effective, he claimed, for it not only humiliated the offender, but also had the virtue of informing the entire school about the seriousness of the offense. Indeed, this method of discipline was so effective, he claimed, that not a single student had been slapped, cuffed, or whipped over a two-year period. The superintendent of Arapaho Boarding School, at first skeptical of the Indian Office's directive against corporal punishment, was also eventually won over. Good discipline had been established in the school for the entire year without resorting to the strap. The single exception was an instance "where a teacher in a fit of passion slapped a boy in the face and in return received a severe blow on the forehead with a slate."[56]

One of the more effective devices used to maintain discipline was to involve the students themselves in the enforcement of rules. Pratt can probably be credited with this idea, as he implemented it at Carlisle scarcely a year after the school's opening. Using a court-martial format, Pratt selected several cadet officers, who were also among the older and most intelligent students, to sit as judges. Precautions were also taken to make sure that as many tribes as possible were represented. Charges were brought, witnesses were examined, a defense was made, guilt or innocence was established, and punishments were handed out. Pratt reserved the right to overrule the court. The court-martial system soon spread to many of the larger schools, and occasionally it was found to work wonders. At the turn of the century, when a new agent, Albert H. Kneale, arrived at Cheyenne and Arapaho Agency, he found conditions to be "notoriously bad" at the boarding school. Faced with the problem of habitual runaways, the former agent had barred the dormitory windows and padlocked all the doors, but to no effect. Kneale struck upon the idea of relying on the honor system. The bars and padlocks were removed, the students organized into companies with elected officers, and a group was designated to pass judgment and carry out punishments for infraction of rules. Kneale then got every boy to pledge obedience to the rule of this group. It worked.[57]

Coping with Disease and Death

"We can not solve the Indian problem without Indians. We can not educate their children unless they are kept alive." This sensational insight, offered by Commissioner of Indian Affairs Cato Sells in 1916, might merit consideration as the most obvious statement ever to be issued by a government agency except for the brutal fact that Indian populations generally and Indian children specifically were being ravaged by disease. The situation was especially acute at boarding schools, where epidemics of tuberculosis, trachoma, measles, pneumonia, mumps, and influenza regularly swept through overcrowded dormitories, taking a terrible toll on the bodies and spirits of the stricken. Tragically, school carpenters were sometimes asked to apply their skills to coffin-making. Every off-reservation school had its own graveyard. Thus, disease and death were also aspects of the boarding school experience.[58]

For Pratt, the health of his students was not just a humanitarian concern, but a political one as well. In the early years, when Carlisle depended upon tribal leaders for recruits, it was vitally important that students be returned as healthy as when they had left. Unfortunately, in the first year alone, six boys died. Another fifteen students were sent back to their agencies because of poor health, and several of these died shortly after their return. In the winter of 1880 the situation worsened. In mid-December, just a day apart, Pratt lost Maud Swift Bear and Ernest White Thunder, both from Rosebud, the largest single contributor of students. Pratt now had reason to worry that his base of support at Rosebud, always tentative at best, might collapse altogether.[59]

The circumstances surrounding Ernest White Thunder's death are somewhat unclear, but the bits and pieces of evidence are suggestive. Pratt writes in his memoirs that when Chief White Thunder agreed to turn over his son, Pratt had promised, "I will be a father to [him] and all the children while they are with me."[60] Although Ernest's feelings about going with Pratt are unknown, it is fair to assume that since so many Sioux were going with their chiefs' blessings, he probably looked upon it as a kind of adventure or perhaps, like Luther Standing Bear, as an act of bravery.

There is no information about Ernest's attitude and behavior in the next few months, but by February it seems clear that he had developed an intense dislike toward the entire Carlisle routine and was terribly homesick. The chief learned about this firsthand in a letter from his son but also secondhand from other parents at Rosebud. When he received a letter from Pratt reporting that Ernest was becoming obstinate and uncooperative, the disappointed father wrote his son.

> My Son: I want to tell you one thing. You did not listen to the school teacher, and for that reason you were scolded. . . . At this agency are over 7000 people and there are four chiefs. These chiefs sent their children to school and others followed their lead.
>
> I want Capt. Pratt to take good care of the children of the chiefs. Your letter did not please me and my people. When the children went to school, many of the people found fault with us for letting them go; and now if what your letter says is true they will find still more fault. Capt. said he would take care of the children the same as

if they were his own, . . . I want you to attend to your books and let play alone.

If you can write a word in English I want to see it and I will be glad. You wrote to me that you were all soldiers and had uniforms. I send you $200 for you to get a large picture in your uniform so that I can see it. I am ashamed to hear every day from others in the school that you act bad and do not try to learn. I send you there to be like a white man and I want you to do what the teacher tells you.

I hope Capt. Pratt will not lose patience with you and give you up for, when I come in the Spring I shall talk to you. You had your own way too much when you were here. I want Capt. Pratt to know I shall talk to you in the Spring and if you don't mind then I shall fix you so you will. I hope you will listen to your teachers for it makes me feel bad when I hear you do not.

Remember the words I told you; I said if it takes five or ten years, if you did not learn anything you should not come back here. Your grandfather and mother would be glad to hear from you if you can write a word in English. When you get this letter take it to Capt. Pratt and have him read it and I hope he will write to me. That is all.

Your Father White Thunder[61]

Pratt did more than read it. In an apparent effort to bring the chief's son into line by humiliating him, he had the letter published in the school newspaper. But there is another news item about Ernest White Thunder on the same page, and it indicates something about the boy's response to his father's deaf ear.

The son of White Thunder has been exceptionally idle, and sometimes disobedient. In answer to some complaints which he made, he received the letter which is published in another column. When asked by his teacher to whom he would write the letter which each student is required to send home at the close of the month, he replied with the utmost nonchalance, "I have no friends to write to; I had one aunt once, but the bears eat her up."[62]

When the chiefs came in the spring, Ernest met with the same response he had received by mail: White Thunder was adamant that his son should remain. Determined to go home, in a desperate act Ernest stole aboard the train as it pulled out of Carlisle. Discovered en route, he was taken off the train at Harrisburg and sent back to Carlisle.[63]

There was more than a little irony in these events. Chief Spotted Tail, who was part of the same delegation, was appalled by what he saw. In par-

Ernest White Thunder, Carlisle, 1879. (Courtesy of the Smithsonian Institution)

ticular, he resented the fact that Sioux boys were being made to drill like white soldiers. And so he removed his own children, informing Pratt that he was taking them home even though they liked the school. Ernest White Thunder, on the other hand, was being forced to stay when he hated it. All this must have eaten away at the boy as he lay awake at night nursing a deep resentment toward both his father and Carlisle. At some point, resentment turned to a deep depression.

The next report about Ernest is that he is severely ill. On December 6, Pratt informed Washington that the outcome was not promising: "White Thunder's son is very sick and I doubt if he recovers. I consider that it is entirely his own fault as I explained to you. He is still very obstinate [and] seems to rather want to die." A few days later Pratt, with a "sad breast," wrote the chief that his son was dead.

> All the time since he got sick I have done everything I could to make him get well. . . . I had to make him go to the hospital and had to take his clothes away from him to keep him in bed. He would not eat and he would not take medicine unless I made him and then he would spit it out. All the time he had the Doctor to see him often every day and night. Whatever was good we got for him, oranges and grapes, and other nice things he had always. After he had been long sick as I told you then he wanted to get well and he began to eat and to take medicine, but he had got so weak that all our care would not save him.

Pratt went on to explain how "all these boys and girls are like my children. It is this that makes me so sorrowful when I tell you about your son." Ernest's friends, especially the sons of American Horse and High Wolf, had been with him almost to the end, but nothing could save him. "Your son died quietly without suffering like a man. We have dressed him in his good clothes and tomorrow we will bury him the way the white people do."[64]

The following day Pratt wrote the chief again. In a long letter, he began by saying:

> I had them make a good coffin and he was dressed in his uniform with a white shirt and a nice collar and necktie. He had flowers around him that some of the ladies brought for the white people love to get flowers for their friends when they are buried. Six of the Sioux boys who were Ernest's good friends carried the coffin into the chapel and then the people sang about the land where people's spirits go when they are dead. And the minister read from the good book and told all the teachers and the boys and girls that some time they would have to die too. He told them they must think a great deal about it and they must be ready to die too, because none of the teachers or scholars could tell when the time would come for them to die.

Pratt explained how the minister prayed to the Great Spirit that the sorrow of Ernest's friends and relatives would pass away and that White Thunder's people "might learn from the good book about the good land of the spirits where good people go when they die." Indeed, teaching Ernest about the Jesus book was the "best thing" the school had done for the chief's son, for "it was what the good book says that we wanted him to know so he could tell you and all your People when he went back because it is that book which makes the white people know so much as they do."[65]

And then Pratt moved on to a matter that was troubling him greatly: how would the news of the two deaths be received at Rosebud? Addressing the issue as delicately as he knew how, Pratt proceeded:

I look upon this detachment of children away from your people somewhat as you would upon a party sent out to gather a quantity of buffalo meat or even sent out to make war upon some other people or to capture horses from some other people. You know how that is my friend, how that very often there are some who never come back and such is the course of things in this life. We must expect death to come to us in a good cause as well as in a bad cause. . . . Never in all the history of your tribe have you sent parties away from it on a better mission than this one and while my heart is pained and sad for the loss that you yourself have sustained in it I am sure your strong good sense will stand by what the Government is trying to do for you and help make it strong. I would be glad to have you write to me and tell me what you think and how you feel about it.[66]

Pratt's letters to Swift Bear are much in the same vein, except that in the case of Maud he was able to argue that the girl's death had nothing to do with her coming east. He reminded Swift Bear that his daughter's lungs were full of disease when she arrived at Carlisle. "Very slowly for years," he explained, Maud's lungs "had been getting worse so that she never could have breathed like other well girls. They were all sore inside." When the tuberculosis turned to pneumonia there was nothing the doctors could do to save her. "This disease would not have been so bad if she had been well like the other girls but it was because her lungs were not sound that it made her die." Surely Swift Bear understood this, Pratt pleaded. "And because you know this I hope you will still help about this good work . . . by making the hearts of the other people strong."[67] A month later Pratt got what he wanted. White Thunder wrote back: "You, my friend, are a good man. For that reason you now have with you children of three of the chiefs. Therefore, my friend, take good care of those children. They belong to us who are chiefs. I am White Thunder who say this."[68]

The correspondence surrounding the deaths of Ernest White Thunder and Maud Swift Bear indicates a good deal about the health issue as a political question, but it reveals little about how such deaths affected the psychological atmosphere of school life. The toll must have been considerable. There is no reason to doubt Pratt's statement to Swift Bear that "the teachers and the scholars all loved Maud and their hearts are full of grief because she is dead. The Sioux girls cried all night." Moreover, Luther Standing Bear, who was at Carlisle during this episode, remarks that deaths like that of Ernest White Thunder "worked on our nerves to such an extent that it told on our bodies."[69]

What was the death rate in Indian schools generally? This is surely an important question, but unfortunately an impossible one to answer. Some of the early reports, especially from off-reservation schools, are alarming. Superintendent Armstrong, for instance, reported in 1881 that of the forty-nine students collected by Pratt three years previously, ten had either died at school or shortly after their return home. Unlike Armstrong, however, most superintendents only reported the deaths of those students who were actually attending school; it was a common practice to dismiss the sickly students. Although this occasionally could be justified on the basis that removing contagious children from the school was necessary to the overall health of the school, it also had the practical effect of lowering the death rate.[70]

Although schools were periodically struck by epidemics such as measles, influenza, and mumps, the most persistent threats to Indian health were tuberculosis and trachoma. Tuberculosis was the most menacing. In its most life-threatening form, pulmonary consumption, the disease attacked a child's lungs, slowly eating away at the afflicted's strength. When it ran its course, coughing, spitting up blood, and hemorrhaging finally resulted in death. Another form of the disease, scrofula, attacked the lymph glands, causing eruptions or running sores in the regions of the lower face and neck. Less life-threatening, scrofula was still debilitating. Both forms of tuberculosis were highly contagious. After the discovery of the tubercle bacillus in 1882, a growing consensus emerged in the medical community that the best defense against infection was strict hygiene, a nutritious diet, plenty of exercise, and well-ventilated living quarters. Unfortunately this understanding only slowly permeated the Indian service.[71]

Because the Indian Office made no systematic effort to gather figures on the state of Indian health until after the turn of the century, it is impossible to estimate with any precision the extent of infection in either the Indian population in general or in Indian schools in particular. What is clear is that the infection level at some schools reached astounding proportions. In 1897, the superintendent at Crow Creek, South Dakota, reported to Washington that practically all his pupils "seem to be tainted with scrofula and consumption." This fact, he went on to observe "steadily and unavoidably affects school work, and subtracts from the results of every kind which might otherwise be achieved." Moreover, the omnipresent reality of disease and death made for a depressing atmosphere.

When a pupil begins to have hemorrhages from the lungs he or she knows, and all the rest know, just what they mean, in spite of everything cheerful that can be said or done. And such incidents keep occurring, at intervals, throughout every year. Not many pupils die in school. They prefer not to do so; and the last wishes of themselves and their parents are not disregarded. But they go home and die, and the effect in the school is much the same. Four have done so this year. As many more have gone out who undoubtedly will never be able to return; and others, in still larger numbers, have had hemorrhages from the lungs, or the terrible scrofulous swellings which we know, and they know, practically certify to their fate. Keeping them in school at all sometimes becomes a rather painful task.[72]

Conditions were indeed horrendous at Crow Creek. Two years later, when Estelle Brown arrived to teach kindergarten, she found that the faces of her pupils shone "with mercuric ointment generously spread over their scrofula sores." In a brutally frank admission, she says that she put the sores to use as identifying marks for remembering the names of her students: "The sores helped. I separated the children with visible sores and so came to identify Sophie Ghost Bear by the running sore on the right side of her neck, Elaine Medicine Blanket had her sore on the left."[73]

Slowly, the Indian Office began to collect reliable data. A survey of Indian service physicians made in 1904 brought the acknowledgement by Commissioner William Jones that tuberculosis was indeed a serious health hazard to Indians, including schoolchildren. A more extensive study funded by the Smithsonian Institution in 1908 studied five reservations and concluded that on average only about 20 percent of the Oglala Sioux, Menomini, Quinaiet, Hupa, and Colorado River Mojave populations were absolutely free of tubercular symptoms. Schools, moreover, were cited for their ineffectiveness in combating the disease. At year's end Commissioner Leupp proclaimed that "the tuberculosis scourge is the greatest single menace to the future of the red race" and shortly thereafter launched the first systematic attempt to eradicate the disease altogether.[74]

The second disease that afflicted large numbers of children was trachoma, or "sore eyes." Shortly after the turn of the century, medical research revealed that trachoma was caused by a specific microorganism and was highly contagious. Until then, Indian service physicians had limited knowledge of the disease. Trachoma proceeds in several stages: the formation of granules on the inner eyelid, followed by the secretion of a pus-like fluid; the growth of blood vessels and ulcers on the cornea; the thickening, drooping, and inward turning of the eyelid, causing greater irritation to the cornea; and finally, the scarification of the eyelid and cornea, resulting in the growth of an opaque substance over the latter. At first irritating, then painful, trachoma is characterized early on by partial loss of sight and if untreated can result in total blindness.[75]

Trachoma was virulent on both reservations and in Indian schools, and, as this remembrance of Jim Whitewolf indicates, it was directly connected with the Indian youth's capacity to benefit from schooling.

> My eyes bothered me. Those days all the children seemed to have sore eyes. I lost the sight in my left eye. I was taken to the eye doctor, and he said that I had bad eyes. They told the agent about it. After that they never bothered me about going back to school. For about two years my eyesight was very dim. I stayed close to home then. I didn't do much of anything. They took me to an Indian woman doctor. She took a piece of glass from a bottle and cut away some white substance that was growing over my left eye. After that I could see better. After she had cured me, my father gave this woman a horse. That was more valuable than money then. Some of the Apache doctors then would require you to bring four things, but this woman didn't. She gave me some stuff, like salt, from the creek and something else to mix with it and told me to put this in my eye. I used this until I saw that my eyesight was all right, and then I quit. I would just go around to dances and visiting, but I never returned to school.[76]

In 1912, Congress funded a major study of trachoma to be conducted by the Public Health Service, and only then did policymakers come to appreciate the magnitude of the situation. For three months thirteen physicians moved through twenty-five states examining 39,231 Indians. The results were truly astounding. Of those examined, 8,940 individuals, or 22.7 percent, were afflicted. Even more shocking was the level of contraction among schoolchildren. Of the 16,470 pupils examined, 4,916 were infected, a staggering 29.8 percent. Moreover, out of the 133 schools surveyed, 37 had a trachoma rate of over 50 percent. In Oklahoma the situation was especially desperate; in the thirty boarding schools examined, 69.14 percent suffered from the disease.[77]

In self-defense, the Indian Office offered its account of the poor state of affairs. How, it asked, could schools maintain high health standards when Congress continued to deny the necessary resources—sufficient boarding facilities, adequate food supplies, and qualified doctors?[78] Second, Indian children often came from filthy, disease-ridden households where knowledge of hygiene was completely absent. It was difficult enough to control and fight infection once the school year was under way; the problem was hopelessly exacerbated at reservation boarding schools where children returned to camp for periodic vacations.[79] Finally, both Indian parents and students alike were still under the influence of savage superstitions. According to Joseph F. Murphy, medical supervisor of the Indian service, the average Indian was "still a believer in the charms and incantations of his untaught medicine man." Parents, agents reported, frequently requested permission to remove a sick child to the village camp so tribal healers could apply their timeworn magical arts.[80] As for the students, they frequently had little faith in white doctors, failed to heed their prescriptions, and all too often displayed a fatalistic attitude toward disease and death. (Indeed, one Navajo woman admits: "I never went to the hospital when I was sick, because I was afraid of the doctors. Also, I had been told that many people died there, and that there must be a lot of children-ghosts.")[81]

But in spite of these explanations, by the turn of the century it was clear that the boarding school itself was a major contributor to the spread of disease. Institutions where no measures were taken to disinfect tubercular sputum, where infected hand towels, drinking cups, schoolbooks, and the mouthpieces of musical instruments passed freely among children, where the diet lacked nourishment, and where two or three students often were forced to sleep in a single bed were hotbeds of contagion. Moreover, off-reservation school presented particular problems: they removed students to a new and sometimes unhealthier climate; the exhausting regimentation wore down the students' resistance; and they exacted severe emotional pain by cutting the children off from family and community. Cora Folsom, director of Hampton Institute's Indian program, would confess in her memoirs, "Homesickness with them became a disease; boys and girls actually suffered in the flesh as well as in the spirit; could not eat, would not sleep, and so prepared the way for serious trouble." Whereas the white student away at boarding school certainly experienced homesickness, "an Indian throws himself flat upon the bosom of mother earth and, scorning the weakness of tears, lies there in dumb misery for hours together, oblivious to dampness, to cold or heat."[82]

By 1910 the campaign to improve Indian health moved into high gear. Superintendents were instructed to guard against overcrowding, to sleep one to a bed, to isolate infected students, to periodically fumigate school supplies, to strategically place cuspidors throughout the school, to introduce personal hand towels in bathrooms, and where possible, to construct open-air sleeping quarters. At a few locations sanitoriums and eye hospitals were constructed. The Indian health service also experimented with various types of eye operations. Most involved inverting the eyelid and then either scraping the inner surface or expressing the infectious matter through a squeezing process accomplished by the utilization of specially designed forceps. Periodic applications of cocaine were used to kill pain. Following the operation patients were kept in a darkened room and for the next few mornings awoke with their eyelids glued together by secretions from their healing wounds. All and all, trachoma operations were both painful and frightening, but when properly carried out were apparently effective.[83]

Much of the health campaign was in the form of preventive education. Superintendents introduced "swat the fly" programs and urged girls to join "little mother leagues." Posters, manuals, stereopticon slides, health talks, and essay contests were used to drive home the message of good hygiene. Students were regularly enjoined not to borrow handkerchiefs, not to spit on the floor, and not to blow their nose in the air with their fingers.[84] Instilling fear was also a useful pedagogical device.

> I am lurking in the dark,
> I am watching for my prey,
> I will attack and leave my mark,
> I am watching for you every day.
> When your strength is getting weak,
> Then I'll take a chance at you,
> I'll feed on blood and pale your cheek,
> I'll devour your lungs through and through.
> Yes, I'll fight with all my might,
> Against your strength, your bones, your flesh,
> When your room is dark as night
> Instead of clean and nice and fresh.
> I sit upon the food you eat,
> Sometimes within the water you drink,
> In filth and dirt I do retreat,
> With joy on yon black grave's brink.
> I am a fiend within the air,
> I ride on particles of dust,
> I'm here, I'm there, I'm everywhere,
> Your ignorance is my sole trust.
>
> .   .   .   .
>
> Do you know the cause of destruction
> In your Lungs, such an oasis,
> Of blood and pus and corruption?
> I am TUBERCULOSIS.[85]

Considerable headway was made just prior to World War I, but the war effort soon forced a reordering of congressional priorities. Appropriations for Indian health, which had jumped from $200,000 in 1914 to $350,000 in 1917, stabilized thereafter, and little progress was made in the immediate postwar era. The impact of this was revealed in a major survey of Indian health conditions carried out by the American Red Cross in 1922 at the request of Commissioner of Indian Affairs Charles Burke. The Red Cross selected Florence Patterson, an experienced public health nurse, to conduct the investigation. Beginning her study in October, Patterson spent nine months in the Southwest surveying conditions for over 40,000 Indians, including schoolchildren. The final report reached the commissioner's desk in June 1924. Burke had wanted a strong report to support increased appropriations. What he got, however, was a stinging criticism of the entire health program. Burke buried the report, and it never saw the light of day until 1928.[86]

The Patterson report was especially critical of boarding schools. Tuberculosis and trachoma rates were again up. At the Pima and Mescalero Apache schools, for instance, 50 percent of the students had contracted trachoma. Even at Phoenix Indian School, which possessed a special eye hospital, 20 percent of the students were infected. Once again, there was the familiar litany of causes: poor diet, overcrowding, lack of sanitation, and the exacting routine of school life, including the heavy work schedule. Indeed, after reviewing a single day's schedule, Patterson issued a blistering indictment of the entire boarding school concept:

> This program, combined with the strain of bells, bugles, and horns, forming in line five or six lines each day, and the mental struggle to combat physical fatigue, could not fail to be exhausting, and the effects were apparent in every group of boarding school pupils and in marked contrast to the freedom and alertness of the pupils in the day schools. One gained the impression that the boarding school child must endure real torture by being continually "bottled up" and that he somehow never enjoyed the freedom of being a perfectly natural child. One longed to sweep aside his repressions and to find the child. As a small child he had undergone a terrific shock in adjusting himself to the school life and routine so difficult from any previous experience in his life. Again, after several years of nonreservation boarding school life, he would have to face a similar shock in returning to reservation life, from which every effort had been made to wean him.[87]

In making these comments, Patterson was going beyond the hard evidence of her investigation and relying on her trained instincts for detecting a fundamentally unhealthy environment. In doing so, she spotted what most students already had discovered firsthand: life at an Indian boarding school was not easy.

CHAPTER FIVE

Classroom

Removing Indian children from their native communities, stripping away the external trappings of their tribal identity, and initiating them into the routine and discipline of institutional life were just a beginning. The battle for children's hearts, minds, and souls could not be won simply with barber shears and marching drills. If Indians were to be prepared for citizenship, if they were to become economically self-sufficient, and if they were to adopt the values and sentiments of American civilization, then they must be instructed to achieve these ends. For this reason, while new recruits were adjusting to life in the total institution, they were also being introduced to the world of the classroom, and with it, the curriculum of the white man's civilization.

In the early years, when students were taken directly from the camp and spoke no English, they entered the classroom with feelings that ran the gamut from hopeful expectation to suspicious hostility. What new experiences, both pleasant and traumatic, lay ahead? Who was this teacher and what would she do? Meanwhile, on the other side of the desk stood the teacher, whose special responsibility it was to reshape every aspect of her Indian pupils' personal and cultural beings. As Cora Folsom, a Hampton teacher, described the scene:

> A class of boys and girls from eight to twenty-five years of age, ignorant of every rule of school or society sits mute before you. The sad, homesick faces do not look encouraging. Everything is new and strange to them. The boys' heads feel bare without the long braids. The new clothes are not easy and homelike. They do not understand one word of your language, nor you of theirs, perhaps, but they are watching your every look and motion. You smile and say "Good Morning;" they return the smile in a hopeless kind of way, but not the "good morning." By a series of home-made signs, which they are quick to interpret, they are made to understand that they are to repeat your greeting, and you are rewarded with a gruff or timid "Good Monink," and thus another gate is opened to the "white man's road."

Other words soon followed: "stand up," "sit down," "walk softly," "speak louder," and "march out."[1]

The first order of business was to teach the Indian children how to speak, write, and read English. At the recommendation of the Indian Office, most teachers employed the so-called objective method of instruction as practiced at Carlisle and Hampton.[2] Under this method students first were shown objects such as books, pencils, and shoes; second, given the English word for the object; and finally, drilled in the proper pronunciation. Lacking objects, teachers utilized object cards, sand tables, wall charts, and occasionally, took students for instructive walks about the grounds. In this fashion, students were also introduced to the alphabet and the written word. Upon seeing a cat or horse depicted on a card, and after learning to pronounce it, students were asked to copy the depicted word on a slate or to trace over words lightly written on the blackboard. In this manner students began to acquire a rudimentary vocabulary and in the process began to speak, read, and write something of the white man's language. As one teacher reported, the pupil soon "glories in being able to name every object with appropriate adjective, from the blue sky above to the green grass beneath." And in the process "he is amused to learn that rakes have *teeth,* that fingers have *nails,* and that tables have *legs.*"[3]

After a few weeks, students were reading simple passages from a reader and copying sentences on their slates. Much of the class time was devoted to drill and reading in concert. The great challenge for the teacher was to move the student from rote recitation to genuine comprehension. As one teacher noted, for many pupils the printed page was "only a mess of words, over which they pore in a dazed sort of way, but from which they fail to extricate any connected ideas which they can express when called upon to recite." The pace, in the beginning at least, was excruciatingly slow. "One lesson is often all that is taught in a week," one teacher reported, "as every step has to be illustrated by drawing, no matter how crude, acted out, or in some way made clear to them." After a few months, however, some students were constructing their own sentences and even paragraphs. Later in the year they moved on to presenting memorized dialogues, answering questions put to them from conversation cards, and writing letters to their parents.[4]

Not for two or three years did teachers begin to teach grammar seriously. One teacher, Helen Ludlow of Hampton Institute, devised an ingenious method for teaching verbs:

Its "principal parts" we know as "chiefs;" the different modes, as so many reservations, in which each chief has a certain number of bands (tenses) that follow him. These bands are numbered as companies doing valiant service in support of the King's English—or the President's American. For many weeks company drill progressed with unflagging interest and patience. To marshal a company on the blackboard for inspection, send it marching into the ears of the audience, and finally to set one or more of its members to work, building sentences, was fun enough for a long time. Battalion drill was proudly gone through at last, and after that height was attained in our system of tactics, to save time, each company is represented by its first sergeant—in other words, each tense by its first person—and they are able to put a very neat synopsis of any verb upon the board, calling upon each other in turn for the tenses, and modes, in successive order or skipping about.[5]

Meanwhile, students struggled. Jason Betzinez, an Apache who came to Carlisle as an older student from Geronimo's band, would later remember: "It was extremely difficult for me to learn to speak English. At first I was unable to make many sounds. I even had trouble pronouncing the letters of the alphabet." Eventually, Betzinez did better, but for the first three years "it didn't seem that I would ever learn." Students who suffered from trachoma faced special problems. One Apache woman recalls: "When I was there, I couldn't see to read. It was all fuzzy. And because of this I can't read and I have to stay after school." For Charles Eastman, who attended Santee School, it was the frustration of recitation: "For a whole week we youthful warriors were held up and harassed with words of those letters. Like raspberry bushes in the path, they tore, bled, and sweated us—those little words rat, eat, and so forth until not a semblance of our native dignity and self-respect was left."[6]

Luther Standing Bear would never forget the day his teacher decided to test her students' proficiency at reading by asking each student to stand and read a designated paragraph from the class text. "One after another the pupils read as called upon and each one in turn sat down bewildered and discouraged." When Standing Bear's turn came he read the paragraph thinking he had committed no errors. However, upon the teacher's question, Are you sure you made no errors? Standing Bear read it a second time. And then a third, a fourth, and fifth, each time receiving no affirmation from the teacher. What had begun as an unpleasant exercise was turning into sheer torture.

> Even for the sixth and seventh times I read. I began to tremble and I could not see my words plainly. I was terribly hurt and mystified. But for the eighth and ninth times I read. It was growing more terrible. Still the teacher gave no sign of approval, so I read for the tenth time! I started on the paragraph for the eleventh time, but before I was through, everything before me went black and I sat down thoroughly cowed and humiliated for the first time in my life and in front of the whole class!

At the weekly Saturday evening assembly, where Pratt regularly singled out individuals for praise or criticism, Standing Bear was certain the superintendent would humiliate him, but quite the opposite occurred. After speaking about the importance of having self-confidence, Pratt called attention to the fact that Luther Standing Bear had valiantly read a passage eleven times in succession without a single error.[7]

The difficulty students experienced in learning English can be explained in several ways. First, there were the normal difficulties encountered when learning a second language. Every language has its own vocabulary, its own phonology or system of sounds, its own morphology or structure, and finally, its own syntax or way of piecing together separate units into complete thoughts. Particularly unique in this instance was the immensity of the linguistic gap separating the students' native language from that of English. Unlike the German- or French-speaking student, to whom similar linguistic patterns would be readily recognizable, the Indian student struggled with a language that was entirely outside his native morphological and syntactical frame of reference. Many Indian languages place little emphasis on time or verb tense; others make little differentiation between nouns and verbs or separate linguistic units; still others build into a single word thoughts that in English can only be expressed in an entire sentence. The point here is not that a given Indian language was necessarily more or less complex than English, but that it was fundamentally different in its makeup. Moreover, when one considers that many classrooms were filled with students speaking a diversity of native tongues, each possessing its own unique linguistic features, and that teachers rarely spoke or had the slightest interest in understanding the particular characteristics of a student's native speech, only then is it possible to appreciate the difficulties encountered in learning to speak, read, and write the white man's tongue.[8]

A second factor relates to the interconnection between language and culture.[9] Learning English meant more than simply learning another language; it also entailed a new way of thinking, a new way of looking at the world. Anthropologists Clyde Kluckhohn and Dorothea Leighton make this point in their classic study, *The Navaho:* "Every language has an effect upon what the people who use it see, what they feel, how they think, what they can talk about." In the case of Navajo, differences in cultural priorities are reflected in the language's grammar:

Take the example of a commonplace physical event: rain. Whites can and do report their perception of this event in a variety of ways: "It has started to rain," "It is raining," "It has stopped raining." The People can, of course, convey these same ideas—but they cannot convey them without finer specifications. To give a few instances of the sorts of discrimination the Navaho must make before he reports his experience: he uses one verb form if he himself is aware of the actual inception of the rainstorm, another if he has reason to believe that rain has been falling for some time in his locality before the occurrence struck his attention. One form must be employed if rain is general round about within the range of vision; another if, though it is raining round about, the storm is plainly on the move. Similarly, the Navaho must invariably distinguish between the ceasing of rainfall (generally) and the stopping of rain in a particular vicinity because the rain clouds have been driven off by the wind. The People take the consistent noticing and reporting of such differences (which are usually irrelevant from the white point of view) as much for granted as the rising of the sun.[10]

Given the immensity of the cultural gulf separating Indians and whites, one can only imagine the difficulties suffered by students because of previous cultural and linguistic training.

The language-culture connection manifested itself in yet another way, namely, the problems students had understanding the meaning of words for which there were no corresponding equivalents in their native language. Frederick Riggs, assistant principal of Santee Normal Training School and a fluent speaker of Dakota, drew attention to this fact on more than one occasion. What, asked Riggs, was the Dakota-speaking child to make of a sentence such as, "One bright summer's day Gracie took Zip for a romp in the orchard"? The white child, Riggs noted, would immediately assume that Zip was a dog, but not a Santee Sioux. The latter would never think of naming a dog; one did not bestow a personal name on something likely to end up in a kettle of soup. And what was the young Dakota speaker to make of the word "orchard," again something outside the child's cultural experience? It was, Riggs claimed, very much like asking the white child to make sense of taking "Zip for a romp in a glacier." Thus, it was one thing for an Indian child to mechanically pronounce words, but quite another for him to genuinely comprehend what he was reading. Words and concepts could not be divorced from cultural context.[11]

Convinced that pupils would never achieve English proficiency unless forced to use it as the sole means of communication, the school service was informed in 1890, "Pupils must be compelled to converse with each other in English, and should be properly rebuked or punished for persistent violation of this rule." The "no Indian" rule, however, was easier to proclaim than enforce, causing school officials to devise all manner of strategies to encourage compliance. At Carlisle, Pratt gave awards to students who went for an extended length of time without speaking their native tongue. At Hampton, Samuel Armstrong called upon each student at evening roll call to confess any violation of the rule." Perhaps the most ingenious solution was that devised by the superintendent of the school at Cheyenne and Arapaho Agency. In this instance students were organized into military companies, complete with sergeants and corporals, solely on the basis of their facility with English and then periodically promoted or demoted in rank on the basis of their adherence to speaking only English. Most, however, relied on administering punishments. Minnie Jenkins frankly describes in her memoirs how on one occasion she laid thirty-five Mohave kindergartners—"like little sardines"—across tables, whereupon she spanked them for speaking Mohave.[12]

The ideal, of course, was to engender in the students a willingness to comply. Pratt, because of his charismatic personality, appears to have been amazingly successful in this regard. Certainly no superintendent could ask more of a student than what Pratt got from one of his Sioux girls in 1881:

Dear Sir Capt. Pratt:

I write this letter with much sorrow to tell you that I have spoken one Indian word. I will tell you how it happened: yesterday evening in the dining-hall Alice Wynn talked to me in Sioux, and before I knew what I was saying I found that I had spoken one word, and I felt so sorry that I could not eat my supper, and I could not forget that Indian word, and while I was sitting at the table the tears rolled down my cheeks. I tried very hard to speak only English.

Nellie Robertson[13]

With characteristic sensitivity, Pratt published this letter in the school newspaper.

How successful were schools at teaching English? At the better nonreservation schools, students could attain a reasonable degree of literacy in a relatively short time. Visitors to Carlisle would always be impressed with that school's accomplishments in this area. After noting the speed with which Carlisle teachers had brought the Apache children of Geronimo's band to a level of basic literacy, one government official was convinced that "no teaching could be better calculated to catch and hold the interest of pupils, unlearned in English or letters, than the teaching of the Carlisle classrooms." One Carlisle staff member went so far as to claim that within the space of six to nine weeks the school could teach children between the ages of six to ten to converse and read in English. Hampton's claims were more modest when it asserted that a "usable" knowledge of English could be acquired by their students in three years. And one of the school's teachers went so far as to say that her students, after a year and a half of instruction, were "able to stand in any service with Bible, prayer or hymn book, and . . . read for themselves the message of good will."[14]

Reservation schools seem to have been far less successful. At San Carlos Agency, Sedgwick Rice reported in 1898 that the children under his charge were making only modest progress. "As they but rarely hear any English outside of the school," wrote Rice, "they cannot be brought to see the need of it, and its use can be insured only by disciplinary measures." Moreover, "the English used among them is so broken that only a careful observer can distinguish it from the Indian tongue, which is very difficult and guttural." John (Fire) Lame Deer, a Lakota Sioux who attended the boarding school at Pine Ridge recalls: "It took me three years to learn to say, 'I want this.'" On a similar note, Frank Mitchell, a Navajo who attended the school at Fort Defiance, recalls: "We did not talk much English; most of the time we talked Navajo, our own language, to one another. They did not understand us and we did not understand them."[15]

Off-reservation schools, of course, had several advantages over their counterparts. For one thing, they tended to be more intertribal in their composition, a factor that both contributed to the use of English as the common language and made the "no Indian" rule easier to enforce. In 1879, for instance, Pratt was able to assign students speaking nine different languages to a single dormitory.[16] Students at off-reservation schools also were thrown into much closer contact with white English-speaking communities. And perhaps, most importantly, off-reservation students were prevented from reverting back to their native speech during summer vacation.

For some schools, all of the object lessons, the copying over of sentences, the recitations, and the letter writing paid off to the point that some students began to lose touch with their native tongue. In 1908, one Haskell student wrote home: "My friend and I, both big Pawnees, have fun trying to make a sentence in Indian without saying a word of English. It is hard as well as fun, when you get ninety in English, to make a good sentence in the Pawnee language."[17]

THE CURRICULUM OF CIVILIZATION

Once students began to understand English, teachers pressed ahead with other areas of the curriculum. The course of study outlined by Commissioner Morgan in 1890 emphasized the following branches of knowledge: arithmetic, geography, nature study, physiology, and United States history. Taught in the proper manner, these subjects would accomplish two things. First, they would introduce Indians to the knowledge of civilization. Second, the curriculum would prepare Indians for citizenship.[18]

In arithmetic the first couple of years were spent on numbers and simple measurements. After eight years students were expected to be able to add, subtract, multiply, and divide whole numbers, fractions, and decimals. During this time some attention was also given to the solution of practical or word problems.[19] As citizen-farmers, Indians must be able to count bushels of wheat, calculate their worth, avoid being cheated by the local trader, manage financial obligations, and construct a house or barn with mathematical precision. For the discerning student, there was a larger lesson as well: the culture that was engulfing him placed a high priority on measuring things; space, time, goods, and money were divided and subdivided to the nearest fraction. The white man's culture was a culture of calculations. This indeed was an important lesson, one that if not taken to heart might bring disaster later on.

Physical geography was also an eye-opening experience. A lecture on the infinite dimensions of the universe, and even on the immensity of the planet earth, left little room for the idea that Indian peoples had dwelt at the center of the world or that the tribal fathers were as wise on questions of cosmology as once supposed. Thus, one teacher noted that she told students very early in her geography class "that the world is round; that the stars are larger than this whole earth; and many other things more wonderful than any legend of [their] fathers." Another teacher reported that after students had completed the assigned task of filling in a map of the Western Hemisphere with pictures of vegetation, animals, and dwellings, one student "was so astonished at his own work that he was found gazing at it with folded hands long after the bell had rung for dinner."[20]

To shrink the vast prairies, northern Arizona's San Francisco Peaks, and even the Grand Canyon into geographical—and actually spiritual—insignificance could not help but shake traditional worldviews to their very foundations. Charles Eastman writes that "when the teacher placed before us a painted globe, and said that our world was like that—that upon such a thing our forefathers had roamed and hunted for untold ages, as it whirled and danced around the sun in space—I felt that my foothold was deserting me." He remembers thinking, "All my savage training and philosophy was in the air, if these things were true." Similarly, Asa Daklugie, an Apache at Carlisle, would never forget the time his teacher showed him Arizona in a geography book. "I was fascinated," Daklugie later recalled. "When she showed me mountains and rivers I could tell their names in my language. I knew the Spanish for some of them and a few in English. She let me take that geography book to the dormitory and . . . I almost wore it out." Edmund Nequatewa, a Hopi at Phoenix Indian School, had a special reason for taking an interest in geography. "I was always thinking of how I could get away from that school. After that I paid more attention to geography lessons, because it is the only way that I can find my way out. I put my whole mind on Arizona, New Mexico and California, studying rivers and mountains in order to find the road that I am going to use to get away from here."[21]

Luther Standing Bear entered Carlisle believing the world to be flat with four corners and recalls that when his teacher told him it was in reality a sphere that revolved on an axis, he could not accept it. "How could we stick to the ground like flies if we were standing on our heads?" But he soon had reason to think twice about challenging his teacher's scientific knowledge. One day an astronomer spoke to his class and predicted that an eclipse of the moon was scheduled to occur at twelve o'clock on Wednesday night of that week. This appeared to go far beyond the primitive claims of any tribal priest, and Standing Bear recalls that "the students laughed and laughed over this, not believing a word of it." But when the appointed night came, the students stayed awake to test the astronomer's predictions. "Sure enough it happened! The moon was eclipsed, and after that, we readily believed everything our teacher told us about geography and astronomy."[22]

But some students were not so quick to accept teachers' claims uncritically. One teacher of geography complained that "it is not easy to give them clear ideas of the relative importance of places and people." When drawing maps Indians unhesitatingly placed their tribal home at "the center of the known world." Moreover, they "place the 'buffalo' among the fierce wild animals of India; decline to believe that an Arab steed is equal to an Indian pony; and after dutifully proclaiming that the Himalayas are the highest mountains in the world, instantly add, 'but not so high as the Rocky Mountains!' " And at least one student was able to question the nineteenth-century's uneasy compromise between science and religion. Hampton's newspaper reported that

> a teacher in endeavoring to overthrow the Indian belief that the earth is flat, stands still, and that the sun passes over and under it every twenty-four hours, said, in conclusion: "So you see, it is the earth that goes around while the sun stands still." A tall boy asked, "Then what for you tell us one story about man in the Bible—I forget his name—strong warrior—fight all day, but get dark so can't fight, and he say 'Sun stand still.' What for he say that if sun all time stand still."[23]

Students also received instruction in the sciences: natural history, botany, and physiology.[24] Most of the instruction went under the title of "observation lessons," although textbooks and simple experiments soon found their way into the curriculum. Probably more significant than the specific content of the scientific curriculum was the deeper message being transmitted. Traditionally, Indian children had been taught to look upon nature in ecological and spiritual terms. To know nature was to recognize one's dependency on the earth and its creatures. The world of nature was inseparable from the world of the supernatural; gods and spirits inhabited the earth, sky, and lakes just as every living creature—the deer, the eagle, the mountain lion—possessed its own distinctive spiritual essence, which, through rites and ceremonies, might be incorporated into one's being as a sustaining source of personal identity and power. In the end, the Indians' knowledge of the physical and natural environment was inseparable from how they approached it—intimately, harmoniously, and with a reverential respect for the mysterious. Whites, on the other hand, objectified nature. Western science was ultimately the search for "laws of nature" and scientific principles that, once established, could be put to the service of technological progress. Nature was to be controlled, conquered, and finally, exploited.[25]

The capacity of the white man to unleash nature's force at will was vividly brought home to some forty Carlisle students when they were marched over to nearby Dickinson College for a lesson on electricity. At one point in the lecture, the professor produced a small bolt of lightening and shattered a miniature house especially constructed for the purpose. But the professor had more surprises in store. According to the newspaper account, "The most amusing thing was when the spark of electricity passed from Roman Nose's nose to High Forehead's knuckle, and while they too were badly shocked, the remainder of the party were convulsed with laughter." The high point came when a circle of students held hands and were hooked up to the professor's "electric machine." Again, according to the newspaper, "most of them found it stronger than they could stand, but a few of the boys held on to the last, although they did get badly jerked."[26] Science too was an expression of the white man's power.

CITIZENSHIP TRAINING

Efforts at citizenship training took place against the background of an ever-changing definition of the Indians' citizenship status. The Dawes Act, it may be remembered, had tied citizenship to allotment, leaving those Indians still living in the tribal relation unaffected. Meanwhile, in 1906, Congress enacted the Burke Act, which altered the provisions of the Dawes Act in two ways. First, it declared that all future allottees would become citizens at the end of the trust period rather than, as the Dawes Act provided, at the time of allotment. Second, under the new law the Secretary of the Interior was authorized to issue fee patents to "competent" allottees before the expiration of the twenty-five-year trust period as originally provided. The Omnibus Act of 1910 offered still another modification. This legislation authorized the Indian Office to create "competency commissions," whose express purpose was to scour allotted reservations for Indians capable of managing their affairs; those examined and found competent would be issued their fee patents and declared citizens.[27]

In 1917 Commissioner Cato Sells announced still another policy for determining Indian competency. Under the new guidelines, patents in fee would be issued to all those with less than 50 percent Indian ancestry and any others determined by the government to be competent. Particularly significant for Indian schools, the declaration provided that all students twenty-one years or older and receiving diplomas for completion of the full course of study were eligible to receive either their patent in fee (if they had received an allottment) or a "certificate of competency." Other paths to citizenship soon followed. In 1919 all Indian veterans of World War I were granted citizenship. Finally, in 1924, the Curtis Act declared all Indians to be citizens of the United States.[28]

It was in this context that school officials turned to the business of instructing students in the principles of republicanism, the rights and obligations of citizenship, and the structure of federal, state, and local governments. Special attention also was given to instilling a heartfelt, patriotic identification with the nation engulfing them. In this connection the subject of United States history was central. But how could Indian pupils be made to identify with the "American experience" wherein Indian-white conflict and the settlement of the West were central themes in the national mythology? Frame of reference was obviously important. In 1890, the Indian Office found what it was looking for in a text by Horace E. Scudder, *A History of the United States of America.* Scudder's approach to the subject was spelled out in the preface, where he expressed his belief that the nation "was peopled by men and women who crossed the seas in faith; that its foundations have been laid deep in a divine order; that the nation has been trusted with liberty." This trust, Scudder continued, "carries with it grave duties; the enlargement of liberty and justice is in the victory of the people over the forces of evil."[29]

Scudder's account of the American past is interesting on a number of counts. First, the book is notable in that very little treatment of Indians is given at all. Although a section of four pages is devoted to the subject of white-Indian relations during the colonial period, there is scant mention of the western tribes and the recent hostilities of the 1860s and 1870s, Indian wars with which students might have been familiar. Second, the book does not completely avoid the question of white responsibility for the sad history of Indian-white relations. It is freely admitted that the Spanish were capable of cruelty and greed, that the Puritans on occasion treated the Indians harshly, and that treaties were often broken. Finally, although references to "blood-thirsty savages" are few, the race is still portrayed in the stereotypical fashion of the nineteenth century. Indians are both noble and savage.

> While the tribes differed from one another, all the Indians were in some points alike. They were brave, but they were treacherous. They never forgave an injury. They could bear hunger and torture in silence, but they were cruel in the treatment of their captives. They were a silent race, but often in their councils some of their number would be very eloquent.

In spite of these redeeming qualities, the first Indians seen by Columbus are described as "ignorant barbarians." Scudder claims that at one time the English considered making servants of the Indians, "but to do this was like taming wild animals." And although the Sioux were in part provoked into war in 1876, the affair at the Little Big Horn is described as an Indian massacre.[30]

Teaching U.S. history to Indians, speaking of savages, civilization, and manifest destiny, convincing pupils that the subjugation of their race was in their own best interest, posed definite problems for the conscientious teacher. One teacher wondered how the textbook's "graphic descriptions of the aborigines, with scalping knife and tomahawk, will strike their descendants, and how they will relish the comments of the historian, sometimes by no means flattering." Another teacher confessed that she found the subject difficult to teach for the reason that she had "the sins of her fathers to answer for before her class." The teacher, she explained, "wants to encourage her pupils to be *civilized* like the white man, to embrace his religion, and follow his example, and yet has to put into his hands a history of broken promises and of a civilization as far from Christianity as the Indian himself is."[31]

The Indian Office had anticipated the problem. "Always seek to create a spirit of love and brotherhood in the minds of the children toward the white people," the office urged, "and in telling them the history of the Indians dwell on those things which have showed nobility of character on the part of either race in their dealings with the other." Moreover, "whenever acts of injustice must be related, show to the pupils that the guilt of the persons committing them does not attach to the whole race, for in every people, no matter how virtuous, there are always a large number of the unconscientious and the cruel."[32] Above all, students should not lose perspective. If students could be brought to the point of believing, on the one hand, that the Indians' future depended upon cooperating with the efforts of the government to transform them, and on the other, that the subjugation of their race was the consequence of inevitable historical forces, then perhaps they would come to look upon their conquerors with reverential appreciation.

The idea of civilized progress was central in this respect. Students should be explicitly told how history was the story of man's progression from savagism, through barbarism, to civilization and how their own native cultures fit into this grand scheme. How this was accomplished is revealed in two short essays written by Indian students at Hampton Institute.

> The Caucasian is the strongest in the world. The semi-civilized have their own civilization, but not like the white race.
>
> The savage race kept their own ways, and they have had these occupations; they were hunted, fished, and foughted to the other people. They beat too.
>
> The white race have three occupations agriculture, manufacturing and commerce.

And the second:

> The white people they are civilized; they have everything and go to school, too. They learn how to read and write so they can read newspaper.
>
> The yellow people they half civilized, some of them know to read and write, and some know how to take care of themself.
>
> The red people they big savages; they don't know nothing.[33]

In teaching the idea of civilization, the aim was to strike a delicate balance between humiliation and hope. Students were to be made to see what they were—savages—but also that the path to civilization was open to them. Philip Garrett attempted to strike just the right note when addressing Carlisle students in 1893:

> The path that lies before you is somewhat different from that of most of those around you. They belong to races which have been gradually developing their own civilization by a power from within, stimulated, as it were, by mere sunshine and rain; you are a race thrown by the Providence of God in the pathway of a mighty and resistless tide of civilization, flowing Westward around you. So mighty is the flood, that resistence is fruitless, and the only choice is between submission and destruction on the one hand, or joining the flood and floating

with it, on the other. . . . But great is the force of example and imitation. You are in the midst of an advanced civilization, which serves you as an object lesson. You have a unique opportunity to show the marvelous change that can be wrought in a single generation by the aid of good schools, and the lessons of centuries.[34]

All the elements are there: savagism, civilization, the idea of progress, humiliation, and hope.

EDUCATION FOR SELF-RELIANCE

Policymakers not only wanted Indian schools to turn out law-abiding, patriotic citizens but also wanted them to produce citizens who were economically self-sufficient. This aim involved a twofold objective: teaching work skills and inculcating the values and beliefs of possessive individualism. Toward the first objective, students spent approximately half the school day either learning industrial skills or performing manual labor. At reservation boarding schools, boys were taught the use of hammers and saws and a variety of skills associated with farming: plowing and planting, field irrigation, the care of stock, and the maintenance of fruit orchards. Some also gained an acquaintance with blacksmithing and harness repair. Girls, on the other hand, spent most of their time learning to cook, clean, sew, and care for poultry.[35]

Because the off-reservation school was a much bigger operation, the curriculum expanded considerably, at least for boys. Larger schools trained students at wagon building, shoemaking, tinsmithing, carpentry, painting, tailoring, and harness making. Most of these departments were run like small shops, managing to turn out a considerable number of articles. In 1881, for instance, Carlisle reported producing 8,929 tin products, including cups, coffee boilers, pans, pails, and funnels, 183 double harness sets, 161 bridles, 10 halters, 9 spring wagons, and 2 carriages, items that on the open market would have had a total value of $6,333.46. Farming, however, continued to be the main pursuit, in part because of the Indian Office's assumption about students' occupational destiny, but also because of its insistence that schools become as self-sufficient as possible. Thus, in addition to raising cows and hogs, school farms, depending on the soil and climate, often grew a variety of grains, vegetables, and fruits. In 1890, for instance, the school at Genoa planted approximately 300 acres, mainly Indian corn, oats, wheat, potatoes, and sorghum. Products of the farm and shop, when not consumed by the school, were sold on the open market.[36]

For girls, the curriculum called for more instruction in the domestic sci-

Wagon shop, Sherman Institute, ca. 1910. (Courtesy of the Sherman Museum)

ences. Sewing, cooking, canning, ironing, child care, and cleaning—the standard duties of Victorian housewifery—were once again the general fare, although a few schools such as Carlisle and Haskell offered special training in stenography, typing, and bookkeeping. If anything, the push for institutional self-sufficiency placed an even greater burden on the shoulders of girls. Thus, in 1890 sixteen girls in Albuquerque's sewing department manufactured 170 dresses, 93 chemises, 107 hickory shirts, 67 boys' waists, 261 pairs of drawers, 194 pillowcases, 224 sheets, 238 aprons, 33 bedspreads, and 83 towels. Pratt proudly announced one year that the girls in the school laundry were washing and ironing about 2,500 items each week "in a very creditable manner." The superintendent at Genoa also reported at one point that fifteen girls, with the help of a few smaller boys, were doing all the school's laundry "in ordinary work tubs." "This method is preferred," he added, "because the girls will have to work by hand when they return to their homes on the reservation."[37]

The question can legitimately be asked: to what extent did the Indian Office's objective of institutional self-sufficiency contradict the principle that industrial education be genuinely instructive? How many pillowcases did a girl have to make to become proficient at making pillowcases? How many shirts to become expert at shirtmaking? Consider the demands made on the boys at Fort Stevenson, Dakota, in 1886. In addition to cutting and hauling 300 posts, fencing in twenty acres of pasture, cutting

Turn-of-the-century conceptions of domestic science, Victorian gender roles, and institutional chores merge in this photograph of Sherman Institute students ironing, ca. 1910. (Bureau of Indian Affairs photo no. 75-L-17B in the National Archives)

over 200 cords of wood, and storing away 150 tons of ice, they also mined 150 tons of lignite coal. Proud of this accomplishment, the superintendent boasted that "a vast amount of hard labor" was required to extract the coal, partly because "about 9 feet of earth had to be removed before the vein was reached."[38]

Occasionally, the Indian Office worried about the problem. In 1895 Superintendent William Hailmann instructed those in the field that "the industrial work of the school should cease to be mere drudgery." Too often, Hailmann claimed, students were being turned into "mere toilers or choremen and chorewomen." But little changed. The push for institutional efficiency was simply too strong. Thus, at Crow Creek, Estelle Brown would always remember how "small girls from the kindergarten daily darned stockings for hours on end." Likewise, Clark Wissler would remember his visit to a school somewhere in Oklahoma Territory, where he observed the boys performing their assigned chores. "A glance at them working under compulsion, feeding pigs, washing dishes and scrubbing floors, revealed the saddest faces I ever saw."[39]

Students had little enthusiasm for chores. One of the greatest complaints was being assigned to a task long after it ceased to have any re-

"Blue Monday" at Crow Agency Boarding School captures the less-than-enthu-siastic attitude that students brought to washing detail, ca. 1890. (Bureau of Indian Affairs photo no. 75-EXE-CROW-8D in the National Archives)

deeming educational value. Henry Roe Cloud, a Winnebago, who eventu-ally graduated from Yale University and Auburn Theological Seminary, recalled at Lake Mohonk in 1914:

> I worked two years in turning a washing machine in a Government school to reduce the running expenses of the institution. It did not take me long to learn how to run the machine and the rest of the two years I nursed a growing hatred for it. Such work is not educative. It begets a hatred for work, especially where there is no pay for such la-bor. The Indian will work under such conditions because he is under authority, but the moment he becomes free he is going to get as far as he can from it.

Similarly, while attending the boarding school at Keams Canyon, Arizona, Helen Sekaquaptewa was never able to escape "bathroom detail." After three months of scrubbing toilets, "how I wanted to get out of being in that old bathroom all the time." But the hoped-for reassignment never came.[40]

Occasionally, the threat of physical punishment prodded students to work harder. Anna Shaw, who attended the Indian school in Phoenix, would always remember the time she spent scrubbing floors in the dining room. "If we were not finished when the 8:00 A.M. whistle sounded," she recalls, "the dining room matron would go around strapping us while we were still on our hands and knees. This was just the right position for a swat—all the matron had to do was raise our dresses and strap." But mostly is was the never-ending drudgery of it all. Irene Stewart recalls in her autobiography:

> Getting our industrial education was very hard. We were detailed to work in the laundry and do all the washing for the school, the hospital, and the sanitorium. Sewing was hard, too. We learned to sew all clothing, except underwear and stockings, and we learned to mend and darn and patch. We canned food, cooked, washed dishes, waited on tables, scrubbed floors, and washed windows. We cleaned classrooms and dormitories. By the time I graduated from the sixth grade I was a well-trained worker. But I have never forgotten how the steam in the laundry made me sick; how standing and ironing for hours made my legs ache far into the night. By evening I was too tired to play and just fell asleep wherever I sat down. I think this is why the boys and girls ran away from school; why some became ill; why it was so hard to learn. We were too tired to study.[41]

By the turn of the century, the balance between academics and industrial training was clearly shifting toward the latter. In 1895 Superintendent Hailmann declared that "the stress of work on the part of the schools should be placed upon industrial and manual training rather than upon literary advancement." Two years later he called upon superintendents to establish an "organic connection" between the two branches. "Literary training should not be neglected," he explained, "but it should be . . . in the service of the respectively fundamental aim of securing industrial fervor and efficiency on the part of the children." This view reached its logical conclusion in the new course of study issued in 1900. Written by Estelle Reel, Hailmann's replacement, it called for the infusion of industrial context in all areas of the academic curriculum. It was not enough that Reel should devote the largest number of pages in the nearly 300-page manual to agriculture (34 pages); this and related subjects now permeated the entire curriculum. Thus, in the sixth year of English, teachers were instructed to draw material from the *Farm Journal* and *Poultry Magazine* for their lessons. When it came to choosing subjects for composition, top-ics should relate to the students' future.

> With the allotment in view, plan what shall be done on every foot of ground there; what shall be raised here, what there, and why; what shall be planted after one crop is taken off; what after that. Study the rotation of crops most successfully followed in the locality. Observe what the land produces best, and let the greatest proportion of the mental strength be devoted to making the land yield every dollar pos-sible.[42]

Reel pounded away at the idea that schools should emphasize the prac-tical over the intellectual. On one occasion, she criticized science teach-ers who instructed pupils in "the chemical and physical properties of mat-ter, a knowledge which will be of little practical value to Indian children." Why not, Reel suggested, instruct them instead in topics related to "ani-mal industry," for example, "the anatomy of the horse's foot?" Such sub-jects would have beneficial carryover to farm life. The same practical fo-cus applied to the education of Indian girls. Too many girls, she complained to the Commissioner of Indian Affairs in 1904, were "practic-ing on the piano" when they should be mastering the "household arts." Henceforth, superintendents should see to it that their "large Indian girls become proficient in cooking, sewing and laundry work before allowing them to spend hours in useless practice upon an expensive instrument which in all probability they will never own."[43]

While students were being taught how to earn a living, they also were being taught a host of values and virtues associated with the doctrine of possessive individualism: industry, perseverance, thrift, self-reliance, rug-ged individualism, and the idea of success. In this respect, reformers and school officials believed they were facing one of their most difficult tasks. And rightly so. Many students did in fact come from cultures where the concept of private property scarcely existed, where extended kinship ob-ligations made the accumulation of personal wealth all but impossible, where one achieved status through generosity rather than accumulation.[44] Hence, the gospel of possessive individualism permeated virtually all ar-eas of school life: the classroom, the workshop, Sunday sermons, evening lectures, and special assemblies. School newspapers were particularly ef-fective forums for indoctrination. Students at Phoenix, for instance, were treated in 1907 to "The Man Who Wins."

> The man who wins is the man who works—
> The man who toils while the next man shirks;

And the man who wins is the man who hears
The curse of the envious in his ears,
But who goes his way with head held high
And passes the wrecks of the failures by—
    For he is the man who wins.[45]

The visit from a prominent public figure was a prime occasion for a lecture on American self-reliance. In 1892 Senator Henry Dawes suggested to Carlisle students that Pratt print over the door of each classroom the words "self-reliance," "self-control," "self-support," and "self-help" and then went on to point out that "no other path of success is possible." In 1907 Commissioner Francis Leupp adopted a slightly different tactic when speaking to students at Sherman Institute. After noting that the school banner, which was monogrammed with the letters "S" and "I," came "pretty near to being a dollar mark," he commented, "Sordid as it may sound, it is the dollar that makes the world go around, and we have to teach the Indians at the outset of their careers what a dollar means." This was, Leupp added, probably "the most important part of their education."[46]

When students understood "what a dollar means," they might want to save them. To this end, off-reservation boarding schools were encouraged to set up a student savings program. Once again, Pratt pioneered the idea. The concept first took shape at Fort Marion, when he allowed the prisoners to earn money by selling articles to tourists, polishing sea beans, and working for local farmers. At Carlisle, Pratt refined the system, and students earned money working on the school farm, in the shops, or from the school's outing program. Although the pay was low, Pratt sought to introduce incentive by instituting a graduated system of pay based on the difficulty and skill of the task, so that an experienced tradesman could earn three dollars a month. Not a sizable amount to be sure, but numerous students managed to save over fifty dollars, and those who participated in the outing program, much more. Student savings were carefully monitored, each student having his own bankbook to keep careful record of his deposits and withdrawals. Since the purpose of the savings program was not just to teach the children how to save money but also the prudent expenditure of it, students were allowed to spend about half their earnings. Before making withdrawals, students were required to submit a price list of all articles to be purchased. All purchases were later submitted for inspection. When Pratt judged that a local businessman had taken unfair advantage of a student, he stormed into town and set matters straight. Like so many of Pratt's initiatives, the savings program soon spread to other off-reservation schools.[47]

Meanwhile, students were receiving mixed messages. On the one hand, they were lectured on the importance of saving, the importance of putting away their meager earnings for a rainy day, perhaps for improvements on an allotment. On the other hand, the culture of consumer capitalism required that they spend their dollars on all variety of material goods produced for the marketplace. Thus, even though conscientious school officials implored students to be prudent consumers, periodic excursions into town and merchants' advertisements in school newspapers were designed to whet students' acquisitive appetites. Indeed, in 1915 one inventive Phoenix businessman sought to link his own economic interest in Indian consumers with those of the school by placing this item in the school newspaper:

> Early to bed and early to rise,
> Love all the teachers and tell them no lies.
> Study your lessons that you may be wise
> And buy from the men who advertise.[48]

THE "OUTING" PROGRAM

Pratt understood from the very beginning that even Carlisle was an artificial experience. Behind the school fence, students could learn about civilization, but they could never come to know it firsthand. This had been the lesson of Fort Marion. It was only when the Florida prisoners had entered into the life of St. Augustine that they gained a genuine sense of how the white man really lived. Out of the Florida prison experiment emerged one of the most distinctive aspects of the Carlisle program and one that would be expanded to several off-reservation schools in the West—the so-called outing system.[49]

Pratt brought the idea to Hampton and convinced Armstrong to place the Indian students on white farms during the summer months. When A. H. Hyde of Lee, Massachusetts, a member of Hampton's Board of trustees and a deacon in the Congregational Church, attended Hampton's commencement in 1878, Pratt proposed that Hyde seek placements for the Indians among the farmers in the Lee countryside. Hyde agreed but shortly after wrote Pratt that no placements could be found; Lee's farmers, just two years after the Custer battle, were leery about taking half-civilized Indians into their homes. Undaunted by this setback, Pratt took his prize Florida boy, Etahdleuh, north to Lee, whereupon Pratt and Etahdleuh addressed a gathering at the Congregational Church and presented their case. The fervency of Pratt, along with the earnest Cheyenne boy dressed in his smart-looking Hampton uniform, was too much for the pious New England farmers. Volunteers came forward and shortly all the Indian students were placed.[50]

After Pratt moved to Carlisle in 1879 he expanded the concept, and it soon came to be a central ingredient of the Carlisle program. Eventually, the outing system took on three forms. Under the basic program, students were sent out for the summer months only. Placed in middle-class farm households, Indian youth were given the opportunity to live, work, and worship alongside other family members on a day-to-day basis. A second version placed students with the family for one or two years. The advantage of this was that it permitted a much broader experience including that of attending the local school. From Pratt's perspective, this second version was the ideal situation, but in fact, the number of year-round placements always remained a fraction of the total. In 1903, the peak year of the outing program, 948 were placed out for the summer, while 305 remained for the entire year. A third version emerged in the 1890s, when Pratt began to place students in industrial and urban settings where they could learn skills other than farming. This was Pratt's least favorite model. "We prefer good country homes or homes in the suburbs," Pratt wrote privately. "Almost every time we have placed students in a city they have dropped into the servant class and became the victims of some degeneracy, unless they happened to be our especially advanced and capable students." By 1910, however, six years after Pratt's departure, over 20 percent of placements were of this sort. Regardless of the type of outing, students were paid a modest wage for their labor, a good share being sent directly to the school to be deposited in their savings accounts.[51]

According to Pratt, the outing program accomplished a number of things. It fostered the acquisition of English by forcing the students to apply their new-found language skills in practical work and family settings. It enabled them to earn money. It broke down prejudice: Indians came to appreciate the goodwill of their white patrons, while patrons gained an increased appreciation of the Indians' capabilities. Students learned the subtleties of civilized living, the little nuances of speech and behavior that could never be fully acquired in the superficial atmosphere of school. In this respect Pratt fully realized the limitations of even the off-reservation school as an agency for accomplishing full-fledged acculturation. "The order and system so necessary in an institution retards rather than develops habits of self-reliance and forethought; individuality is lost. They grow into mechanical routine." Pratt also argued that the outing system gave Carlisle students the "courage of civilization." It allowed them to test their capacity to compete with whites in the struggle for existence. "The result of this is the gradual building up of an idea . . . that they can with safety break away from the tribal commune and go out among our people and contend for the necessities and luxuries of life."[52]

During Pratt's tenure at Carlisle the program was carefully administered, and great care was taken in the selection of patrons. In this regard

Pratt benefited from the fact that Carlisle was surrounded by farmers, many of them Quakers, who were generally sympathetic to the school's aims. Indeed, the outing system became so popular with whites that Pratt always had a surplus of patrons from which to choose the most qualified. Two form letters were used in the selection process. The first explained the basic guidelines of the program, including how students were to be paid (depending on their worth, girls from two to eight dollars per month, boys from five to fifteen dollars per month). Patrons also were asked to respond to a series of questions designed to reveal the nature and overall character of the household ("Is the use of tobacco or liquor allowed in your household? Does your family attend religious services, and would the pupil have the same privilege?"). A second letter was sent to a person of reference who again was asked a series of questions to verify the suitability of a given patron. Was he a man of good habits? What class of employees did he hire? Was he kind to his help? Once Pratt was satisfied about a patron's motives and qualifications, he was eligible to receive a student.[53]

For a student to participate in the program, he was required to have a basic understanding of English. Since students were not forced to have an outing experience, they had to make a formal request for placement. This request actually doubled as a sworn statement whereby students agreed to obey their employers, bathe regularly, attend their patron's church, refrain from leaving the farm without permission, avoid drinking, gambling, or smoking, and generally to behave in a manner that would bring honor to themselves and to Carlisle. Students also agreed to write home once a month, detailing their progress as well as the benevolence of their patron family and employer. Where students were actually placed depended on several factors: the age and sex of the student, the nature of the work to be carried out, and the religious affiliation of both the patron and the student. Pratt also tended to place students a considerable distance from the school to discourage runaways, and generally speaking, avoided the practice of placing students too close to one another.[54]

Pratt put a great deal of pressure on students to succeed. An extreme example of this can be seen in his selection of Luther Standing Bear for a position in John Wanamaker's Philadelphia department store. Pratt apparently saw Wanamaker's request as something of a breakthrough and took great care in filling it. With characteristic drama, he announced his final selection at the Saturday evening meeting in the school chapel. Calling Luther Standing Bear to the front, Pratt placed his hand on the boy's shoulder and said for all to hear:

> My boy, you are going away from us to work for this school, in fact, for your whole race. Go, and do your best. The majority of white

people think the Indian is a lazy good-for-nothing. They think he can neither work nor learn anything; that he is very dirty. Now you are going to prove that the red man can learn and work as well as the white man. If John Wanamaker gives you the job of blacking his shoes, see that you make them shine. Then he will give you a better job. If you are put into the office to clean, don't forget to sweep under the chairs and in the corners. If you do well in this, he will give you better work to do.

As if this were not enough, Pratt continued:

Now, my boy, you are going to do your best. If you are a failure, then we might as well close up this school. You are to be an example of what this school can turn out. Go, my boy, and do your best. Die there if necessary, but do not fail.

Finally, Pratt asked all to say a silent prayer for the boy's success.[55]

Once in the field, Pratt took great pains to monitor students' progress. Patrons were supplied with a list of outing regulations and were required to submit monthly reports. Special "outing agents" also periodically checked up on students as well as the overall conditions surrounding the placement, including the patron's character. Students' letters also were an important source of information, although Pratt was generally unsympathetic to their complaints. In 1881, when Pratt received a letter from Maggie Stands Looking stating that "these folks have no bathe place," he wrote back:

Dear Maggie:

When I was a boy on my grandfather's farm there was no "bathe place." It was a log house and two of us boys slept in the attic, to which we had to climb by a ladder through an opening left for that purpose. We washed out the wash tub, then carried it and several buckets of water up the ladder and had fine baths.

Many times in my travels I have been in frontier hotels having no bath tubs, and by filling the large wash bowl with water and taking one of the towels for a wash cloth and rubbing my body well, have had a bath that made me feel as good as jumping into a river.

Your friend and school father,
R. H. Pratt[56]

Overall, patrons gave students high marks. One farmer praised his Indian boy by saying he was "right good with horses and knows how to handle young colts. Like him pretty well." Another typical response: "She makes very good bread and can cook an ordinary meal as well as I could desire. The best of all is her pride and interest in her work and her ambition to learn." And: "I shall always feel indebted to you for your kindness in sending me dear L_____. She is a jewel. We love her so much and are already beginning to feel the parting." From another,

> Her health is much better, and we are glad; she is very trustworthy, nothing would induce her to be sly or untruthful. If anything like a dish or china gets broken, she is so frank and honorable about it. Without any help she made some fine butter and the most delicious ice-cream.[57]

When patrons praised students, it was usually for their diligence, honesty, obedience, and a general willingness to learn. When they complained, it was because they lacked these same qualities. "He is a very trying boy at times, will not obey. He is stubborn and sullen," wrote one patron. Another reported: "He is very provoking sometimes, pretends not to understand what we mean when I think he does. He goes out at night much too often. Pretends to go to the creek to bathe, but just walks over it and on to the neighbors and comes home after we are in bed." From another:

> The boy arrived all right but I am afraid he is not going to suit here; has milked twice and hasn't milked the cows clean either time. Tonight I am going to correct him, and if he doesn't do better he is no good to me; he is an older boy than I cared about. He says he is twenty-two. I would rather have one sixteen or seventeen. He knows more than I do myself he thinks.[58]

What is much more difficult to assess is the students' attitude toward the experience. From the numerous letters regularly reprinted in Carlisle's newspaper, however, it is clear that many students regarded the outing as one of the bright spots in their school experience, particularly when they fell into a warm and loving family that treated them as one of their own. "I don't think anybody could find fault about these people they are just the kind of people to live with," one student wrote. Another girl wrote Pratt: "I am up in my small cosy room. I love this place, they are so kind. I have a good kind father and mother and two little sisters here. They are very sweet little sisters to me." One boy volunteered:

> I am very much oblige to you Capt. and I did not know nothing when I first came here and this time I knew everything I got to do. I

like farming very well and I think I am going to be a farmer when I get home. No more walking around hunting work. I am going to work for myself, like out here. I don't abused his horses and cows. I try to be kind to them. If any of you school boys and girls want some muscles just come out to the country and work and learn some useful things.

According to another:

Oh Capt. I do have such a nice place here. . . . Captain I do wish you would let me stay out all the year as I have much lovely home and good wadges for the work I have to do. And I could go to school very easy the school house is not far. Let me stay till Christmas anyway then if you think I ought to be back I will gladly return to dear Carlisle, but I want to assert up on staying till Christmas anyway *please*. I often thank you for your kindness by sending me in such a lovely place to such kind people.[59]

But again, just as some patrons were disappointed in the students Pratt sent them, so many of the students found the outing experience a long and trying ordeal. A particular problem was being cut off from friends and classmates. One girl, shortly after reaching her assigned destination, took pen in hand and wrote Pratt:

I never have been so lonesome in all my life and I hope I never will again. I cannot eat my meals. And here while I am writing the tears keep dropping so that I cannot hardly see the lines of my paper. I don't go up in my room but I can't help but cry. I will never bother you to come out in the country again. And if you think it is best I will be willing to bear any punishment you are mined to put upon me, I will try and bear it cheerfully; if I may but come back.[60]

Other students objected to the conditions under which they were expected to live and work and with good reason. One frustrated student reported: "She always calls us Dunce, careless, lazy, ugly, crooked, and have no senses. I never heard anybody call me that before. What do you think of them names, do you think they are pretty names for us? We don't think so and I know you don't either." Another boy wrote Pratt, "I am sorry to tell you that this man is not fit to have any Indian boys on account the way he behaves, he is very careless about his work and the way he treats me." Nothing angered students more than the idea that they were being exploited. "I don't want to stay and work low wages, if he want cheap boys let him get some other boy," complained one student. From another, Pratt received this letter:

The man is good but the wages and food are very poor indeed. Am doing a man's work. Of course he might tell you that I am not a good farmer, but I am sure that I am doing more work than the boys around here. Well Capt. to make the story short, I will say that I want to change my place. If you don't think that you could find a place for me will I try to find it myself.[61]

But again, such letters were in the minority. Although there were numerous complaints about working conditions, mainly wages, most students' letters indicated satisfaction with being able to experience the white world beyond the gates of Carlisle.

Policymakers praised the outing concept as a powerful mechanism for carrying out the government's assimilationist aims. The question that soon presented itself was this: could the Carlisle system, which relied upon eastern patrons, many of them Quakers, be carried out as successfully in frontier settings, where whites might regard it as an opportunity to exploit Indian labor? Superintendent of Indian Schools Daniel Dorchester foresaw the problem in 1892. After praising Pratt's program, he went on to remark that the Carlisle outing system simply would not work in most western locales. "With too many the common idea is that the Indian is a creature to be cheated, debauched, and kicked out of decent society. Young Indians from the schools can not be safely located among such people." Haskell's superintendent, Charles Meserve, confirmed Dorchester's suspicions two years later while speaking at Lake Mohonk. "If I were asked to give my experience in a word," related Meserve, "I should say that there has not been enough of the feeling that the Indians are human beings and are capable of being civilized." Pratt agreed. Writing to General Oliver Howard in 1895, Pratt confided, "You know and I know that frontier 'outing' is and must be a flat failure."[62]

Still, throughout the 1890s the Indian Office pressed for expansion of the idea. In the coming years several off-reservation schools, including Haskell, Carson, Albuquerque, Genoa, Phoenix, and Sherman Institute, developed outing programs. But just as Dorchester had predicted, western outing programs were often exploitive. The superintendent at Phoenix, where ranchers and farmers were constantly pressing the school for laborers, freely admitted in 1894 that citizens in the area seldom looked upon the outing system "from a philanthropic standpoint."[63] The superintendents at Haskell and Carson City, moreover, reported having trouble getting patron housewives, who had grown accustomed to Indian domestic help in the summer months, to turn loose of their Indian girls for the fall school term. In a similar vein, Sherman Institute was struggling to "disabuse the general public of the idea that this is an employment agency or intelligence service."[64]

In fact, at some schools the outing system had degenerated into exactly that. Perhaps the most blatant example of this was the practice of sending out work gangs in groups of 50 to 100 to work for farmers and ranchers. Genoa, Chilocco, and Albuquerque, for instance, regularly sent out contingents to the beet fields of Colorado.[65] Likewise, Sherman boys were sent out to southern California ranches to harvest cantaloupes and oranges.[66] In such cases, students labored monotonously in the hot sun from daybreak to sunset, often sleeping in barns or tent camps at night, never seeing the inside of a Victorian parlor, let alone being taken in as members of a middle-class family.

Surely there was something to be gained from such experiences. For one thing, there was an opportunity to earn money. For another, students acquired habits of discipline that could contribute to long-term self-sufficiency. But perhaps most important, students learned something about the marginal terms upon which they would be incorporated into frontier society—as common laborers and domestic servants—if whites had anything to say about it. In any event, for both boys and girls, whether they attended Carlisle or Phoenix, the outing experience constituted an important element in their education.

CHAPTER SIX

Rituals

Social life, wrote Sally F. Moore and Barbara G. Myerhoff, "proceeds somewhere between the imaginary extremes of absolute order, and absolute chaotic conflict and anarchic improvisation." Accordingly, collective ritual or ceremony may be seen as an "attempt to bring some particular part of life firmly and definitely into orderly control." Rituals "lend authority and legitimacy to the positions of particular persons, organizations, occasions, moral values, view of the world, and the like." In short, ritual and ceremony "structure the way people *think* about social life," which, paradoxically, leads to another characteristic of ritual: its capacity to transform or alter attitudes and values. Again according to Moore and Myerhoff: "Ritual may do much more than mirror existing social arrangements and existing modes of thought. It can act to reorganize them or even help to create them."[1] In this chapter I analyze the boarding school as a ritual system, specifically, how four areas of ritual life—religion, athletics, gender relations, and holiday celebrations—functioned simultaneously as legitimizing and transformative processes.

Missionaries and policymakers alike had always regarded the Indians' conversion to Christianity as essential. Thus, there was nothing startling in Haskell Superintendent H. B. Peairs's assertion, "A really civilized people cannot be found in the world except where the Bible has been sent and the gospel taught; hence we believe that the Indians must have, as an essential part of their education, Christian training." In addition to bringing Indian youth to the "one true God," Christianity promised to reconstitute their moral character, strengthen their attachment to the nuclear family, promote their love of flag and country, and finally, encourage the process of individualization. Needless to say, the great majority of philanthropists would have liked to see Indian students protestantized, not just Christianized, but most could appreciate the larger issue at hand. Even Herbert Welsh, well-known for his anti-Catholic sentiments, could utter that "the great religious bodies, the Roman communion on the one side, and the Protestant communion on the other, should try and recognize the value of each other's work, at least as an instrument of civilization."[2]

Students entered boarding school with vastly different religious backgrounds. Some came already converted to Christianity. In this regard, schools were reaping the harvest of missionary efforts across Indian country. Thus, shortly after a group of Dakota children arrived at Hampton in 1879, they sang for the student body "Nearer My God to Thee," although in a language unrecognizable to all but a few.

> Mita Wakantanka,
> Nikiyedan,
> Kakix mayanpi xta,
> He taku ani;
> Nici waun wacin,
> Mita Wakantanka,
> Nikiyedan.

"My thoughts went to and fro," reported one observer of the scene, "and when I looked at their beaming faces and knew that they understood the words they were singing, for they sang in their own language, I felt that they were nearer to Him at that hour."[3]

Most, however, came from cultures still permeated by a traditional religious outlook. What were the common denominators of this worldview?[4] First, traditional Indian cultures were so thoroughly infused with the spiritual that native languages generally had no single word to denote the concept of religion. It would have been incomprehensible to isolate religion as a separate sphere of cultural existence. For the Kiowa, Hopi, or Lakota, religion explained the cosmological order, defined reality, and penetrated all areas of tribal life—kinship relations, subsistence activities, child raising, even artistic and architectural expression. The theistic structures of native religions differed greatly. Some religious systems were polytheistic, but others, as Joseph Epes Brown observes, represented "a form of theism wherein concepts of monotheism and polytheism intermingle and fuse without being confused." Thus, the Lakota universe, to cite just one example, was populated by a pantheon of gods, spirits, and personalities, but pervading all was *Wakan-Tanka,* or the "Great Mysterious." Hence, Brown quotes Black Elk, "Wakan-Tanka, you are everything, and yet above everything." The spirit world pervaded all.[5]

A second theme was man's fundamental interrelatedness with nature. Unlike Christianity where God and man stood apart—really above—nature, Indians lived in ecological harmony with their environment, approached it with reverential humility, and ultimately, ascribed to it a spiritual significance unknown to European-Americans. According to the Indian worldview, all creatures—the buffalo, the eagle, the spider—and the inanimate world as well, possessed their own unique soul or spiritual essence. In such a world, nature was filled with spiritual lessons, to be read and interpreted just as the white man read his Jesus book. Nature, moreover, was not something to be objectified and conquered, nor to be seen as merely a source of sustenance and shelter; it was, rather, a profound source of spiritual awareness from whence man could reaffirm his elemental relationship with all living things.[6]

A third characteristic was the richness and variety of religious expression. On one level this manifested itself in elaborate tribal ceremonies—the sun dance of the Plains peoples, the kachina dances of the Pueblo, the Midewiwin of the Objibwa, the chantways of the Navajo, to name just a few. Added to these are the culturally prescribed provisions for individual religious expression. Particularly noteworthy in this regard are the role of dreams and the almost ubiquitous vision quest. In the latter instance the supplicant sought direct communication with the supernatural, which might appear in the form of a hawk, a fox, an ant, or perhaps a "thundering being." The knowledge and power gained from such an experience often shaped the entire life course and personality of the vision seeker. Also, most cultures singled out those significant transitions in the life cycle—birth, puberty, marriage, and death—for public ceremonial recognition, although again, the manner of expression differed greatly from one culture to another. Finally, each religious system possessed its own songs, dances, myths, and ritual dramas.[7]

Fourth, and by way of comparison to Christianity, Native American religions tended not to conceive of personal morality or ethics as the special domain of religion. Although it is true that all cultures certainly knew of "evil" and possessed their own definition of proper social behavior, the social regulation of interpersonal behavior had its source in the larger social fabric of tribal existence. This, of course, was in direct contradiction to Christianity, which, from the Indians' perspective, seemed preoccupied with "sin" and provided a biblical prescription for nearly all aspects of social relations. It was for this reason that Indians who had converted to Christianity soon discovered they had embraced not only a new God but an entirely new way of life. An extension of the morality issue was the whites' conception of heaven as the exclusive destiny of the righteous, as compared with the Indians' view of the afterlife, which was rarely as restrictive. What Henry Warner Bowden says of northeastern cultures applies to Indians generally: "They thought the gods would punish sacrilegious acts almost immediately, just as socially destructive behavior met with swift communal justice. But they assumed that everyone would eventually reside in the same place after death."[8]

If Christianity and traditionalism were the polar extremes of Indian religious belief, by the turn of the century other forms of religious expression had come upon the scene. By the 1880s, for instance, some tribes in the Northwest were converting to Shakerism, which took its name from the fact that its followers frequently achieved a trembling, trancelike state in the course of praying, singing, and dancing—in all, a ritualized synthesis of white and native religious expression. An even more powerful movement was the rapid spread of the so-called peyote religion, later designated the Native American Church. The most sensational aspect of this new faith involved chewing peyote buttons, which produced powerful and transcendent visions wherein the worshiper achieved an enhanced sense of self, power, and spiritual consciousness. Beyond this, the new religion proved to be a highly flexible configuration of native and Christian traditions: core elements included the worship of a supreme being (the "Great Spirit" or God); the belief in both white and Indian spirits (angels, the devil, the thunderbird), the fusion of Christian ethics with native values, and the blending of native and Christian ritualistic practices. Finally, discussion must include the brief but ill-fated ghost dance religion that swept across the Central and High Plains in the late 1880s, culminating in the tragic episode at Wounded Knee in December 1890. Given the brevity of the movement, its long-term influence on Indian youth is questionable. Still, some students home for the summer surely observed relatives swept up in the fervor of the moment, observed the dancing and ritualized trances, and heard firsthand accounts from dancers who told of seeing the utopian world to come, a world without whites, where Indians would be reunited with fallen warriors and the prairies once again would be teeming with bison.[9]

What else can be said about the religious background of students? For one thing, many students came from communities characterized by religious factionalism and thus may have arrived deeply divided themselves. On the other hand, many students came from cultures that either had managed to integrate various aspects of Christianity into their own religious system without destroying the latter's essence or had simply accepted and compartmentalized it in the spirit of what one scholar has termed "nonexclusive cumulative adhesion."[10] Finally, and this point cannot be overstated, except for the early years when schools recruited older students fully enculturated into tribal ways, nearly all students entered boarding school with only a partial understanding of their tribal belief system and ceremonial cycle. Reservation boarding schools cut students off from religious experiences that by tradition could only be had in the fall, winter, and spring. For nonreservation students the deprivation was even more complete.

It was in this context that boarding school superintendents waged an aggressive campaign of Christianization. By the 1890s Indian Office rules stipulated, "Pupils of Government schools shall be encouraged to attend the churches and Sunday-schools of their respective denominations." Even though local churches were encouraged to open their doors to Indian students, schools also were expected to develop a systematic program of religious instruction. A typical week's activities included Sunday morning, afternoon, and evening services, daily morning and evening prayers, and a special Wednesday evening prayer meeting. As for the content of religious instruction, teachers were encouraged to emphasize the Ten Commandments, the beatitudes, and prominent psalms. Superintendent William Hailmann urged in 1894, "Prayer, song, and Bible reading should be wholly free from mystifying allusions and sentiments, but rich and forceful in the simple earnestness with which they lead the heart to God, to virtue, to benevolence, to reverence, to self-abnegation, and to devotion."[11]

For younger children, Sunday school was probably the most effective format for instruction. In Sunday school, Hampton Institute reported, "the teacher endeavors to put into these almost empty minds the simplest, and at the same time the most strengthening, truths of God's Word." Bible stories, especially when given a creative rendering by an enthusiastic teacher, were a favorite of students. According to one account: "As soon as an Indian understands enough English to follow the simple stories, he can never get enough of them. Some of the friskiest boys will sit like graven images through a whole evening, listening to them." Stories of David and Goliath, the separation of the waters, the slaying of the Philistines, and the resurrection of Christ were easily the equals of the wonders told by tribal medicine men. "When I found the place in the Bible," one teacher related, "and read about the holy city which we all hope to enter, their merry eyes opened wide and their little faces grew thoughtful, and they wondered if the little boy who died last autumn went there, and asked 'Did the angels come to take him?' "[12]

An inordinate amount of time was spent on moral training. In the eyes of educators, Indian children were products of cultures that placed little emphasis on "virtue," at least as it was understood in the context of Christian ethics. In the words of one Indian agent, "The Indians are simple children of nature, and many things condemned as immoral among whites are with them without offense."[13] In particular, Indian children needed to be taught the moral ideals of charity, chastity, monogamy, respect for the Sabbath, temperance, honesty, self-sacrifice, the importance of pure thoughts and speech—indeed, an almost endless array of personal characteristics important to the formation of "character."

Fundamental to this aim was implanting the idea of sin and a corresponding sense of guilt. And sometimes it worked. One Carlisle boy caught writing "vile thoughts" to a friend was moved to write to Pratt:

> I want to tell you that I cry inside of my heart when I was in church for the bad and sin I have done. Oh I am very *sorry,* but Captain I only believe that God has power to take way our sins. So please Cap-

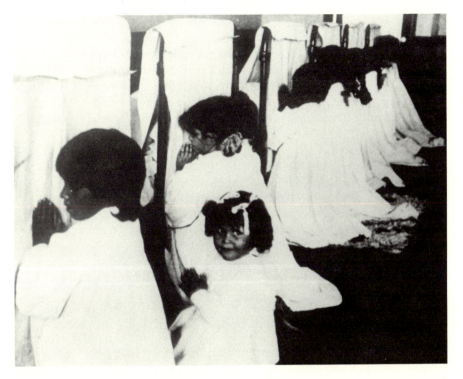

Prayers before bedtime, Phoenix Indian School, 1900. (Bureau of Indian Affairs photo no. 75–EXP-2B in the National Archives)

tain help me and pray for me to come out of this wrong where I am in. I will promise you that I will *never* write nor say such words to any body here after this.

I will do what you told me, that is if I get a letter from some one is bad, I will throw it in stove or I will not answered it.

Captain Pratt now from today I will commence my way to follow the Christians. If I do fall into sin I will get up again. Ever since I get into trouble I feel as though I am by my self. But I have parents and I must try to do what is right to see that I am in right side here after this.

Captain I hope to help me and pray for me that I may become Christian and I will give my self to Christ. I have long sin and gives me but a sorrow life. Now Captain Pratt I will not mind any one that will try to pull me down and lead me into wrong direction.[14]

Efforts to build Christian character were not limited to Sunday sermons and prayer meetings. McGuffey Readers were hardly deficient in moral content, nor were most teachers shy about offering advice on moral questions; indeed, they were expected to. Student essays were yet another medium for reinforcing the character theme, and one example was the Indian Office's efforts on behalf of temperance. Because alcoholism was both a health and moral issue, in 1915 it became the subject of a systemwide essay contest. Student response to the issue, at least measured by several seventh grade essays printed in Haskell's newspaper, was deeply felt.

> Alcohol wrecked my life, but two years ago I reformed and am trying to lead a good life. Alcohol has wrecked the lives of many people and is still at it. I have seen men killing each other, cutting up each other, frozen to death, killed by railroad trains because they were going home along the track and were to drunk to get out of the way. Whose fault is it? Who is to blame? Alcohol!

According to a second:

> We once had a nice home but after alcohol entered it kept on going down and down until we had no home. Papa drank up everything. He caused mother to sell her land and now mother has no home at all. She works. If I had the power, I would crush every saloon to pieces. Fight well, hard and forever until this great enemy is banished from our Nation. I pray God to give us strength to fight this enemy.[15]

Undoubtedly, many students could identify with admonitions against alcohol because they had seen the havoc it could wreak on an Indian community.

More difficult to assess is their overall response to the constant proselytizing. Some students were apparently confused by it all. In some schools pupils were forced to repeat the words of Bible verses and hymns with no explanation of the meaning behind the phrases. For younger students, language presented a problem. A former student at Tuba City Boarding School bitterly remembers two-hour Sunday sermons, even though "some of us who did not understand the full meaning of the sermons would get bored and fall asleep." Similarly, Frank Mitchell, who attended Fort Defiance, recalls that when the priests and missionaries came to school: "We did not know much English, and we did not understand what they were talking about half of the time. They talked about God, and most of us did not understand it. So I guess they were just talking to themselves."[16]

The pressure to convert was sometimes immense. Jason Betzinez, an Apache student at Carlisle, recalls that "the most powerful influence on my life at this . . . time was my introduction to the teachings of Christianity. . . . This influence became stronger and stronger as I came to understand English better. It changed my whole life." Similarly, Thomas Wildcat Alford, who, before leaving for school, was warned by Shawnee chiefs against converting to the white man's religion, eventually fell under the spell of the evangelical promise. In time, he came to know "deep in my soul that Jesus Christ was my Savior." Even Don Talayesva, who was torn between his ancestral Hopi beliefs and Christianity while at Sherman Institute, and who would promptly reject Christianity upon his return to Oraibi, managed to conjure up this sermon for a school YMCA meeting.

Well, my partners, I am asked to speak a few words for Jesus. I am glad that I came to Sherman and learned to read and cipher. Now I discover that Jesus was a good writer. So I am thankful that Uncle Sam taught me to read in order that I may understand the Scriptures and take my steps along God's road. When I get a clear understanding of the Gospel I shall return home and preach it to my people in darkness. I will teach them all I know about Jesus Christ, the Heavenly Father, and the Holy Ghost. So I advise you boys to do your best and pray to God to give us a good understanding. Then we will be ready for Jesus to come and take us up to heaven. I don't want any of my friends to be thrown into the lake of hell fire where there is suffering and sorrow forever. Amen.[17]

The evidence about students' reaction to conversion efforts is sketchy at best. But most students, like Helen Sekaquaptewa, probably went through the motions, kept their counsel, and endured the hours of preaching and praying as best they could.

I remember one preacher especially, although they were all about the same. I couldn't understand a thing he was talking about but had to sit and listen to a long sermon. I hated them and felt like crying. If I nodded my head going to sleep, a teacher would poke me and tell me to be good. It seemed as if this preacher would talk all night. He put a great deal of emotion into his sermons. He would work himself up to a climax talking loud and strong, and then calm down to a whisper, and I would think, "Now he is going to stop." But no, he would start all over again and go on and on.[18]

How many students simply rejected the school's conversion efforts outright? Again, the evidence is sketchy. Helen Sekaquaptewa relates that the various missionaries "were always urging and bribing us with little presents to join their church," and then goes on to say: "It didn't appeal to me and I didn't join any of them." Even more suggestive is a mission-ary newspaper's account of Pratt's effort at a school assembly to extract from students a public declaration of their religious inclinations. When asked how many were already Christian, thirty-four students stood. When asked how many were "trying" to become Christians, another seventy-two rose from their seats. Interestingly, this account was presented as evidence that the school's missionary program was rapidly winning converts. But it also provides an indication of the number who remained skeptical of the Christian message; the vast majority had remained seated.[19]

A particularly intriguing question for which there is no answer is how many students surreptitiously carried out native rituals in defiance of the official religious program? Also, how many students were involuntarily visited by visions or dreams, traditionally powerful mediums of religious experience? Consider the truly extraordinary account left by Don Talay-esva of his spirit journey back to Hopiland while laying unconscious and hospitalized at Sherman Institute.[20] Several examples of religious counter-culture are presented in Morris E. Opler's *Apache Odyssey: A Journey Between Two Worlds.* Discussing his boarding school experiences, Opler's Mescalero informant relates how one boy sought to acquire power from the towhee bird. "He used to tie the feathers to his bed. At night he used to say he wished to see the bird so that it might show him something." The ritualistic approach to the bird apparently had its effect.

> So one night the towhee came in and slept under his pillow. He spoke to the bird that night, and the bird stayed right there. Early in the morning the boy got up, and the towhee flew out. Others tried to catch it, but it came to this boy, and he held it in his hand. Others asked for it, but the towhee told the boy to turn it loose, and he did. It came for the next three nights too. But no one but the boy saw it these other times. He learned supernatural power from it.

Indeed, the bird became a powerful spirit guide and protector. When the boy was selected for transfer to an off-reservation school, the bird's power was invoked to reverse the superintendent's decision. "He got the help of the towhee, and he didn't go. He stayed right where he was."[21]

Another instance occurred when a school employee purchased a large quantity of bear meat. A Mescalero schoolboy crippled with a bad leg managed to get a piece of the roasted meat and ate it in the belief that the power of the bear might correct his deformity. According to Mescalero tradition, bear meat, ritualistically eaten under the direction of a shaman, possessed special healing power. In this case, however, the ritual prescriptions had been forgotten, which constituted a reckless and stupid act. Indeed, the bear's spirit was angered.

> About midnight we heard this boy crying. The bear was after him; he saw it go out the door. The boys tried to keep him quiet but they couldn't. And so he kept crying 'til morning and also vomited. He said the bear was coming in and putting its paws down his throat, trying to catch something. He was very sick all that day. They didn't know what to do. The doctor gave him some medicine, but it didn't help him. The relatives of the boy were told, and they went to Swinging-Lance, who was a chief. . . . Swinging-Lance talked to the agent, who was his friend, and got the boy out of school, for that boy saw the bear every night, and every night it put its paws in and out of his mouth, and he cried.[22]

After the boy was taken from the school, his relatives found a shaman who carried out a public curing ceremony, which included, among other things, a ritualistic feeding of bear meat. Somehow, the boy recovered. The Mescalero present were understandably impressed. "The white doctor said that the boy just had an upset stomach, that there was nothing wrong with him. But the Mescalero said he had Bear sickness and would have died if it weren't for them."[23] Presumably, once word spread back to the school, many students adopted the same opinion. What the episode illustrates beyond all doubt is the complex configuration of the forces shaping Indian students' religious attitudes.

GENDER RELATIONS

In the eyes of reformers no sphere of Indian life was more reprehensible than the relations between the sexes. There were two aspects to the issue. One concerned the low status of women in tribal society, the proverbial image of the degraded "squaw," totally subservient to the whim and will of her hunter-warrior husband. Second, most Indian societies lacked the rigid moral code necessary to govern sexual conduct along ethical, that is to say Christian, lines. In any case, a primary objective of the boarding school program was to reconstruct students' attitudes toward gender roles and sexual mores. Once again, savage habits of mind must give way to more civilized ones, and ritual could be instrumental in accomplishing the transformation.

As reformers imagined it, Indian women were accorded a status in tribal society scarcely above that of wild beasts. Although the nature of this debasement differed from tribe to tribe, the features of native life most frequently mentioned were polygyny, wife selling or forced marriages, and a division of labor that relegated women to the role of drudge. In the words of Carl Schurz: "The Indian woman has so far been only a beast of burden. The girl, when arrived at maturity, was disposed of like an article of trade. The Indian wife was treated by her husband alternately with animal fondness, and with the cruel brutality of the slave-driver." Commissioner Oberly concurred: The traditional warrior's "squaw" was little more than his slave: "With no more affection than a coyote feels for his mate, he brought her to his wigwam that she might gratify the basest of his passions and minister to his wants. It was Starlight or Cooing Dove that brought the wood for his fire and the water for his drink, that plowed the field and sowed the maize."[24]

The assessment in the field was pretty much the same: Indian women lived a pitiful existence. Agents reserved their most scathing attacks for the Indian practice of arranging marriages. In 1897 one agent in the Southwest reported that in the last four years several "full-blooded" school girls in their early teens had been given away in marriage during the summer months. In the midst of "wild orgies," several "poor little girls were induced to marry in Indian fashion; to be forever afterwards deprived of all the opportunities and advantages of school life." Because the Indian girl learned her lowly status early in life, reported one teacher, the immediate challenge before the school was to awaken her to her possibilities. "Her whole home training has been to keep down anything that her male relatives might consider ambitious and consequently she has very little self-respect. This makes her slow and diffident in class and not a social success at first." But this would change in time.[25]

How accurate were reformers' perceptions of women's status in tribal life? Although the subject is immensely complex, contemporary scholarship would seem to support two generalizations. First, in most cultures the status of women was neither that of slavery nor of complete equality but somewhere in between; second, there was considerable variability in women's status from culture to culture. Reformers quite correctly pointed to some practices—for example, forced marriages and female disfigurement as a punishment for adultery—that were hardly indicative of high status. Where such practices existed, Indian women certainly stood to benefit from the white man's definition of women's rights. Still, it is important to note that reformers clearly overlooked the disquieting fact that in many cultures Indian women were accorded a status and performed roles largely unknown to their white counterparts. Many Indian cultures, for instance, were matrilineal and matrilocal in their social organization. In some societies women owned and controlled property, performed vital economic functions, wielded political influence, and were revered for their healing powers. It is also worth noting that Indian religions were generally less patriarchical than the white man's Christianity, often giving considerable theological status to female deities and spirits.[26] Thus, reformers' perceptions were only partly accurate; although some Indian girls stood to improve their status from white schooling, others suffered a net loss. Victorian America was hardly a prescription for female equality.

But what school officials wanted to do, of course, was to transform Indian girls into bronze embodiments of Victorian womanhood. As mothers of the next generation of Indian children, they needed to be taught the domestic skills of homemaking as well as their role as moral guardians in a Christian home. Boys, moreover, must be made to recognize women's role in the new order of things. Commissioner Jones made special note of this when speaking to an assembly at Hampton Institute in 1898. Noting that several previous speakers—Indian boys—had slightly turned their backs to the girls separately seated in the audience, the commissioner made a point of bowing to the girls, commenting, "Don't be discouraged, girls, much more depends upon you than upon the boys, and we look to you to carry home the refinement that shall really elevate your people."[27]

The message went forward in various fashions: domestic science classes, McGuffey Readers, and Sunday morning sermons. In the end, however, the Victorianization of male-female relations needed the support of ritualized social activities. A logical place to begin was the dining room. Thus, in the 1890s the Indian Office recommended that boys and girls sit at a common dining table. The sexes, one superintendent argued, "should be thrown into each others' society that the girl may have an opportunity to exhibit her self-possession, to acquire ease and grace in company, and the young man may respect and acknowledge her acquirements and be taught that the woman is not the inferior creature she is generally considered by the Indian race."[28]

At Crow Creek, Estelle Brown tells us that one of her first duties was to monitor the dining room, where the superintendent had recently decided upon the policy of forcing boys and girls to eat at the same tables. Brown soon noticed, however, that integrated tables worked to the distinct disadvantage of the girls. At issue was a single pitcher of black molasses served every morning with dry bread. The problem was that the boys drained the pitcher, leaving the girls with none. Unable to monitor twenty tables at once, Brown complained to the superintendent. Why couldn't each table have two pitchers? The reason was simple enough: Crow Creek's yearly ration of molasses wouldn't last at the rate of two pitchers per table. At this point Brown was given a brief lecture, the main point being that for centuries the Sioux had treated their women like "chattels," and that the integrated tables were instrumental to making them equal. "Do you still think," the superintendent concluded, "that molasses is more important than sex equality?" Brown writes: "Perversely, I did. I felt that

In this photograph, "A Domestic Science Dinner," male and female students at Phoenix Indian School prepare to demonstrate their knowledge of the Victorian dining ritual, 1900. (Bureau of Indian Affairs photo no. 75–EXP-2F in the National Archives)

if I were a small Indian girl I would prefer getting enough to eat to gaining highly doubtful equality with boys. I'd try to get that for myself and, meanwhile, be sure of my share of molasses." In so many words she informed the superintendent to this effect. But to no avail.[29]

The Indian Office was not about to listen to complaints from an overworked employee from Crow Creek, or for that matter from anyone else who might suggest that Victorian America was a flawed blueprint for "woman's sphere" in civilized society. And if it was difficult getting the boys at Crow Creek to share the molasses, the situation appears to have been somewhat better at other schools. One off-reservation institution claimed that every boy "sits at the table with girls, and instead of being helped first, he finds that he must see that every girl is supplied with food before he dares think of himself. If a girl happens to be without a chair, he must rise and give her his." Similarly, at Carlisle one observer noted how "the girls are first waited upon, and there is a pleasant interchange of thought between the sexes, showing that the germs of pure social life are taking root."[30]

Other than in the classroom and the dining hall, the only other time that the sexes mixed were on those occasions when they were allowed to "enjoy each other's society." According to Indian Office guidelines "such occasions should be used to teach them to show each other due respect and consideration, to behave without restraint, but without familiarity, and to acquire habits of politeness, refinement, and self-possession." In short, male-female relations must be ritualized according to civilized standards. Sometimes students socialized at picnics or in sitting rooms, both carefully chaperoned. More common were Saturday night socials, where students played checkers, worked puzzles, tossed bean bags, blew soap bubbles, and passed rings along ropes. On other occasions marches, promenades, and dances were the order of the day. In her memoirs, Minnie Jenkins recalls arriving at her new post, Fort Mohave, on the evening of the Saturday night dance. Boys in grey uniforms and girls in white dresses danced the two-step, schottishe, waltz, Virginia reel, and an occasional square dance. "The pupils' manners were excellent," she remembers. "A boy bowed before a girl when requesting a dance, conducted her to her seat afterward and thanked her."[31]

Jim Whitewolf would always remember his first promenade. The affair was arranged so that the girls invited the boys, but none of the boys knew which girl had selected him for a partner. Whitewolf could only hope that it was a Comanche girl who, a few weeks before, had secretly written him a note asking him to be her "sweetheart." On the night of the big event he bathed, put on his best Sunday clothes, and polished his shoes.

We had hair oil on our hair, and we had flowers in our buttonholes, handkerchiefs in our pockets, and our neckties all tied. All of us boys marched in by twos. We stood real straight and had our coats buttoned up. There were about ten of us, and we were all seated on a bench in a row. We were facing a big crowd of all the students there. I noticed that there was a chalk line drawn around the floor along the edges where we were all seated. Pretty soon, as we were sitting, all the girls came in dressed in white, with red flowers on. They were sure pretty. My heart was just shaking. I didn't know which was the girl who had invited me. The girls knew who they had invited, and they each sat down beside the boy they invited. A girl came over and sat down by me. I just sat there real straight. It was the Comanche girl who had written me that note before.

At the appointed moment the couples began their promenade around the room keeping time with the music, the winning couple to receive a cake, a pair of gloves, and a scarf. After several passes around the floor, Whitewolf realized that he and his Comanche admirer were one of the two finalists.

Instruction in gender rituals began at an early age as evidenced by this scene at Haskell Institute in which boys and girls are apparently learning a children's game or perhaps how to promenade. (Courtesy of Watkins Community Museum, Lawrence, Kansas)

And then the judges dismissed the other couple as well—the girl was seen chewing gum. After Whitewolf and his partner received their prizes, all the couples were invited to talk with their dates. "I was about fifteen years old at this time. It was the first time I ever had a date with a girl and talked with her like that."[32]

But most of the school's energy was invested in keeping the two sexes apart from one another. In the eyes of the Indian Office, most Indian children had "no inherited tendencies whatever toward morality and chastity."[33] Until the sexes were thoroughly Victorianized, free association on the playground or in sitting rooms could only result in disaster. Surveillance was the key. But monitoring the behavior of so many Indians wasn't easy, especially at reservation schools where schools were frequently understaffed, where the layout of buildings often worked against segregation, and where would-be suitors beyond the school fence kept a watchful eye on girls of marriageable age. One superintendent likened the challenge to the following: "Round up 95 or 100 fleas in your beautiful homes, and after feeding them well let them out for exercise two or three times a day, and see if you can keep track of all of them."[34] An unfortunate analogy to be sure, but it illustrates the impossible task superintendents faced in trying to regulate relations between the sexes.

In the end, adolescent yearnings managed to find expression. There was, for example, the ubiquitous classroom love note. "Hear me," one Hampton young man declared, "this all I am going to say. I like you, and I love you. I won't say anything more. My whole heart is shaking hand with you. I kiss you." Anna Moore, a Pima girl who at the age of fourteen met her future husband, Ross Shaw, at Phoenix Indian School, recalls: "We wrote notes because the matron was very strict and only let us see each other at social functions. But sometimes Ross would sneak over to the girls' side of the campus, where we would play croquet until the matron discovered us and shooed Ross back where he belonged." But true romance was not to be denied. "Soon we were going together. We were truly childhood sweethearts."[35]

For the most part such goings-on were within the boundaries of Victorian propriety, but there were also secret activities of a more illicit character. While at Keams Canyon, Don Talayesva recalls: "I had occasion to see some of the boys masturbate until they ejaculated. Sometimes we played a little with each other. One boy wanted me to pretend that I was a girl with him, but I did not want to do it." Later at Sherman Institute the boys were given a pamphlet on the evils of masturbation. "It said that the practice ruined a boy's health and caused him to go insane. But I saw the boys doing it right along. They did not mind being watched by other fellows."[36]

For the bold and the brave, masturbation was a poor substitute for genuine lovemaking. Edmund Nequatewa recalls that it was "customary" for the older Hopi boys at Keams Canyon to slip out at night to visit their girlfriends in the other dormitory. "These things must have been planned ahead, because when they got around to the girls dormitory, the girls had hung down their sheets to pull up the boys." Indeed, Talayesva, who was at Keams Canyon about the same time, recalls one occasion when thirty of the older boys and a good number of girls received a severe thrashing when boys were found in the girls dormitory. One might think that the incident would have discouraged Talayesva, but not so.

> One Saturday afternoon, as I worked alone in the kitchen, I spied Louise on the porch of her dormitory and beckoned through the window for her to come over. After feeding her, I hugged her warmly for the first time, told her that she was a sweet little thing, and that I wanted her for my wife. Then I moved with her gently into the pantry, and locked the door. The little room was crowded and we had to stand and be quick; but she knew what to expect and seemed experienced. It was the first time that I had found and given real pleasure in lovemaking. After that I cared more for her than ever.[37]

One should not conclude from such accounts that illicit lovemaking was rampant in boarding schools. Carlisle, for instance, would admit to only seven pregnancies by 1901, two of these occurring during outing.[38] On the other hand, superintendents were generally hesitant to talk about such matters for the simple reason that it reflected poorly on their management abilities. There is no record of how many girls were quietly dropped from the rolls for reasons of pregnancy.

There were cases of genuine tragedy. In *Red Moon Called Me*, Gertrude Golden tells the story of "Ada," who is described as an "intelligent, trustworthy and industrious young lady" about nineteen or twenty years old. Like all students at Fort Defiance, Ada lived on the reservation during the summer months. But when she returned in the fall of 1914 for her graduation year she was not her normal cheerful self. At social affairs Ada remained uncharacteristically aloof from the other students and sat quietly against the wall with the teachers. In early spring, the school seamstress was suspicious when she discovered, in the midst of measuring Ada for a new dress, that the girl's waist was much larger. She reported this fact to Golden, but the latter was unwilling to admit to herself that something might be wrong. She later regretted this.

> About a month before the closing of school, and our graduating exercise, Ada appeared in line for breakfast one morning looking very white and weak. The assistant matron noticed her and helped the girl back to bed. The doctor who called a little later saw immediately what had happened, although the poor girl denied vigorously that she had given birth to a child in the night. Examination of her trunk revealed a dead infant, new born. Then, and only then, did Ada give way. She confessed fully, telling what had happened during the summer at the home of her cousin and how she had suffered during the following months in an effort to conceal her condition. She had tried to stop the cries of the child and, in doing so, had choked it to death.[39]

Golden, it turns out, felt some responsibility for the whole episode. In the past few weeks, as the principal teacher, she had taken over the task of religious instruction for the Catholic girls while the padre was away. "I had been very, *very* emphatic in stressing the wickedness of doing anything that would bring illegitimate children into the world—children who would be without father, home or name and who would suffer the disgrace all through their lives." Golden now feared she had lectured the girls too "forcefully" on the subject. The superintendent, meanwhile, did his best to hush up the whole episode and transferred Ada to another school. But as Golden goes on to relate, "the shock, the shame, the separation from her companions were too much for the poor girl, and she died of quick consumption within a year."[40]

Estelle Brown tells a remarkably similar story about "Lucy." Indeed, since this story also occurred at Fort Defiance in approximately the same year, and since Lucy's age is given at nineteen, Lucy and Ada may in fact be the same person. According to this version, Lucy was married in traditional Navajo fashion during the summer vacation but was determined to return to school to complete her last year of school. Because Lucy carried "too much flabby, unhealthy flesh" to begin with, none of the employees noticed the gradual swelling in the girl's abdomen over the course of several months. One night in April, Lucy locked herself in the girls' bathroom and gave birth to a baby which she quickly strangled and hid in her trunk. The following morning when Lucy failed to appear for breakfast, the matron found her wasted and bedridden, the same matron who had lectured Lucy fervently for months on the hellish fate that awaited those who conceived children outside Christian wedlock. The school physician was called in and once he surmised what had happened, he asked Lucy why she had murdered her baby. Lucy could only glance at the matron and reply: "So she wouldn't know. She say it is a sin, to marry so. Her God will burn me forever if He finds out. Now she will tattle to her God and He will burn me."[41]

Brown comments at one point that "no employee could have suspected the conflict that must have raged in this girl's mind, a mind hopelessly confused by the beliefs and customs of her own people and by the faith and moral precepts taught her at the school."[42] The truth of the matter is that school employees never knew what was going on in their students' minds. In Lucy's case, the collision of worldviews had produced a desperate mental state, one that finally resulted in the dreadful act of infanticide, something forbidden by both the Navajo and Christian ethical systems. One thing is certain: neither the Sunday morning sermons nor the Saturday night promenades had done much to improve the quality of Lucy's life as an Indian woman in the new America.

INDIAN FOOTBALL

Sometime in 1893 Pratt was visited by about forty of the school's athletic boys. The purpose of the visit was to convince the captain to revoke his ban against football, a decision made three years earlier when, in a contest with nearby Dickinson College, one of the Carlisle players had broken his leg. Pratt, who wanted to civilize Indians, not kill them off, had declared the sport simply too dangerous to play. But now he was being petitioned to reverse his decision. Pratt finally agreed to lift the ban, but only under two conditions: first, the players must promise to be models of sportsmanship, never bringing disgrace to the school or their race; and second, they must promise to beat the greatest football teams in the land. After some discussion, the boys agreed to both challenges. Carlisle would play football. In later years, other off-reservation schools would also take to the gridiron.[43]

The Indians played their first full season in 1894, winning only a single game. The 1895 season was much more impressive, and their win-loss record improved to 4 and 4. Even more significant was that the four losses came at the hands of the University of Pennsylvania, Navy, Bucknell, and Yale. More important, Carlisle was beginning to gain respect.[44] Even though Carlisle lost to Pennsylvania by a score of 36–0, the press had nothing but praise for the Indians' performance. One reporter went so far as to claim that "they have by far the best team of tacklers playing football today, excepting none." Another wrote, "The Indians played a hard, aggressive game from start to finish, and had they a coach who would teach them . . . teamwork, it is safe to say that they would be the equal of any team now playing."[45]

In the next several years, Pratt came to the same conclusion: the Indians needed a first-rate coach. In 1899, at the advice of Walter Camp, he signed on Glen Warner, a former Cornell football captain with coaching experience at the University of Georgia. The acquisition of Warner proved to be a stroke of genius. A tough disciplinarian, Warner put his Indian players through grueling practice sessions, concentrating on endurance and precise execution. A brilliant innovator, he introduced new elements into the Carlisle program—and for that matter, the game itself—including the huddle, the idea of numbering plays, the double wing formation, the body block, the spiral punt, and the "crouching start."[46] A master strategist, Warner devised trick plays, which in an era of vague game rules left much to the imagination. A classic example was the famous hidden ball play that Carlisle sprang on Harvard in 1903. After receiving the ball, the Indians quickly grouped and slipped the ball under the sweater of one of the guards, who then ran for a touchdown before any of the Harvard players could see what happened. Three years later in a game with Syracuse, Carlisle players appeared on the field wearing sweaters with patches that matched the color, size, and shape of footballs, a ruse that made it extremely difficult for opposing players to spot the ball carrier. Warner would later claim, "I have never been able to get any team of college boys to work tricks as smoothly as did the Carlisle boys." With the exception of a three-year interlude, "Pop" Warner would remain at Carlisle until 1914.[47]

The Warner years were Carlisle's glory years (see Table 6.1). Season after season, Carlisle not only chalked up an impressive win-loss record, but

Table 6.1. Carlisle's Football Record, 1894–1917

	Games Won	Games Lost	Games Tied	Total Carlisle Points	Total Opponents' Points
1894	1	6	2	62	108
1895	4	4	0	88	114
1896	6	4	0	176	90
1897	6	4	0	232	98
1898	5	4	0	188	93
1899	9	2	0	338	44
1900	6	4	1	211	92
1901	5	7	1	135	168
1902	8	3	0	251	51
1903	11	2	1	275	46
1904	9	2	0	335	44
1905	10	4	0	354	55
1906	9	2	0	244	36
1907	10	1	0	267	62
1908	10	2	1	212	55
1909	8	3	1	243	94
1910	8	6	0	235	68
1911	11	1	0	298	49
1912	12	1	1	504	114
1913	10	1	1	295	63
1914	4	7	1	99	151
1915	3	6	2	84	196
1916	1	3	1	55	65
1917	2	7	0	129	264

Source: John S. Steckbeck, *The Fabulous Redmen: The Carlisle Indians and Their Famous Football Teams* (Harrisburg, Pa.: J. Horace McFarland, 1951), 133.

did it by defeating the major football powers of the day. The 1907 team, which Warner later described as "about as perfect a football machine as I ever sent on the field," rolled over the University of Pennsylvania, University of Minnesota, University of Chicago, and even Harvard, ending with a win-loss record of 10 and 1. This was just the first of many such seasons. Such feats were all the more remarkable when considering that Carlisle was usually outweighed, used fewer substitutes, often played a more demanding schedule, and rarely played on its home field.[48]

The political and cultural meaning of the Carlisle football story brings two broad questions to mind. First, where did the football program fit into Carlisle's larger institutional objectives? Specifically, what political and educational goals did Pratt hope to achieve through football? Second, what deep social or historical meaning can be read into the story? "All play means something," writes Johan Huizinga.[49] Hence, the question, What was the meaning of Indian football as deep play, as secular ritual?

For Pratt, winning football games was not an end in itself but a means to a larger objective: winning support for the idea that Indians, if given the opportunity, were capable of competing with whites not only on the football field but in society as well. "If, through football, Indian boys can kick themselves into association and competition with white people, I would give everyone a football," Pratt wrote to one of the school's supporters. Through football, Pratt believed, Carlisle's work would gain wider notoriety. "Nothing we have ever done," he once remarked, "has so much awakened the attention of the country to the possibilities of the Indian." Watching his football team play Harvard and Yale not only reaffirmed Pratt's philosophy on the Indian question, it provided deep satisfaction. "I have considerable elation and reward," he confided, "in seeing my boys shake up and even overcome the trained college athletes with all their centuries of development and intelligence." On the other hand:

> I am keeping my hand on the throttle, and watching carefully the ongoing of this train. So long as I believe as I do now that it is doing good to the cause and will probably lead to deeper public thought as to what is best and right for the Indians I shall accelerate it. If I discover that the contrary is likely to result I will stop it. In the meantime I think we had better have work a plenty, study a plenty, civilized experiences a plenty and play a plenty.[50]

But keeping his "hand on the throttle" proved no easy matter. There was, for instance, the issue of recruitment. Here, Pratt walked a delicate line. Certainly he was not averse to attracting potential football talent, on one occasion writing to an agent, "if you should by chance have a sturdy young man anxious for an education who is especially swift of foot or qualified for athletics, send him."[51] Still, he appears not to have succumbed to the natural temptation to recruit students solely for their prowess on the gridiron.

He certainly had opportunities to do so, especially after Warner signed on in 1899 and unabashedly began his own recruitment campaign. In reply to an inquiry from a student who expressed interest in coming east to play football for Carlisle, Pratt answered, "My hope is that if you come here it will be for the purpose of getting an education letting football be secondary, very secondary." Should the school become fixated with the idea of turning out sports "champions," he added, "I will have to break up football altogether." In reply to a request from a former player, who, probably at Warner's instigation, asked to return to school to resume his old football career, Pratt responded: "You are pretty well equipped for the duties of life and I feel assured that turning your attention to football rather than to more important things is not helpful to you and I regret to see you inclined to do that. Take my advice and let football go." On the same matter, Pratt lectured Warner: "I do not think it is well to let Frank Beaver come back to Carlisle just for football purposes and I wish you would not ask me to do that. He is through with Carlisle and let him go out into the world and take care of himself." As it turned out, Frank Beaver did actually return to Carlisle, which suggests that even Pratt was not entirely consistent on the issue. Still, during Pratt's years football was largely appreciated for its instrumental value.[52]

Pratt also believed that football was a powerful tool for acculturating Indians to the American value system. From football Indians would learn the value of precision, teamwork, order, discipline, obedience, efficiency, and how all these interconnected in the business of "winning." Football also built character by teaching prized American values like hard work, self-reliance, and self-control. It also gave ritualistic expression to one of the cardinal elements in American social thought, survival of the fittest.[53] Indeed, one Carlisle player wrote his mother:

> I have been played in football. I played on second team here at Carlisle. I used to play at halfback and could do better there but they put me in the right end and I have a hard time trying to ketch who got the ball, but sometimes I get a chance to ketch him. Sometimes I have to do to throw myself down when they come around on my side and they all fall on top of me. But as school book say, a genius capacity for taking infinite pain.[54]

And so Indians should play football. It would win them white friends, and once more, it would show them they could only "win" by becoming white men. Pratt made both points one Saturday night when speaking to a cheering throng of Carlisle students just returned from parading through the streets of the town. The celebration had been prompted by news of a great football victory; the Indians had defeated Cornell 10–6. The phone was ringing constantly, Pratt told the crowd. Local citizens were calling to congratulate the Indians on their victory, which caused Pratt to ask, what would the townspeople's response have been just twenty-five years earlier if a party of Indians had gone streaming into Carlisle? They knew good and well; the women would have scrambled for the cellar, and the men would have reached for their rifles. But now, "Our friends and neighbors, the white people, join in our rejoicing when we succeed even though those we overcome are their own race." Students must not forget this larger meaning of the school's victories on the gridiron: Indians had defeated white men at their own game precisely because they were becoming white men. Pratt bellowed: "We put aside Indian thoughts, and Indian ways, Indian dress and Indian speech. We DON'T want to hold onto anything INDIAN."[55]

But there was still another meaning to the Indians' feats on the playing field, one that Pratt seems not to have anticipated and that stemmed from the very nature of the game. Football at its most fundamental level is a contest for yardage, a bone-crunching struggle for the control of territory. It is this aspect of football, James Oliver Robertson asserts, that has always explained Americans' special fascination with the game. It "ritualizes the moving frontier, and the teamwork, cooperation, and individual heroism necessary to resist the moving frontier." And then he adds, "Football players are pioneers *and* Indians at the same time."[56]

At first, Robertson's hypothesis, which is offered in the spirit of speculation, may seem a bit farfetched. It is highly questionable, for example, whether spectators actually viewed a Yale-Harvard game, two exclusively white teams, as a symbolic conflict between pioneers and Indians. But what of a contest between Indians and whites? Such a racial clash would have, of course, left much less to the imagination, and spectators could clearly identify who was who, pioneers and Indians. Consider this reporter's account of the Harvard-Carlisle contest in 1896:

> Never was there a spectacle so calculated to impress an imaginative mind. All the manifold interests of the present and the past, the near and the far, were collected on the instant on Soldiers' Field. Over 500 years of education were represented by the young palefaces in crimson, while centuries of fire and sun worship, medicine men incantations, ghost dances and mound building were flooded before the inner vision by the appearance of the young men from Carlisle. Every glance at their swarthy faces and crow-black hair wafted the mind back to the days of Pontiac, King Philip, Samoset, to the time of Hannah Dustin's escape, to Lovewell's war and Marquette's trips of discovery in a fabric of birch bark.[57]

As it turns out, press accounts of Indian-white football contests were filled with allusions to frontier conflict. For instance, when the Indians played the "palefaces" of Illinois, the *Chicago Chronicle* reported that the latter had "its line shot and shattered by arrowlike plunges and its advances balked as a tomahawk would stop the rush of an unarmed opponent." The Illini planted their men "before the chalk line that separated victory from defeat, but the red giants tore through them and toppled them this way and that." Likewise, the *Philadelphia Press* described the Princeton-Carlisle game as the "fiercest struggle ever witnessed" and went on to report that "the tug, the strain, the resounding thwack of shoulders on head and knee on hip, the crunching of shoes on fallen limbs, told of a struggle in which race was matched against race. And the race with a civilization and a history won the day."[58]

What is one to make of such accounts? "The contrast between play and seriousness is always fluid," writes Huizinga. "Play turns to seriousness and seriousness to play." It follows that play or contests are often capable of creating a "real world" of their own. In such instances they become a "representation *of* something."[59] Huizinga's insight helps to explain the deeper meaning of Indian-white football. Given the history of Indian-white conflict, spectators were quick to create a "real world" of their own as they watched the two races invade and defend one another's territory. More than a game, Indian-white football constituted a dramatic reenactment of frontier conflict. Thus in the Princeton-Carlisle game in 1896, "the sons of civilization overcame the children of the wilderness."

Football was not only the moral equivalent of war, it was a special kind of war. "Custer's last stand on the Little Big Horn," the *Boston Globe*'s account of the Harvard-Carlisle game read, "was never more fiercely assailed than was the stand of [the] Harvard eight." At one point in the game, Carlisle's warriors had moved the ball "foot by foot and yard by yard" down to Harvard's five-yard line. The fighting was fierce. "There was piling and crunching and tumbling and twisting like that of a drive of logs in ugly water, but the men of Harvard stood as firm as a hill. At them went the Indians like buffalo charging in the van of a prairie fire, but the human wall could not be breached." In the end, Harvard accomplished what Custer could not, and the Indians were defeated 4–0.[60]

The *New York Herald* described the 1896 Yale-Carlisle game in similar terms. In a closely fought battle that Yale barely won, it was said that the Kiowa, Comanche, and Apache "whooped and grunted and tore holes through Yale's rush line, through which they poured like fire water from a bunghole, or buffalo through a mountain canyon." Meanwhile, "all along the side lines danced the medicine men, with their buckets and sponges and incantations, praying and conjuring in their native tongue, and doctoring everybody that needed it."

> Three thousand spectators saw the delirious battle. They saw Yale hurled back foot by foot, and yard by yard. They saw the half-wild men, whose ancestors made things pleasant for us in the olden times with tomahawk and scalping knife, knocking the breath out of the pale faced lads whose fathers took their muskets afield to protect themselves from possible scrimmages.[61]

And what of the Indians? Did Carlisle players view Indian-white football clashes in the same manner? One reporter for the *New York Journal* suggested as much and tried to imagine what the Indian players must be thinking:

> They [whites] had stolen a continent from us, a wide, wide continent which was ours, and lately they have stolen various touchdowns that were also ours. . . . It is too much. Let us, then brothers, be revenged. Here is an opportunity. The white men line up in their pride. If sacrifice of bone and sinew can square the thing, let us sacrifice, and perhaps the smoke of our wigwam campfire will blow softly against the dangling scalps of our enemies.[62]

What in fact was the attitude of the Indian players? The evidence is sketchy, but it appears that this reporter's hunch was not far off the mark. Pop Warner, for instance, tells us that his Carlisle players never possessed "school spirit" in the same way that his white college teams possessed it. "When playing against college teams," Warner claims, "it was not to them so much the Carlisle School against Pennsylvania or Harvard, as the case might be, but it was the Indian against the White Man." Warner noted on another occasion, "It was not that they felt any definite bitterness against the conquering white, or against the government for years of unfair treatment, but rather that they believed the armed contests between red men and white had never been waged on equal terms." It is an open question whether Carlisle players never felt "bitterness against the conquering whites," but Warner is surely right when he suggests that his players appreciated the "even break" they could get on the football field. Nor is there any reason to think that Indian players would view the game in any different terms than white spectators, a ritualistic replay of frontier conflict. Hence, Warner's recollection that "if there was one team that the Indians liked to beat more than another, that team was the Army."[63]

Down on the field, in the midst of the tackling and crunch of bodies, the Indian players were fully capable of making pointed historical references. In the 1896 Pennsylvania game, for instance, when one of the Quakers, William Bull, was knocked to the ground, one Carlisle man was heard to remark to a teammate while pointing to the fallen player, "Sitting Bull." On another occasion, when a furious Warner learned in the midst of a game that one of his players had been illegally kneed, he asked the injured player, "Didn't you say anything?" The Indian replied, "Who's the savage now?"[64]

The evidence from two football players' letters is also suggestive. One Haskell player wrote home in 1914:

> Our football men are busy each day putting in hard practice for the coming war. We have been mobilizing our troops since the first of

September and they are now trained and equipped for the coming campaign. They have done considerable skirmishing and I was wounded on the right shoulder.

Similarly, after a game with the University of Pennsylvania, one Carlisle player wrote to his parents:

We had a hard time playing football last Saturday. We play with Quaker team at Philadelphia. They were pretty good play and heap much bigger but we beat him anyhow us Indian boy side. We too slick for him. Maybe white men better with cannon and guns, but Indian just as good in brains to think with.[65]

As Richard S. Gruneau reminds us, "sports, like all cultural products, have the capacity to be either reproductive or oppositional, repressive or liberating." Nor are these functions necessarily mutually exclusive. Games and sports can be hegemonic instruments of social integration and acculturation and at the same time dramatize deep social tensions. "Games," in the words of Brian Sutton-Smith and John Roberts, "exist to render conflict malleable. They do not merely socialize by mirroring. They socialize by mirroring and inverting. They are radical as well as conservative."[66]

So too was Indian football full of multiple meanings. Consider Carlisle's 1897 football banquet. On this special evening the players dined on soup, chicken salad, turkey, creamed oysters, ice cream, and cake, all served on place mats cut in the shape of footballs. From the ceiling hung game balls bearing the scores of Carlisle's gridiron victories.[67] There was much to celebrate. Although the school had by no means proven itself a flawless football machine, having won just six of its ten contests, it was gaining recognition as a rising football power. On one level, the banquet was a celebration of the fact that Indians were proving themselves fully capable of defeating white teams at a game requiring technical skill and physical and mental toughness. The school's football heros were living testimony to those qualities—perseverance, obedience, self-sufficiency, the competitive spirit—so necessary for success not only on the gridiron but in the game of life as well. The football banquet, moreover, was a time to celebrate the fact that Carlisle's football victories were winning friends for the Carlisle philosophy, for the Indian and his possibilities.

But in the midst of all the ceremony and speech making, there were other notes sounded as well. One such moment came when Bemus Pierce, the team captain, reviewed the season highlights. Earlier in the evening, A. J. Standing, Carlisle's assistant superintendent, had patronizingly commented that although the Indians were to be congratulated for their gritty performance on the field, they "still need a white man to coach, and to manage their finances." Later, Pierce, unwilling to let Standing's comment go unanswered, decided to add a few additional remarks to his planned speech.

> Now, I am glad to say we have a white man for a coach, but we have no white man on the team when we are on the gridiron. Therefore, I say if the Indian can do this, why can he not as well handle the team, and handle the financial part? If he can do so well in this game, I believe in time he can do most anything.[68]

Two years later, Pierce was coaching football at the University of Buffalo.

Another telling moment came in the remarks of the school's bandmaster, Dennison Wheelock. Speaking for the school, but also as an Oneida, Wheelock attempted to spell out for the players the larger meaning of their football victories.

> At this school, we are trying to bring the Indian up to the position that the white men occupy. Long ago, it was said that the Indian could not understand civilization. It is repeated even at the present time. I deny it. I assert that what the Indian could not understand was the greed, the grasping selfishness of the white man in this country and when the Indian learned that his habitation and the hills he so dearly loved were being invaded, he justly cried, "There is eternal war between me and thee." And when he resisted, who will say that he did not do right? Who will say that he would not have done the same? He resisted with a thousand warriors, but he had to retreat westward like a hunted fox. . . . Today the Indian is beyond the Mississippi. The only way I see how he may reoccupy the lands that once were his, is through football, and as football takes brains, takes energy, proves whether civilization can be understood by the Indian or not, we are willing to perpetuate it.[69]

A game, writes Huizinga, "is 'played out' within certain limits of time and space. It contains its own course and meaning." Moreover, once on the playing field, "the player can abandon himself body and soul to the game, and the consciousness of its being 'merely' a game can be thrust into the background."[70] So Indian-white football was more than just a game. Football was about boundaries, crossing boundaries, and defending boundaries. It was about another time and space. It was about the frontier and about Crazy Horse and Custer. It was about history and about myth. Indian-white football was deep play.

CALENDAR RITUALS

In the world of the boarding school, part of becoming civilized was learning how whites kept track of time and the various meanings they ascribed to time. On the one hand, this meant learning about clock time, how whites divided each day into hours, minutes, and seconds. In this connection students learned how "being on time" and "making use of time" were important elements in the white belief system. A second scheme for measuring time was calendar time, the white man's system for counting years, months, and days. It was at this point that students learned that whites attached special significance and meaning to particular days of the year.

The idea of a ritual calendar was hardly new. Virtually all native societies set aside certain occasions for ceremonial observance. But now Indians were acquiring a new identity, becoming a new people. Hence, they must come to identify with the myths and rituals of the society engulfing them. The school's annual ritual calendar—beginning with Columbus Day and ending with the Fourth of July—would facilitate the forging of this new identity. And at various points, the process would directly relate to one of the age-old issues facing the republic: the question of the Indians' past and future place in the American empire.[71]

Columbus Day

At the direction of the Indian Office, Indian schools began celebrating Columbus Day regularly on October 21, 1892. Although the nature of the program of activities was left to the imagination of each school, the Indian Office decreed that "the interest and enthusiasm of the children in these proceedings should be thoroughly aroused and the day of the celebration made to exert as inspiring an influence over them as possible."[72] What students were being asked to do, of course, was pay homage to the courageous voyager who, while sailing west across the Atlantic in search of Asia, "discovered" the New World instead and proclaimed the local natives to be *los Indios.* By the nineteenth century, the year 1492 had already been thoroughly mythologized. It signified the grand beginning of the American story. Before Columbus, the myth said, America was a place outside of time and space, a continent peopled by savages, a continent waiting to be settled, civilized, and exploited. Columbus Day celebrations at Indian schools had a special obligation, and it was not an easy one. Indian students must be made to see that Columbus's accomplishment was not only a red-letter day in history but also a beneficent development in their own race's fortunes. Only after Columbus, the myth went, did Indians enter into the stream of history; only after Columbus did Indians begin the slow and painful climb out of the darkness of savagery.

Perhaps the most auspicious Indian celebration of Columbus Day was in October 1892 when Pratt took large contingents of students to New York and Chicago to march in parades commemorating the four hundredth Columbian anniversary. To New York, Pratt sent 322 boys and girls, including the school's thirty-one-piece marching band, all clad in their finest school dress. Carrying American flags and marching behind a bright silk banner, "Into Civilization and Citizenship," the battalion smartly stepped their way through cheering onlookers. New York's enthusiastic response was duplicated ten days later when Pratt personally led a battalion of 305 boys in a Chicago parade, part of the opening ceremonies of the World's Columbian Exposition. Again, the banner and marching band led the way, but in this instance the remaining marchers were divided into ten platoons, each representing some department of the school's work, each boy carrying a tool or specimen of the classroom or workshop.[73]

Press accounts were wildly enthusiastic, and excerpts were printed in the *Red Man* so students back on campus might vicariously experience the meaning of Indians marching in a Columbus Day parade. One New York paper reported that Carlisle's participation was the highlight of the day, noting that "the descendants of those first Americans who were here before Columbus discovered the West Indies, are in themselves an unmatched proof of our progress, and show that what Columbus hoped—the conversion to Christianity of the natives of the Continent, is now at last in a fair way of accomplishment." Commenting on the Chicago parade, the *Springfield Union* announced that Indians had good cause to celebrate Columbus and then went on to observe: "The students of Carlisle, PA., Indian school represented the savages Columbus found. But instead of appearing as savages, they marched in their present character as intelligent, well-dressed and well-bred young men, each company carrying the symbols of its profession or trade." Columbus had catapulted the Indian into history. "But for the coming of the white man these Indians would be savages still, but today they are in a fair way to become the equals of any of us in civilization and citizenship."[74]

Thanksgiving

As the myth goes, in late December 1620 the *Mayflower,* carrying some 102 English voyagers in search of religious freedom, dropped anchor off the coast of New England. After a year of disease and starvation aggravated by a terribly harsh winter, half of the settlers of Plymouth colony were in their graves. By the following autumn, however, the small colony was beginning to flourish. Cultivated fields yielded a bountiful harvest of corn, beans, and squash, more than enough to sustain the settlement through another winter. In recognition of their good fortune, the colony's governor, William Bradford, declared three days of thanksgiving. He sent out hunters to shoot turkeys, ducks, and geese for the festivities, while Chief Massasoit, a local Wampanoag chief who had made peace with the settlers, brought ninety of his braves and a large quantity of fresh venison. For three days, whites and Indians feasted and engaged in target shooting and other leisurely activities. Meanwhile, Bradford's followers gave prayerful thanks for the blessings bestowed upon the beleaguered settlement.

Bradford had good reason to invite the Indians to the festivities, for in all probability the colonists could never have survived without them. A few months after the Pilgrim settlement, Samoset, an Indian from the coast of Maine who had been brought south by English fisherman eight months before, strolled into Plymouth speaking broken English, and to the delight of the Pilgrims, provided invaluable information on the surrounding countryside and its inhabitants. Shortly thereafter, Chief Massasoit and a delegation of Wampanoag appeared. Among this group was the legendary Squanto, who had been kidnapped by the English in 1614 and taken to England where he lived until 1619 before being returned to Cape Cod. Squanto's linguistic skills were of inestimable value in negotiating a treaty of peace with Massasoit and the potentially dangerous Wampanoag. From Squanto, Plymouth villagers learned how to plant and fertilize corn, where to find game and fish, and what wild fruit and berries were safe to eat.

Columbus Day celebrations taught students how Indians had been "discovered," how they had come to be called Indians, and how the date 1492 was the beginning of their history and civilization. In the observance of Thanksgiving—through classroom discussions, special programs, prayers, and the ritualistic feast (determined by the limitations of the school commissary)—students learned how the brave pilgrim fathers had settled in the wilderness, possessed the land in the name of their God, and how "good" Indians had aided them in the process. How noble red men like Samoset, Squanto, and Massasoit had earned a special place of honor in the nation's history. Thus, Indians as well as whites had reason to celebrate Thanksgiving, or so the teachers claimed. At Blue Canyon, Arizona, Minnie Jenkins constructed the day's program around a Sunday school chart depicting the Pilgrims and Indians feasting together at Plymouth in 1621. "This chart was an inspiration," Jenkins writes, "and never was there a lesson more appreciated by our Indian children than this picture of 'The First Thanksgiving.'" Or so she thought.[75]

Christmas

Many Indians experienced their first Christmas while at boarding school. Not surprisingly, although most celebrations included special programs and church services and the ritualistic singing of Christmas carols, most students soon came to identify the day with Santa Claus and gift giving. Helen Sekaquaptewa recalls that her first knowledge of the holiday was at the Keams Canyon school, when a local trader and another man appeared at the dormitory to distribute boxes of apples, oranges, and candy, saying: "This is for Christmas."[76]

Similarly, Jim Whitewolf experienced his first Christmas in 1892 at an Oklahoma boarding school. He first heard of the holiday from some older boys, who regarded it as one of the high points of the year. The day was indeed special. At noon, the dining room tables were filled with turkey, chicken, beef, pork, oranges, and apples. Before eating, an "old man" prayed aloud. "I didn't understand what he was praying about—he was just talking." Later that evening a beautifully decorated fir tree was unveiled, and gifts were distributed to those having their first Christmas. Whitewolf's gifts included candy, cakes, nuts, a scarf, a pair of gloves, and a shirt. At the sight of the tree, he recalls: "My eyes went wide open. I really was looking at it. I think this was one of the biggest Christmases I ever saw.[77]

Things didn't always go smoothly. One Christmas celebration at Truxton Canyon, Arizona, was almost a disaster. As Flora Gregg Iliff, principal at the time, tells the story, before she came to Truxton neither the Walapai nor the Havasupai had much knowledge of the white man's Christmas. Although some of the older children had received gifts in years past, the figure of Santa Claus had never made an appearance. Determined to make up for this, Iliff set about making plans for an elaborate Christmas Eve program, and to make the celebration even more special, she decided to invite Walapai adults to witness the festivities.[78]

All through December teachers made preparations for the big day. Donated toys from eastern merchants were unboxed and wrapped; bags of candy and fruit were made ready; students rehearsed holiday sketches; and Joe Iliff, the industrial teacher (and Flora's future husband), known by his Walapai name "Suspenders-crossed-in-the-back," perfected his Santa Claus outfit. As a precautionary measure the school doctor began preparing the superstitious Walapai parents for the white-bearded apparition they had never seen before. "You savvy Santa Claus?" the doctor began asking villagers. Invariably the response was "no savvy." So the doctor told them about the white-bearded, red-suited, jolly man who flew across the sky and brought gifts. Word quickly spread. As the appointed day came closer, more and more Indians approached the school with the question, "San Claw—how many suns—he come?" As the days passed, the doctor held up fewer and fewer fingers. The parents were clearly interested, although unbeknown to Flora Iliff, the suspicion was being voiced quietly among the Walapai that the white man's Santa Claus might in reality be *Quiqete,* the great evil spirit of the Walapai.

On Christmas Eve, the auditorium was filled to capacity and the air was "electric with expectancy." The hour-long program went smoothly enough, the parents beaming with pride at their children's performance. And then:

Suddenly in a tense silence there came the jingle of sleigh bells, a loud pounding on the front door and a demand for admittance. Every eye focused on the entrance. No one stirred or seemed to breathe until the door was thrown open and old Santa, with a monstrous pack on his back, bounded in. Not an Indian in the hall had ever in his life seen anything that resembled that apparition. The ruddy-complexioned, bewhiskered mask, the long white hair, the red coat with its white cotton trim, and the high rubber boots made a bewildering combination.

The children at this point sat rigid and wild-eyed with excitement, but the villagers were not so sure. Indeed, as students stood transfixed, one of the tribe's old wisemen jumped up, waved his arms, and with fierce emotion, screamed—"*Quiqete, Quiqete!*" At this, complete chaos erupted. Walapai parents bolted for the doors while "pandemonium broke loose among the children." Some followed their parents' cue that the strange figure was in fact *Quiqete* and stampeded out of the hall. Others stood their ground. Many of the kindergartners "ran to the teachers . . . and clung to us, tears rolling down their fat cheeks while they sobbed, 'No good! No good!' " In the midst of the din, teachers tried to restore order. Indian policemen circulated through the crowd outside, assuring the parents that there was nothing to fear from the red-suited visitor. At length, calm was restored, both students and adults back in the hall. And so the program continued.

Don, Seth, Sam, and a few of the older boys . . . had volunteered to distribute the presents, but they did not recognize their teacher in his disguise and refused to go near him. The audience was quiet while Santa told of his home in the North and of his long drive over ice and snow to bring gifts to the children at Truxton. While he talked, some of our small girls leaned forward, intently peering up under the front of his long, red-flannel coat, whispering. The peeping and the whispering spread from the small children to the older ones. Santa was betrayed. They had seen three sofa pillows pinned to his suspenders to make his stomach look plump and round as it looked in the pictures we had shown them of Saint Nicholas. They recognized the cushions. They had seen those cushions many times on a certain couch at the school. That planted suspicion in the minds of Don and Seth, so they listened to Santa's voice. Suddenly one of them exclaimed, "Mr. Iliff!" and the tension eased. They spoke Joe's Walapai name to the older Indians; all repeated it. They knew "Suspenders-crossed-in-the-back" and were not afraid.

With the crisis over, Santa began passing out gifts—horns, drums, whistles, games, dolls, ribbons, and neckties. Again absolute bedlam broke out as children tried out their toys, horns blasting and drums rumbling. The roar was deafening. Principal Iliff called for silence, but "their wild emotions were too deeply stirred now; there was no stemming the hysterical outburst through which they were finding release." Finally, the promise of bags filled with candy, nuts, and oranges brought a degree of order. After distribution of the candy, the children were immediately marched back to the dormitories whereupon toys were put away and children put to bed. "But long after lights were out," remembers Iliff, "the chatter went on until nerves relaxed and everyone fell asleep." Christmas had come to Truxton Canyon.

New Year's Day

Although New Year's Day was officially a national holiday, schools seem to have done very little to celebrate it, apparently because the day was largely devoid of either political or religious significance and lacked a rich ceremonial tradition. Its chief function was to remind Indians of how whites kept track of the stream of time, how they divided the year into months and days, how days filled up months, and how months added up to make a year. In this manner whites systemized time, planned the future, remembered the past. Moreover, certain years were more important than others, dates like 1492, 1620, 1776, 1887.

Indian Citizenship Day

Especially created for Indian schools, Indian Citizenship Day, or Franchise Day, commemorated the passage of the Dawes Act on February 8, 1887. The idea for creating a special Indian holiday appears to have originated with Samuel Armstrong at Hampton Institute. Two years after the General Allotment Act became law, the Indian Office directed all schools to prepare programs designed "to impress upon Indian youth the enlarged scope and opportunity given them by this law and the new obligations which it imposes."[79] Because the Dawes Act combined two favorite themes in Indian reform—private property and citizenship—celebrations of the holiday went to extraordiry lengths to imbue the law with deep symbolic meaning. Indeed, one thoroughly indoctrinated Hampton student proclaimed:

> Now we are citizens
> We give him applause:
> So three cheers, my friends,
> For Senator Dawes![80]

Speeches by prominent government figures, dramatizations, and pageants were the order of the day. A particularly extravagant stage production, "Columbia's Roll Call," performed at Hampton in 1892, deserves special examination.[81] Written by Helen Ludlow for an all-Indian cast, the script was a patchwork of narrative and poetry designed to honor familiar American heroes. The pageant's structure revolves around the mythic American goddess Columbia, who summons forth, one by one, familiar historical figures upon whom she bestows a badge of citizenship. Wrapped in an American flag, she begins by proclaiming:

> Heralds of Fame and History
> Unroll your scroll of mystery;
> Then with your silver trumpet's blast
> Unloose the shut gates of the Past,
> And call Columbia's heroes forth,
> Proclaim them—East, West, South, and North

The first figure to step forward is none other than Columbus. In a long poem he relates his voyage of discovery. The meaning of his accomplishment is made clear when he describes that moment when land is sighted.

> Then boomed the Pinta's signal gun!
>   The first that ever broke
> The sleep of that new world—the sound
> Echoing to forest depths profound,
>   A continent awoke!

As the story unfolds, the savage land slowly begins to awaken from its sleep. Captain John Smith comes forward and reminds Columbia of the triumph at Jamestown.

> I see a train of exiles stand
>   Amid the desert desolate,

Cast picture for "Columbia's Roll Call," 1892. (Courtesy of the Hampton University Archives)

> The fathers of Virginia's land;
>   The daring pioneers of fate
> Who braved the perils of the sea and earth,
> And gave Columbia's boundless empire birth.

But Jamestown is only a foothold of civilization in a howling wilderness. Columbia asks, "The Pilgrim fathers—where are they?" Miles Standish and Priscilla Alden step forward, followed close behind by John Eliot, the Puritan missionary. George Washington also makes an appearance. In the procession of heroes, all white, each has bestowed upon him the coveted badge. But Columbia has yet to honor an Indian, nor is it clear what the fate of the Native American is to be in Columbia's empire. The issue is finally raised by an Indian petitioner who pleads:

> You have taken our rivers and fountains
>   And the plains where we loved to roam,—
> Banish us not to the mountains
>   And the lonely wastes for home!
> Our clans that were strongest and bravest,
>   Are broken and powerless through you;

> Let us join the great tribe of the white men,
>   As brothers to dare and to do!

Indians were now willing to join the white man's march of progress:

> And the still ways of peace we would follow—
>   Sow the seed and the sheaves gather in,
> Share your labor, your learning, your worship,
>   A life larger, better, to win.
> Then, foeman no longer nor aliens,
>   But brothers indeed we will be,
> And the sun find no citizens truer
>   As he rolls to the uttermost sea.

Columbia replies by challenging the Indians to name individuals of their race equal to those white heroes "that have made me great and established my throne in the New World." In the developments that follow, it becomes eminently clear what Columbia's standard is for a place of honor in Indian history. One by one they come forth. There is Samoset, whose lines are, "I said to my paleface brother, welcome Englishmen." There is the chieftain who says to Washington, "We welcome you to our country." And an Indian convert recites a Bible verse in Algonquian.

In the end Columbia is convinced. She gazes upon a group of Indians dressed as farmers, teachers, and mechanics. Their plea for a place of honor and citizenship seems too reasonable to deny, and she says to her Indian wards: "You have gained your cause. Your past, your present, and your purposes for the future prove your right to share all I have to give. Take my banner, and your place as my citizens."

A major theme in Indian Citizenship Day celebrations was the virtue of work. In another Ludlow production, successive waves of students, organized by trade, came forward to sing of their particular contribution to the world of productive labor. The farmers bellow:

> We're a band, we're a band
> Of farmers good and true;
> We've a title to our land,
> And we'll occupy it too.
> We will plow, we will plant,
> Not a lazy one shall roam;
> Then H'rah, H'rah, H'rah
> Shout the merry harvest home.

And the laundresses say:

> Dash, dash, dash—pour the water in the tub;
> Plash, plash, plash—so the clothes we gaily rub;
> Then we'll hang them in the sun,
> And we'll iron them aright,
> And when our work is done,
> They'll be clean and smooth and white.
> A civilizing power is the laundress with her tub;
> We are cleaning more than clothes, as we rub, rub, rub.[82]

A particularly troublesome area for such celebrations was the issue of land loss. Under the terms of the Dawes Act, all surplus reservation lands beyond that needed for allotment were to be sold off to white settlers, the proceeds to be deposited in a tribal trust to be spent, among other things, on education. Thus, if students were to embrace the Dawes Act, they must be divested of the impression that the price of citizenship came at too high a cost. This was exactly the issue addressed in a poem recited at Carlisle's celebration in 1890. In this instance the poem was written by one of the school staff but read by a student, Jemima Wheelock. "A Message from Carlisle Students to the Indians" begins by noting that taking land from Indians was an old American story.

> You say we are poor, though a splendid dominion
> Of forests and rivers and mountains of gold
> Were ours, e'er the greed of the white man detained it;
> You are sorry and grumble that now it is sold.

The poem continues by pointing out that the government was now offering redress to the Indians. Education will compensate for the past dispossession of Indian lands and presumably for those lost as well as a consequence of the Dawes Act.

> But welcome the ruin, if now by our losses,
> We gain thousandfold in a better estate.
> A man may be chief in the empire of reason.
> Education, not land, makes a citizen great.[83]

Such school celebrations sought to convince Indian students that the benefits of the Dawes Act—allotment, citizenship, education—far outweighed the dispossession of "surplus" land. And apparently some were won over. Exuberant over Indian Citizenship Day ceremonies, one student, still struggling with his English, wrote home:

Well, I am going to tell you what is reason we do all that. Well, reason for celebrating Tuesday was the Indians are going to be citizens now and be free now, and take their lands and make a good farm for themselves and try to do what the white people do, and you are citizen now and I tell you all this because I thought you would like to know it if you didn't all hear it yet.[84]

Washington's Birthday

The ritual calendar wheel had scarcely turned two weeks when school children were celebrating one of the nation's oldest national holidays. By the early nineteenth century, George Washington the man had become Washington the monument, a venerated symbol of American nationalism, republicanism, and independence. Mythologized by painters, sculptors, and biographers, Washington was revered as "the Father of his country," a semidivine embodiment of American character traits—courage, honesty, strength, and devotion to freedom. A portrait of Washington hung in virtually every schoolhouse in America; the cherry tree story, first mythologized by Parson Weems and then reworked for McGuffey Readers, was a staple of every young American's education.[85]

Surely there were aspects of Washington's character that Indians could admire. Strength, courage, bravery, quiet humility, were attributes held in high regard in Indian society. But thoughtful students might legitimately question Washington's claim on Indian hearts. What of Washington the Indian fighter? What of Washington the land surveyor? What of Washington the "Great White Father?" But such questions were not likely to surface with students' first exposure to the Washington myth. One Haskell student wrote home in 1911:

> We had a holiday yesterday and a social last night. George Washington was old yesterday and next year day, February 22, 1912, George Washington be old again. He left a good house and mother and father to see Washington. George Washington liked to work and he liked to go to school. He went to study books. He liked to play soldier. And Washington love country. He have wagon and horse, one horse Washington.[86]

Washington was just the first of many "great white fathers," and occasionally students had the opportunity to see one in the flesh. In 1901, for instance, Phoenix students were paid a visit by President William McKinley. Like all such occasions, the affair was carefully scripted, complete with drill routines, fluttering flags, and marching bands. According to a local news account, the drill routines were "executed like clockwork, unmarred by a single mistake or bungle." The highlight of the ceremony came when, at the sound of a bugle, 700 students snapped a salute to the president, then cried out in perfect unison, "I give my head and my hand and my heart to my country; one country, one language, and one flag."[87]

McKinley was not the last to visit Phoenix. Within a decade Presidents William Howard Taft and Theodore Roosevelt also made appearances. For one new recruit in 1909, it was all terribly confusing. At the first sight of the massive Taft on the reviewing stand, all he could do was utter, "Gee! George Washington is fat."[88]

Arbor Day

There is a delightful moment in James Fenimore Cooper's *The Prairie* when Leatherstocking, now some eighty years old, is asked why he has trekked so far west. The reason, the reader learns, lies in the landscape itself, the fact that there are so few trees. Past the forest line, the venerable hero explains, he is beyond the reach of "Yankee woodchoppers" and therefore will not have to look upon the "madness of their waste." "It was a grievous journey that I made," the old frontiersman reflects, "a grievous toil to pass through falling timber and to breathe the thick air of smoky clearings week after week as I did!" And so he sought out a landscape beyond the "deafening" sound of the ax "in search of quiet."[89]

Most Indian students had never heard of Cooper or of the fictional pathfinder. But they knew about George Washington, and they also knew about the cherry tree affair. Tree chopping is, of course, at the very heart of the Washington myth. Accused of chopping down his father's cherry tree, young George confesses, "I can't tell a lie, Pa; you know I can't tell a lie. I did cut it with my hatchet." In a brilliant analysis of Weems's story, James Oliver Robertson observes:

> We insist on believing that the child cut down a tree—the one central act all Americans know as the act of civilizing the wilderness. The trees had to be cut, the great forests leveled, in order to make civilized land out of the wilderness; in order to clear the land and plant it and make it grow; in order to build log cabins for civilized shelter; in order to get fuel for warmth and cooking; in order to split rails for fences to make boundaries and keep animals and other uncivilized things in their place; in order to build stockades against the Indians; and, in a more modern world, in order to have lumber for houses and paper to read from. The backwoodsman, the tree-cutting harbinger of civilization. the hardy pioneer, rail-splitting honest Abe, lumberjack Paul Bunyan can all be summoned up by the vision of an eighteenth-century Virginia boy in silk breeches with a hatchet in his hand—when that boy is Father of His Country.[90]

Robertson goes on to note that one of the functions of myths—and one might add rituals as well—is to resolve deep-seated tensions and paradoxes in the society. Hence, schoolboys hearing the cherry tree myth fully acknowledge that young Washington was wrong to chop down a perfectly good cherry tree. On the other hand, Weems's story is hardly about saving trees. Upon George's admission of guilt, his father proclaims: "Glad am I, George, that you killed my tree; for you have paid me for it a thousandfold. Such an act of heroism in my son is worth more than a thousand trees, though blossomed with silver and their fruits of purest gold."[91]

By the late nineteenth century, Americans increasingly turned to the practice of planting trees and even created a new holiday to emphasize the importance of doing so. Curiously enough, the movement began in the High Plains country, the very site of the aged pathfinder's last days. In 1872, J. Sterling Morton, a member of the Nebraska State Board of Agriculture, proposed Arbor Day as an official state holiday to be commemorated with ceremonial tree planting. The first year, 1 million trees were planted and by 1898, some 16 million. Virtually all the states followed Nebraska's lead, each designating its own calendar date consistent with the region's seasonal climate. In 1885, the National Educational Association adopted a resolution calling upon all schools to observe the day, and in 1890, the Indian Office followed suit.[92]

Several themes—aesthetic, romantic, patriotic, economic—are discernable in Arbor Day celebrations. In poems and orations, students declared trees to be symbols of regeneration, knowledge, and civic pride. Trees were living reminders of the beauty in nature's gift and God's great plan. Planting trees, moreover, was an investment in the nation's most precious natural resource and its economic future. Arbor Day, proclaimed a Department of Agriculture bulletin, "directs the eyes of all not toward some achievement of the past but to a goal to be reached in the future. It celebrates not what we have done but what we hope and determine to do now and the days to come."[93]

Indians were to be a part of that future just as they had been part of its past. Once upon a time, the myth went, Indians had been part of the "howling wilderness," impediments to progress and the nation's destiny. But the children of Columbia had entered the wilderness; they felled the forests, plowed the land, and made a garden. Indians, meanwhile, had either been killed, tamed, or driven west. Now a new generation of Indians was being civilized. It followed—indeed, the myth required—that Indians ritualistically participate in civilizing the landscape. By participating in Arbor Day celebrations, by planting trees along the school's walkways and along the roadsides, Indians were helping create the garden. By planting groves of cedar and elm on Nebraska hillsides, nourished by the bones of

Leatherstocking, Indian children were making way for the sound of the ax.

Memorial Day

"We learned a verse about Memorial Day," one Haskell student wrote home in 1906. "On Memorial Day," he continued, "we went to chapel at four o'clock. Then we went down to the cemetery and decorated the graves. We sang America and the band play."[94] Originally designated as a holiday to remember those who had died in the Civil War, by the end of the century Memorial Day, or Decoration Day, had evolved into an occasion for memorializing all soldiers who had fallen in arms and for honoring the deceased in general. Indian schools noted the holiday with varying degrees of tastefulness.

Haskell used the occasion to honor students who had died while at school. The 1914 program was probably typical. It began when 600 students marched from the school to a nearby graveyard. The procession included the school band, 50 Haskell girls wearing white dresses (each girl carrying a bouquet of flowers), and several companies of uniformed students in their finest school dress. Moving toward the graveyard the band played "Onward, Christian Soldiers." After passing through the cemetery gates, the entire body gathered in formation around some fifty student graves, after which the band played "America." A chaplain offered a few words of prayer. And then, to the strains of "Nearer My God to Thee," the Haskell girls in white stepped forward, each placing a bouquet on one of the graves. The ceremony concluded with "the sweet sad tribute of the bugle" and a few remarks on the meaning of the holiday. As the last rays of sunshine were cast over the graveyard, students made their way back to the school grounds.[95]

Some superintendents used the occasion to honor Indian figures who had distinguished themselves as friends of the government, even when it involved killing Indians. In 1893, for instance, Agent James McLaughlin sent the Standing Rock brass band over to Fort Yates to participate in the unveiling of a monument dedicated to several Indian policemen who were killed in 1890 during the arrest of Sitting Bull. In 1900, among the graves decorated by Piegan students was that of Billy Jackson, described by the agent as "one of Custer's most trusted scouts." A year later, the agent at Klamath Agency, Oregon, reported that "the graves of men like Chief David Hill, who was always a leader in civilization and a noted ally of the whites during both the Paiute and Modoc Indian wars, have been carefully decorated and marked by placing the nation's flag over them."[96]

In two of the instances noted above, students may very well have found nothing objectionable in the ceremonies. The Piegan were no friends of the Sioux. Likewise, the Klamath had little affection for the Modoc and Paiute peoples. But acknowledging Indian sentiments was not really what such ceremonies were about. Indeed, some superintendents seem to have gone out of their way to offend their students' hereditary loyalties. Alice Fletcher, for example, after visiting Lapwai Boarding School in 1890, wrote to a friend:

> On Decoration Day we happened to see the procession of school children going out to decorate the graves of the soldiers who slew their fathers in the Joseph war. The graves lie outside the school grounds and nearby are some smaller mounds of the little ones who died here last winter. The procession limped disjointedly along, the children doing their best to keep step with no fife or drum, but singing "John Brown's Body Lies A-mouldering in the Grave" and bearing aloft, tied to a fish pole, a diminutive flag, borrowed for the occasion, from the school doctor. As the procession passed, we followed, and when the little girls placed the wreaths they had made upon the soldiers' graves, we saw . . . [the superintendent] draw a handkerchief from his pocket and turn his back upon us all.[97]

In this instance, the pathetic scene of Nez Percé children decorating the graves of those "who slew their fathers" was even too much for the superintendent to endure. Still the ritual was carried out, as it was elsewhere. At one point in his autobiography, Don Talayesva matter of factly recounts how one day in May "we had a Decoration Day celebration. We stuck little flags in our caps, took bunches of flowers, and marched out to the graves of two soldiers who had come out here to fight the Hopi and had died."[98]

Independence Day

Only those students in summer attendance at off-reservation institutions regularly participated in school-sponsored July Fourth celebrations. Most outing students probably accompanied their patrons into a nearby town to celebrate the nation's oldest holiday. Meanwhile, Indian agents on reservations marked the holiday with a modest celebration, which at the very least included a brief speech, acknowledgment of "old Glory," and some fireworks. The agent at Klamath, however, allowed the Indians to perform the "long departed war dance" and to conduct mock Indian raids. In the latter instance, braves raced through the woods "dressed in all their barbaric splendor, mounted on fleet horses, filling the welkin with the soul-curdling war whoop." The rationale for allowing such displays was that they were a lesson to the schoolboys of "the wonderful advancement made in a few years, under reservation training, from active savagery to a position well advanced toward practical civilization."[99] One can only wonder what the students' thoughts were.

Back in school the next fall, the ritual calendar would begin anew with Columbus Day. Once again, the dramatic renderings, the pageants, the parades, the fluttering banners, the praying, the hymn singing, and the graveyard observances were all designed to explain to Indians who they were, where they fit in the American story, and what they must become if they were to be part of America's future. Rituals helped point the way.

PART THREE

Response

CHAPTER SEVEN

Resistance

The Indian agent Eugene White would never forget the day one seven-year-old Ute boy was enrolled at Uintah Boarding School. The induction should have gone smoothly. Even though the lad was brought in "wild as a jack rabbit," he was delivered to the school by his father, normally a strong indicator that the boy would be cooperative. As a matter of procedure, White turned the youngster over to Fannie Weeks, the school superintendent, and Clara Granger, the matron, and invited the boy's father into the office for a bit of friendly conversation. It was all a matter of routine. The father would seek assurances he had done the right thing in bringing the boy in; the agent would praise him for his intelligence and foresight in doing so and would promise to watch over the boy like his, the agent's, very own son.[1]

All was proceeding according to script until, as White later recounted: "I heard a tremendous disturbance break out up at the schoolhouse. Tables and chairs were being hurled about, women were screaming, children were running in every direction." When White reached the schoolhouse he could scarcely believe the scene before him. In one part of the room Superintendent Weeks was almost in a "swoon." "Her dress was torn, her face badly scratched, and two-thirds of her hair missing." In another stood Mrs. Granger, "her face and neck showed several ugly fingernail scratches, one ear was bitten almost off, and her nose was swollen to ridiculous size, and bleeding profusely." Meanwhile, crouched upon a corner woodbox was the silent but defiant culprit, "the worst scared little animal I ever saw."[2]

Calm restored, White reconstructed events. After the boy had been turned over to the two women, they had "petted" and fed him, all the while coaxing him, in a tongue he had never heard before, to speak to them. Then Miss Weeks turned to other duties, and Mrs. Granger was to lead him to the storeroom for a new set of clothing. When Mrs. Granger

stooped to take his hand, the little fellow sprang up on her shoulders and went to snatching, biting, and pulling hair like a real wildcat. Of course, when Miss Weeks heard the screaming she rushed heroically to the rescue of Mrs. Granger. In trying to pull the boy loose she bent Mrs. Granger over on the table. The little Indian jumped off on the table, kicked Mrs. Granger on the nose, leaped upon Miss Weeks' shoulders and commenced to pluck her head. She struggled and screamed tremendously at first, but in a little while she dropped on her hands and knees and commenced to pray. When she sank entirely to the floor the little fellow jumped off, ran to the far corner of the room and climbed up on the woodbox. The ladies said he did not utter a word—did not even whimper—during the melee, and did not look at all mad, but just seemed to be scared almost to death.[3]

What is one to make of this episode, especially considering the fact that the defiant youth eventually became "one of the brightest and most amiable children in school"?[4] Is it possible that once acclimated, the boy found boarding school life completely agreeable? Perhaps, but not necessarily. As will be shown shortly, the fact of resistance need not take such dramatic form. What was the reason for the boy's rebellion? Was it simply a matter of fear or the pain of being separated from his father? Was it possibly a reaction to the cultural assault about to be performed? Perhaps both of these. One wonders also if the boy's eventual cooperation was elicited by virtue of the fact that his father had voluntarily brought him to school. How different would the young Ute's adjustment have been if the agent had been compelled to take him by force?

Although the evidence for this particular episode is incomplete, the historical record on student response in general makes one thing abundantly clear: students, often in collaboration with their parents, frequently went to great lengths to resist. In this chapter, I explore the manner, extent, and motivation for such a response.[5]

PARENTS' OPPOSITION TO BOARDING SCHOOLS

The opposition of Indian parents to white schooling was both deeply felt and widespread. "The Indians have a prejudice against schools," the agent at Sac and Fox Agency reported in 1882, and another agent complained, "The Crows are bitterly opposed to sending their children to school and invent all kinds of excuses to get the children out or keep from sending them." Similarly, the Lemhi in Idaho were said to be "constantly at rebellion against civilizing elements," of which the school was a prime irritant. The problem, the agent lamented, was that the Indians in his charge had "not yet reached that state of civilization to know the advantages of education, and consequently look upon school work with abhorrence." Frustrated over recruitment problems, the superintendent of one school could only conclude that the average Indian had as much regard for education "as a horse does for the Constitution."[6]

When parents refused to enroll their children in school, agents normally resorted to either withholding rations or using the agency police. When one agent at Fort Peck met with resistance, he sent the police to round up the children, denied rations to the parents, and then, to drive the point home, locked several of the most intractable fathers in the agency guardhouse. In any event, the forced procurement of children was usually unpleasant business.[7] In 1886, the agent to the Mescalero Apache reported:

> Everything in the way of persuasion and argument having failed, it became necessary to visit the camps unexpectedly with a detachment of police, and seize such children as were proper and take them away to school, willing or unwilling. Some hurried their children off to the mountains or hid them away in camp, and the police had to chase and capture them like so many wild rabbits. This unusual proceeding created quite an outcry. The men were sullen and muttering, the women loud in their lamentations, and the children almost out of their wits with fright.[8]

Resistance to the annual fall roundup took a number of forms. Most dramatic were those instances when an entire village or tribal faction refused to turn over their children. Sometimes parents simply slipped away from the main camp for several weeks until the pressure for students had let up. Another response was to offer up orphans or children living on the fringe of extended kinship circles. Occasionally, resistance took the form of bargaining. This occurred on those reservations where the school-age population was in excess of dormitory space, thus allowing tribal leaders and agents to negotiate a family quota until the school was filled. In other instances, the whole matter was simply dropped in the lap of tribal policemen, who in turn might put the agonizing question to a mother—Which child to give up, which to hold back? In his memoirs, Frank Mitchell readily admits that he was the first child to be given over because he was the "black sheep" of the family. Indeed, he argues that when Navajo policemen were looking for children, they consciously avoided taking the "prime." Rather, "they took those who were not so intelligent, those the People thought could be spared because of their physical conditions, and those who were not well taken care of."[9]

Even after children were enrolled, parents still found ways to oppose the school. In the face of a particularly obnoxious school policy, or in time of crisis, parents were known to withdraw their children en masse or to encourage runaways. Sending delegations to the agency, drawing up petitions to Washington, and catching the ear of an inspector were other methods of protest. From the Indian Office's point of view, the most insidious form of resistance was the conscious efforts of tribal elders to undermine the school's teachings during vacation periods by enculturating youth in the curriculum of traditional culture, a phenomenon that, it may be remembered, was one of the major reasons for policymakers' preference for off-reservation schools. And finally, after 1893 some parents took full advantage of their legal right to deny the transfer of older students to off-reservation institutions.

What prompted such resistance? In part, the answer lies in the distinction Edward Dozier makes between "forced" and "permissive" acculturation. "The forceful imposition of religion, ideologies and behavior patterns by the dominant society on a subordinate one appears to be met in every case with resistance and rejection," writes Dozier. On the other hand, when cultural interchange takes place free of compulsion in a "permissive contact situation," then "the resultant product is a new cultural whole where the cultural traits of both groups are fused harmoniously in both meaning and form."[10] To be sure, Dozier's distinction overstates the case; forced acculturation need not always result in resistance. Still, the argument is sound in the main. Conquered and colonized, Native Americans were hardly of a mind to view government policies, including that of compulsory education, as benign.

If nothing else, the policy of forced acculturation exacerbated an age-old characteristic of native life, tribal factionalism.[11] "Upon close study," Hamlin Garland observed in 1902,

> each tribe, whether Sioux, or Navajo, or Hopi will be found to be divided, . . . into two parties, the radicals and the conservatives—those who are willing to change, to walk the white man's way; and those who are deeply, sullenly skeptical of all civilizing measures, clinging tenaciously to the traditions and lore of their race. These men are often the strongest and bravest of their tribe, the most dignified and the most intellectual. They represent the spirit that will break but will not bow. And, broadly speaking, they are in the majority. Though in rags, their spirits are unbroken; from the point of view of their sympathizers, they are patriots.[12]

Although Garland's analysis fails to do justice to the complexity of tribal opinion, it does offer a major motivation for resistance, namely, that a significant body of tribal opinion saw white education for what it was: an invitation to cultural suicide. If white teachings were taken to heart, almost every vestige of traditional life would be cast aside. At the very least, whites expected Indians—and here, of course, the extent of the list differed with cultures—to abandon their ancestral gods and ceremonies; redefine the division of labor for the sexes; abolish polygyny; extinguish tribal political structures; squelch traditions of gift giving and communalism; abandon hunting and gathering; and restructure traditional familial and kinship arrangements. Across campfires, tribal elders weighed the issues. And many, like this Papago parent, asked:

> Now, are we a better people than we were years ago when we sang our own songs, when we spoke to the Great Spirit in our own language? We asked then for rain, good health and long life. Now what more do we want? What is that thought so great and so sacred that cannot be expressed in our own language, that we should seek to use the white man's words?[13]

When such attitudes translated into a complete indictment of white ways, the agent's call for students was almost certain to meet with staunch resistance.

But opposition to schools did not always spring from a comprehensive rejection of white ways. It might just as well represent opposition to some selective aspect of the school program: punishing children for speaking their native tongue, pressuring them to convert to Christianity, forcing them to perform manual labor. Especially obnoxious to some was the school's manner of disciplining Indian children, and even more, the practice of dressing and drilling them like soldiers.[14] One of the reasons given by Spotted Tail for withdrawing his children from Carlisle in 1880 was his discovery that Pratt had turned the school into "a soldier's place."[15]

Parents also were certain to dig in their heels if they suspected that a superintendent was unusually mean-spirited. In early 1890, for instance, it appears that one of the major reasons for the Navajos' refusal to fill the agency school at Fort Defiance was the widespread belief that Superintendent G. H. Wadleigh, nicknamed "Billy Goat" by the local Navajos, was mistreating their children. In a special investigation, one Navajo mother testified how her eight-year-old son, Henry, was confined in the school belfry for two days, only to be released in leg irons. In this condition the boy ran away, and his mother found him

> crawling on his hands and knees. His legs were tied up with iron shackles. I picked up and carried him in my arms. When I got my boy home—the Billy Goat came after the boy, and said he wanted to take him to the school again. . . . I told him to take the iron strings off of my son Henry, and I would let him go—he took the iron strings off and left my house returning to the school leaving my son with me, telling me not to tell the agent. Next day I sent the boy back to school—he is there now.[16]

One of the headmen in the area, Sour Water, frankly told the inspector that Billy Goat Wadleigh was a major cause for parents holding back children. "I told Mr. Wadleigh," the old man related, "that we put our children into school to learn to read and write. That we did not want our children whipped. That the school was no jail for them."[17] At the recommendation of the inspector, Wadleigh was eventually removed; meanwhile, the school had received a setback.

Many parents also had suspicions that boarding schools posed a threat to their children's health. When the agent at Uintah went looking for students in 1900, one of the major reasons for opposition was the school's high death rate. Still, by November the school had managed to boost its enrollment to sixty-five. And then, in the words of the agent, "came the catastrophe"—an epidemic of measles. After word reached the villages, parents swooped down upon the school and carried their children off to camp, turning them over to medicine men. Upon hearing that the Indians planned to burn down the school, the agent called in a troop of cavalry. Meanwhile, the school staff listened to the "tom-tom and the barbarous howl of the medicine man at night, and the death wail from the same wickiup in the morning." A few students were coaxed back again and things began to improve until it was announced that the children were to be vaccinated. Not waiting for their parents this time, the frightened students bolted for home, and there they stayed until the year's end.[18]

Parents especially associated off-reservation schools with death. In 1889 Washington received word from Navajo Agency that since two boys of a leading chief had died at Carlisle, "no Navajo will listen to a proposition to send a child of his to an eastern school."[19] By 1891, the Spokane, who had lost sixteen of twenty-one children sent to eastern schools, also were fed up with the idea of off-reservation schools. "I made up mind that my people were right in being afraid to send the children away," one chief declared. "My people do not want to send their children so far away. If I had white people's children I would have put their bodies in a coffin and sent them home so that they could see them, I do not know who did it, but they treated my people as if they were dogs." But then, in reference to an old government promise to build the Spokane their own school, the old man continued: "They should give me that school house. When they buried sixteen of our children they should pay by building a school."[20]

For some parents the distinction between reservation and off-reservation schools was a fundamental one. "Why is it," one Ute parent asked, "that Washington does not build a school-house here, as he agreed to when we sold him our lands in Colorado?" Similarly, at Rosebud, the agent was informed: "We have been promised for a long time by the Great Father that we should have a boarding school at this agency. Why do we not have it? Have such a one built here or at other agencies and we will send our children. We do not want to send our children from home."[21]

The bottom line was that parents resented boarding schools, both reservation and off-reservation, because they severed the most fundamental of human ties: the parent-child bond. The reservation school, by taking the child for months at a time, was bad enough; the off-reservation term of three to five years was an altogether hellish prospect, especially if the child had been shipped off without the parent's consent. "It has been with us like a tree dropping its leaves," one distressed Navajo parent protested in council.

> They fall one by one to the ground until finally the wind sweeps them all away and they are gone forever. . . . The parents of those children who were taken away are crying for them. I had a boy who was taken from this school [Fort Defiance] to Grand Junction. The tears come to our eyes whenever we think of them. I do not know whether my boy is alive or not.[22]

THE CRISIS AT FORT HALL

In 1892 the Indian Office experienced a year of crises. During the course of that year several tribes in the Far West—Navajo, Hopi, Apache, Bannock, Shoshone, and Southern Ute—made a defiant stand against compulsory schooling. Not surprisingly, these acts of resistance came in the last year of Thomas J. Morgan's term as Commissioner of Indian Affairs as that year marked the peak of the government's efforts to enroll children in school. As Morgan soon discovered, it was one thing to convince Congress to build schools but quite another to fill them. In 1892 the question facing Morgan was, In a supreme test of will between the Indian Office and Indian parents, if withdrawing rations and sending out the police failed to accomplish their objective, could his superiors be counted upon to enforce attendance?

The situation was particularly critical at Fort Hall, Idaho, home to nearly a thousand Northern Shoshone and half as many Northern Paiute, called Bannock. Although the reservation had been established in 1867, the Fort Hall Indians had been largely ignored until the early 1880s, when the government began instructing them in agriculture.[23] But plowing the earth did not come easy, especially to the formerly nomadic, buffalo-hunting Bannock. In 1885 the agent concluded that the Bannock were both "intractable and very improvident." Rather than till the soil, they held fast "to the primitive idea that they were not made to work, resisting stubbornly every effort to induce them to improve their condition." The

Shoshone, on the other hand, were making commendable progress at becoming "provident and industrious." Six years later, Inspector Robert Gardner noted the same distinction. Although the Shoshone displayed some disposition to farming, the Bannock largely resisted it. Indeed, "a little moral suasion, and perhaps force may be required to make them settle down, and make homes for themselves." As things stood, the Bannock preferred horse racing and gambling to plowing.[24]

In 1880 the Fort Hall Boarding School opened its doors. Although at first underfunded and too small to offer both an academic and an industrial curriculum, by 1892 the school was reportedly a first-class operation with classroom and dormitory space for 200 students.[25] The problem was enrollment; only 62 students were in attendance. One-half to two-thirds of the Indians at Fort Hall wanted no part of the school, and with this fact in mind, Agent S. J. Fisher, with the help of a school supervisor, began beating the bushes for students in January 1892. Lecturing parents in council and rounding up a few orphans boosted the enrollment to 88, still far below an acceptable figure.[26]

But Fisher pressed ahead, informing Morgan in March that "things are assuming a more serious aspect every day." Fisher reported that he had personally "taken quite a number of school children by force," but it hadn't been easy. On one occasion, he even had been compelled "to choke a so-called chief into subjection" to get hold of his children. The new crisis, Fisher went on, stemmed from the complete breakdown of the police system. In particular, the five Bannock policemen had recently declared in tribal council that they would no longer force parents to give up children. Hearing of this statement, Fisher called the policemen to his office and ordered each one to produce a Bannock child by the end of the week or face dismissal. When no children were brought in, Fisher, true to his word, discharged them. At that point, one of the policemen, who was also a "war chief," announced that no other Bannock would serve on the police force. This proved to be no idle threat, and Fisher could not induce any other Bannock to wear a badge. Meanwhile, their counterparts, the Shoshone policemen, stated flatly that they would not force Bannock children into the school. And so, there were only twelve to fourteen Bannock children in school, and there was no prospect of increasing the number. "As matters now stand," Fisher informed Morgan, "there are but two alternatives. Troops must be sent at once, or it must be admitted that the Bannocks with a few of their Shoshone followers are on top."[27]

Why such opposition to the school? Actually, there appear to have been several reasons. Surely a major factor was the threat that white education posed to traditional ways. In the words of the agent, Fisher, before moving to the reservation, the Bannock had been a "wild, restless, and nomadic" people, and the path to status and manhood had included stealing horses, war, and hunting, certainly not the plow. Hence, "There are a good many Indians on this reservation," proclaimed one observer, "who would much rather see their children with painted faces and decorated with feathers, spending their time in idleness about the camps than attending school."[28]

By 1890 this aversion to the "new way" had intensified because of the ghost dance. Many Indians in the Fort Hall area had been practicing a version of this dance since 1870, and a new "Messiah craze" now increased old revivalistic longings. The ghost dance religion promised much: if the Shoshone and Bannock would but carry out prescribed rituals and remain true to tradition, the white man would vanish, deceased tribesmen would spring to life again, and the hills would be full of deer and buffalo.[29] The impact of the movement on the school was catastrophic. As the school superintendent explained at year's end, when the envisioned paradise failed to arrive in late summer, "the defense of the medicine men was that too many parents were sending their children to the white man's school."[30]

J. S. Leonard, special Indian agent, concurred that the "religious fanaticism" of the ghost dance religion was a primary cause of opposition to the school.

> The medicine men predicted during the winter that great floods would destroy the whites, and curiously enough there have been unprecedented rains this spring, which has so emboldened the most fanatical that they are prepared to resist any efforts to stop the dances, extend farming operations, or to put their children in the school. The coming of the Indians' Messiah, according to the revelations of the medicine men, is conditioned upon the firm resistance to white man's ways. While I am of the opinion that only a few of the whole number would resort to violence, yet a great majority are dominated by the medicine men. Many of those whose children are in school seek to take them out, and no runaway is permitted to return to the school.[31]

A second reason for resistance was the school's poor health record. Indeed, School Superintendent George Gregory, in a letter to Morgan in late 1892, cited the "unusual amount of sickness" and the "large number of deaths" as the primary reasons for parent opposition. In November 1890, scarlet fever had swept through the dormitories, striking down sixty-eight children. During the next two months, eight children died in school and another thirty, removed from the school by their parents, died at home, dropping the enrollment from 105 to 68. And that was not the end of it. In 1892 the agency physician reported that "quite a number of school

children have died during the last year from various diseases but principally consumption." In self-defense, Fisher assured Washington that sani-
tary conditions were excellent. What he failed to mention was what government physicians actually knew to be the case: dormitories were
hotbeds of contagion. Fisher, meanwhile, assessed the situation by saying
that "these Indians are so badly blinded by superstition that it is impossible to reason with them." But such excuses did little to alter the fact that
many of the Indians at Fort Hall viewed the school as a death house.[32]

There is also a third possibility: parents were holding children back in
protest of white encroachment and treaty violations. The Indians at Fort
Hall had much to complain about. In 1888 President Cleveland had
signed a bill negotiated and ratified a year before that sold some 1,600
acres to the Union Pacific for its Pocatello station, where a small but thriving white community had settled on reservation land. The following year
saw implementation of a treaty, originally negotiated in 1880, that sold
some 297,000 acres to whites who had illegally settled on Shoshone-Bannock land. Meanwhile, the Indians harbored grievances over the failure of
the government to keep whites off the reservation. In a petition sent to
Washington in 1895, Shoshone-Bannock chiefs protested the fact that
white farmers were stealing their water, cutting their timber, and home-
steading on reservation land. Although this petition was drafted three
years after the crises of 1892, it surely represented long-standing resentments. Moreover, when Inspector William Jenkin went to investigate
events at Fort Hall in November 1892, his report to Washington made a direct connection between treaty violations by whites and the Indians' resistance to schools. After noting that the Indians pay "no attention to the
treaty clause wherein they agree to send children to school," he observed
that they were quick to "refer to the violations of the treaty by the
whites." Indeed, "they regard themselves as nations, and ask that all obligations beneficial to them be observed, but are not willing to observe
those binding on them." Although Jenkin was clearly unsympathetic to
the Indians' position, it is clear that the Indians believed they had legitimate reasons for complaint.[33]

Finally, the Fort Hall school was hardly a smooth-running educational
machine. Staff turnover was the major problem, and as early as 1885, the
agent complained that he was having "great difficulty" obtaining teachers
"adapted to the work" of teaching Indians. In 1888 another agent confessed that it was a "wonder" how the school could function effectively
"amid the many changes and mutations" in the staff. Indeed, the record
shows that in just two years, eight different men had served in the capacity of superintendent. For the 1887–1888 school year alone, only one of
ten employees served for the complete duration of the term, making effective management impossible.[34]

In 1890 it appeared that John Williams, the new superintendent, might bring some stability to the school. An inspector visiting the agency in November reported that the entire staff was not only of good "moral character" but seemed "capable, efficient and industrious, and taking an interest in the proper discharge of their duties." But any enthusiasm Williams may have had for the job received a crushing blow in January 1891 when the same scarlet fever epidemic that killed some forty schoolchildren struck down the superintendent's own four-year-old daughter, described by a grieving Williams as "the pet of the Indian children and the idol of our home." On January 19, she died, sending Williams into a depressed state that eventually drove him to periodic bouts with alcohol. By April 1892, word of Williams's condition had reached Washington. Knowing that his future employment was hanging by a thread, Williams wrote to Morgan pleading for his job, to avoid, he said, "bringing my little family into disgrace by having a father and husband discharged from the service for intemperance." Williams claimed, "I never tasted stimulants 'till we lost our little girl and with God's help (which I have) I will meet her, before I again touch anything of the kind." Williams claimed to have taken his last drink on April 4. On that date, "I went to my room and made a solemn declaration before my God and Mrs. Williams that I would die before I would use any kind of stimulants for medicine or otherwise. I have kept it and by the grace of God I will keep it 'till I die." So he was throwing himself upon the mercy of the commissioner: "I have sinned against you and merit your rebuke in the severest manner. God has forgiven me, cannot you?"[35]

Morgan could not, and Williams was relieved. What impact, if any, did Williams's problems have on Indian opposition to the school? Probably very little compared to the health issue, but when Superintendent of Indian Schools Merial Dorchester visited Fort Hall in December of the same year, she made special note of the fact that "the lax management of the school under Mr. Williams has left a bad impression on the reservation at large." The most frequently uttered criticism by the Indians was Williams's failure to keep the boys and girls separate from one another, especially after dinner when they were permitted to escape to a thicket of bushes below the school buildings.[36]

Staff problems continued under the next superintendent, G. P. Gregory. By late October 1892, both teachers at the school had resigned. The reasons for the first resignation are not clear, but in the case of Lena M. Tife they are spelled out in an acrimonious letter to Morgan. She had several complaints. In addition to her teaching duties, she had been ordered to go to the girls' dormitory after supper to patrol them by the "flickering light of one tallow candle." One Sunday, she had been forced to lead the pupils in religious singing for an hour, even after "I told Mr. Gregory that I *could* not play the organ and sang too indifferently to lead." All this while other employees—at least one of whom had musical ability—were allowed to lounge about the agency. In addition, she complained that before the break of dawn she was expected to "light up the school house . . . going down alone in the dark." And then there was the question of the laundry. The superintendent "has *compelled* us to let our washing be done by the laundress and Indian girls, though I much preferred mine done in town as I am afraid of catching some 'Indian disease.' "[37]

Particularly noteworthy are Tife's complaints about backbiting factionalism. "Things have been very unpleasant here for some time," she informed Morgan, "owing to the unpleasantness existing between the superintendent and some of his employees." According to Tife, Superintendent Gregory took umbrage at the slightest criticism. Moreover, "he has spies here who tell everything and his idea of 'taking sides' means listening to other pupils' conversations and reporting, a thing which I will not do for $600 a year." The outrageousness of it all! "Mr. Morgan I have not refused to obey a *single* command, have not uttered *one* disrespectful word, *tried* to keep neutral, but *would* not play spy for anyone." And so she was leaving: "I can not live happily in such turmoil."[38]

It is impossible to assess if the Indians were aware of these problems or, for that matter, what they would have made of them. But they offer further evidence that there were various reasons why the Indians at Fort Hall might have chosen to oppose the school.

Meanwhile, Morgan was presented with the problem of how to fill the school.[39] On March 11, 1892, scarcely a week after Agent Fisher had requested troops, Morgan recommended to Secretary of the Interior John Noble that the necessary military support be dispatched to Fort Hall. Noble, in turn, sent the recommendation to President Harrison. In early May, Morgan received the following memorandum from the president: "I do not like to resort to extreme measures in these cases, and hope that this matter can be successfully managed by the agent and his police. Of course, if the resistance to the authority of the agent continues I will reconsider the question."[40]

Morgan was furious, as the whole point of the request was that the agent was not capable of dealing with the situation. But the commissioner refused to give up. Indeed, perhaps in anticipation of Harrison's opposition, Morgan had already dispatched Special Indian Agent J. A. Leonard to Fort Hall to assess the situation. Not surprisingly, Leonard's recommendation was the same as Fisher's: troops were required if the school were to be filled. With this additional support from the field, on June 15, 1892, Morgan requested a second time that Secretary Noble present the issue to the president. Did the president, Morgan asked Noble, really understand the issue? Approximately 100 children at Fort Hall were being kept out of school by parents "under the influence of ignorant medicine men" opposed to all civilized influences. As for the possibility of an actual military clash should soldiers be sent, in all likelihood they would not have to "lift a finger"; a simple show of force would settle the issue. But Morgan's second request failed to get as far as the first. On June 21, Secretary Noble replied that he had chosen not to pass on the recommendation and added this bit of advice, "It will be best, I think, for you not to apply for a military force in the future."[41]

Morgan was astounded. If the situation at Fort Hall had been an isolated instance of Indian defiance, perhaps patience would have been in order, but the Navajo, the Hopi, and the Ute were also creating problems.[42] It was time to make a stand, and if the government would not support him, then the forces of philanthropy must be alerted. In the fall of 1892, before Mohonk and other reform groups, Morgan pounded away at a single theme: the entire civilization program was in jeopardy unless the government renewed its commitment to place all Indian children in school, at gunpoint if need be. At Mohonk, Morgan ended his address by proclaiming, "It *will* be done if public sentiment demands it; it will not be done if public sentiment does not." Mohonk's president, Merrill Gates, immediately jumped to his feet and shouted, "Do it."[43]

Had Morgan not been in the last days of his term, he probably would have resigned. His final annual report, written in November 1892, amounted to a thinly veiled denunciation of the government's inaction. The Indian Office, Morgan wrote, was "confronted with a crisis." Although "the rights of parents" should not be tread on lightly, "I do not believe that Indians like the Bannock and Shoshones at Fort Hall, the Southern Utes in Colorado, the Apaches and Navajos of Arizona—people who, for the most part speak no English, live in squalor and degradation, make little progress from year to year, who are a perpetual source of expense to the Government and a constant menace to thousands of their white neighbors, a hindrance to civilization and a clog on our progress—have any right to forcibly keep their children out of school to grow up like themselves, a race of barbarians and semisavages." But Morgan had been denied soldiers. As things stood: "I have exhausted all the means at my control. Some of the Indians are . . . in a state of open rebellion against our Government. Their agents are powerless; this office is helpless."[44] So ended Morgan's tenure as Indian commissioner.

Meanwhile, the situation at Fort Hall would not go away.[45] The issue finally came to a head in 1897, when a new agent, F. G. Irwin, sent out the police (now back in force) to round up more students. In this case, however, the police proved to be a bit overzealous and brought in a kicking, screaming, fourteen-year-old girl who claimed to be married. The furious husband and several younger men shortly descended upon the school, disarmed and humiliated the police, and left with the grieving bride. The situation grew decidedly worse when a group of old women protested that almost all of the older girls in school were married. Next, a number of Indians began interfering with police attempts to round up students. Agent Irwin then did what Fisher had done five years before: he called for a troop of cavalry. This time, however, the request was granted.[46]

On Sunday, September 26, 1897, some forty-three men of Troop F, Fourth Cavalry, boarded a train at Boise for Fort Hall Agency. A crowd assembled to watch as railroad cars were loaded with baggage, horses, pack mules, thirty days' rations, rifles, and ammunition—200 rounds for each man. "When the train pulled out," a reporter for the *Boise Statesman* recorded, "nearly every member of the departing troop had promised one or more scalps for his friends upon his return." As it turned out, there would be no opportunity for taking scalps. Just as Morgan had predicted, the mere sight of the troops was enough. Some 40 students were collected in a single day, and by year's end, the school boasted an all-time high enrollment of 207 students. After the show of force, Superintendent Hosea Locke reported in 1898, "The opposition soon melted away, and some of the worst Indians seemed reconciled and in favor of the school."[47]

STUDENT RESISTANCE

In spite of the fact that boarding schools were total institutions, their control over students was not absolute. For one thing, weekends and holidays usually allowed some opportunity for relaxation and reflection. Also, boarding schools were hardly impervious to outside influences. At reservation schools, and even a few off-reservation schools, students were permitted to return home in the summer. Scenes of agency life beyond the school fence and visits from parents and relatives also brought relief. To be sure, off-reservation schools were more confining, but students were not entirely cut off from reservation life. Tribal delegations occasionally showed up, and letters between students and parents crisscrossed the miles. Furthermore, outing programs, although hardly a reprieve from white society, also provided a change of scenery and a manner of escape from the grind of institutional life. Finally, in both reservation and off-reservation settings, all students carried within themselves, although in varying degrees, memories and knowledge about traditional lifeways. For all these reasons, many students, even after years of schooling, still possessed the intellectual and psychological resources to assess and respond to the institution that would transform them.

Students resisted for several reasons. First, there was the deep resentment occasioned by the institution itself. The forced separation of parents and children was traumatic for the children, and following that they were thrown into a completely alien environment where strangers (white ones at that) stripped away all exterior indicators of tribal identity, even to the point of changing names. And then there were other adjustments: the constant marching, the regulation of every aspect of daily existence, the humiliating punishments. It is hardly surprising that in the first few days and weeks the tortured sound of grieving children crying themselves to sleep was a regular feature of institutional life. And also the genesis of resistance.

Second, resistance was in part political. For older students especially, it took little imagination to discern that the entire school program constituted an uncompromising hegemonic assault on their cultural identity. As already observed, many Indian parents were quick to see boarding schools as yet another attempt to destroy Indian lifeways. Before leaving their homes, children were surely reminded of this fact. Moreover, once at school the day-to-day message only served to reaffirm parental fears: whether on the drill field or in the classroom, Indian children were expected to look and act like white people. In time, perhaps, they would come to *think* like whites, and for all practical purposes, *be* white. For some students, the curriculum of civilization constituted so much contested territory where textbook lessons on westward expansion and Wednesday night prayer meetings were regarded as invasions of their personal and cultural being. From this perspective, acquiescence was tantamount to racial betrayal.

Finally, resistance can be explained in psychological terms. In the context of severe cultural conflict, students were experiencing education in terms of what anthropologists have come to call "acculturation stress," "cultural discontinuity," and "cognitive dissonance."[48] Especially relevant in this connection is the concept of "cognitive control." According to George Spindler, "each psychocultural system is made up in part of a unique way of viewing, sorting, and synthesizing the things and events believed to exist in the world. This is a cognitive process. Cognitive control is the maintenance of the organization of this process." But what happens in situations involving severe cultural clash? "When divergent cognitive systems confront each other in the perceiving, thinking, and action of members of the confronting cultural systems," Spindler explains, "the need for cognitive control is accentuated because the effectiveness of this control is challenged as well as the very assumptions about reality upon which it is based." Indeed,

Confront a native who is already operating with a complex cognitive system with another that is equally complex and divergent in a conflicting way and the result may be failure—a breakdown in the ability to think at all. His cognitive control may be threatened and disaster face him, for without cognitive control man is doomed. He has no ability to predict, to plan, to choose, to put first things first, to keep his wits about him.

In such situations, the individual may consciously or unconsciously attempt to "exclude" the source of this discontinuity from his mind altogether.[49] He might, in fact, choose the path of resistance.

How did students resist? Some chose the path of escape and ran away. The situation facing Superintendent George Scott at Fort Stevenson, Dakota, was typical. In 1886 Scott explained the school's low enrollment by citing his Sioux boys' "pernicious habit of running away." A year later he was still plagued with the same problem: "An Indian child will run away whenever the roving disposition seizes it." In this instance, escape happened to be quite easy because of a nearby swamp. Once the runaway reached this point, "all hope is lost in catching them until they arrive at the agency." Scott surmised that the only way to prevent escape would be to construct a high wall around the entire school, and even then, sentinels would have to be posted.[50]

But even walls, gates, barred windows, and padlocked doors could not hold the determined runaway. The promise of freedom and the pull of family were simply too strong. For some students the desire to attend a tribal ceremony supplied the necessary motivation. Students learned the time and whereabouts of these events in various ways: a surreptitious message from a relative; the glow of firelight in the distant sky; the sound of drums reverberating against the mountains. Thus, in 1891 the agent to the Omaha and the Winnebago was angered over the fact that parents were in the habit of giving "notice of the time of dances and their whereabouts to the pupils." Several years later the situation had not improved. This time it was the complaint that the "Omahas have been so continuously engaged in dancing, feasting, racing, and similar pastimes during the past year that it has been impossible to secure large boys who would be desirable apprentices in the shops." A few large boys had been enrolled in the winter months, "but as soon as the 'tom-toms' summoning the people to the feasts and dances sounded on the neighboring hills in the spring," the boys were gone.[51]

Runaways were a problem for off-reservation schools as well. Chilocco records indicate that in a four-month period in 1927 the desertion rate was 111 boys and 18 girls. Minnie Jenkins recalls that during her year at Fort Mohave, "The pupils ran away in droves, the worst offenders being the wee kindergartners." At one point, the problem became so serious that several of the worst offenders were locked in the school jail. And then, Jenkins relates, a most extraordinary thing happened. At breakfast one morning the employees heard a series of loud, crushing blows. Investigating, they discovered the unimaginable: using a large log as a battering ram, the kindergartners who were not locked up had broken through the jail door, and the entire class had headed for the river bottom. Jenkins reports that the school staff could scarcely believe it possible that kindergartners could pull off a jailbreak. But the evidence was there. "At the sturdy jail, there lay the sturdy door, broken from its hinges. There lay the log, a big one, and the many pieces of rope. We were amazed!"[52]

At the Phoenix School, Pima and Papago boys felt the pull of not only their homes but also the pleasures to be enjoyed in a frontier city, which lay, by way of citrus orchards and cow pastures, just three miles south of the school. Although some students occasionally wandered into gambling casinos and houses of prostitution, most simply sought relief from the routine of school life. Peter Blaine, a former Phoenix student, remembers that after the night watchman made his final rounds, some of the older boys would make a "dummy" in their beds out of pillows and sheets and then slip off to the lights of Phoenix. "They weren't mean," Blaine recalls. "They did it just for fun. They would go out, play around." A more dramatic story is the attempt made by a group of Yavapai boys in 1902 to reach their homes in the Verde Valley. The journey involved a hundred-mile trek, some of it over difficult terrain. Remarkably, without food or water and in spite of freezing rain and snow, they made it.[53]

Even Carlisle had its problems. In 1901, Pratt reported that of the 114 boys discharged that year, 45 were dropped for running away. The vast majority of this group were characterized as "chronic runners." Tracing the history of several of these offenders, Pratt came to the conclusion that many in fact had been "educated to run away" while attending reservation schools. Because "no material punishment is attached to running away from these schools, it comes to be for the boy only a nice little lark." In short, Carlisle and other institutions would have had fewer problems of this kind if reservation superintendents were tougher.[54] Pratt's charges were, of course, grossly exaggerated. The historical evidence would suggest quite the opposite, that superintendents resorted to all sorts of measures—strapping, confinement, and public humiliation—whatever it took to convince runaways to remain in school.

At reservation schools probably the most effective deterrent to desertion, beyond the student's fear of getting lost or being attacked by a wild animal, was his knowledge that he would probably be captured before ever reaching his destination. In this connection the ability and loyalty of agency police were vital to keeping the problem under control. Indian police were usually excellent trackers; they often knew the runaway's family and could therefore anticipate the direction of flight; and finally, they knew the country, the canyons and hollows where a child might get lost or hide. On the other hand, when the police were unreliable, the superintendent had a much tougher time of it. Consider this episode that Helen Sekaquaptewa witnessed at Keams Canyon.

> One Saturday morning when we were out on the playground, our attention was drawn to the yard of the main office where many Navajos, among them many policemen, had ridden up on horses. We could not hear them but concluded they were talking loud, because of the violent gesturing. Then one policeman dismounted and, stepping forward, took off the shirt of his uniform and threw it on the ground at the feet of the Superintendent. Next he stripped off his pants and followed with his cap and belt and gun, and threw them on the ground before the Superintendent. He had other clothes on under his uniform. Then he jumped on his horse and snatched the bridle of an extra horse standing conveniently nearby and went galloping down to the bottom terrace below the school grounds. I had noticed the two Navajo girls sitting on the lowest step of the lowest terrace, each holding in her hand a little kerchief-tied bundle and watching the commotion in front of the main office.

Perhaps the events unfolding were set in motion by a love affair; perhaps in fulfillment of some promise to assist the girls' return to their families. In any event, the two girls were prepared to leave and the policeman was determined to assist them.

> When the policeman started toward the girls, they stood up. He stopped in front of them, took the hand of one girl and helped her mount behind him on the horse, while the second girl leaped to the back of the second horse. We all watched as they raced up the canyon, to freedom? When we turned our eyes back to the group of men the crowd was dispersing. Nobody made any effort to go after the runaways. The Navajo policemen did not want to bring the girls back.[55]

Some students were inveterate runaways. In his autobiography, Jim Whitewolf confesses to running away three times. On the first occasion Whitewolf and two other boys, knowing that their parents were scheduled to receive their beef ration, slipped out of school before breakfast and headed directly to camp in order to watch the "butchering." That evening, Whitewolf voluntarily returned to school whereupon he was given a choice between two punishments: having his palms switched or spending the next day sitting alone in the school chapel. Whitewolf opted for the latter. Three months later, he and two other boys ran away again, this time motivated by the news that there was to be a big "hand game" at camp. The superintendent sent a wagon to bring back the escapees and the choice of punishments was more humiliating: a severe thrashing or working in the girls' laundry for two days. Whitewolf chose the latter:

It was hard work. I had to work at washing dirty socks. There was a Kiowa woman boss there. I wanted to have a good time with those girls in the laundry, but that Kiowa woman boss kept watching me. . . . Every day I had to put on an apron and wash clothes. The girls thus made fun of me. I couldn't help it. Some of those dirty socks and girls' underdrawers sure did stink. I had to help the girls carry out the tubs of dirty water and dump them. That was hard work. Those girls would tease me and say, "We got a boy here who sure can wash good!"[56]

The third occasion had a happier ending. It began when Whitewolf and several others were caught in the stock pens mercilessly chasing the hogs. The boys' punishment was to take a wagon out to the sweet potato patch and load bags of potatoes all day. Fearing that they still would be whipped at day's end, Whitewolf and his fellow pig-chasers lit out for the camps. They eluded the police for two days but on the third were captured and returned to the school. At this point they were assigned to the school farmer, a Mr. Bight, who, under order by the superintendent, put the boys to work hauling dirt. After three days of backbreaking labor, the superintendent appeared on the scene with a strap and directed Bight to give each of the runaways ten licks. Bight refused. "Mr. Bight told him that we boys had worked hard three days and that we were tired. He said he wasn't going to beat us on top of it." In joyous disbelief, Whitewolf watched as the standoff between the superintendent and the farmer quickly degenerated into a full-fledged slugfest. By the time it was over, the superintendent had received a thorough thrashing and was considerably humiliated. Whitewolf never did receive the licking. In fact, the superintendent would soon be dismissed for mistreating his students. Whitewolf, however, had learned his lesson. Partly to please his father, he never ran off again.[57]

But some students never seemed to learn, as indicated by this note from the clerk at Albuquerque Boarding School to the superintendent of Southern Pueblo Agency:

Joseph Siow, age fourteen, a Laguna from Casa Blanca, deserted last night some time after the bed checks were taken. Joseph is a chronic run-a-way, he having deserted several times last year, and if I remember correctly, in order to get him back at one time the ex-governor had to be threatened with a jail sentence if the boy were not brought back. It is my recollection that the father must somewhat aid and abet his continued desertions and it will be very much appreciated if you will take the necessary steps to have this boy brought back immediately to school. The last time he deserted it took us thirty days to get him back and . . . [the] sentence was one day in jail for each day's absence, but he was let out on good behavior in twenty days.[58]

Joseph Siow apparently made it home, safely. Others were not so lucky. In 1891, three Kiowa boys ran away from the boarding school at Anadarko, presumably in response to harsh punishments handed out by one of the teachers. The runaways' destination was a Kiowa camp some thirty miles from the school. Before reaching the camp, however, a severe blizzard struck and all three boys were later found frozen to death. A similar fate awaited Pius Little Bear, age twelve, who in the dead of winter ran away from the school at Cheyenne River in 1903. "Every effort was made to overtake him," the agent later reported, "and I succeeded in getting the two boys who had started with him, but he had wandered from the road and I missed him. He died from cold and exhaustion before being found."[59]

The mystery surrounding several runaways from Grand Junction would never be solved. Originally seven boys ran off. The superintendent apparently did all that could be done, sending trackers into the mountains and telegraphing civil authorities along expected escape routes in hopes of intercepting them. Two of the boys made it back safely to their homes. A third joined the army. As for the remaining four, officials never could account for their whereabouts. It was thought that Arthur Ducat, one of the two who had made it home, might shed some light on the mystery, but all efforts to extract information from him elicited nothing helpful. "Several statements made by him," Washington was informed, "have been followed up and found not to contain one iota of truth." The missing four were never heard from again.[60]

It was partly out of fear for their students' lives that school officials pleaded with students not to run away. Indeed, it was while Gertrude Golden was lecturing her Yuma pupils on the dire misfortunes that could befall a runaway that she violated an old tribal taboo. One of her students had recently run off, and though the boy was found, it was only after suffering from exposure. Not long after, he contracted pneumonia and died. "In attempting to impress the other children with the terrible consequences of running away," Golden relates, "I inadvertently mentioned the fate which had overtaken their playmate. When I mentioned the boy's name, my usually mute, repressed flock broke forth in an indignant hiss, while the whole class cast insulted, angry, outraged looks at me." Shortly, a young girl explained to Golden what she had done. By Yuman custom the names of deceased ones could never be spoken. Presumably, Golden continued to lecture her pupils on the dangers of running away, and indirectly may have even cited the case of the boy in question, but as she makes clear to her readers, out of sympathy for native ways she never again uttered the name of the dead.[61]

A second form of resistance was to set the school on fire. Agent reports make clear that "mysterious" fires were commonplace throughout the school service. The agent at Fort Stevenson, for instance, remarked in 1886 that "fires during the winter months were of frequent occurrence." A few years later the agent at Santee wrote: "The burning of the boarding school and laundry buildings the past spring was a serious loss to the reservation. It still is a mystery how the fire originated in the school room proper." Many such fires can be attributed to shabby construction, outdated heating systems, and sheer carelessness. But not all. In 1899, the agent at Blackfoot Agency informed Washington that "two school boys remembering that when the building burned the previous year several boys were released from further attendance at school, became possessed of the idea that should another building burn the entire school might have a prolonged vacation, started a fire."[62]

Unfortunately, reliable figures on the number of fires, let alone what proportion were acts of arson, are not available. What is certain is that the Indian Office took the problem seriously. Shortly after leaving office, Commissioner Francis E. Leupp confessed that student incendiarism was one of his most worrisome concerns: "Remonstrances, explanations of the perils as well as the wickedness of such actions, and even the ordinary penalties which lay within the power of the teachers to impose, were alike powerless to break up this wanton fancy for the firebrand as a panacea."[63]

In 1897, two Carlisle girls conspired for two weeks on how to burn down the girls' dormitory and nearly succeeded in doing so. Elizabeth Flanders, a Menomini, and Fannie Eaglehorn, a Sioux, carried out their scheme on a Sunday evening. At the sound of the supper bell, the two girls slipped into the reading room, set some newspapers ablaze, and then scurried to join the march to the dining hall. The fire was quickly discovered and squelched, however, and did minimal damage. An hour and a half later they made a second attempt. When the bell rang calling the girls to chapel, the conspirators placed a pillowcase full of paper in an isolated closet filled with dresses, torched the bag, and then hurriedly fell into line for chapel. Fortunately, another girl late for chapel discovered the fire, signaled the alarm, and the building was again saved. Pratt immediately launched an investigation. According to an account of the episode in the *Red Man,* there was so much "indignation" among the other girls that one of the guilty parties was driven to confess. Both eventually pleaded guilty after which Pratt turned them over to local authorities for prosecution. The court in turn sentenced both girls to eighteen months in the penitentiary and issued a $2,000 fine.[64]

The Indian Office dealt with the threat of arson in two ways. The first was to institute safeguards to protect innocent children from injury. The horrific prospect of a throng of panic-stricken students trapped inside a collapsing two-story wooden dormitory engulfed in flames was to be avoided at all costs. By the turn of the century, several preventive measures were in place. At remote schools the first line of defense was to scatter buckets of water throughout the building. Primitive as it was, this policy was credited with preventing numerous minor fires from escalating into major ones. Fire escapes were also a regular feature of dormitory construction, and fire drills were part of every school's institutional life. A circular issued in 1899 directed superintendents that "all pupils from the smallest tot up to the largest should be taught how to march speedily, quietly, and with military precision out of their respective dormitories and rooms . . . whenever the first signal calls them." Given the regimentation of school life, these exercises came easily for students. Indeed, there was collateral value in fire drills: they would give students "the moral qualities of self-control, precision, and obedience to the orders of a superior."[65]

A second remedy was to hand out stiffer punishments to arsonists. Notwithstanding Pratt's stern treatment of Carlisle's two arsonists, it was not until the Leupp administration that the Indian Office decided to prosecute offenders with the full force of the law. The new policy took effect in 1905 when two Menomini girls burned down the reservation boarding school. Indicted and tried, Lizzie Cardish, the principal offender, was sentenced to life imprisonment at Fort Leavenworth, Kansas. By design, the story was widely circulated in school newspapers as a warning to those who might contemplate similar acts. Haskell's *Indian Leader* carried a letter from the commissioner's office stating that "the punishment for the crime was very severe, but it should be a warning to all pupils in Indian schools throughout the United States that this Office will not tolerate crimes of this character."[66]

The message was reinforced two years later when Haskell students read the following item:

On the evening of December 7, an attempt was made by three girls, Angeline M-jes-sepe, Maggie Levier and Lucy E-te-yan, pupils of the Pottawatomie school, to burn the girls' building. During the evening play hour these girls gained access to the sewing room and saturated the floor and clothing with kerosene. The odor of kerosene was detected by the employee in charge and investigation found these girls in bed with matches in their pillows. They made a full confession, stating that about midnight when all were asleep they intended to set the building on fire.

As the article went on to explain, the girls were placed under arrest by the county sheriff and eventually sentenced to a state reform school. The message to be learned from such stories was clear: arsonists would pay a heavy price for their deeds. "The lesson evidently sank into the hearts of our pupils all over the Indian country," Leupp later wrote, "for the riot of incendiarism ceased from that day."[67]

Probably the most pervasive type of resistance is the most difficult to document—passive resistance. Scholars who have examined Indian education in more recent contexts have identified a wide range of student behaviors designed to undermine the schools' objectives: willful acts of defiance, disruptive pranks, "work slow downs," refusing to participate in competitive exercises, and perhaps most common, adopting a general posture of nonresponsiveness.[68] Thus, Estelle Brown describes her students at Crow Creek as so many "mute, graven images," and within a month after her arrival she determined that she was not cut out to teach Indians. "It was not so much an inability to understand their mentality," she writes, "as it was my being unable to cope with their refusal to respond to my efforts."[69]

What Brown and others came to understand was that students, not teachers, often determined the pace of classroom work. Perhaps most unnerving was the students' uncanny ability to dutifully go through the motions of compliance while inwardly resisting the teachers' efforts. When students were most obdurant, teachers could only guess at the thoughts masked by the expressionless faces staring back at them. On one occasion, students volunteered what those thoughts might be. When a group of Navajo students were invited to construct a poem about school, they responded with:

> If I do not believe you
> The things you say,
> Maybe I will not tell you
> That is my way.
>
> Maybe you think I believe you
> That thing you say,
> But always my thoughts stay with me
> My own way.[70]

Students seem to have been endlessly inventive in finding ways of "counting coup" on a system that sought to debase all things Indian. They hatched ingenious plots designed to disrupt school routine and devised pride-enhancing coping strategies that made boarding school life psychologically bearable. For instance, when Lakota girls at Pine Ridge wished to protest some aspect of school policy, they sometimes plucked their eyebrows and braided their hair in the traditional Lakota manner, both expressly forbidden by the school rules. Autobiographical accounts indicate that students feigned illness to miss class, stole food, and on occasion succeeded in bringing a complete halt to the educational program. Francis La Flesche, for instance, describes in his autobiography how he and several conspirators loosened the joints of the stovepipe so that when students marched into class the pipe collapsed, spilling smoke and soot over the desks and floor. Their reward was a "half holiday" from school. In another instance, La Flesche and his Omaha friends strategically sprinkled corn just beyond a weak section of the hog fence and achieved the desired effect. Just as his geography class was in the middle of naming the rivers of South America, the superintendent burst into class crying, "Hurry, boys! The pigs are out and going to the Indians' cornfield!" The rest of the afternoon was spent chasing hogs.[71]

The distinctive method of resistance chosen by the Hopi boys at Keams Canyon came in direct response to the superintendent's order to padlock the dormitory at night to prevent escape. What angered the boys was that the building was without toilet facilities. To urinate the larger boys now had to climb up to the windows, and the smaller ones used knotholes in the plank floors. When warm weather set in, Edmund Nequatewa recalls, "the whole place stunk." Regulating their bowels posed a special problem. Concluding that they would have to choose between not eating supper or defecating on the floor, the older boys decided on a most unique strategy of protest. In Nequatewa's words, they decided "they will just crap all over the floor, which they did." The following morning when a furious disciplinarian asked the guilty parties to step forward, all the "big husky boys" readily identified themselves and announced that messing the dormitory would be a regular practice until the padlocks were removed. The issue was then taken to the superintendent, who, although determined to keep the boys locked up, was willing to meet the protesters halfway by supplying the dormitory with a quantity of buckets. The solution was not what the boys had hoped for but at least they had made their point.[72]

Probably one of the safest ways of fighting back, and one of the most satisfying as well, was to tag a hated school official with an insulting Indian name. If Indians could be renamed by whites according to their fashion, why couldn't whites be renamed, albeit secretly, according to Indian fashion? Frank Mitchell recalls that Navajo students at Fort Defiance named one teacher "Miss Chipmunk" because she was so "mean and skinny," and a particularly ugly woman was called "The Woman Who Makes You Scream." The girls at Phoenix took the process a step further. In this instance the butt of their scorn was the dormitory matron, whose distinguishing trait was her mean-spirited propensity for applying the strap. So the girls began calling her "Ho'ok," the name of a legendary Pima witch. One girl even went so far as to imitate the matron on her nightly bed check. "She tied some large nails together so they would jingle like old Ho'ok's keys. Then she would call out in a nasal tone, 'Girls! girls!' How she giggled when she saw us scattering in every direction like scared rabbits!" A protest ritual of sorts and another small victory.[73]

What is one to make of Chester Yellow Bear's behavior at Wind River Boarding School? As Albert H. Kneale tells the story in his account of his years as an Indian agent, the episode began when Mr. Jones, a teacher for whom students had an intense dislike, complained to Agent Kneale that Yellow Bear had called him "Crazy Jones." Jones demanded retribution. Kneale knew some sort of punishment was called for, and so it was decided that on the following morning at chapel exercises Yellow Bear should publicly apologize for his insolence. When Kneale first confronted the boy with his crime, Yellow Bear remarked, "He don't ought to be so crazy." But Yellow Bear said he would cooperate and apologize. Kneale claims that the boy was "none too bright," so they carefully rehearsed his statement, which consisted of a single sentence, "I am sorry I said Mr. Jones is crazy." On the following morning, Jones was in charge of the exercises and at the prearranged moment called Yellow Bear up front to make his apology. The boy did make his statement, but its form was slightly different from the original. In a loud falsetto voice he expressed what Kneale admits to have been "general sentiment" among the students, "I am sorry Mr. Jones is so crazy." Kneale asserts that the altered statement was purely accidental, that the boy "had not the intelligence" to intentionally alter the words in so subtle a fashion. Perhaps. But the agent may also have underestimated the capacity of Yellow Bear to publicly "count coup" on Mr. Jones.[74]

Yet another form of resistance was to engage in clandestine acts of cultural preservation. There is some evidence to suggest, for instance, that students sometimes went to great pains to instruct one another in the legends, folktales, and stories that they had heard from elders. La Flesche confesses that he and his Omaha friends regularly retreated to a small storeroom, where by candlelight they told stories and ate pemmican secured by secret raids on nearby camps, an old Omaha ritual. Irene Stewart also matter-of-factly remembers, "During evenings we told Navajo stories." One Apache student recalls of his boarding school days: "Even when we were in school we used to think about our own people and our own ways. Someone in the dormitory would start telling a Coyote story.

While it was being told everyone would be quiet. Then, at the end of the story, all would break out laughing." Even at Chilocco, one of the Indian Bureau's largest off-reservation schools, students engaged in all manner of activities the authorities frowned upon but could not prevent. On weekends, holidays, or as part of a late night escape plan, groups of Creek, Choctaw, and Cherokee boys spread out over the school's 8,000 acres, seeking nearby ravines or wooded areas where they gathered in makeshift campsites. Safely away from the school they hunted squirrels and rabbits with bows and arrows, parched stolen corn on dormitory dust pans, and performed variations of the stomp dance around evening campfires. Meanwhile back in the dormitory, Ponca girls sustained their spiritual and emotional needs by carrying out midnight rituals totally antithetical to the school's religious program—peyote meetings.[75]

At Pine Ridge the school playground became the arena for transmitting traditional Lakota ways. Thisba Huston Morgan, a teacher, recalls what a group of girls did with materials salvaged from sewing class—bits of cloth, a little thread, a few needles, some small boxes, and empty spools.

> Thus equipped, following the life patterns they knew, they would set up camps in the several corners of the playground, complete with tepees made of unbleached muslin, about two feet high for the families of Indian dolls made from sticks, covered with brown cloth, with beads for eyes and real hair clipped from their own braids. Their dresses were cut Indian style, decorated with the tiniest of belts and necklaces and moccasins. Wagons would be made of the boxes and spools, to convey them and their belongings when on visits to a camp in a neighboring corner. There a feast would be prepared from scraps brought from the kitchen. One could see as many as fifty tepees at one time. One group would be encamping, another decamping, and another moving their heavy laden wagons. Sometimes another touch of reality would be added to the camp when a travois would be seen near a tepee, a tiny horse or dog, molded from the sticky gumbo with twigs for legs and dried in the sun, would be between the poles.

The teachers chose not to interfere. But Morgan well knew that this was more than idle child's play. For as she goes on to observe, the playground display attracted the curiosity of older Indians just beyond the fence. "Frequently, there could be seen a dozen or more braves squatting on the high ground looking down upon these miniature camps with nostalgic interest. They said it reminded them of their camps in the hills and they would recall their exploits on the Little Big Horn."[76]

Although escape, arson, passive resistance, nicknaming, and cultural maintenance constituted the main lines of resistance, three others deserve mention. The first was not so much a form of resistance as it was a way of manipulating the Indian school bureaucracy, namely, the habit of some students to drift from school to school until they found a location to their liking. Charles Meserve, superintendent at Haskell, was one of the first to spot the phenomenon. "Now and then," he wrote the Indian Office in 1892, "I meet Indian men and women that have spent a term of two or three years in one institution, a like term in another, and a like term in still another, and then wish to enter Haskell." Communication with other superintendents confirmed his suspicion that the problem of the "student tramp"—a term Meserve coined—was a serious one, especially at off-reservation schools where the competition for students was often fierce. One such student was James McCarthy, a Papago who entered Phoenix in 1906. McCarthy was an inveterate runaway and over the course of the next eleven years enrolled himself at Santa Fe, at Phoenix a second time, and finally at Albuquerque, where the Indian Office finally caught up with him and forced him to return to Phoenix—for the third time.[77] By this time the Indian Office had taken measures to control a problem that was clearly getting out of hand. After 1915 a student wishing to transfer from one off-reservation school to another would no longer be permitted to do so without the express recommendation of both the student's former school and the Commissioner of Indian Affairs. Meanwhile, a number of students manipulated the system to their own advantage.[78]

Second, students occasionally sought relief by ingesting substances known for their capacity to produce hallucinations, and even death. Flora Gregg Iliff would never forget the time at Truxton Canyon when she was summoned to the dining room by a frantic matron who reported that the girls assigned to clean-up duty were acting "crazy." Iliff was understandably shocked by the scene before her.

> The twenty girls moved about with a dazed look on their faces, some with arms outstretched, hands groping. Their eyes had the wild glitter and the inability to focus that sometimes characterizes the eyes of the insane. The color had drained from their faces. Habit asserted itself, and some of the girls went about their usual task, trying to remove the dishes from the tables. Their dazed minds could not estimate distances; their shaking hands groped for the dishes, trying to grasp those beyond reach. Bertha, a tall, thin girl, daughter of a chief, carried her dishes to the kitchen sink, washed them, reset the table, then immediately picked up the dishes and went through the same performance, repeating it several times. Dot ran about the dining hall lunging at imaginary mice, then baffled, stared at her empty, trembling hands. Mabel, in a daze, went from one girl to another under

the delusion she was picking lice from their heads and cracking them between her teeth as she had seen a few of the older women do. The matron was frantically trying to learn the cause of the girls' behavior.[79]

An investigation revealed that during noon break the girls had found a patch of wild Jimsonweed in the nearby hills, a plant known by the Walapai for its hallucinogenic properties. The girls recovered, but Iliff was clearly worried when other children began experimenting with the drug. Taken in excess, the plant might cause permanent mental disability. To prevent a wholesale epidemic, immediate action was called for. Iliff lectured students on the poisonous effects of the plant, and the guilty parties were denied special privileges. Meanwhile, the school staff scoured the immediate countryside, destroying any weeds in sight. What finally put an end to the threat, however, was the observed effect on yet another victim, a particularly bright boy named Jim. Always the first to complete his fractions, now he "stood at the blackboard with a pained expression on his once bright and handsome face, trying to force his dull mind to perform tasks to which it was no longer equal."[80]

Why, Iliff asked several of her male students, had they ingested the plant, well-known by their parents to be dangerous? Some responded they had just wanted to experiment, to discover what it was like to "get drunk." But she suspected the explanation given by one of the boys was closer to the truth, that they had eaten the plant "because they were not allowed to hunt rabbits and quail, to climb mountains and to ride their ponies when they pleased." Illif continues, "When confused or angry, the Walapai turned to trickery: the children missed the complete freedom they had enjoyed at home, and this form of revolt gave them a peculiar satisfaction." Fortunately, the devastating effects of the plant on Jim had a profound impact. Several of the boys "forgot their resentment at the loss of their freedom" and willingly joined in the work of destroying nearby plants.[81]

Finally, a few students learned how to exploit the machinery of bureaucratic protest. Consider the case of one Navajo youth saddled with the name of Rip Van Winkle. By 1894, young Van Winkle had been enrolled at the school in Grand Junction, Colorado, for over four years. Taken to Grand Junction without his father's consent, he wanted to come home. Van Winkle initiated the process with a handwritten letter to Edwin H. Plummer, the agent at Fort Defiance. Although the boy's powers of communication were severely limited, the gist of his message is crystal clear.

February 20, 1894

Dear sir:

I am going to write to you this morning I dont like stay here. I want go home. I have stayed here over 4 years and half pretty nearly five years. I want to write the commissioner for me so I can go home. I want to see my folks. I have been here along enough I think so I wish you to write to the commissioner for me. I think you know my grandfather. I can not spell his but I can tell you where he lives. I think you will know him. He lives at foot of the mountains on the road that goes to the saw mill. I wish you would tell I said. If does not who I am tell to ask George Bancroft. He can tell him who I am. Tell him I am not feeling well and want to come home I want to see my grandfather pretty bad. He is getting old and nobody to do his work I think. I think you would not know what tribe I am from. I am from the navajo tribe. I am getting tired of this place and want come home this summer if you will be kind anough to write to Washington for me. If you will I'll obliged most all of the navajo boys want to go home to see their people. They are anxous to go home. That is all for this time. Hoping to hear from you soon.

From you truly

Rip Van Winkle[82]

Just how unhappy the boy was is reflected in a second letter written to his brother a month later.

March 28, 1894

Dear Brother Will Price

I am going to write to you this afternoon. I stay house and three day. I dont feel better every day. I dont think stay here but I like go home this summer. I am very sorry all time and the boys march with the brass band and I think they play pretty good. I wish you would tell my grandfather if you see him. I do not like to stay here because the supertendent don't like the navajo boys. I will ask him if I can go home summer. If he dont let me go, I will run away from him. He told me. He said put me guard house and stay four day said that. if you will write *to me* again.

from your brother

Rip Van Winkle[83]

This second letter was apparently brought to the agent by the boy's father, who also requested that his boy be sent home. Agent Plummer, in complete sympathy with the request, sent both letters on to Washington and recommended the boy's release, which he eventually attained.[84]

Rip Van Winkle succeeded in using the Indian Office's own machinery to gain his freedom. But as is indicated in the letter to his brother, had his request to Plummer failed to gain his release, he was prepared to run away and apparently at one point indicated as much to the superintendent. Van Winkle and his friends may also have engaged in other resistance behaviors: tagged the superintendent who "don't like navajo boys" with a choice nickname; played the role of the stoical Indian; and told coyote stories in the late-night hours. These matters are open to speculation as is this Navajo boy's overall disposition toward white schooling. It is quite possible, for instance, that he genuinely liked boarding school for a time. Or that after returning home for the summer, he enrolled in another school, such as Santa Fe or Albuquerque. If these possibilities seem unlikely, it is only because the full range of ways in which students responded to boarding schools has yet to be examined.

CHAPTER EIGHT

Accommodation

Exactly when Charles Marshall, an eighteen-year-old full-blood Sioux on the Cheyenne River reservation, decided he wanted to attend Hampton Institute is not known. It may very well have been a snap decision, arrived at when he heard that a representative of the school was in the region collecting students. In any event, on the appointed day of departure, Marshall rode some thirty miles to the agency to join a party of recruits. One can only imagine his alarm when he discovered that the group had already departed for the Missouri River where a boat waited to take them south. Remounting, he rode furiously to the river, only to be informed that he didn't have the necessary physician's report. Undaunted, Marshall galloped back to the agency in search of the doctor, who, once located, performed a perfunctory examination. With the examination certificate in hand, fully confident that all obstacles were removed, Marshall rode back again to the river, skidded to a halt in a dust cloud, turned his pony loose, and presented himself to the Hampton recruiter. At this point Marshall was given the devastating news that the doctor had declared him "unsound." Completely distraught, Marshall pleaded to be taken anyway. He *must* go to Hampton, even if it meant dying there. So intense was his appeal that the recruiter finally relented. Marshall remained at Hampton for four years and eventually returned to Cheyenne River as a farmer and stock raiser.[1]

Whereas Marshall's attitude toward school was one of unbridled enthusiasm, that of Charles Eastman was one of tortured ambivalence, partly because of a division of opinion within his family. When the young Lakota ran away from a mission school his grandmother passionately argued against sending him back, saying: "The Great Mystery cannot make a mistake. I say it is against our religion to change the customs that have been practiced by our people ages back—so far back that no one can remember it." Eastman's father, however, believed that the next generation must learn to live alongside whites and that cultural isolation was simply not possible. Finding his father's logic persuasive, Eastman finally agreed to enroll in Santee Indian School. But the doubts remained, and he oscillated between attachment to his Lakota heritage and the pull of the "white man's road" as represented by the school. "At times I felt something of the fascination of the new life," he later recalled, "and again there would arise in me a dogged resistance, and a voice seemed to be saying, 'It is cowardly to depart from the old things.' " At one point Eastman "retired to the woods" to clear his mind.

> When I came back, my heart was strong. I desired to follow the new trail to the end. I knew that, like the little brook, it must lead to larger ones until it became a resistless river, and I shivered to think of it. But again I recalled the teachings of my people, and determined to imitate their undaunted bravery and stoic resignation. However, I was far from having realized the long, tedious years of study and confinement before I could begin to achieve what I had planned.[2]

Eastman was by any standard a remarkable student and later graduated from Boston University's School of Medicine.

If many students resisted the boarding school, others reached an accommodation with it. For some this came in the form of a grudging acceptance of the institutional pressure for compliance, the need to go through the motions and bide one's time until the ordeal was over—resistance in the guise of accommodation. But others, as the instances of Marshall and Eastman suggest, actively cooperated with the institution that would transform them. As illustrated in the discussion that follows, the response of accommodation could take any number of forms, ranging from complete identification with white ways to a pragmatic strategy of cultural adaptation.[3] In any event, learning something about the white man's language and lifeways did not necessitate a wholesale abandonment of one's Indian self. Accommodation was not synonymous with surrender.[4]

MAKING THE CASE FOR EDUCATION

As the Eastman case clearly demonstrates, gaining the children's cooperation was considerably easier when parents were persuaded that schools offered the next generation distinct advantages. Because policymakers and educators clearly understood this they sometimes went to great lengths to convince students that tribal elders were slowly coming around on the education question. As already noted, tribal leadership in fact was often deeply divided on schools. Students knew this, and school officials knew that students knew it. The challenge for educators was to convince students that "progressive chiefs" were carrying the day. And so, school officials searched for ways to manipulate student opinion.

One of the most inventive strategies was to devise fictional accounts of old-time Indians having educational conversion experiences. Consider the three-act play, "Chief Strong Arm's Change of Heart," performed by

Haskell Institute's senior class in 1909.[5] Written by a teacher, the play opens with a nostalgic camp scene where buckskin-clad villagers, to the accompaniment of tom-toms, are joined in traditional dancing and singing. The mood quickly changes as the solemn-looking Chief Strong Arm steps to center stage and delivers a long speech expressing his deep anguish over the plight of his tribe. His people have been robbed of their lands; the bison are gone from the prairies; the children can no longer gain glory on the warpath. He calls a council to consider the future and invites a neighboring tribe, led by Chief Eagle Feather, to join them. In the next scene, Strong Arm speaks to the larger council. Pondering the future, he asks:

> Must we assume the yoke of the toiler?
> Yield without murmur the joys of our past?
> Must we take on the new way of living?
> Join in the struggle for raiment and food?
> Must we now wrestle with earth and with moisture?
> Wearily sow that we may enjoy bread?
> Troubled is Strong Arm, your chief and your brother
> Burdened with sorrow, he shows you his heart.

Eagle Feather is younger and more progressive, and in response to Strong Arm's pessimism, counsels his friend, "We must turn our faces forward." The Indians' only hope, he suggests to Strong Arm, lay with their children.

> I've a son, he now is with us;
> He's been learning at a school;
> Every inch he's as the white man,
> Save in color, still our own.
>
> He will tell you what he's learning,
> He will tell you how to win;
> We are passing as the Indian,
> But we're ever to be men.

Eagle Feather's son, James, then proceeds to tell Strong Arm's people about the faraway school he attends, Haskell, and how he is learning the skills necessary for survival. Similar sentiments are expressed by a young woman who is also attending school, Margret Shining Eyes. So persuasive are the two Haskell students that Strong Arm consents to let his daughter, Moonbeam, and others join them next fall. But Strong Arm is still suspicious. He promises to visit Haskell in a few months to make sure no harm has come to them. Act I closes as Moonbeam and other children say their tearful farewells as they depart for Haskell.

Act 2 opens with the new recruits arriving at Haskell and adjusting to school life. In rapid succession, snapshots of Haskell life are re-created: upbeat depictions of dormitory life, lawn socials, lighthearted games, and snappy bugle calls. Shortly, Strong Arm arrives for his inspection visit. The chief visits classrooms, observes children learning various trades, and is treated to a quickstep drill routine. The chief is bewildered by much that he sees but cannot help but be impressed with Moonbeam's and the others' enthusiasm and progress. A later scene introduces a note of romance: James Eagle Feather and Margret Shining Eyes have fallen in love, presumably at one of the lawn socials, and they announce that upon graduation, they intend to marry. Act 2 closes with a surprise engagement reception.

Act 3 shifts the story to Chief Eagle Feather's village, where Strong Arm is paying his old friend a visit. James Eagle Feather and his new bride, equipped with their Haskell education, are now living in a modern house in the fashion of whites. Shortly, Moonbeam and Henry Lonewolf, another Haskellite, proclaim that they too are in love and ask for Strong Arm's blessing, which he graciously bestows. It is clear from the couple's manner that they also plan to live like the white man. And so the old chief sees that there is no turning back. The ways of his ancestors will surely pass away altogether. Somehow, the chief is reconciled to this fact, knowing that his people's survival depends upon their joining the white man's march of progress. Flanked by Moonbeam and several of her generation, Strong Arm closes with:

> The past seems lost,
> Far, far away as in the night;
> Alone I seem to stand—
> I find no pathway leading to the light.
>
> But when I turn,
> And look into your faces bright,
> And there behold your joy, your hope,
> My heart is soft and light;
> And Strong Arm yields, yes, yes!
> It must be right.
>
> Now golden sunbeams pierce the gloom,
> A way appears in light;
> A radiance steals into my heart.
> Clearing the darkness from my sight;

I only turn me back to say,
Farewell, O night!

Another example of parental change of heart can be found in William Justin Harsha's short story "Ros-sa-bee's Ruse."[6] In this instance the plot revolves around an Arapaho mother, Ros-sa-bee, being told by the new schoolmaster at the agency that she must send her children to school. Because Ros-sa-bee is a superstitious "squaw," resentful of the changes being forced on the Arapaho, this news is devastating. At the center of her life are her husband, Lame Bird, and her two sons, Hio Bird and Red Bird. The anguish of having to part with the two seven-year-olds is more than she can bear. Ros-sa-bee angrily wonders, "Who is this schoolmaster that he can talk in such a manner? Is he a chief? Has the Great Father set him over our tribe that we must trot after him like dogs?"

Perhaps her husband, who has been at the agency, will bring better news. But Lame Bird arrives only to confirm her worst fears. He has talked with the agent, Johnny Smoker, and the order must be obeyed. Lame Bird laments: "The road of freedom is cut off. We must walk the way of *nea-tha,* the white man. Yes. The last string has been tied on our wrists. Our children must go to school." When Ros-sa-bee protests, Lame Bird adds that Johnny Smoker has threatened to cut off their rations. There is nothing to do but cooperate.

But Ros-sa-bee cannot reconcile herself to the reality that Hio Bird and Red Bird are to be taken from her. And so she devises an ingenious plan to circumvent the agent's dictum, a plan devised from the fact that neither the schoolmaster nor the agent know how many children the couple has and from the fact that the two boys are twins. Ros-sa-bee's ruse comes down to this: she will send both Hio Bird and Red Bird to school, but she will send each one on alternate weeks. While one is in school being made to learn the white man's ways, the other will be at home learning the traditional Arapaho ways. The schoolmaster will never know the difference.

At first it appears that the scheme will work. Hio Bird is sent off to school decked out in his finest Arapaho garb, his long hair tied and adorned with a brilliant feather, his face painted in circles of pink and blue. At week's end the entire family awaits the boy's return and is shocked at his appearance. The long hair, the paint, the beaded buckskin are gone. This leads to a terribly painful moment on the eve of the second boy's departure, since he must be made to look like Hio Bird. And so Ros-sa-bee, with shears in hand, must play the role of the school matron: "Eight black eyes ran with hot tears and four quivering mouths moved in choking agony when the blades of the cruel shears came together through the raven-black hair of the lad." The first crisis passes, Red Bird is sent in Hio Bird's place, and the plan is saved.

At several points, Ros-sa-bee's stratagem is nearly exposed. The young schoolmaster from Boston is puzzled by what he comes to describe as the Indian's "alternating mind," the fact that he retains only that knowledge acquired every other week. At one point Ros-sa-bee paints a red scar on the neck of one boy to match a real one received the week before by his brother. Later, one of the boys is whipped by the schoolmaster (henceforth named "stickmaster") for forgetting a lesson taught the week before. This provocation nearly results in disaster when Ros-sa-bee, who comes to the school to confront the teacher, almost succeeds in plunging a butcher knife into his heart, save for the timely arrival of the agent. What finally exposes all, however, is a totally unexpected development, and one Ros-sa-bee could never have anticipated. As Harsha explains, both boys "fell quite in love with both the school and their teacher. Each would beg to be allowed to take two consecutive weeks, then they united to ask that they might go together."

Ros-sa-bee is at first hurt, then angry, but finally, because of her unbounded love for her two sons, cannot deny their request. Harsha's moral tale ends with Ros-sa-bee attending the school's commencement ceremony. By ones, twos, and threes, students step forward to recite a poem, give a recitation, sing a song.

> Hio Bird spoke a piece; Red Bird sang a song. As each stepped to the platform and stood before the audience in pigeon-toed fright and awkwardness Ros-sa-bee thought she would surely choke with pride. A moral earthquake overturned her soul. Old things passed; all things became new. She did not understand the fine English her boys were using so boldly. She rather thought the simple tune that Red Bird essayed too operatic for reservation use—it was so different from the singing of her fathers. But a great new thought was impressed upon her mind. She gave expression to it that night after supper as they all sat on the ground before the smoldering fire.

Beaming with pride and newfound conviction, Ros-sa-bee announces: "The *neatha's* road has some sense after all, . . . my boys are to be men now, like Johnny Smoker and the stick-master. Yes, the old trails are cut off. We have found a better way."

The Parental Factor

How students viewed such fictional presentations is difficult to say. Although some surely dismissed them for what they were, carefully scripted conversion tales, others were able to see in them an element of logic, a logic born of the fact that in actuality many tribal elders were coming to accept the necessity, even desirability, of children acquiring some schooling. This fact could not help but weigh on their minds and condition their response.

Meanwhile, the Indian Office, fully realizing the value of parental support, did what it could to manufacture it and sometimes with considerable success. One method employed at reservation schools was to encourage parents to visit classrooms to witness their childrens' progress. "The parents came in larger and larger numbers, until there was rarely a day without visitors," Jenkins remarks at one point in her memoirs. They "entered quietly, seated themselves on the floor with their backs to the wall with eyes for no one but their children who had learned to read and write *marks* just as Melicanos [Americans] do."[7]

A second strategy was to involve the tribal community in the school's operation. One of the best examples of this is the arrangement negotiated at Cheyenne and Arapaho Agency in 1893. Under this agreement the agent appointed a board of three school trustees selected from prominent headmen. The board was granted two concessions: they would make periodic inspections of the school, and they would inform the agent of parent complaints. In return, the Indian board agreed to support the school superintendent in his exercise of authority over students, to report all the names of parents who failed to send their children to school, to assist the agent in the return of all runaways, and to encourage parents to voluntarily return children to school at the end of summer vacation. Although some agents were loath to give up any authority, a few realized that in the long run involving tribal leaders made their job much easier. If nothing else, it sent a powerful message to students—namely, that their parents were fully implicated in the school's efforts to educate them.[8]

Probably the most effective way of securing support was to bring selected tribal leaders east by railroad so they could see for themselves the geographical scope of the nation's industrial and material might.[9] A classic example of this technique occurred in 1893, when the Navajo agent Lt. Edwin Plummer conceived of the idea of taking a group of conservative-minded Navajos east "for the purpose of seeing something of the educational methods of Americans, and the power, extent and advantages of civilization." Plummer proposed that the Navajos be selected from those Indians "living most remote from civilization and from those opposed to adopting civilized modes of living and the educational advantages offered for their children." In a letter to Herbert Welsh, Plummer explained that some of the younger Navajo men were "rebelling against and opposing the efforts to educate and civilize the children, and . . . think that they are stronger than the whites." The proposed trip would presumably dispel any such illusions. As it turned out, Plummer was unable to raise suffi-

Family photograph, Fort Yuma Reservation, Arizona, ca. 1890. (Courtesy of the Arizona Historical Society Library)

cient funds to take the group as far as Washington, but he could do the next best thing; he could give them a splendid dose of civilization in Chicago. What better way of exposing these Indians to the wonders of civilization than by treating them to that grand spectacle of the age of progress, the World's Columbian Exposition?[10]

It all went as planned, and on October 13, Plummer's party left Gallup, New Mexico. Included in the group were eleven men and three school-children. After the train passed through Kansas City, three of the headmen asked to speak to Plummer. As Plummer later recounted, the delegation told him "they had always supposed that they knew all about the country we were traveling through from their ancestors, but that they now saw that they were mistaken." Before traveling east, they explained, they had "supposed that there were very few white men in that part of the country, but they saw that it was full of them." If the journey by train impressed the Navajo with the geographical expanse of white society, the World's Columbian Exposition in Chicago impressed them with its power.[11]

Camping on the fairgrounds, the Indians spent days taking in the sights and sounds of one of the major cultural events of the nineteenth century, a nationalistic and gaudy display of American materialism and utopian yearnings. Highlights of the visit included tours of the great "White City," testimony to man's cultural and technological achievements, and the mile-long "Midway Plaisance," which included cultural exhibits laid out sequentially to represent mankind's evolutionary progress from savagism to civilization. Here the Navajo surely took note of the fact that the location of the Indian villages clearly depicted Native Americans as representative of man's earlier stages in social evolution. Elsewhere on the fairgrounds, the Navajo were led to two other exhibits, one by the Indian Office and another by Carlisle, each depicting the progress being made by Indians through education. This, of course, was the point of the whole venture: to convince the visiting Navajo that education held the key to their future.[12]

It was a sobering experience. When the group arrived back at the agency, several in the delegation made speeches to a number of Navajo awaiting the sojourners' return. One after another, they related the strange and marvelous sights they had observed and all confessed their conversion on the education question. "I want the people to send their children to school to learn to read and write," one speaker told the crowd. "I want the boys to learn to read and write, so they can deal with [the] white man. I am glad we went to the fair. I never knew how the white people lived until I saw it." Another advised, "No difference how much you love them [children], better let them go to school."[13]

Plummer was convinced the Chicago trip had created a "revolution" in the tribe's attitude toward schools. In February 1894, he wrote Welsh that the enrollment at Fort Defiance was now up to 148, nearly double what it had been the year before. Once more parents were voluntarily enrolling their children in school and were returning them when they ran away.[14] Although Plummer's optimism was surely exaggerated, it was not entirely unfounded. Minnie Jenkins, who was teaching at Blue Canyon six years later, tells how one day a Navajo parent strode into class and began lecturing students—on what subject she was not sure. The only words she could catch in the flood of Navajo were "Fort Defiance," "Chicago," "Wash'ton," and "Great Father." Later, a translation revealed that this parent had taken it upon himself to admonish students on the necessity of education and in the process had made special note of what tribal elders had seen at the great "White City" in Chicago. Plummer's plan was still paying dividends.[15]

Tribal delegations were also frequently invited to visit off-reservation schools. By the early 1880s, Pueblo, Ojibway, Crow, Shoshone, Bannock, Cheyenne, Arapaho, and Lakota delegations had all visited either Carlisle or Hampton.[16] Such visits not only had the effect of building support among tribal leaders, but they also offered a splendid opportunity to parade noted chiefs before student assemblies where they could give ringing endorsements of the school program. One Lakota chief, Like-the-Bear, stood before students and said to Armstrong: "I see you are making brains for my children; you are making eyes for them so they can see well. That is what I reach out to the Great Spirit for." On another occasion, a Lakota chief, Wizi, said at Hampton:

Looking at our children here, I think how sometimes I put seeds into the ground. If I don't see them growing after a time I feel uneasy. Then I look again, and if I see them sprouting, I feel glad. so I feel about our children. I see the seed is growing here now, and by and by it will do good among my own people.[17]

Even better known chiefs frequently admonished students to learn all they could while at school. When speaking at Hampton in 1883, Red Cloud, once a symbol of Indian resistance, made note of Armstrong's presence by saying, "You see that man standing there—who has charge of you. I want you to listen to all he says. He has brains, he has eyes, he will take good care of you. I like all his work, and I am very glad to see it." When Armstrong asked through an interpreter how parents back on the reservation felt about Hampton, the old chief replied: "The Indians love their children but they sent them here, a great ways off, to learn the white man's ways. This shows what we think of it." Similarly, in 1904, Chief Joseph would sit on Carlisle's stage with Gen. Oliver Howard, the chief's adversary in the Nez Percé War, only to say that he was "thankful to know there are some of my children here that are struggling to learn the white man's ways and his books." Even Geronimo was convinced. Speaking at Carlisle he lectured students: "You are here to study, to learn the ways of the white man. Do it well." In reference to Pratt, the legendary Apache added: "Your father is here. Do as he tells you. Obey him as you would your own father . . . obey all his orders. Do as you are told all the time and you won't get hungry."[18]

Such statements on behalf of education were more than stagecraft. This can clearly be seen in the letters that parents, with the aid of the agent or a missionary, wrote to their children away at school. To be sure, superintendents welcomed such communication when it supported the school's interests. Pratt and Armstrong regularly informed parents on the status of their children, sometimes enclosed a photograph, and urged parents to send a word of encouragement to struggling offspring. Many superintendents also required that students write letters home, an exercise usually carried out in English class. Overall, such communication seems to have worked to the school's advantage. This is clearly revealed in an Indian father's response to a letter and photograph sent by Samuel Armstrong:

> MY FRIEND: You got my letter and you answered it, and when I saw your letter my heart was very glad. But when I saw your face in it I was most pleased of all. Then I made a feast and called the parents of the children that had gone to school. They were also very glad, they passed it around and each one gave it a kiss. So now we have all seen you, and it seems as if we can now trust you to take good care of our children. Perhaps you don't know that Indians think of their children a great deal, and don't know how to have them out of their sight one day. So now, my friend, you know how I felt about my two boys, but I can trust you now, anything happens to them I want you to tell me soon. Your friend, FAT MANDAN.[19]

And so the letters fluttered across the miles, from agency to school and back again: from superintendent to parent, student to parent, and from parent to student. "I told you both before you went away how much I wanted you to learn English to read and write like white people," one father wrote his daughter. A father from Crow Creek gave this advice: "Don't run away from school. It will be your own good if you learn. Do all the work they tell you to do, and learn to be a carpenter and a blacksmith. . . . Learn to talk English; don't be ashamed to talk it." Bobtail, a Cheyenne, wrote this to his son: "Those who went to Carlisle are on a good road. I think they will learn English fast and understand the white man's road quick. So they can bring it back to their people."[20]

Two letters from Black Crow at Rosebud to his daughter at Carlisle suggest the mixed feelings that many parents had about their decision to

Bobtail, a Cheyenne, visiting his son at Carlisle, ca. 1880. (Bureau of Indian Affairs photo no. 75–1P-3–44 in the National Archives)

send their children so far away. Shortly after he received a letter in which his daughter expressed her longing for home, Black Crow wrote back: "I think you must be homesick. If this is so, the feeling will soon wear away. I would rather you would stay there and learn; we all want you to learn." Then Black Crow received news, probably in a letter from Pratt, that his daughter was not applying herself. What was the truth of the matter? It was good that his children should learn something of white ways, but had Pratt somehow deceived him? Was his daughter being mistreated? If only his daughter could write like the white man.

My girl I want you to write me yourself. And tell me if you can understand my words yet in English. I am anxious to know if your mind is on what you went to school for. If there is anything there that is not right I want you to notify your father. I think you have a good home—but I think sometimes that some one might abuse you in some way that is why I ask you these questions. So I may know from your own mouth how these things are. I suppose my daughter you have very good clothing and very good bed to sleep in—and I think there are very good white people to look after you—that is what I want to know from you.[21]

But parents could also be stern taskmasters. "You say in your letter that you felt bad because they cut your hair," Cloud Bull wrote to his son. "Never think anything of that kind. You have gone there to learn to be a white man." In a similar vein, Long Face, at Rosebud, wrote his daughter Red Rose:

You wrote me to send you some money and moccasins. By the advice of your teacher I think it is best not to send them, as it makes you think about going down to the town to spend the money, and sell the moccasins, in that way you forget your books and what you went to school for. I want you to learn every day, to listen to what the teacher tells you as that is what I sent you there for.

Also from Rosebud came this father's query: "Why do you ask for moccasins? I sent you there to be like a white girl, and wear shoes."[22]

Some parents lent moral support by describing their own efforts to walk the white man's road. One Lakota, Cloud Shield, wrote to his son away at Carlisle:

I send my picture with this. You see that I [had] my War Jacket on when taken, but I wear white man's clothes [now], and am trying to live and act like white men. . . . All our people are building houses and opening up little farms all over the reservation. You may expect to see a big change when you get back.

Another wrote:

MY DEAR DAUGHTER—Ever since you left me I have worked hard, and put up a good house, and am trying to be civilized like the whites, so you will never hear anything bad from me. When Captain Pratt was here he came to my house, and asked me to let you go to school. I want you to be a good girl and study. I have dropped all the Indian ways, and am getting like a white man, and don't do anything but what the agent tells me. I listen to him. I have always loved you, and it makes me very happy to know that you are learning. I get my friend Big Star to write. If you could read and write, I should be very happy.

Your Father,

BRAVE BULL[23]

Pratt and other superintendents surely appreciated the political value of such letters. To the extent that parents saw the need to learn white ways, so much greater was the school's psychological claim on the students' minds and souls. Thus, Hampton's Indian dormitory supervisor—none other than young Booker T. Washington—delighted in telling readers of the *Southern Workman* how the father of one of the Indian girls, Ziewie, was making remarkable strides toward self-transformation. When Ziewie had left Crow Creek Agency, Washington related, her father, Unapesni, was indistinguishable from countless other long-haired, blanketed Indians clinging to a world that no longer existed. But Ziewie's leaving for school had wrought a miraculous change in the old man. Step by step, he began abandoning traditional Lakota ways for those of the white man. First, Unapesni cut his hair and began wearing "citizen clothes." Then he purchased some goods and opened a small store, which was so successful that he soon had a bank account of $3,000. Next, he abandoned his tepee and built a house, furnishing it in the manner of neighboring white men's houses. Finally, Unapesni changed his name. Translated into English, Unapesni meant "Don't Know How." Unapesni's new name, which he painted on a sign in front of his house, read "D. K. Howe." In Washington's account of the story, he suggested that a more appropriate Indian name for Ziewie's father would be "Do Know How." In any case, "how pleasant it will be for his daughter Ziewie to go back and find her father so far on the road to civilization."[24]

There is no way of knowing whether Washington's description of Unapesni's—or D. K. Howe's—transformation is entirely accurate. Washington claims to have based it on a letter to Hampton written by the agent's wife. Assuming that the story was true, one can only wonder what impact it had on Ziewie, who was undergoing her own transformation at Hampton. Indeed, for Ziewie, and for countless others as well, the knowledge that a significant body of tribal sentiment favored some sort of accommo-

Ziewie, a fifteen-year-old Sioux girl from the Crow Creek Agency, at the time of her arrival at Hampton Institute in 1878. (Courtesy of the Hampton University Archives)

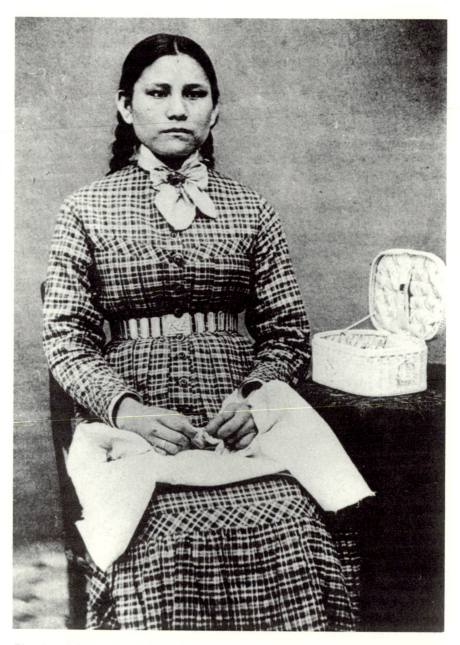

Ziewie, a fifteen-year-old Sioux girl from the Crow Creek Agency, in 1879, four months after her arrival at Hampton Institute. (Courtesy of the Hampton University Archives)

dation with their colonizers must have been a major influence on their own disposition toward schooling.

Yet the question remains: Why did students cooperate as much as they did? Pressure from tribal elders certainly was an important factor, but it does not begin to explain the fact that many students, quite independent of parental influence, not only reached a grudging accommodation with the boarding school but came to see it as a positive experience. This again presents the question: What factors prompted the response of accommodation?

PATTERNS OF ACCOMMODATION

Some students internalized the ideological underpinnings of the school program—the civilization-savagism paradigm. This of course was an extreme form of accommodation, but the evidence suggests that a significant number of students, although certainly a minority, responded to this motivation.[25] In reference to an upcoming celebration of "Indian Citizenship Day," for instance, one Hampton student editorialized that the occasion "gives us the opportunity to reclaim ourselves from an obscure life of barbarism, to climb the ladder of civilization. We rejoice that at last we are emerging from unknown ages of darkness on this great continent, and we are beginning to cooperate in the work which God has intended for all men to do." Much the same sentiment was expressed by another Hampton student: "Christian nations are the greatest—Christian civilization is the greatest. So if we hope to succeed and make our people who are last, among the first, we must carry to them Christian knowledge, Christian example, and Christian civilization."[26]

When students embraced the civilization-savagism dichotomy, it shaped their perspective on the meaning of Indian-white history. Witness this student's interpretation:

Centuries ago we undoubtedly held full control over this fair land— this vast domain from east to west. Bodily we were free to roam, but our freedom of thought lay dormant as we slumbered heavily by the campfires of prosperity. What did the fertile valleys, the rich plain, the mineral treasures concealed in the hillsides mean to us? They simply told us that here was a good hunting ground, and there a good site for temporary habitation. But when the white man came he put everything in a new light. He saw how everything in nature could render him a service. 'Twas not long before we saw his engines making their way across our domains west-ward. Mountains were in his way but he climbed them. Rivers were there, but he crossed them.

When he was killed by our arrows, he as it were, sprang up from his own ashes. He brought with him civilization and freedom. These constituted the power which made him a most formidable adversary. Our wanderings along his track proved a hindrance to his progress and we were driven away until finally we found ourselves penned on reservations with nothing to do and nothing to expect. . . . Since then we have entered upon a stage of civilization which brings with it problems hard for us to handle. This is our past.[27]

Several themes followed from such an analysis. Indians were savages, but, like whites, could climb the ladder of civilization. To accomplish this feat they must sever all ties with the past: their communal lifeways, their barbaric religious rituals, and perhaps most important, their aversion to manual labor. The last point could not be stressed enough. "Work is the birth and civilizer of the human race," proclaimed one Haskellite in a graduation address. And by this measuring stick, "Indians are the most uncivilized race of our land today. Why? For the simple reason they are lacking in knowledge of manual training."[28]

And in their quest for knowledge, one Haskell student explained, Indians must understand that they suffered from a distinct disadvantage.

When the white boy leaves home to attend school, he goes with his work already half prepared, or the fundamental ideas of his education are already laid. His moral education has duly been taken up at his home. These elements of civilization develop as he grows. He goes to school seeking the opportunity to prepare himself for some profession, through which he may conquer the hardships of after-school life. With the Indian it is quite different. He is born a savage, nurtured by superstition in the very midst of ignorance, and he lacks from the first those advantages that his white brother has. He is absolutely bound to the customs and habits which have characterized his people for unknown centuries, and these ways are entirely foreign to conditions of civilization.[29]

Because of the environmental disadvantage, reaching the higher rungs of civilization's ladder would not be easy. "The progress of the Indian is not so rapid as it ought to be," lamented one Lakota boy away at school, "but we cannot expect a whole race to reach the topmost round of civilization in a single generation."[30]

When students were reduced to conceptualizing the history of Indian-white conflict as the conflict between levels of civilization, and then were able to conquer the self-hatred that this conceptualization implied, the motivation to achieve could be intense. "We can take two roads, one where we only pile up decayed things, and the other which is like piling up gold and silver," one Carlisle student wrote his parents. Another wrote, "I expect, mother, you are looking for me to come home this summer, and no doubt you look toward the north where the hill is and wonder if I will come home over it as I used to when I came from school when I was with you." But he would not be coming home, not this year. "Remember," he concluded, "that I am here to learn still better way of the civilized people."[31]

Although some students saw education as a path to civilization, others cooperated for more pragmatic reasons. This pragmatism took several forms. Some pessimistically concluded that the options facing Indians were exactly as policymakers defined them—assimilation or extinction. If the course of Indian-white history taught anything, it was the sobering lesson that whites would never allow Indians to live on their own terms. The buffalo had been exterminated and other subsistence patterns were being seriously threatened. The flood of whites moving west was never ending, and always there was the demand for Indian land and resources. In such a world how could Indians hope to survive unless they recognized their ever-increasing dependency on white society and then adapted somehow to changing circumstances?[32] The agent to the Crows was quick to spot this line of reasoning. The Indians, he noted, "are not slow to realize the changes that are taking place around them and the necessity of their accommodating themselves to the inevitable results effected by the irresistible progress of American genius and industry."[33]

By this line of reasoning, education was essential, not because it facilitated one's climb up the ladder of civilization, but because it ensured racial survival. This logic was clearly at work in "A Sick Indian and His Starved Horse," a fable published by the Society of American Indians, a pan-Indian organization composed largely of former boarding school students. In this imaginary tale a sickly young brave lies stretched out under a tattered canvas tent observing his pony, which is slowly starving to death. His sole possessions are two peyote fans, a few crackers, a little coffee, and a few tins of beef. This pitiful figure, the reader learns, is a school dropout who has a 160-acre allotment, which he has rented out to a white farmer, and also a legal claim to some tribal trust money. But he is unable to collect his allotment rent, and a dishonest agent is cheating him out of his trust money. Thoroughly destitute, he laments:

I am sorry I didn't stay at school longer. . . . I might have learned more so I could have stood on my own feet. I think my education is like my pony out there. He's weak and starved. He couldn't carry me out of danger. He would fall down and the wolves would eat both of us. I have lain here a long time and I have seen the picture of myself well and strong and my horse sleek and full of life. Now if I had stayed at school I would have had an education that would have carried me a long way out of danger; I would have been strong. I would have had a steed that would have won the race to success. Yes, I thought of education that way.

This story was clearly aimed at students and ends with this admonishment:

Remember the young Indian, his tattered tent, his starved pony. Remember he had every capacity for learning and had a fine but undeveloped mind. So he became sick, was cheated and was miserable. Are you going to live that way and allow the wolves to gnaw your ice-chilled bones? Or are you going to help yourself by your own strength and with its over abundance help others also?[34]

Many old and young alike were asking themselves this same question and coming to the same conclusion: education was central to an Indian's future.

This was precisely the argument advanced by Pratt that convinced Spotted Tail to send several children to Carlisle.

Spotted Tail you are a very great man. You are the chief of all these people. You have no education. If you had been educated like the white man you would have known that there was gold in the Black Hills, and might lead all these people to dig it out. If you were all as smart as the white man, you could take care of yourselves, just as the white man does, and would not need an agent. The white man gets ahead of you all the time, because he is educated and you are not. You have to leave your affairs in the hands of the white man, and there are so many changes of your agents you come to grief all the time. The way to avoid that is to become the equal of the white man. You may not greatly change yourself, because you are too old, but your children can easily equal the white man by being educated. You can remember when you did not see a white man out here. You had all this country to yourselves, and you were not disturbed; but the white man is coming on and on, and you cannot help it. He will walk right over you, unless you get up and stand in front of him as his equal. The way to do this is to get his education.[35]

Along similar lines, Luther Standing Bear recalls his father telling him that the Long Knives (whites) "keep coming like flies." His conclusion: "So we will have to learn their ways, in order that we may be able to live with them. You will have to learn all you can, and I will see that your brothers and sisters follow in the path that you are making for them." This statement would prove to be a major factor in Standing Bear's adjustment to school. Similar logic convinced Benjamin Brave to leave Brule country. The Hampton recruiter, Brave later recollected, had pointed across the Missouri to where the growing town of Chamberlain stood. Someday, she forewarned, the prairies would be covered with white farms. "So, my friend," she advised, "if you make up your mind to go with me and learn something about white people's ways, then you will be able to stand and live among this flood."[36] Her argument made sense.

Consider the case of a ten-year-old Maricopa boy, Hezekia, who led a "strike" against speaking English, boldly announcing to his teacher that he saw no need for learning the white man's language. The following dialogue reportedly ensued:

Teacher: Hezekia, can your father talk English?
Hezekia: No, sir.
Teacher: When he wants to write a letter what does he do?
Hezekia: He gets somebody who knows English to write for him.
Teacher: He knows Indian, why don't he write it?
Hezekia: We can't write Indian.
Teacher: Oh, I see; when you get to be a man you want somebody else to write your letter for you?
Hezekia: No, sir (and he began to look abashed).
Teacher: When your father goes to the store to buy something, how does he do if he cannot tell what he wants?
Hezekia: He has somebody talk for him.
Teacher: But if nobody there can talk Indian what can he do?
Hezekia: He points to what he wants.
Teacher: But if he can't see what he wants what does he do?
Hezekia: He don't get it.
Teacher: So you want to do like that when you are a man, do you; have somebody talk for you at the store, or go around pointing to this or that, holding up your fingers to show how many you want and saying "muncha"; then pay for one thing and get your change, and pay for another and get your change—all because you can't count how much they all cost, and being afraid all the time you are being cheated and not getting all you pay for; or have to go away without what you want, all because you cannot talk English like almost everybody around here can do? I don't believe your father and mother want you to do that way, and I can't think you want to do that way yourself.[37]

In the end, Hezekia thought better of his resistance to learning English.

The pragmatic rationale, as this exchange suggests, sometimes had a distinct political edge, the idea that education was an essential weapon in the next generation's defense of tribal interests. It was clearly in this spirit that one Lakota, Robert American Horse, lectured students at Hampton on the need "to learn to do everything well, . . . because we have to live among white people, and the only protection we have is a boundary line." Even more pointed was another Hampton student's address on "The Cheating of the Indians." The basis for Joseph Du Bray's speech was an old tribal legend about a trickster spider who persuaded a group of ducks that if they would dance in a circle with their eyes closed, he would sing them beautiful songs. The ducks fell into the spider's trap—and paid the price. As they danced, the spider killed them, one by one. "So today," Du Bray suggested, "the bad whites are making the Indians dance with their eyes shut, and will take all their land away from them." But there was a solution: "If the Indian is to hold his own, he must fight the white man with his own weapons. They have a sharp weapon, called knowledge. They are fighting the Indians with this knowledge. . . . If we get this weapon of knowledge we shall get along with the white people."[38]

A final version of the pragmatic response can be seen in those students who chose school as a temporary escape from conditions at home. Poor food and clothing, an unhappy family situation (including the prospect of an arranged marriage), the diminished expectations of reservation life, and even the oppressiveness of tribal tradition could induce children to prefer school over camp life. "Hungry children would need little urging to become inmates of boarding schools with well-spread tables," mused Commissioner Price. Similarly, the superintendent at Mescalero Agency was of the opinion that the school's high attendance "must not be attributed to a thirst for knowledge, but rather to a longing for something to eat and wear. The Indians have been on a starvation basis for years." The superintendent at Fort Yuma concurred; the Yumas did not want knowledge so much as food and clothes.[39]

Several autobiographical accounts support this interpretation. In *Apache Odyssey,* Morris Opler's informant recalls: "I had to be caught to go to school. I didn't want to go. But when they got me there, they gave me bread and I liked it pretty well. It was that big white bread. I wanted to stay then." For Don Talayesva, it was the conditions at home that prompted him to reenroll at Keams Canyon. "By the end of summer," he recalls, "I had enough of hoeing weeds and tending sheep. Helping my father was hard work and I thought it was better to be educated." Frank Mitchell also wished to escape distasteful aspects of home life: the traditional Navajo requirement that boys run several miles at sunrise, but also a dreaded uncle who was constantly scolding him. Beyond this, Mitchell was more than a little pleased with the provisions he received at Fort Defiance. "When I entered school there was plenty to eat there, more food than I used to get at home," he recalls. "I was willing to go to school if they were going to feed me like that." Mitchell, moreover, was glad to exchange his old clothing for the standard school allotment. "I was proud to look at the clothes and the shoes, and to walk around in them."[40]

Finally, accommodation was sometimes rooted in the fact that students genuinely came to enjoy school life. Once the trauma of loss, separation, and homesickness faded (for some it never did), children could discover unexpected pleasures in their home away from home. "I enjoyed school and was eager to learn," recalls Helen Sekaquaptewa. "I was a good reader and got good grades. The teachers favored me and whenever visitors came they always called on me to recite."[41] Beyond the joy of learning, there was the sheer adventure of it all. At reservation schools, but especially at off-reservation schools, students were introduced to endless new experiences—the wider world beyond the reservation.

Consider the experience of Albert Yava, a Tewa-Hopi who entered Keams Canyon Boarding School in 1896. It was at Keams Canyon that Yava was introduced to electric lights and steam heat. His transfer to Chilocco brought a series of adventures. First, there was the excitement of the train ride. As the locomotive rolled out of Albuquerque, he ate his first banana. "My banana was sweet inside, but the rind was pretty tough. When I was about half through eating it my brother asked me what I'd done with the peeling. I said, 'What peeling?'" At a layover in Kansas he sat on his first restaurant stool "and kept falling off because I felt like I was still riding and swaying." At the station curio shop he purchased a pair of "specs" and a box of pencils. "I was always curious about specs, and wondered what you could see through them." As for the pencils, he had come to associate them with "being educated." Perhaps the most unforgettable moment was when he was taken into the Chilocco dormitory. What surprised Yava was that most of the other boys were "light skinned." At first Yava thought he was in a white school. "I found out later that they were Indians, all right, but they were Cherokees and other tribes. It was the first time I ever knew that Indians came in different colors." After a period of adjustment, Yava came to like Chilocco; he applied himself to his studies, played football and baseball, and earned money in the summer by thinning beets in Colorado. Thus, even though Yava tells us that his overall motivation to learn sprang from his desire to learn to "cope" with the white man, it is also clear that school was a genuine adventure.[42]

Other students developed a strong affection for their teachers. Even Pratt, the supreme eradicator of all things Indian, frequently evoked feelings of deep respect. In some cases, students were clearly infantized. There is the former student who writes, "I am not a shining star but, Daddy Dear,

I have been plugging along and still climbing to a higher round on the ladder which I hope to surmount some of these days." There is the student who recalls that Pratt "made a fine appearance, especially when we passed in review before him during parades. He was over six feet tall, had broad shoulders, and stood erect. We greatly admired his military bearing." But there was also the Pratt who took a kindly interest in all his charges, the man whose door was always open to a troubled student. Another aspect of Pratt's appeal was spotted by Elaine Goodale during her visit to Carlisle, the fact that he made no allowance "for the Indian boys and girls as *Indians*." According to Goodale: "They are not petted and praised for doing well *considering*. They are expected to do well as a matter of course, without any consideration at all." In short, some students found at least a modicum of self-respect in Pratt's philosophy that Indians were potentially the equal of white men, that civilization was not in the genes.[43]

Pratt was not the only one to evoke such responses. "We had no school last week and I was wishing to go to school all that time," one Haskell student wrote home. "Oh Papa," she continued, "you do not know how much I love my teacher." Another student claimed, "We have the best teacher in Haskell, the best teacher that I have had since I have been going to school." Cut off from family and community, it is understandable that small children developed strong attachments for kind and warmhearted teachers. Thus, shortly after Gertrude Golden transferred schools she received a letter from a former student asking: "How are you getting along these days? Every morning we sing gypsies' song and Concha and Lillie and I always cry. The school room is lonesome without your sweet smiles. I wish I could see you but I cannot get my wish." She continued:

> It is so lonesome over here without your sweet face I just only wish I could see you once more and then I won't wish for anything else. Your room looks so lonesome without you too. All the Home Three girls said hello. We don't have our exercises any more like we used to have. Miss Golden, that drawing always makes me cry. All the crying I did I waste my tears. Sometimes I am thinking about you and I call Miss Phillips Miss Golden.[44]

Because there were many Miss Goldens in the Indian school service it is hardly surprising that some students followed the path of accommodation, even to the point of forging strong affiliative ties with the institution designed to reconstruct their cultural beings. One student at Sherman Institute rhapsodized:

> We pupils come from far and near
> Seeking the knowledge that we find here,

While teachers patiently strive to show
What every pupil will need to know.
To make these moments clear and bright
We each should work with all our might,
And when the time of schooling ends
Will leave us one of Sherman's friends.[45]

THE EFFECTS OF TIME

In explaining the response of accommodation, the factor of time deserves special mention. The years between 1880 and 1920 brought immense changes in Indian lifeways. As acculturative forces took their toll, boarding schools became, if only slightly so, less forbidding arenas for cultural conflict. Moreover, after the first generation of students returned home, the boarding school became a less mysterious institution; veterans of the system could now prepare the next generation for the ordeals that lay ahead. And paradoxically, by the turn of the century, boarding schools had become part of the Indian experience. To be an Indian in white America meant being carried off to a faraway place where the white man cut off your hair, put you in a uniform, and told you that your ancestors were savages. Thus, Lucille Winnie writes in her memoirs that her graduation from Haskell in the 1920s was the fulfillment of her father's dream that she attend the same institution he had attended a generation before.[46]

Time also operated on a psychological level. The days, months, and years at boarding school could fundamentally alter a student's outlook. The story of Irene Stewart, whose early life was spent in the Canyon de Chelly region of the Navajo reservation, clearly illustrates the process.[47] Irene was born in 1907 and given the Navajo name "Goes-to-War-With." At the age of three, after her mother died, Goes-to-War-With was raised by her father and grandmother. Her early life was typically Navajo: hogan life, herding sheep, listening to elders tell the old legends, and learning the ways of Navajo womanhood.

At about the age of six, however, it was time to go to school. Because her grandmother was adamantly opposed to the girl's leaving, her father, who was more agreeable to the idea, informed the agency superintendent that it would be best to send a policeman. And so, Irene recalls, "the policeman took me on horseback all the way to the school at Fort Defiance." Next came the strange new world of the boarding school. "I feared everything, especially the people and the strange facilities." Shortly after entering the girls' dormitory "I was taken to a huge bathtub full of water. I screamed and fought but the big girl in charge was too strong. She got me in and scrubbed me." After this ordeal, Irene was given underwear, a dress, a pair of "strange and heavy" shoes, and a nightgown. That night she slept in a bed for the first time in her life. "There was always someone crying," she remembers. The dormitory was full of homesick children.

The first year at Fort Defiance was difficult. In addition to missing her family, there were the new surroundings, the new clothes, and the new foods. During the winter she came down with pneumonia and was placed in the hospital, where a nurse force-fed her jello. Fortunately, Irene's first teacher was a caring, gentle woman. Still, Irene missed home terribly and looked forward to summer when she could go home. But when her grandmother showed up to take Irene's older sister home, the old woman explained that Irene would have to wait for her father, who was her legal guardian. Irene became hysterical and pleaded to be taken also, and the superintendent finally agreed. Later, Irene was reunited with her father, but when she told him how lonely she was at school, he insisted that she return. "You have no one but me," he emphasized. "Your mother has been dead these three years. Someday you will take advantage of your education."

And so she returned in the fall, in fact every fall for the next five years. There was much to resent: the "no speaking Navajo" rule, the regimentation, the strict teachers, the drudgery of the chorework, the time she was slapped in the face for looking out the window. But Irene had been warned by her father not to run away. A bear or wolf might get her before she reached home. Besides, she would only be brought back, and she knew full well the punishments handed out: she would either be spanked, locked up in the school jail, or forced to walk back and forth in front of the dormitory in boy's clothing. And so she suffered the homesickness, learned her lessons, and obeyed the rules.

But sometime—Stewart thinks it was about fifth grade—she began to discover unexpected joys in school life. She developed a talent for singing, lost some of her shyness, and enjoyed participating in the school holiday programs. She enjoyed the schoolyard games and made many new friends. "By the time I entered fifth grade," she writes, "I had forgotten about my grandmother [now dead] and other relatives. I was no longer always lonesome and homesick. And when I was home on summer vacations, I missed the fun I had at school." On June 2, 1922, Steward graduated from sixth grade.

Nearly all the graduates were persuaded that they should continue their education at an off-reservation school—Albuquerque, Santa Fe, or Haskell. When it came to Stewart's turn to register, only Haskell was open so she took it. The next fall, she and several others piled into an old army truck that took them to Gallup, New Mexico, where they boarded the train for Kansas. "Just before I climbed in, father hugged me and blessed me with his corn pollen. I cried as I took my seat."

Life at Haskell was different from that at Fort Defiance, and Stewart roomed with girls from different tribes. Moreover, by the 1820s Haskell had dramatically liberalized its dress code: fashionable dresses, contemporary hairstyles, and makeup were all permitted. Stewart had her hair cut and styled to look like Clara Bow, complete with "spitcurl." Still, Stewart recalls that her first two years at Haskell were miserable, and she missed home. Indeed, at one point she wrote letters to her uncles, one of whom had accompanied Agent Plummer to the Chicago World's Fair in 1893, asking them to remove her from Haskell. But they only replied that she would eventually get over her homesickness; getting an education was more important. And things did get better. By the third year, "I had begun to like Haskell," Stewart recalls. She made new friends, joined the glee club, and played on the girls' basketball team. Moreover, with new resolve she applied herself to her studies. "Before I knew, the four years were up. I was anxious to go home, and at the same time reluctant to leave Haskell." The superintendent pleaded with her to stay, but Irene decided it was time to return home.

The reunion at Fort Defiance was awkward. Her father appeared much older, so frail in fact that his daughter scarcely recognized him. And the daughter had changed as well: her bobbed hair, her new way of dressing, the subtle little behaviors that came with living among whites. Stewart was confused. Had she done the right thing in coming home? "I felt out of place again. How these sudden changes make a Navajo student feel is only to be understood by one who has experienced them." Later she adds, "The school regimen was hard to break away from; it had left me with problems unsolved." So Stewart made a snap decision. Rather than go home with her father she would stay at the agency for a while, find employment, and return later in the summer. After working for the agent a few weeks doing housecleaning, she did return only to have her worst fears confirmed. "When I had left the Navajo country years before, I felt heartbreak; now I was disappointed in it." Hogan living, Stewart decided, "was not for me."

At the end of the summer she decided to register for Albuquerque Indian School and finish her education. A tonsillitis operation at Fort Defiance weakened her, but "live or die, I was going back to school." Albuquerque turned out to be a disappointment. Unlike Haskell, she found that many students at Albuquerque regularly reverted to their native tongue once beyond the reach of the school staff. Because Stewart was determined to improve her English, she only associated with those who bided by the "no Indian" rule. Graduating from Albuquerque in 1929, she always regretted not having finished at Haskell. "I lost quite a big opportunity by not returning to that fine school."

Several factors seem to have brought about Stewart's change of heart. Certainly one factor was her father's and uncles' belief that she should acquire an education. Another factor seems to have been the futility of escape. "I had known about those girls and boys who had tried running away," she recalls. "Few succeeded. The others were caught and brought back. One boy ran off in mid winter and froze his feet. A girl, caught not far from the school, received a whipping from the head matron." But one also must not underestimate the factor of time, how it slowly wore away at her resentment and eventually dulled her desire to resist. The time factor worked in two ways. On the one hand, it cut her off, at least partially, from crucial aspects of traditional Navajo life. "My attempt to live the traditional Navajo way of life was chopped up with school life," she admits. On the other hand, it allowed Stewart to discover unexpected pleasures of boarding school: new friends, singing, and basketball. Somewhere along the line, she also grew accustomed to modern comforts: electricity, flushing toilets, cooking stoves. She wanted an income and an opportunity to better herself. In short, the years at school had transformed her into something quite different from her former self. But what? Was she totally acculturated to white ways of living and thinking? Not really. As Stewart makes clear in *A Voice from the Tribe*, she remained in touch with her Navajo past and identity, even to the point of rediscovering the pleasures of hogan life.

THE ROLE OF CHOICE

As anthropologists have shown, just as the acculturation process may involve the complete abandonment of one belief system for another, it can also be a selective process of sorting some things out for adoption and others for rejection. Policymakers and school authorities never anticipated that Indian students would be active participants in the acculturation drama. Presumably, the self-evident superiority of white civilization, together with the malleability of youth, were sufficient to guarantee the children's cooperation. But those in the field sometimes admitted the truth of the matter, namely, that the nature of student response was far less predictable than originally assumed. Not only did some students continuously exhibit patterns of resistance, but even those who cooperated often did so on their own terms.

Flora Gregg Illif, superintendent at Truxton Canyon, Arizona, discovered just how complicated the accommodationist response could be when she attended a Walapai curing ceremony. It all began when "Mab," one of her schoolgirls, contracted a bad cough that eventually turned to tuberculosis. Thus afflicted, the girl was soon begging to go home. Illif was without a hospital, so finally gave her consent. In a matter of days, word reached the school that one of the Walapai medicine men was being brought in to work a miracle. Meanwhile, Mab, now failing rapidly and barely coherent, made known her desire for the taste of oranges and crackers, items only available in the school commissary. Illif obliged Mab's father's request without hesitation, and apparently for this reason she and another staff member were allowed to attend the curing session.[48]

Even before reaching the location of the ceremony, Illif could hear the sounds of gourds and chanting. Stepping into the hot, dirt-floored shack she immediately took notice of the emaciated patient, Mab, and the old shaman who was working on her. But she also noticed "Don," the dying girl's brother, who "was one of my most advanced pupils, a large husky lad, fully grown. I saw his face freeze in an expression of hostility. He was a leader at the school and an officer in charge of a company of boys, but, while he conformed to the white man's regulations at the school, he obviously resented any prying on our part into the Indian's way of life. He knew that we had come to witness a ceremony in which we had no confidence."[49]

Illif would never forget what she observed that night. "We were witnessing something beyond our known world." The old shaman, stripped to a loincloth, with trickles of sweat dripping from his limbs and with eyes fixed in an otherworldly trance, chanted and rattled his medicine gourd. The crucial moment came when the old man attempted to literally suck the sickness—the evil spirit—from the girl's chest. "He pressed his thin lips hard against the girl's flesh, making coaxing noises; from his throat came gurgling sounds as if he was swallowing something he had drawn from her emaciated body." But, as Illif was told by a Walapai interpreter, the cure was not going well. Shortly, the shaman enjoined the faithful to help him, desperately pleading for them to join in the singing and shouting: "Drive out these things that make her sick! It is hard, very hard. I cannot do it alone."[50]

Meanwhile, the patient, now near death, turned her head from side to side, breathing with great difficulty. "Nothing they could do to her now could cause suffering. She was beyond the reach of pain." At about 3:00 A.M., Illif became panic-stricken. What if the Walapai faithful, now "possessed by a fury that was beyond my comprehension," should blame the ceremony's failure on the presence of white visitors? This possibility evoked one overwhelming desire—"we wanted just one thing, escape." With hearts thumping, Illif and her companion stepped into the cold mountain air and attempted to appear calm as they made their way back to the school.[51]

Once in the safety of their rooms, Illif reflected upon the night's events. Several scenes were indelibly imprinted on her mind. One was the savage superstition that lay behind the ceremony. Another was the pathetic figure of Mab slipping into death. Still another was the figure of Don, one of her prize students, totally swept up in the emotion of the ritual.

> The muscles of his face were drawn in tight ridges, sweat rolled down his cheeks and dripped from his chin; his eyes were those of an Indian, a fanatical Indian, straining with all that was in him to lay hands on that magic power. He would support with the last breath of his life that thin, mummified zealot that sucked and gurgled and screamed in a wild frenzy. And I wondered: "tomorrow will he stand in front of his company at school and give his commands to his boys? Will he sit at the head of his table in the dining room and help serve the younger children? Tonight he is steeped in Indian tradition. Can he change by the time the breakfast bell rings in the morning?"[52]

The answer came the next morning when Don, "red-eyed and weary," assumed his usual position as head of his breakfast table. But a deeper question remained. If this seemingly model Indian student was not uncritically absorbing the school's teachings, what exactly was he absorbing? Precisely, what was being selected out for incorporation and for rejection? And were the terms for his accommodation different from the other Walapai? What Iliff seems to have been on the verge of discovering is what the historical record clearly verifies: Indian students were not passive players in the acculturation drama.

On the other hand, the cultural options available to Indians were hardly unlimited. Consider the sketch made by Wohaw, one of Pratt's Kiowa prisoners at Fort Marion. The sketch clearly depicts Indians at a fateful crossroads in history. On one side, below a large bison, are a tepee and bison herd, symbolizing the traditional life of a nomadic hunter. By contrast, on the figure's left side, the artist has drawn a spotted cow, a farmhouse, and sections of plowed earth, representing a life of stationary agrarianism and stock raising. It is clear that Wohaw has chosen this second way of life. With his face turned to the spotted cow, he literally has planted his foot on the white man's path. There are no clues as to the reasons for his choice. Does he view white ways as superior to the old Kiowa ways? Or is it merely an acknowledgment of the fact that much of the old Kiowa life will soon vanish altogether, a coming to terms with Pratt's insistence that the only alternative to assimilation was racial extinction?

Whatever the reasons, Wohaw's sketch is a stunning portrayal by one Indian of the life choices ahead of him. But it is also important to realize that this depiction only represents Wohaw's thinking at a particular point

Wohaw's sketch, 1877. (Courtesy of the Missouri Historical Society)

in time, during his incarceration at Fort Marion. Indeed, scattered records suggest that the life choices made by Wohaw after he returned to Kiowa country were not as one-directional as his prison sketch would indicate. Although it is true that at various periods he attended school, worked as a policeman, farmed an allotment, raised stock, and educated his children—all consistent with the new way—this was only the half of it. In later years, to Pratt's great disappointment, Wohaw also took up the ghost dance, and eventually, the peyote religion.[53]

As the case of Wohaw suggests, any analysis of student response cannot be restricted to the years of school attendance. Pratt and the Indian Office always understood that the ultimate test of the boarding school, especially the off-reservation model, was whether its graduates would live up to policymakers' expectations. And in this hope is the genesis of one of the most heated and perplexing controversies of the day, the so-called returned student problem.

PART FOUR

Causatum

CHAPTER NINE

Home

The final week of school was both hectic and exciting. So much to do. The packing of the trunks, the last-minute purchases in town, the long farewells. Some students no doubt marked the final days and hours by counting down the small rituals that had regulated their lives: the last bugle call, the last morning inspection, the last prayer service, the last forbidden late-night dormitory talk session. And then there were all the preparations for the going-away ceremony: the construction of the reviewing stand, the pressing of dresses and uniforms, the polishing of band instruments, the manicuring of the school lawn, the setting up of exhibits. Slowly, the days and hours fell away, the anticipated event nearly at hand. It was only fitting that the long ordeal should culminate in one final act of splendiferous ritual.

"Never in the history of Haskell," proclaimed the *Indian Leader,* "has there been a more beautiful commencement day than June 25, 1902." The day began with guests strolling through classrooms and corridors, where hundreds of exhibits displayed specimens of student accomplishment, ranging from hem-stitched flannel shirts and crocheted napkins to bridles and harnesses. Later, in the school chapel, on a stage adorned with potted palms, delicate ferns, and dozens of flower blossoms, the official program unfolded. At this commencement, State Superintendent Frank Nelson lectured graduates on the prerequisites of "correct living." H. B. Peairs, Haskell's superintendent, spoke next and addressed what he presumed were the inner thoughts of home-goers, their fear of failure. Instead of asking themselves, "If I succeed" or "If I find work," Peairs advised graduates that they should be thinking, "I WILL succeed, I WILL find work." Graduates then stepped forward to deliver their orations on "The Value of Domestic Training" and "Emancipation Through Work." Interspersed with all the orations were several musical numbers, including a girls' vocal quartet rendition of "Welcome Primrose Flower" and a mixed chorus performance of "The Nightingale and the Rose." Finally, Superintendent Peairs handed out the diplomas.[1]

In the early evening hours, guests were directed to the marching field to witness a display of drill routines. With students in company formation, the Haskell band struck up a lively marching tune, whereupon, according to the Lawrence *Journal,* "The evolutions of a battalion were gone through with a military precision that was beautiful to see, and that brought round after round of cheers as the boys and girls passed the reviewing stand." Next, the crowd was treated to a drill contest between four of the boys' companies, with the prize being awarded to the smallest company—"the little tots"—who for their age went through their routines with remarkable discipline and poise. Not to be surpassed, sixty girls then entered the field for a demonstration in club drilling. "The swinging of the clubs in unison as the band played, the harmony of the dark skirts and light waists worn by the participating young women, the gay crowd of spectators, all combined to make the scene one of rare beauty."[2]

Clearly, such carefully orchestrated ceremonies were designed to strengthen support for Indian education among white citizenry. But there was also a more profound purpose to commencement rituals: it was the last opportunity to impress upon graduates the deep meaning of their school experience. Two themes permeated commencement rhetoric. The first was transformation; Indians had arrived in a state of savagism but now returned thoroughly civilized. This had been the school's quintessential mission. "The Indian is DEAD in you," Reverend J. A. Lippincott proclaimed at one Carlisle commencement. "Let all that is Indian within you die! . . . You cannot become truly American citizens, industrious, intelligent, cultured, civilized until the INDIAN within you is DEAD." Pratt was so impressed with the reverend's remarks that he immediately jumped to his feet to add the postscript: "I never fired a bigger shot and never hit the bull's eye more center."[3]

Second, commencement offered a ceremonially sanctified opportunity for passing on philosophical truisms and heartfelt advice. As speaker after speaker emphasized, the travails ahead would be numerous. Only moral courage, stiff backbones, and right attitudes could carry the day. Thus, Commissioner Morgan lectured a group of Carlisle graduates, "If you insist and overcome temptation, you will be rewarded with victory; if you yield to it, it will sweep you to destruction, as it has tens of thousands of white boys and girls." The secret was to adhere to those values that had been at the center of the school's program: piety, frugality, honesty, and industry. Such time-honored values had raised them out of savagery; if cherished, the same values would keep them from slipping back. Whatever home-goers did, they should not make the mistake of letting down. There would be a natural temptation, Pratt warned one graduating class, to spend their personal savings on new clothes and to celebrate homecoming with several days of relaxation. The boys "will want to wear a flashy necktie with a pin in it, and make a splurge; and the girls of course will want an extra ribbon in their hair, a ring or two, a dress with tucks and frills, and other embellishments." Such self-indulgence, Pratt thundered, was sheer nonsense, the sure path to self-destruction and disgrace. No, the path to success began elsewhere.

> Begin immediately! Work first and visit when work is done. . . . Take hold of the work that lies next you. You don't need to go to the agent and ask him to give you something to do. Work for all you can get, but WORK. Work for nothing rather than not work. You can work your way up and out, but you can't PLAY your way up and out, you can't IDLE your way up and out.[4]

Students were going home, and the great question was about to be answered: Would returned students serve as a vanguard for progress and civilization or would they sink once again into the morass of self-destructive tribalism? Policymakers were worried on two accounts in this regard. Some feared that students, although genuinely converted to civilized ideals, would succumb to the countervailing influence of traditionals. What would happen, for instance, to Ralph Feather, who, after three years at Carlisle, was moved to write home; "Father, I think of you all, but I don't like your Indian ways, because you don't know the good ways, also you don't know good many things." How would this high-spirited Dakota boy fare once thrown back into the Indian camp? As Margaret Napawat, a Kiowa at Carlisle, wrote in her graduating essay: "Think of all the temptations and influence of my people I have to face. This is the commencement of a hard life for me. Alone, in the midst of wickedness I have to struggle. Will you blame me if I fail." The issue of blame aside, that question spoke to reformers' darkest fears.[5]

Even more sobering was a second prospect, that the school experience had succeeded only in changing a student's outer appearance, that under the veneer of civilization still beat an Indian heart. Clark Wissler wondered as much when comparing a set of ubiquitous "before" and "after" photographs shown by an enthusiastic schoolmaster. In the first instance a student was shown as he arrived, the epitome of the young warrior—painted face, braided hair, decorated with eagle feathers, and beaded buckskins and moccasins. The second photo presented an image altogether different, the archetypal reconstructed Indian—short-cropped hair, black suit, stiff collar, and oversized necktie. Here was the proof, the schoolmaster offered, of the school's great accomplishment. But Wissler, who had seen much of Indian life, was not convinced that the two images told the whole story. "I secretly suspected that there was still a pagan heart concealed by those plain black clothes and that if the boy lived to return to the reservation he would let his hair grow long, own a beaded shirt and a blanket, and on occasion pray to the pagan gods of his tribe."[6]

In any event, the moment of truth was at hand.[7]

Homecomings and Reservation Realities

As they told the story at Warm Springs, a boy of fifteen had left the reservation for the school at Forest Grove looking every inch a wild Indian, dressed in moccasins, a filthy trade blanket, and shoulder-length hair. Looking much the same, his father, already an old man, came to the agency to bid his son farewell, and before the boy departed, enjoined his son to obey his teachers and to learn something of the white man's ways. There was nothing particularly distinguishing about the scene. Every September there were hundreds of such dramas, heartsick parents and anxious children saying their farewells before the long separation.[8]

Three years passed, the day of homecoming finally at hand. In physical appearance, demeanor, and dress, the figure who stepped off the train bore little resemblance to the boy who had left. In his short haircut and new suit of clothes, the young man of eighteen, now several inches taller, had the erect carriage of one who had spent hundreds of hours on the drill field. Indeed, the boy who had left three years before was so utterly transformed that his father, standing on the station platform among the welcoming crowd, was unable to recognize his own son. Meanwhile, the son excitedly scanned the faces of parents, searching for his father. This search too was in vain, for unknowingly, the old man, in an effort to impress his returning son, also had undergone a major alteration. In his new citizen's suit and short hair, only the holes in his ears and nose bespoke the fact that he once had lived in the fashion of his ancestors. So the father and son looked for each other, the father privately worried that his son had missed his train, the son fearful that his father had fallen ill or, worse yet, was dead. Finally, after several minutes of fruitless searching, each took his separate path back to the agency. Only later, when the two happened upon one another and realized their mistake, did the long-awaited reunion take place.[9]

Assuming that this returned student had genuinely adopted the ways of the white man, the son would find the days ahead considerably easier if blessed with a "progressive" father. Most students, however, would not be so fortunate. Indeed, superintendents worried much about the sort of reception returning students would receive from reservation Indians, particularly those unsympathetic to the school's aims. "If . . . you chiefs when you go back," Pratt lectured a delegation of Sioux chiefs visiting Carlisle, "will go to work and make the Indians stop their dances, change their Indian habits and dress for civilized ones and make different and better surroundings for our returned pupils, the boys and girls . . . will remain as we send them, and be glad to." Whatever Pratt's hopes, the hard truth was that many reservations were bastions of traditionalism or deeply factionalized. For the returning student who, in the words of one agent, "bears the burden of his people's redemption," the challenge was monumental. "We catch him like a wild animal, and, when properly domesticated, throw him back into the jungle to survive."[10]

Although many seem to have made the transition quite easily, the evidence suggests that many others—particularly those committed to living their lives in accordance with school teachings—had a difficult time of it. It was at homecoming that parents and children first came to realize the cultural chasm that now separated them. Imagine the scene of parents dressed in blankets, shawls, and moccasins catching their first glimpse of sons and daughters stepping from the train or wagon dressed in the "latest styles," boys in tailored uniforms or suits and patent leather shoes, girls in store-bought dresses, silken hose, high-heeled shoes, and hats of the "latest creation." Agent Albert Kneale, who observed many such scenes, recalls: "I have seen these girls, when they first cast eyes upon their parents, stare in abject horror, then as the truth dawned upon them, burst into tears. I have seen parents glance fleetingly on these visions of civilized loneliness, then turn away in disgust, returning to their homes, leaving the children to shift for themselves."[11]

This, of course, was an extreme reaction. Most homecomings were touching, affection-filled reunions. Still, as the joy of reacquaintance settled into the routine of daily living, many households became settings for dramas involving deep intergenerational and cultural conflict. Whereas the cultural clash between whites and Indians had once been fought on battlefields and in treaty councils, now it advanced to parent-child disagreements over campfires and across kitchen tables—whether to farm or lease an allotment, whether to boil the dishwater, whether to offer a prayer of thanks for a slain animal's spirit.

Points of contention festered over seemingly minor but telling issues that could turn a harmonious homecoming into a fractious, tension-filled moment. When the differences touched fundamental cultural concerns, families could descend into irreparable conflict. "Why haven't you bought a white man's bed to sleep on?" Polingaysi Qoyawayma remembers asking her Hopi parents after returning from Sherman Institute. "And a table? You should not be eating on a floor as the Old Ones did. When I was a little girl I did not mind sleeping on the floor and eating from a single bowl into which everyone dipped. But I am used to another way of living now, and I do not intend to do these things." This daughter of traditional Hopi parents came home from school with many new ideas. She refused to grind corn in the laborious manner of Hopi women; she used three "precious eggs" to make a white man's cake; she threw valuable apple peelings into the scrap pail while making a pie. Surely these behaviors were irritating but hardly sufficient cause for a family breakup. But Qoyawayma's rejection of Hopi ways was more fundamental. During the kachina homecoming dance, one of the Hopi's most sacred ceremonies, she refused to sit with her parents and eat food "sacrificed to the devil." In a matter of months, to the relief of both her and her parents, she left the village to live with missionaries. As the title to her autobiography conveys, there was *No Turning Back*.[12]

The pressure exerted on returned students could be intense. In some communities, ridicule and ostracization, traditional methods of social control in native society, were unmercifully employed to force returnees back into the tribal fold. "I don't think the Hampton boys are keeping up as they ought to do," one boy wrote Armstrong concerning the situation at Yankton Agency. "They hear the Indians talking around them and they are getting a little down and down." The situation was all the more complex if a student's homecoming reawakened old cultural allegiances. As Thomas Wildcat Alford wrote Armstrong in 1888, "the returned student has still his natural propensities which were only made dormant." Once back in the Indian camp, Alford explained, the advantage in the tug-of-war for the student's soul abruptly shifted from the school to the tribe, "and unless the student has something to do to direct his thoughts, or is uncommonly decided in his convictions . . . no one can fail to see which of these two forces will come out a conqueror."[13]

The interaction of these two factors—the recession of the school's influence and the corresponding increase in that of the reservation environment—are clearly revealed in two areas where returned students sometimes faced almost insurmountable obstacles in their quest to live up to school expectations: their newfound religious convictions and their efforts to become economically self-sufficient.

In the first instance they were clearly waging an uphill battle, the religious crosscurrents in Indian country being multiple and complex. Many students, however, eagerly joined the crusade against "heathenism" in whatever form it manifested itself. One student, still having trouble with English, wrote:

> I work among my people: teach that I learn better life than the old way. When I came back from Hampton. I went out among the camp, and have them sit around me and read the Bible to them. I do that about month. And after that I build log house. We have church every Sunday and meeting in the evening. I put up United States flag. Because I have no bell.

Such proselytizing often bore spiritual fruit. When Fred Big Horse, a former member of Carlisle's Young Men's Christian Association, came upon a band of ghost dancers still suffering from events at Wounded Knee, he took it upon himself to preach to them on "what it meant to worship a true God." And apparently with considerable success. "At first they doubted," Big Horse reported, "but at last, one by one, I won them over to my faith, and then they wanted a church built right away so they could worship on every holy day."[14]

Adherents to native religion of whatever form hardly consumed Christian doctrine uncritically. When former Hampton student Charles Clifford attempted to convince a group of ghost dancers at Pine Ridge that they were following a "false religion," his arguments seemed only to deepen their fervor,

> because when I told them the story of our Savior, they would compare it with the story of their Christ, and say that he is the same Christ come again the second time to save the Indians from the land of bondage, like Moses saved the children of Israel from the land of the Egyptians. They were told by their prophets that this Christ came to whites the first time to prepare them for the life to come, but they despised Him and hung him upon a cross and put Him to death, so he gave up this work among the whites, who are now slowly starving the Indians to death to get them out of their way.

Likewise, Frank Black Hawk had trouble converting the Indians at Standing Rock. As Black Hawk explained in a letter to his school, he preached.

> But they asked me many questions I was not able to answer. Here is some of the questions they asked me. If God made men and women his own image why is it they are so many different colors of nations in the world and why did the white people killed Jesus Christ? You say he was the son of God and could do everything. Why he did not save himself when they was going to kill him? And what is the reason his Father did not save him when he prayed so many times, and so hard? All of these I was not able to answer and many others.[15]

At least Black Hawk and others were allowed the freedom to roam around the agency in search of converts. In those cultures where the social organization was much more close-knit, returning students were almost immediately subjected to a wide range of time-honored practices designed to force wayward villagers into conformity. Students returning to the pueblo villages of New Mexico and Arizona, for instance, endured all manner of publicly sanctioned disciplinary pressures, ranging from social ostracism to public whippings. When Talayesva, recently returned from Sherman Institute, displayed some hesitancy about being initiated into the Wowochim society, one of the primary Hopi religious societies, he was subjected to relentless pressure to fulfill his religious obligations.

> I knew that it was a Hopi rule for boys to take this important step into manhood. Some of my uncles had told me that if I were not initiated, the people would call me a boy all my life. They said that my childish name, Chuka, would stick to me forever and that the girls would not regard me as a man. I was not sure that I wanted to be initiated now, but feared that if I refused all my uncles and relatives would be against me.

Later he says, "I could not put off initiation into the Wowochim." In addition to the urgings from the village war chief, he was constantly being badgered by his mother and father, grandfather, great uncles, ceremonial father, clan father, godmother, and clan mothers. Up against such a formidable group, Talayesva finally relented. Moreover, after his initiation, "I regretted that I had ever joined the Y.M.C.A. [at school] and decided to set myself against Christianity once and for all."[16]

Pueblo students were not the only ones to succumb to community pressure. At Osage Agency, returning Carlisle students faced a difficult choice indeed: either participate in tribal dances or pay the price by giving up a pony or accepting a whipping. According to the agent, many "choose the dance in preference to either of the alternatives." Similarly, when Jason Betzinez returned from Carlisle to the Fort Sill region in 1900, he was disgusted to find many of his Apache classmates half-naked, participating in the medicine dance. Besides finding their behavior religiously reprehensible, Betzinez objected to their participation on health grounds. For one thing, the dance was performed in January and lasted all night, with the consequence that "many of the dancers fell to the ground in a stupor induced by prolonged exertion, self-hypnosis, bad liquor, or a combination. Here they lay for hours before waking." The result was often pneumonia, and the passing of masks from dancer to dancer led to the spread of tuberculosis. Many of the backsliders surely understood this but beyond the reach of the school's influence were unable to resist the temptation to join in. "If you minded your own business and tried to live in the white man's way," Betzinez later recalled, "then the Indians branded you as being some kind of an outcast who no longer loved his own people."[17]

Another area where returned students apparently experienced frustration was in their efforts to attain economic self-sufficiency. The first challenge was to find work. Sometimes students returned to allotments and took up farming, but as many found out, this was often an impractical solution. In some regions the lack of irrigation, poor climate, and absence of "start-up" resources made this a dubious enterprise. Other sources of employment were equally limited. Reservation economies were usually wastelands of opportunity, with a few agency jobs constituting the major source of employment. Off-reservation employment was certainly available in some locales, but the work was often seasonal with the pay low and meant contact with prejudiced whites. Perhaps the greatest shock to returned students was the discovery that their industrial training was almost useless. Few reservation Indians had a crying need for tin spouts, hard-soled shoes, or tailored suits.[18]

Thus, even when students returned to their reservation homes imbued with a desire "to strive and succeed," such good intentions often withered on the hard rock of circumstance. "I have been thinking about the talks you used to give us on Saturday nights about earning our money and living," one student wrote back to Pratt. "I am very thankful to you for all the kindness you have done for me. I am going to stand for Carlisle." And perhaps he did. For others, however, the quest for self-sufficiency was illusive at best. Only a year or so after Quoyonah, one of Pratt's Florida prisoners, was resettled back at Fort Sill, he was reduced to writing Pratt:

> You first taught me the white man's road. I am now very poor and disconsolate. All you gave me is gone, and if you can send me any clothes or something to work in I will be thankful. I have no tools to work with, or plows to work the ground to make corn. Can you send me some? I am again a *Comanche*. I was compelled to go back to the old road, though I did not want to, but I had no pants and had to take leggings. I never have any money, for I cannot earn it *here,* and my heart told me to come to you for help, and perhaps you could send these things to me. I have no piece of ground for my own, and now when I want to work the white man's road and learn it, I have nothing to do it with. I am working first on this man's ground, then on somebody else's, and I am never settled in any place. I have made a great many rails so you see I have not forgotten what you told me. I haven't a horse of my own. I am very poor. When you come to see us I shall have nothing to show you—no corn—no house—nothing at all. A poor county and a bad ground. I don't sleep well. I am afraid.[19]

Another obstacle to self-sufficiency was the traditional Indian ethic of sharing. "With the Indian, he is richest who gives most; with us, it is he who keeps most," mused William Hailmann, Superintendent of Indian Schools, when discussing the problems facing returned students. Although overly simplistic, Hailmann's point touches upon one of the most difficult dilemmas confronting the student saturated in the ideology of rugged individualism. It was one thing at school to memorize the poem, "The Man Who Wins," including the sentiment,

> And the man who wins is the man who hears
> The curse of the envious in his ears,

and quite another to act upon this sentiment after going home.[20]

For one thing, tribal society valued hospitality. "The old Indian instinct of tribal communism and unlimited hospitality is still a great barrier in the way of young people and their prospect of 'getting ahead in the world,'" Cora Folsom observed after visiting several reservations. "No sooner does a young man, or woman, get a good salary than all his relations . . . immediately spring up in poverty and distress, and are really so needy that it requires a strong heart to turn away from them." The temptations to participate in elaborate gift-giving ceremonies, traditional mechanisms for cementing tribal ties and redistributing wealth, constituted another obstacle. Consider Pratt's response to the news that one of his former prisoners, Chief Killer, had celebrated his daughter's homecoming from school in the traditional manner of bestowing gifts.

> I am sorry that you are so foolish as to give away horses and spend money because Maud came home. It is a very foolish Indian way. No man will ever prosper and get rich who does that way. You must not only learn to earn money and increase your cattle, but you must learn to save them. I have always hoped that you would some day be a rich, influential farmer among the Cheyennes, but you never will be, if you throw away what you work for, in that manner.[21]

Chief Killer certainly knew Pratt's views on the subject and may have even subscribed to them, at least while imprisoned at Fort Marion. But living among the Cheyenne again, it was a different matter.

The challenge of economic self-sufficiency fell largely on the shoulders of returning male students. For girls it was how to apply the lessons learned in domestic training class to the primitive conditions of camplife. "I note . . . that you incline to the duties of home making, which is commendable, because there is nothing in the world that helps more to make people happy and progressive than well-ordered, efficient, and refined housekeeping," Commissioner Cato Sells wrote Belle Peniska, a Carlisle graduate, upon her receipt of a certificate of competency. "High-minded, sweet-tempered home-keepers are the bringers of strength and virtue to social welfare. Hold fast to your highest ideals; they will be among your best friends in any work you do." High-sounding rhetoric to be sure, but as many enthusiastic housekeepers discovered, the lessons of domesticity were not easily adapted to dirt-floored tepees and cabins without tables, beds, washtubs, or cooking utensils, innovations often viewed by unsympathetic parents as needless conveniences, inappropriate for Indians. When this reality of homecoming was compounded by others, for instance, the intense pressure to resume tribal dress ("the Indians laugh and make so much fun of us") or the prospect of an arranged marriage, the challenge of living up to "civilized" expectations could be indeed enormous.[22]

Did women have a more difficult time readjusting to reservation life than men? In the long run probably not, at least when viewed through the anthropological lens of "role continuity." In a now classic study of Menomini adaptation to cultural change, Louise and George Spindler argue that acculturating males and females confronted distinctively different challenges in their adjustment to white society. To cite just one example, Menomini males, who historically assumed a major responsibility for earning a livelihood, were now expected to adopt an altogether new set of values and behaviors to fulfill this traditional role: "He must learn to be punctual in his arrivals and departures, and run his daily and weekly cycle by the clock and calendar. He has to learn that accumulation of property and money is the way 'to get ahead.' . . . There are no precedents for these and many other expectations in the traditional pattern of instrumental roles for males in Menomini culture." For Menomini women, on the other hand, basic role expectations—notably those of wives and mother—were relatively unchanged by the assimilationist forces pressing upon Menomini society. Because of this role continuity, the Spindlers hypothesize, Menomini women have not found "the flux and conflict of rapid culture change as disturbing as do the males."[23]

Although the above thesis is entirely plausible in a general way, it still does not alter the fact that males and females alike faced an uphill struggle of monumental proportions. As one girl wrote back to Hampton from somewhere in Montana, "It is so easy for Indian school-boys and girls to say 'I am going back to help my people and teach them the right way to live.' But what a different thing to do it!" Reverend Hollis Frissell, a member of the Hampton staff, got a glimpse of just how difficult it was in 1885 when canvassing Sioux country for more students. Visiting an Indian cemetery, the agency interpreter led Frissell to a Hampton student's grave and, in a tribute of respect, uttered in broken English, "He try hard to walk to white man's way; *Too* hard for him."[24]

Frissell was evidently touched by the episode but remained undaunted in his enthusiasm. This student had "died in the struggle," but others were making it. The year was 1885. The first contingent of Hampton students was back in camps leading their people toward the path of civilized progress. The work of philanthropy was about to gather its harvest.

THE RETURNED-STUDENT QUESTION

In the spring of 1881, Hampton Institute said farewell to one of its favorites. James Bear's Heart, now in his late twenties and one of Pratt's original

"Florida boys," was going home. Here surely was a living embodiment of reformers' vision of the "before" and "after" Indian. As Indian Supervisor Booker T. Washington wrote in the *Southern Workman,* Bear's Heart, before his capture, had been "clad in a blanket and moccasins with his long hair flowing down his back, his ears jingling with ear rings, and his tomahawk and bow and arrows swinging from his side." Now, six years later, "instead of his blanket he wears back a neat suit of the school gray uniform decorated with a sergeant's and color-bearer's stripes. . . . Instead of the tomahawk, he takes back a chest of carpenter's tools; instead of his bow and arrows, he takes the bible and many other good volumes." The newspaper account continued: "His long hair and moccasins he has long since forgotten, and instead of the weak, dirty ignorant price of humanity that he was, with no correct ideas of this life or the next—his only ambition being to fight the white man—he goes back a strong, decent, Christian *man,* with the rudiments of an English education, and hands to earn himself a living at the carpenter's bench or on the farm."[25]

Before departing, Bear's Heart took a few moments to advise Indian students that they should obey their teachers, study their books, and pray to the white man's God. "You must all try for yourselves and learn how to read and write: that is what you all left your homes for; . . . for some people think that Indians can not learn, so I will say once more try hard in your study. I bid farewell to you all." With his trunk packed with gifts for relatives, Bear's Heart left for the Far West. By the end of April, he was back in Indian territory, writing to Armstrong: "My dear friend: —I got home all safe. I was very glad to see my mother and my sister and all my relations. They were glad to see me. All of them well, none have died."[26]

But how would this returned student conduct himself after the initial activities of feasting and gift giving, when the traditional temptations of camp life reasserted themselves? The answer soon came in a letter from Agent John Miles.

> Bear's Heart reached home in due time, and after visiting his friends in camp for a few days *only,* applied at my office for work; said he could not be idle, and he had no desire to remain idle in camp—but was anxious to show his people that he had been taught to work, and that it *pays* to work, and that it is honorable to work. He told his people the first Sabbath in Sabbath school that "the *Bible religion* has work right along with it." I put him in the carpenter shop, where he seems quite at home, and I am confident his example and influence will be on the right side.

Miles ended with, "*Send us more such men.*"[27]

But in late September, Pratt received word that "Bear's Heart is at present on the sick list, having overheated himself in helping unload a train." Whether this condition contributed to his contraction of tuberculosis is not clear. In any event, his health continued to deteriorate and in January 1882, less than a year after his return, he died. Until that time, the young Cheyenne had completely fulfilled Pratt's and Armstrong's expectations. The young man's "whole heart is for progress among his people, and both by preaching and practice he endeavors to help his people forward," Miles had observed of the industrious Cheyenne before his death. The great tragedy, of course, was that Bear's Heart's influence for good was cut so short. Still, if reformers sought evidence to support their faith in the transforming power of education, the life of James Bear's Heart was a stunning illustration.[28]

The task that Pratt, Armstrong, and their supporters faced was that of convincing policymakers and the public at large that the vast majority of returned students were, like Bear's Heart, a progressive force for civilization.[29] And indeed, through the mid-1880s, reformers' optimistic reports generally carried the day. In the spring of 1886, however, the reform cause received an unexpected setback. On March 10, 1886, during the House debate on Indian appropriations, Indiana Congressman William Holman, chair of a special committee to investigate the results of Indian schools, reported on the committee's findings. Holman made an astounding charge: returned students almost invariably relapsed into barbarism. Illinois Congressman J. S. Cannon, a member of Holman's committee, concurred, asserting that except for those returned students employed by the government, "we could not find that there was one student of all the hundreds educated at Carlisle or Hampton or in any of the schools off the reservation but had gone back to their savage life in a very short time." In short, returned students were essentially blanket Indians.[30]

A week's recess in the House debate gave reformers the time needed to deflect Holman's attack,[31] but Holman's charge proved to be just the opening round in a protracted debate on the so-called "returned student problem." "Go to Pine Ridge or Rosebud," one journalist proclaimed, "and select from the thousands the most gaudily dressed of the young savages, those whose faces are continually smeared with paint, whose feet now know no covering but heavily beaded moccasins, those whose blankets are decorated to excess, and you will discover a Carlisle or Hampton boy."[32] Sociologist Frank Blackmar lent scholarly credentials to such claims in 1892 when he published his findings based on sixty-seven Cheyenne and Arapaho returned students, all former students of Haskell. According to Blackmar, only three of the group "were pursuing anything beyond the life of an ordinary camp Indian," and many had even taken up the ghost dance.

Another young Cheyenne who spent four years at Haskell . . . has gone the way of the useless and the do-less. Although in Haskell he was adjutant of the battalion and was noted as a superior officer. He was a good farmer and could read [and] write English well. He owns 160 acres of land and his squaw owns another tract of the same size. But in practice he is a veritable camp Indian. He receives his rations from the government and does nothing towards his own support. He lives with his family in a tepee about six by eight feet, and just high enough to receive his standing. He is now living with his second woman since leaving school.[33]

Such accounts only fueled a growing impression that the average returned student was a backsliding, relapsing, retrograding Indian.

Over the next forty years, school superintendents and other "friends of the Indian" would do everything in their power to defend the record of returned students. One strategy was to bury critics' charges with an array of countervailing appraisals from those in the field. For every example of relapse came counter images of former students leading their people toward agriculture, Christianity, and education.[34] Reformers also attacked critics for basing their conclusions on superficial impressions. Critics, it was said, were often unfamiliar with either Indians or reservation life, and they were consequently ill-prepared to interpret the genuine meaning of a returned student's life. As Cora Folsom of Hampton pointed out, upon seeing returned students lounging about the agency in soiled clothes, moccasins, and long hair, the "casual visitor" was apt to judge the educated Indian as a complete failure. But further investigation would probably prove this initial impression to be unduly harsh. If the visitor bothered to follow the student back to his home, more than likely he would discover "a brave and earnest struggle after better things, a larger farm, a neater house than his neighbors, many of the comforts of civilization and . . . the children brought up in the ways of civilization."[35] Indians, like books, could not be judged by their covers.

Another strategy was to publish statistical summaries of students' performance after leaving school. Hampton Institute, perhaps because it was a contract school, was especially conscientious in its record keeping. Under a succession of Indian program directors—Helen Ludlow, Cora Folsom, Carol Andrist—information was collected from survey questionnaires, student letters, and firsthand observations by agents and missionaries. Particularly effective were reservation inspection tours carried out by a member of the school staff. On more than one occasion, Cora Folsom crisscrossed the Dakotas in a horse and buggy in search of answers to telling questions: Were students self-supportive or were they dependent on government rations? Were they farming an allotment? If so, how many acres? What were their homes like? Did they sleep in a bed? Was there a clock in the house? Who did they marry? Was their spouse educated? Were they Christian? Did they attend church? Were their children in school?[36]

Back at Hampton the information was sifted, recorded, and interpreted, whereupon each returned student was placed in one of five categories: excellent, good, fair, poor, and bad. The first three categories were in turn collapsed into "satisfactory," the latter two into "disappointing." The basis for the classification scheme, as explained by Cora Folsom, was as follows:

Excellent: Those who have had exceptional advantages and used them faithfully, or those who by great earnestness and pluck have won an equally wide and telling influence for good.

Good: Those who have done their best and exerted a decidedly good influence, even though it may not have been very wide. They have married legally, have been honest, industrious and temperate, and lived a life to which we can point as an example for others to follow.

Fair: Those who live a fairly proper life; who mean to do well, but from sickness, peculiar temptations, or unfortunate circumstances, do not at all times exert a good influence. Many . . . are placed here because they have married in the Indian way.

Poor: The shiftless and fickle ones. Many do well; go to church, work their land, and appear very well for a time, then turn about, go to Indian . . . dances and so spoil all the good influence they have really tried to exert. Those who have been known to drink or refuse to marry legally are on this list. Many are poor wrecks when they came to us and soon returned.

Bad: Those who have done wrong while knowing better, yet, with few exceptions, those from whom no better was expected.[37]

To be sure, the system was hardly scientific. Even assuming that the information on individual students was accurate, there was still considerable leeway for interpretation and judgment. It must be remembered too that the school staff desperately *wanted* their students to succeed and therefore were understandably predisposed to see evidence that validated

Hampton's approach to racial uplift. On the other hand, there is no evidence whatsoever that the staff were consciously dishonest in their record keeping. As new information came in, the staff regularly updated their figures, frequently moving students up or down in the classification as the evidence indicated.

Still, it cannot be forgotten that publications documenting returned students' records ultimately were political documents designed to win policymakers' support. An impressive illustration of this is Hampton's report to Commissioner Morgan in 1891, summarizing thirteen years of the school's work with Indians. Published as a Senate document, the report was distinctive in several respects. First, there were the raw figures. Of the 318 Indians who had passed through Hampton's gates, 72 were judged excellent, 149 good, 62 fair, 23 poor, and 12 bad. Overall, 283 were classified as satisfactory and only 35 as disappointing. Second, the report presented a brief background sketch on each student. The entry for Samuel Medicine Bull, for instance, reads:

> A son of the Chief Medicine Bull, and a young man of strong influence and force of character. In the year that he taught at home he so influenced his father that, instead of opposing everything progressive, he became a leader in the opposite party. Samuel returned to Hampton for two years, and has, since 1886, been teacher at his father's camp, and catechist there and at St. Albans. He is industrious, and has a good farm and herd; is a carpenter on occasion, and wields a powerful influence for good in a quiet way that is very telling. He married a Christian girl.

Third, the report was illustrated with several photographs giving visual reinforcement for the report's written claims, striking images of Indians in civilized dress, posing in front of wagons or houses constructed with Hampton know-how. Finally, the report included a foldout map of all the reservations to which Hampton students had returned. On each reservation stars, dots, and the squares were coded to represent broad categories of employment in which returned students were engaged. To a generation that scanned maps of Indian country for evidence of military posts, the multitude of symbols could not help but conjure up images of frontier warfare. In this instance, however, it was the returned students waging the war against savagism.[38]

Although other schools produced less elaborate reports, the conclusions were similar. Carlisle, which used evaluation categories identical to those of Hampton, claimed a somewhat lower but still impressive level of success. In 1898, out of 1,021 former students, only 171, or 17 percent, were judged to be a disappointment. Haskell and other schools were scarcely more modest in their claims. Thus, when Commissioner of In-

Table 9.1. Known Occupations of Living Carlisle and Hampton Returned
Students, 1912 and 1918

Occupation	Carlisle (1912)		Hampton (1918)	
	N	%	N	%
Farmers/ranchers	769	26.2	269	31.6
Housewives	677	23.1	236	27.7
Laborers	328	11.2	62	7.3
Agency/school service	245	8.4	94	11.0
Trades	229	7.8	51	6.0
Living with parents	202	6.9	24	2.8
Clerks/salesmen/ self-employed	166	5.7	33	3.9
Domestics	116	4.0	16	1.9
Professions	77	2.6	12	1.4
Students	58	2.0	15	1.8
U.S. government	46	1.6	13	1.5
Mission work			17	2.0
Miscellaneous	18	0.6	10	1.2
TOTAL	2,931		852	

Sources: Red Man, March 1912 (reprint, New York: Johnson Reprint Corporation, 1971):
282–83; and Records of the Board of Indian Commissioners, National Archives, Reference
Material, 1875–1933, Tray 120.

dian Affairs William Jones addressed Carlisle's graduating class in 1899, he
went out of his way to point out that the Indian Office's statistics clearly
indicated that graduates of off-reservation schools, as a rule, "do not go
back to their old habits." The truth of the matter, Jones said, was that
"seventy-six percent of the graduates of Carlisle and kindred institutions
are leading correct, honest, and upright lives." Jones wondered if the
common schools could claim a higher "percentage of profit" with white
students. Two years later, Jones, in his annual report, made similar claims,
citing a recent Indian Office survey as evidence.[39]

The search for supportive data prompted some schools to periodically
publish occupational profiles of former students[40] (see Table 9.1). Taken at
face value, the figures reported by Carlisle for 1912 and Hampton for
1918 were impressive. Most male students took up farming and ranching,
while a much smaller percentage became laborers, tradesmen, and employees of the Indian service. Women, for the most part, became housewives, although a few entered the Indian service as teachers, matrons, and
seamstresses. On the whole, such data projected the image of returned
students leading productive, purposeful, successful lives. The problem
with such reports, of course, was that they left unanswered several troubling questions. In the case of Carlisle, for instance, what became of some
1,220 students, unaccounted for, who for all practical purposes disap-

peared from the face of the earth? Another troubling question was the impossibility of assessing with any precision the extent to which students' occupations could be directly attributed to schooling. In some instances the connection was clear, but it is also clear that the vast majority of Indian women would have become housewives, and a smaller number of men would have landed jobs as laborers without any schooling whatsoever. In addition, identifying one's occupation as "farmer" spoke only indirectly to the question of whether the student was a "successful" farmer; it failed to address the issue of whether the student was economically self-reliant, independent from government rations. Still, on the surface, such figures substantiated off-reservation schools' claims.[41]

Critics, reformers maintained, also failed to distinguish between those returned students who *attended* off-reservation schools and those who actually *graduated,* which, unquestionably, was one of reformers' most persuasive counterarguments to the charge of relapse. As a matter of fact, when Holman and other skeptics began their attack on Hampton and Carlisle, only a small percentage of students had actually mastered the entire course of study, by and large the equivalent of a grammar school education. Thus, by 1892, only 31 of Hampton's 318 former students had actually graduated. The situation was much the same with Carlisle. Not until 1889 did Pratt award any diplomas, and even then only 14 students graduated out of the 178 leaving for home, all having spent five years at the institution. The ratio of Carlisle's graduates to nongraduates would improve slightly over the years, but the fact remains that by 1909, after some 4,151 students had attended the institution, only 532, or approximately one-eighth, had received diplomas. The same year, Haskell reported that 400, or 20 percent of its 2,000 former students, were certified graduates.[42]

Actually, former students could be categorized into three groups: graduates; nongraduates who had remained in school for a full term of three to five years, and those who attended for only a brief period of time. (In the last category were those who either ran away or suffered from severe health problems.) What infuriated reformers was the failure of critics to note any such distinctions. Therefore, it is no surprise that the Indian Rights Association criticized a news story in 1890 which claimed that all fifty Carlisle graduates returning to Osage Agency were unable or refused to speak English and had immediately reverted to the old ways. After investigating the story, the association reported the charges were largely unfounded. Although some fifty Osage youth had indeed returned from Carlisle, and some had undeniably retrograded, not one, technically speaking, was a graduate. Moreover, many of the nongraduates who had relapsed had attended Carlisle only as small children, and even then only for a few months, hardly enough time to wash out their primitive Osage natures. Was this a fair test of the returned student question?[43]

Surely reformers had a legitimate argument, but it also reveals something of a strategic retreat from their initial claims. Reformers knew that lumping all returned students into a single group placed their defenders in the impossible position of having to defend the record of all students, regardless of the duration of their schooling. On the other hand, to defend only graduates meant defending a very small percentage of the total number of returned students, hardly a convincing argument for continued investment in off-reservation schools. But why did reformers feel compelled to surrender so much ground to begin with? This brings up one of the most intriguing and paradoxical aspects of the controversy: the reformers' tendency to defend returned students' records while simultaneously acknowledging that relapse did indeed occur.

In 1885, well before Congressman Holman's charges, Superintendent of Indian Schools John Oberly confessed at Lake Mohonk: "The Indian boys who return to the camps from Hampton and Carlisle do not exercise the good influence they should exercise among their people. Most of them sink into obscurity; and I am not putting it too strongly when I say that a majority of them go back to the blanket." The same year, Philip Garrett, a member of the Board of Indian Commissioners and recently returned from an inspection tour of several reservations, told Lake Mohonkers that their expectations for returned students were overly optimistic. The returned student might do well enough to earn a good rating from his former superintendent, but such ratings hardly told the whole story. Firsthand observations convinced Garrett that, after two or three years, the average returned student "is not distinguishable from those he left behind when he went away. The refined, civilized, scholarly boy or girl of the school becomes an Indian again."[44]

Certainly, on fundamental principles, there was no reason to be discouraged. Boarding schools, particularly the off-reservation type variety, *had* proved to be effective instruments for assimilating Indian children to white ways of thinking and living, at least temporarily. The root of the problem lay elsewhere—namely, with the reservation system itself. As Superintendent Oberly told Mohonkers in 1885, the returned student

> does not go back to savage life because he cannot accept civilization, but because after his graduation, . . . he returns to a social condition in which civilization must necessarily perish—a stagnant social condition—a condition in which nothing that he has learned can be of any use to him. The tribe . . . does not advance or go back; it stands still; it is not progressive and it is not conservative, it is motionless—a pond of impure water with no inlet or outlet, the surface of which is never disturbed by moving keel, or foot of swimming bird, or mo-

tion of fish, or active wind, or gentle breeze. It is a condition of stagnation in which civilization cannot survive.[45]

Returned students needed help, but what sort of help? In their answer to this question, it is not surprising that reformers' first instinct was to advocate increased efforts in the areas of education, civil service reform, and allotment. Reformers' appeal for increased educational expenditures was consistent with one of their most fundamental assertions, namely, that the war against savagism could only be won if it was total and uncompromising, that is, if *all* children were exposed to the elevating influence of the schoolhouse. Was it any surprise, one superintendent asked, that the returned student would be "scoffed and sneered at by the stay-at-home bucks and squaws?" Charles C. Painter made virtually the same argument in *A Plea for Enlarged School Work*. In answer to the problem of why returned students were taking up the blanket, Painter asked, "why not try the experiment of putting the three-fourths of the boys who have not been in school, but who laugh at the boy who has, also in school and educate them to the point where they will stand with and help those who otherwise are under great temptations to go back to the old life?" For Painter, the solution was simple: the answer to the returned student problem was to create more returned students.[46] Civil service reform and land allotment also were central to the returned students' success. Civil service reform would result in the appointment of more qualified agents, the single most important individual responsible for keeping the returned students on the path of civilization. Allotment, on the other hand, would break the stranglehold of the tribal relation, reward the values of frugality, hard work, perseverance, and self-sufficiency, and move the returnees toward citizenship. What was needed was not retreat from the original principles of Indian reform but a more aggressive pursuance of the same.[47]

Another means of supporting returned students was to step up the war against tribal culture. Even though plural marriages and various "heathenish" dances were officially banned by the 1890s, native culture proved stubbornly resilient.[48] This prompted Commissioner William Jones to issue his infamous "short hair" order in 1902. "The returned male student far too frequently goes back to the reservation and falls into the old custom of letting his hair grow long," Jones began. "He also paints profusely and adopts all the old habits and customs which his education in our industrial schools has tried to eradicate." Jones instructed agents:

You are therefore directed to induce your male Indians to cut their hair, and both sexes to stop painting. With some of the Indians this will be an easy matter; with others it will require considerable tact and perseverance on the part of yourself and your employees to successfully carry out these instructions. With your Indian employees and those Indians who draw rations and supplies, it should be an easy matter, as a noncompliance with this order may be made a reason for discharge or for withholding rations and supplies. Many may be induced to comply with the order voluntarily, especially the returned student. The returned students who do not comply voluntarily should be dealt with summarily. Employment, supplies, etc., should be withheld until they do comply and if they become obstreperous about the matter a short confinement in the guardhouse at hard labor with shorn locks, should furnish a cure. Certainly all the younger men should wear short hair, and it is believed by tact, perseverance, firmness, and withdrawal of supplies the agent can induce *all* to comply with this order.

The order went on to state that all males should be strongly encouraged to wear "citizens' clothing" and reiterated the office's prohibition against dances and feasts, many of which were "simply subterfuges to cover degrading acts and to disguise immoral purposes."[49]

Jones's rationale for the order partly had to do with health considerations. The use of facial paint in the hot summer months could cause irritation, infection, and possibly blindness. But Jones's concern was clearly deeper than that of health. After some agents raised objections to the circular, the commissioner justified the measure by emphasizing its symbolic importance. After making the incredible assertion that there was never any intention "of interfering with the Indian's personal liberty," he continued, "It was not that long hair, paint, blankets, etc., are objectionable in themselves—that is largely a question of taste—but that they are a badge of servitude to savage ways and traditions which are effectual barriers to the uplifting of the race."[50] In any event, by prohibiting paint and long hair and by encouraging civilized dress for all Indians, it would make the ordeal of the returned student so much easier.

Returned students also needed jobs, especially in those regions where farming and stock raising offered limited opportunities.[51] Part of the solution lay in employing returning students in the burgeoning Indian service bureaucracy. The problem here was the growing number of occupations falling under civil service classification. The solution was to grant Indians special status, and it was in this direction that the Indian Office, with the full cooperation of the Civil Service Commission, moved. In 1895 graduates of normal programs were made eligible for employment as assistant teachers or day school teachers "without further examination." The following year all positions below that of superintendent, teacher, industrial teacher, kindergartner, and physician were declared exempt from civil service competition. As for the higher positions, those might be filled on the basis of "noncompetitive examination." Although most returned students entered the service in lower rank positions, the impact of giving Indians preferential status was considerable. Whereas only 18 percent of school service positions were held by Indians in 1888, by 1896 it had climbed to 28 percent. Just one year later, the figure had jumped to 37 percent, or 648 out of a total of 1,774 employees. According to the Superintendent of Indian Schools, the experiment was working well and clearly established that Indian employees "are not inferior to white employees."[52]

Another approach to Indian employment was launched in 1905, when Commissioner Leupp established the Indian Employment Bureau. Leupp originally had toyed with the idea of appointing "employment clerks" at larger reservations to assist returning students. The creation of a centralized office was mainly an expansion on the idea. Leupp instructed the new bureau's director, Charles Dagenett, a Carlisle graduate, "Gather up all able-bodied Indians who . . . would like to earn some money, and plant them on ranches, on railroads, in mines—wherever in the outer world, in short, there is an opening for a dollar to be gotten for a day's work." Some schools also ran their own employment bureaus, matching returned students with job openings, mostly of the low-paying manual or domestic labor sort and much of it seasonal. Whether run by the national bureau or by the schools themselves, the programs worked more to the advantage of white employers than to the Indians.[53]

Besides jobs, returned students needed direct material assistance. Although some did return from school with a small savings, and others received occasional payments in the form of government annuities, large numbers arrived home with good intentions but little else. In 1885, Commissioner John D. C. Atkins suggested that returning students should be provided with start-up funds for building a modest house and for purchasing farm tools. Actually, the commissioner's proposal was based on a program initiated by the Women's National Indian Association, whereby married couples trained at off-reservation schools were granted $300–$400 loans to build homes. Since Congress was unwilling to fund the idea, the number of students who actually benefited from such loans was small. Still, a few recipients received a much needed boost in their efforts to make use of their education. In 1885, Alice Fletcher received this letter from Minnie Stables, living on the Omaha reservation.

> My Dear Friend: We are all well; we are very busy out here; Philip he most finish our house, two rooms down-stairs and two rooms up stairs and kitchen. Philip he building alone by himself and he was so

slow. I think he going to finish it next week; we have hard time all this summer; live in a tent all summer; it is very hard for me. I just hate to live in a tent now; we live in yet, but our house is most finish it.[54]

Another strategy was the organization of so-called returned student associations. As early as 1883, a former Hampton student confessed: "It is very hard to stand alone. But if we get more on our side, and all keep together and have a young men's meeting and make rules, we can keep up, and by and by more boys will come on our side." By the late 1880s, associations had been established at several of the Sioux agencies with Hampton students leading the way. The Lower Brule organization underwent several name changes—the Brotherhood of Christian Unity, the Hampton Association, and finally, the Returned Students and Progressive Indian Association. Benjamin Brave, an officer in the Lower Brule organization, wrote Cora Folsom in 1887:

We are trying to [do] right among our people who are now in negligences and ignorances of our mighty God. We hope that do more good works among our poor savage race. I am very sorry for them sometimes. Because they do not [what] is best for them to do in our future life.[55]

Agents were instructed to encourage such associations, in part because they provided an organizational base for converting traditional Indians to civilized ways, but more important because they offered psychological support for those tempted by the allurements of traditional culture.[56]

The school itself could play an important role in boosting returned students' spirits. Scanning the pages of Carlisle's *Red Man,* Phoenix's *Native American,* or Haskell's *Indian Leader,* one could pick up news of old friends, relive a victory on the gridiron, and read the superintendent's views on a pressing Indian question. But personal letters were preferable, and students sometimes literally grieved for contact with their old school. "I have received the papers which you sent to me last week," a lonely Benjamin Brave wrote Cora Folsom at one point, "but still I like to hear from you very much. How [come] don't you Hampton friends do *not* answer my letters? . . . I am afraid that you have forgotten all about me." Actually, Brave had received several letters from Folsom and would receive several more; Folsom simply had difficulty keeping up with her mounting correspondence. Pratt too was conscientious about keeping in contact with former students, writing to them years after leaving his post at Carlisle. When Carlisle graduate George Balenti received a letter from Pratt, he wrote back, "There are lots of things I would like to write about but I am so excited over this grand opportunity that I can't think." In any event, he hoped that Pratt would write again, "for you never fail to give us old children of yours good advice."[57]

Another school-initiated strategy for reinvigorating flagging spirits was the returned student conference. Phoenix Indian School seems to have led the way in this regard, partly because so many former students—Pima, Papago, and Apache—lived within a day's journey of the school. Held once a year, returned student conferences offered alumni an opportunity to renew school ties and listen to pep talks from one another and members of the school staff. "I am sorry to say," one graduate lamented at the 1914 conference, "that there are some who are going the other way. They are trying to introduce the old way of living, dancing at night, singing at night . . . they are going backward instead of pressing forward." Various prescriptions were offered on how to prevent such relapses. Perhaps returned students simply needed to grow thicker hides to repel the abuse and ridicule directed at them. Or perhaps, as another speaker suggested, the returning student needed a "guide" to sustain him in the dark days of depression, a guide on the order of Jesus Christ. Then again, the answer might lay in reminding themselves individually, in forums such as these, of their monumental responsibility to lift up those still wallowing in ignorance.[58]

Reformers were continually searching for new ways to prop up school graduates. The most radical proposal, one advanced by Philip Garrett, was to colonize educated Indians on special reservations, each settler being provided with a plot of land, a house, a few animals, and necessary tools, all provided in the form of low-interest government loans. In another version of the colonization concept Garrett discussed the possibility of settling returned students on the edge of existing reservations where they would constitute a buffer zone between Indian barbarism and white civilization. The great drawback in this plan, Garrett confessed, was that the educated Indian would still be "too near to a barbarism for which he would have filial respect, and would be liable to its contagion." Another proposal, one advanced by Superintendent of Indian Schools Daniel Dorchester, was to extend the term of off-reservation schools to perhaps as many as ten years. And finally, the Board of Indian Commissioners suggested in 1918 that the Indian Office establish reservation "community centers" modeled after the immigrant settlement house. Such centers would be a "God-send" to young women who "are shocked when they return to the homes of their parents to find nothing which can give them even a chance to live as they had been living at school." In the end, proposals for colonization, term extension, and settlement centers all fell on deaf ears. Congress, which had the ultimate responsibility for funding such schemes, found them either too expensive or too inadequate for the problems at hand.[59]

Through it all, a few reformers continued to make the point—one remarkable for its profundity—that there would be no returned student problem if there were no returned students—if graduates would choose to make their way in the wider world rather than return to their homes. This idea became the great lament of J. B. Harrison, who confessed his urge to shout: "Escape for your lives! Run away, get over the line, and keep going till you are so far away that it would be hard to get back. Work on a farm: do anything that is honest; live among men, and become a man." This, of course, had always been Pratt's solution, one he never tired of advancing. To Fred Big Horse, a former student, he wrote at one point:

> You ask me to tell you the quickest way for the Indians of the reservation to become citizens. I will name you the very quickest: let them move right out from the agency among citizens, locate here and there, settle, determine to be the equal of the white man and to contend for all the necessaries and the good things of life with the white man; this is the very quickest way I know and I think it the best way. You ask me what is the slowest way. I say, stick to your reservations, hang together, demand rations and support from the Government, and you probably never will be citizens.[60]

Whether Big Horse took the advice is not clear; most likely he didn't.

For all practical purposes the returned student controversy was finally put to rest in 1918 when the Board of Indian Commissioners released its report on a yearlong study of the question conducted in conjunction with the Indian Office. Late in 1916, agency and school superintendents were surveyed on the question, Why do so many graduates of nonreservation schools fail—and seemingly deliberately fail—to advance in civilization, industry, application, and intelligence? The manner in which the question was framed is particularly noteworthy. Superintendents were not asked *whether* relapse was pervasive, but *why* it was pervasive.[61]

As reports from the field drifted in, both the Indian Office and the Board of Commissioners spotted a major problem with superintendents' replies, namely their failure to distinguish between ex-students and graduates. The term "returned student," the Indian Office noted in an interim report, "seems to have lost its original meaning for, as commonly used, it no longer is restricted to designating only those who are graduated from Indian non-reservation schools but includes ex-students of any Indian school." After acknowledging that the imprecision of superintendents' replies made it "well nigh impossible" to evaluate the record of actual graduates, the board's final report then proceeded to gloss over the distinction between graduates and ex-students altogether. Amid this confusion, the board offered its judgment: the average returned student retrograded to the point of becoming "a typical reservation Indian." What is surprising is that the judgment met with little or no response from reform circles, perhaps because the report identified conditions on the reservation as the major cause of student relapse, a point that reformers had been making for years.[62] In any event, policymakers now apparently accepted as fact what an earlier generation of reformers would have hotly contested— large numbers of returned students were forsaking their schooling.

Still, one cannot easily ignore the claims of select institutions, notably Carlisle and Hampton, that their students disproportionately lived up to institutional expectations. Carlisle and Hampton, it must be remembered, shared several unique characteristics. Both were led, for a time at least, by charismatic figures, and both institutions mainly enrolled students who came voluntarily (the forced assignment of approximately 100 Apache to Carlisle in the late 1880s was an aberration). Both were distinctive for the extent of the intertribal mix of their student bodies; both drew their students (in the early years) from tribes experiencing severe cultural strain; both were located in regions where prejudice against Indians was muted if nonexistent, affording students a more rewarding outing experience; and both took special care in the selection of teachers. Finally, both bene-fited from additional funding, largely a result of Pratt's and Armstrong's resourcefulness in attracting private donations. All of these factors lead one to conclude that even though their claims were surely exaggerated, their success rate was probably higher than other schools.[63]

MORE THAN RETROGRESSION

Clearly, reformers had badly miscalculated the outcome of the returned student issue, which prompts the question, Where did they go wrong? From reformers' perspective, of course, the problem stemmed from the halfhearted manner in which the government pursued the assimilation program. Only when the reservation system was totally obliterated, only when all Indian children were enrolled in school, only when the cultural option of native traditionalism was thoroughly cut off, they argued, could returned students legitimately be expected to carry out their assigned roles as cultural transformers. Although there is a certain logic to this posi-tion, a close reading of the evidence suggests that the origins of the re-turned student problem were much deeper than reformers supposed.

For one thing, reformers had clearly overestimated the capacity of schools, even boarding schools, to fully eradicate the students' ties with native culture. As already observed, reformers never really understood the motivations behind students' cooperation with the boarding school program, that the response of accommodation was often little more than a pragmatic adaptation to changing historical realities. What reformers could never admit was that many students looked forward to their home-coming, not because it offered an opportunity to proselytize, but because it allowed them to renew the familial relationships and cultural habits of their youth. It is hardly surprising that Carl Sweezy, who genuinely liked Carlisle, still confesses that "it was good to come back . . . once more, to hear Arapaho spoken and to take part in Arapaho ceremonies and eat Arapaho food." Or that Don Talayesva, after several years at Sherman, would hardly reach the reservation boundary before longing to become "a real Hopi again" and to sing "the good old Katcina songs."[64]

In making their case for education, reformers had simply promised too much. It would have been one thing to argue that education would facilitate Indians' gradual adaptation to white society and institutions, and quite another to promise that it guaranteed the wholesale transformation of their hearts, minds, and souls. If policymakers had argued that schools gave Indian youth a rudimentary understanding of English, a host of new industrial and domestic skills, and an enlarged understanding of the values and attitudes of white society—no small accomplishment—their defense of returned students would have been made substantially easier. But reformers had promised more than this, and in doing so, they set a standard for success that made critics' charges of relapse all that more believable.

Leo Crane, Hopi agent, spoke to this very issue in his lengthy reply to the Indian Office's returned student survey. Crane, who had little regard for Hopi tradition and was one of the most despised Hopi agents, was nevertheless a prescient observer of the cultural and circumstantial pressures exerted on returning pupils. Crane began his report by explaining how Hopi children spent the first seven years of their lives steeped in a pueblo culture that had changed very little since the thirteenth century. During these formative years, a Hopi child, Crane explained, lived and breathed all things Hopi, eating Hopi foods, speaking the Hopi language, unconsciously internalizing Hopi values, mores, and a distinctive Hopi worldview. Once more, "he learns Indian legends, attends Indian dances and ceremonies much more colorful and appealing than any later white man's entertainment."[65]

About the age of seven, the child was forced into a day school where he struggled to make sense of the white man's way. The schoolteacher, no matter how gentle, could not begin to counter the influence of the pueblo that still held sway over the child's mind. "Everything learned during the day has been ironed out of him at night, through ridicule and adverse criticism of that fool white teacher." In a few years this child moved to the reservation boarding school at Keams Canyon, removing him from daily contact with the pueblo but failing to entirely eliminate its influence. Parental visits and summer vacations only deepened his Hopi identity. Even at school "he still plays Indian games, and when out of sight of his teachers will unconsciously sings Indian chants. He is AN INDIAN under instruction." And then came the off-reservation school. Here, the Hopi adolescent genuinely enjoyed the "innovations" of white society—electric lights, flushing toilets, sewing machines—but could not help but ask what any of these things had to do with the thirteenth-century pueblo to which he would surely return. Meanwhile, the military regime grated on his nerves and he missed terribly the desert home of his childhood. In his mind's eye, he longed for his mother's *piki* bread, the excitement of a kachina dance, the scent of crackling juniper logs.[66]

Still, the average student returned home with the idea of improving his life and that of his people. But "the hand that has been firmly thrusting between his shoulder blades for fifteen years, has suddenly been removed." All the industrial training, he finds, is next to worthless. He is a carpenter in a land without lumber, a painter with nothing to paint, a tailor where clothes are fashioned from flour sacks, a shoemaker among moccasin wearers. The agent, he learns, is unable to employ him at the agency. And so the retrogression process begins. "First: the money goes; then the good clothes and the 'regal' shoes wear out; third, nature is busy on his hair. He binds up his hair with a gaudy handkerchief as do the others; he begins to make . . . a pair of moccasins." Meanwhile, "the old people, in strict patriarchal fashion, have set aside and maintained all this time for him, a few horses, cattle, and sheep. Gradually he accepts that which he has. He ceases his visits to the agency, asking for a job. The old life is before him. He has, apparently, become an Indian of the Indians."[67]

But not entirely, which was Crane's point. The appearance of relapse was terribly misleading. In actuality, white schooling usually left a decided imprint on students. More often than not, returned students were able to converse in English, desired the luxuries and conveniences of modern life, were more attuned to hygiene, were more suspicious of old superstitions, and would see the advantage of education for their offspring. For these reasons, Crane adamantly insisted, "I do not concede that the popular impression is a correct one—that so many returned students actually FAIL." No, a returned student only failed to the extent that *"he is not what the taxpayer expected him to be. He is not what the faddist and sentimentalist tried to make him."*[68]

That the boarding school left a lifelong impression on students there is little doubt. More difficult to assess is the collective impact of returned students on their home communities. In the final analysis, Ralph Linton has written, cultural change is "a matter of change in the knowledge, attitudes and habits of the individuals who compose a society."[69] From this perspective it would appear that boarding schools necessarily had a profound influence on native society, for if white schooling did anything, it introduced Indian children to new ways of thinking and behaving. And as already discussed, although many rejected the school's teachings out of hand, many others embraced them, if only selectively. In one way or another this latter group returned to their tribal homeland in the capacity of cultural brokers. Because of their familiarity with the white "outside," returned students were uniquely situated to mediate between Indian and white worlds, uniquely situated to assist tribal elders, "progressives" and traditionals alike, in their negotiation of the cultural borderlands just beyond the reservation line. And if the effect of their efforts was sometimes to facilitate the hegemonization of white ways, at other times it was to engineer pragmatic adaptations to changing circumstances.[70]

But reformers had wanted to obliterate Indian lifeways, not simply modify them. This, combined with the fact that returned students were sometimes terribly unreliable, gave policymakers considerable cause for concern.[71] It also reemphasizes the point that reformers had clearly miscalculated how the acculturation drama would play out. Late-nineteenth-century Indian policy was based on the doctrine of social evolution, a concept that presupposed a replacement model of cultural change. Old values, habits, and beliefs would be discarded, the theory went, as newer, more civilized ones were taken on. The same theory was applied to individuals. Cultural identity was perceived as a zero-sum phenomenon: one was either more or less an Indian, progressing or retrograding as the case might be.

In retrospect, this model of acculturation seems terribly simplistic. As anthropologists have clearly demonstrated, when individuals are placed in situations involving cultural contact, they often respond in ways that defy the replacement model. Reformers could not anticipate that many students, caught between the contesting claims of native and white outlooks, were not prepared to abandon one in the process of acquiring the other, that just as an assimilationist education might win converts to white civilization, so it was just as likely to produce the bicultural personality. Acculturation, it turns out, is often a willed, thoughtful, and imaginative process, simultaneously involving acts of selection, resistance, and conjoinment, a creative process in which the individual actively participates in the shaping of his or her own identity.[72] Thus, Albert Yava, a Hopi, who it may be remembered was an eager student, relates:

Ever since the white man appeared, we have been changing, adapting to new ideas and ways of bettering our condition. It has been pretty painful at times. The white man brought, you might say, a new order of nature. It was as if our whole environment, the things we had to contend with, had turned into something new. To survive, we had to do things we never did before. We had to reorganize our thinking, and while we were doing this we lost a firm grip on our old traditions. For a while we were halfway there and halfway here. We wanted to cope with a new culture without giving up our old one. Some of those old traditionalist leaders thought we could stay the way we used to be. I have always thought that the only way we can save the old traditions is to recognize the new forces at work in our lives, accept that times have changed, and become part of the modern world. That way we can survive and preserve a part of our minds for the old values. If you don't survive, you don't have anything.[73]

Yava, like countless other returned students, was clearly not a passive player in the acculturation drama.

Consider the instance of Albert Hensley.[74] Born about 1871, Hensley's Winnebago youth seems to have been one of general despair. By the time he was seven, both his mother and grandmother were dead, leaving his father—"a drunkard and a horsethief"—as his main protector in the world. In one of Hensley's two autobiographies, he would recall, "If at anytime of my life I was in trouble it was then. I was never happy. Once I did not have anything to eat for four days." In 1888, at the age of sixteen, things took a turn for the better. At Winnebago Agency, in Nebraska, young Hensley met the allotting agent, Alice Fletcher, who urged him to enroll at Carlisle Indian School. When Hensley's father refused to give the necessary permission, Fletcher and Hensley concocted an escape plan that landed the latter on an eastbound train for Pennsylvania. Nearly thirty years later, he would recall the date of his arrival at Carlisle—December 22, 1988. "I wanted to lead a good life. At school I knew that they would take care of me and love me."

Hensley thrived at Carlisle. Preparing himself for "success" in the white man's manner, he learned the trades of steam plumbing, carpentry, and blacksmithing. He had two outings in the Pennsylvania countryside, and even though on one occasion his patron was a "mean man," only paying Hensley $10 a month, "I worked as hard as though I was getting $40.00 a month." When not on outings, Hensley dutifully followed the school's routine, soaking up the air of "civilization," including a knowledge of Christianity. He remained at Carlisle nearly six years and was in his third month of his "senior" year when he was diagnosed as having tuberculosis. On June 15, 1895, in an apparent effort to keep the school's mortality rate down, he was sent "back to Nebraska to die."

Back home, however, Hensley quickly recovered and for a while, at least, lived the life of a model returned student. He secured employment at the agency, first as chief of police and then later as blacksmith, interpreter, and assistant to the allotting agent. He was elected county commissioner and joined the Episcopalian church, promising "never to forsake the religion of the Son of God." But then, just when it appeared that his life had all the earmarks of another Carlisle success story, things took a turn for the worse. "At that time the Winnebago with whom I associated were heavy drinkers," he recalls, "and after a while they induced me to drink also. I became as wicked as they. I learned how to gamble and I worked for the devil all the time. I even taught the Winnebago how to be bad."

On the path to self-destruction, neither his faith in Episcopalianism nor the memory of Pratt's stirring lectures provided sufficient sustenance. Hensley now wandered in the wilderness of utter spiritual despair. At this point, however, he was drawn to a new religion rapidly gaining adherents among the Winnebago—peyotism. "I ate the peyote and liked it very much," he recalled years later. "I continued eating peyote and enjoying it. All the evil that was in me I forgot. From that time to the present my actions have been quite different from what they used to be. . . . This (peyote) religion was good. All the evil is gone and hereafter I will choose my path carefully." Precisely what it was about peyote that gave him a renewed sense of purpose and meaning—the colorful and transcending nature of the visions, the rituals of the peyote meeting, or the general sense of well-being derived from the entire experience—Hensley does not reveal, but clearly his conversion was a transforming experience. Meanwhile, Hensley conducted other areas of his life in a manner consistent with his Carlisle training. Married with five children and resolving "never to be idle again," he farmed a 160-acre allotment and always remained a staunch supporter of education.

What Hensley's narratives do not reveal, but which other sources clearly establish, is his leadership role in the peyote community. By the turn of the century, peyotism, although a pan-Indian religious movement, had split into two loosely associated sects: one patterned along aboriginal lines, the other a blend of native traditionalism and Christianity. The Winnebago followed a variant of the latter, the so-called Cross Fire ceremony. Along with native peyote practices, the Cross Fire ritual embraced several Christian strains, including baptism, the prohibition of tobacco, the construction of churches, but most principally, the singing of hymns such as "Christ Is the Way of Life" and the "Lord's Prayer."[75]

What is particularly significant is Hensley's role in reshaping the peyote ritual. In addition to introducing additional Christian elements into the ceremony (most notably, the open Bible as an altar for the peyote buttons), he actively defended peyote against growing white sentiment to prohibit its use. In 1908, after hearing that the Indian Office would under-

Albert Hensley delivering two daughters and two nieces to boarding school, ca. 1915. (Courtesy of the National Archives)

take a scientific investigation of the plant, in a long letter he proclaimed: "We have tasted of God and our eyes have been opened." Furthermore:

It is utter folly for scientists to attempt to analyze this medicine. Can science analyze God's body? No White man can understand it. It came from God. It is a part of God's body. God's Holy Spirit enveloped in it. It was given exclusively to Indians and God never intended that White men should understand it, hence the folly of any such attempt. It cures us of our temporal ills, as well as those of a spiritual nature. It takes away the desire for strong drink. I myself, have been cured of a loathsome disease, too horrible to mention. So have hundreds of others. Hundreds of confirmed drunkards have been dragged from their downward way.[76]

Albert Hensley was just one of many returned students to turn toward peyote. When congressional hearings were held in 1918 on a bill designed to outlaw its use, an effort that ultimately failed, observers were struck by the number of former Carlisle students who came forth to testify against the measure, each offering testimony in direct contradiction to that given by their former "school father," Richard Henry Pratt, who was ardently opposed to the plant.[77] As the testimony offered by James Mooney, director of the Bureau of American Ethnology, suggests, the connection between having attended Carlisle and support for peyote was more than coincidence.

The Indians now are largely civilized; they are becoming citizens; they are educated, and they travel about and take an interest in each other. A great many of the young men who have been sent to eastern schools, in a climate damper than the one to which they have been accustomed, come back with weakened lungs, coughs, and hemorrhages, and they are told by their Indian friends at home that if they use the peyote it will relieve the coughs and check the hemorrhages, and they have found that to be true. That is the universal testimony of the Indians. . . . The result is that the young men, not the older uncivilized ones, but the younger, middle-aged, and educated men, have taken up the peyote cult and organized it as a regular religion, beyond what they knew before among the various tribes.[78]

Coming at about the same time as the Board of Indian Commissioners' returned student survey, the peyote hearings only served to remind policymakers that boarding schools, especially the off-reservation variety, were a dubious investment. Too many returned students had failed to walk the straight and narrow path of civilization. If former students like

Albert Hensley were not examples of absolute retrogression, they still were not what reformers had originally promised they would be, what the doctrine of social evolution had proclaimed they would become. Hence, the shift toward a more realistic Indian policy, something already well under way, seemed more than justified.

CHAPTER TEN

Policy

In 1901, Commissioner William Jones began his annual report with a remarkable admission: the nation's Indian policy was a miserable failure. In the last thirty-three years, Jones observed, the government had spent over $240 million in an attempt to civilize Indians. At public expense, they had been given food, clothes, plows, seed, wagons, and schools, all in an effort to ease the transition from hunter to agriculturist, from dependency to self-reliant manhood. And what were the results of this enormous investment? The fact of the matter was that Indians were still largely living on reservations, still prisoners of their tribal outlook, still wards of the "Great Father" in Washington. The hard truth was that the average Indian "is little, if any, nearer the goal of independence than he was thirty years ago, and if the present policy is continued he will get little, if any, nearer in thirty years to come." After many "well-meant mistakes," it was time to reassess.[1]

The current approach to Indian education was of particular concern. In the past twenty years some $45 million had been spent on the education of 20,000 youths, most of the amount swallowed up in an immense network of boarding schools. Through a combination of cajolery, threats, bribery, fraud, persuasion, and force, Indian children were annually swept from their camps and deposited in institutions hundreds of miles from their homes, whereupon teachers, farmers, matrons, seamstresses, industrial teachers, and disciplinarians undertook the arduous work of civilization. Twenty years of such a policy had revealed an unpleasant truth: reformers had clearly expected too much of the off-reservation school. Even though returned students were certainly a positive force, they were incapable of single-handedly transforming Indian society. Perhaps policymakers should direct their efforts closer to the source of savagism. "The key to the whole situation is the home," Jones flatly proclaimed. "Improvement must begin there."[2]

The campaign against off-reservation schools was waged with even stronger conviction by Jones's successor, Francis Ellington Leupp. Unlike Jones, who had no particular background in Indian affairs, Leupp was well suited for his new post. A highly respected journalist, Leupp developed a keen interest in the Indian problem in the early 1890s, visiting several reservations to witness Indian life and the impact of government policies firsthand. In 1895 he was appointed by Herbert Welsh as Washington agent for the Indian Rights Association and a year later joined the Board of Indian Commissioners, both positions offering an ideal forum for deepening his reformist propensities. In 1905, as a friend of Theodore Roosevelt, he was a natural replacement for outgoing Commissioner Jones. For the next four years Leupp worked assiduously to reorient Indian policy.[3] At the center of this reorientation was the idea that Indian assimilation must necessarily be a gradual process and in the end might never be entirely achieved. Moreover, the Carlisle approach to education was fundamentally wrong. "It is a great mistake," Leupp wrote in his first annual report, "to start the little ones in the path of civilization by snapping all the ties of affection between them and their parents, and teaching them to despise the aged and nonprogressive members of their families. The sensible as well as the humane plan is to nourish their love of father and mother and home . . . and then to utilize this affection as a means of reaching, through them, the hearts of the elders."[4]

By the turn of the century the reform outlook typified by Thomas J. Morgan and Richard Pratt was clearly losing sway in the councils of Washington. Indeed, Jones's 1901 report marks the opening phase of a gradual thirty-year retrenchment from the ideal of immediate assimilation to one of gradualism.[5] As part of this retrenchment, policymakers from widely different ideological perspectives would whittle away at the boarding school as a central component of Indian education. The following discussion will examine the evolution of this reorientation, pausing along the way to highlight those events—including the closing of Carlisle in 1918—that signaled the shift was under way.

THE CASE AGAINST OFF-RESERVATION SCHOOLS

Between 1900 and 1920 the case against off-reservation schools was made along four lines: the belief that Indians, either because of inborn racial traits or sheer obstinacy, were incapable of rapid assimilation; the belief that boarding schools, however effective, were unjustifiably cruel to both parents and children; the belief that such institutions encouraged long-term governmental dependency; and finally, the belief that Native American lifeways, rather than being condemned as universally worthless and thereby deserving of extinction, might serve instead as a fruitful foundation for educational growth. It is important to emphasize that just as these strands of opposition were not necessarily interconnected, neither were they necessarily mutually exclusive. Taken as a whole, they offered policymakers compelling reasons to reassess an earlier generation's assumptions about Indian education.

One of the major reasons for calling into question the investment in off-reservation schools was the growing belief that Indian assimilation would at best be a slow process and might in the end even be unachievable. This idea, of course, constituted a sharp break with the view that Indians, under white tutelage, could traverse the distance between savagism and civilization in a single generation. By 1903 Commissioner William Jones had concluded that civilizing Indians was like taming wild birds. "The young of the wild bird, though born in captivity, internally retains the instincts of freedom so strong in the parent and beats the bars to secure it, while after several generations of captivity the young bird will return to the cage after a brief period of freedom." Each succeeding generation of school-children, Jones asserted, would lament less the "loss of freedom" and exhibit an increasing desire "to be in touch with the dominant race." Meanwhile, the instinct for freedom, as the problem of student relapse illustrated, could only be eradicated over time.[6]

Similarly, the overriding theme in Leupp's views was gradualism. "The trouble with our efforts in the Indian's behalf," Leupp asserted, "has always been that we have expected too much of him right away." If the problem of student relapse proved anything, it proved that "race characteristics which have been transmitted from generation to generation for centuries are not to be uprooted in a day, or a year, or a good many years." Crossing the "boundary between barbarism and civilization" could take time, in part because the race possessed those primitive qualities "common to all mankind in the lower stages of social development," in part because of inherited "mental and moral traits." Whether this last statement was in reference to a basic genetic deficiency is not entirely clear, but Leupp seems to have flirted with the possibility. In any event, he questioned whether the race could ever be completely assimilated. "Ethnically he will always remain an Indian, with an Indian color, Indian traits of mind, Indian ancestral traditions and the like."[7]

The new mood can clearly be seen in the remarks delivered by S. M. McCowan, superintendent of Chilocco, to a group of Indian educators. Indians, McCowan claimed, "cannot understand our civilization in a minute, or a generation; and not understanding it they cannot appreciate it, and will not follow it." Years in the school service had taught him "that Indians are just the same as white people; that they have the same elements of manhood; that they have the same talents; and that the same processes of evolution that have been followed so successfully in the cultivation of the white races will be followed with as much success in the cultivation and development of the red race." McCowan's list of assertions was fully congruent with those expressed in the heyday of reform in all but one area: the time required for the social evolutionary process.[8]

For the most part the gradualist doctrine was simply a call for patience.

But the movement clearly drew support from an emerging body of social thought that held that inherited race characteristics, not environment, were the source of primitive man's backwardness.[9] The view inevitably found its way into discussions of Indian education. At a special session on the subject at the National Education Association meeting in 1909, one speaker proclaimed: "The races of men feel, think, and act differently not only because of environment, but also because of hereditary impulses."[10] Similarly, in response to the Indian Office's request for opinions from field personnel on the cause of student relapse, the superintendent at Truxton Canyon, Arizona, offered an explanation faintly reminiscent of Commissioner Jones's "wild bird" theory.

> Blood is an important factor in this discussion. You may find a nest of wild duck eggs; bring them home and place them under the gentlest, quietest old biddy hen on the ranch and when they hatch, you may feed them, have the hen take care of them and bring them up with the utmost care until they are well grown and you think thoroughly domesticated, but some day a flock of wild ducks come flying overhead and there is a fluttering of wings and your ducks are gone. Why? Because they are *wild* ducks. Yet our domestic ducks are descendants of wild ones, but it has taken many generations to make them tame.[11]

The logical by-product of such skepticism was a reduced faith in schools as hotbeds of assimilation.

Another criticism of off-reservation schools was that they encouraged attitudes of dependency. Given the fact that a central argument originally made on behalf of such schools had been that they would effectively instill the attitudes and values of rugged individualism, this allegation was particularly devastating. The charge here was that an Indian child plucked directly from the camp and taken to Carlisle or Sherman was, in effect, transported from an environment of poverty and filth to one of wonder and comfort. As a guest of the "Great Father" the urchin was fed, clothed, housed, pampered, and cared for by a legion of matrons, cooks, and seamstresses. And then there were the modern conveniences: the hot baths, the electric lights, the flushing toilets, the steam heat. For entertainment there were thrilling athletic contests, musical performances, and special activities for socializing between the sexes. A student received all of this, Commissioner Jones pointed out, without "a single effort of his own or of his people." In effect, the Indian youth was a "modern Aladdin, who has only to rub the Government lamp to gratify his desires." One could scarcely imagine a system more designed to perpetuate pampering and dependency. Given the fact that the entire system had been created to foster self-reliance, the actual consequences were a cruel joke for all concerned, Indian students and policymakers alike.[12]

Meanwhile, others attacked boarding schools for being inherently cruel and inhumane. This third criticism focused on the questionable moral justification for separating children from their parents, maintaining that separation for months, even years at a time, all the while forcing children to submit to an institutional routine completely foreign to their background. "The theory that to civilize the red man it is necessary to disrupt families and to smother natural emotions by teaching the child to abhor his parents," declared novelist Hamlin Garland in 1902, "is so monstrous and so unchristian that its failure was foretold to every teacher who understood the law of heredity." Another critic, Charles F. Lummis, a California-based conservationist and magazine publisher, waged a relentless campaign against a system that looked upon Indian parents as nothing more than "breeders of pupils" for government factory schools, where "pin-head" employees waged constant psychological warfare against helpless captives.[13]

The most devastating attack along these lines came in the form of three semi-autobiographical essays written for *Atlantic Monthly* by a young Sioux author who had experienced life in an Indian boarding school firsthand.[14] In the first article, "Impressions of an Indian Childhood," Zitkala-Sa (Gertrude Bonnin) describes her idyllic youth spent within the comforting confines of the Yankton Sioux community. The essay, however, ends on an ominous note: Quaker missionaries arrive to recruit pupils for White's Manual Institute in Wabash, Indiana. The girl of eight is enthralled with the missionaries' promises, including a ride on the "iron horse" to a land where big red apples, a particular favorite of Zitkala-Sa's, are but for the asking. She begs her mother to let her go to the faraway Quaker School, and finally her mother assents.

> Wrapped in my heavy blanket, I walked with my mother to the carriage that was soon to take us to the iron horse. I was happy. I met my playmates, who were also wearing their best thick blankets. We showed one another our new beaded moccasins, and the width of the belts that girdled our new dresses. Soon we were drawn rapidly away by the white man's horses. When I saw the lonely figure of my mother vanish in the distance, a sense of regret settled heavily upon me. I felt suddenly weak, as if I might fall limp to the ground. I was in the bands of strangers whom my mother did not fully trust. I no longer felt free to be myself, or to voice my own feelings. The tears trickled down my cheeks, and I buried my face in the folds of my blanket. Now the first step, pointing me from my mother, was taken, and all my belated tears availed nothing.[15]

The next installment, "The School Days of an Indian Girl," begins with a description of her journey east on the iron horse. Zitkala-Sa stares out the train window, somehow gaining comfort from the endless row of telegraph poles passing by. She has seen such poles not far from her mother's dwelling. "Often I had stopped, on my way down the road, to hold my ear against the pole, and, hearing its low moaning, I used to wonder what the paleface had done to hurt it." Her first glimpse of the institute is at night. She is struck by the brightness of the lights that pour forth from the buildings. Entering the dormitory, she clings to the wall. "The strong glaring light in the large whitewashed room dazzled my eyes. The noisy hurrying of hard shoes upon a bare wooden floor increased the whirring in my ears. My only safety seemed to be in keeping next to the wall." She cries herself to sleep wondering what awaits her in the coming days. The next day she resists having her long hair cut and has to be tied in a chair. "I cried aloud, shaking my head all the while until I felt the cold blades of the scissors against my neck." It was at this point, she relates, that she lost her spirit of rebellion. "In my anguish I moaned for my mother, but no one came to comfort me. Not a soul reasoned quietly with me, as my own mother used to do; for now I was only one of many little animals driven by a herder." And so, Zitkala-Sa succumbs to the "iron routine" of boarding school. The days turn into months, the months into years. She goes through the motions of learning "like a dumb sick brute."[16]

After a few years at White's Institute, she returns home, only to find after a while that she is terribly unhappy. To the disappointment of her mother, she returns to school and after graduation decides to enroll in Earlham College in Richmond, Indiana. As the only Indian, she is terribly lonely. She hides in her dormitory room and weeps, "wishing I had gone West, to be nourished by my mother's love, instead of remaining among a cold race whose hearts were frozen hard with prejudice." Gradually, however, she becomes acclimated to her new surroundings and in her classwork demonstrates a considerable talent for writing and public speaking. She is persuaded to compete in the annual interclass oratorical contest. Taking first prize, she is chosen to represent Earlham at a statewide contest, where she wins one of the two top prizes. But "the little taste of victory did not satisfy a hunger in my heart." She longs to go home.[17]

But as she explains in the third installment, "An Indian Teacher Among Indians," her fate is to travel still further east. She cannot resist the opportunity to teach at Carlisle Indian School, where she is immediately impressed with the charismatic Pratt and at first seems pleased with new position. But she is soon weighed down by exhaustion, depression, and finally illness. Pratt decides to send her home to restore her spirits but also to recruit more students. Back at Yankton her health improves, but she is incensed at the sight of white settlers encroaching on reservation land. With a new sense of foreboding she returns to Carlisle. Now among youths who, like herself, had traveled east on the iron horse to attain a white education, Zitkala-Su discovers the deep source of her long despair: "Like a slender tree, I had been uprooted from my mother, nature and God. I was shorn of my branches, which had waved in sympathy and love for home and friends. The natural coat of bark which had protected my over sensitive nature was scraped off to the very quick." She ends by speculating on the inner thoughts of the endless stream of "Christian palefaces" who regularly walk through the school's corridors, examining specimens of student work and peering in classrooms at children bending over their books. Mostly, she suspects, the visitors feel pride and self-satisfaction "at seeing the children of savage warriors so docile and industrious." Zitkala-Sa wonders if the visitors have ever bothered to ponder the unthinkable—"whether real life or long-lasting death lies beneath this semblance of civilization."[18]

At the heart of Zitkala-Sa's writings was the fourth and final criticism of the off-reservation schools. Always at the core of the off-reservation philosophy was the assumption that eradication of the children's native identities must be an essential component of the educational process. By the turn of the century this assumption was being called into question by new developments in educational theory, notably the ideas of G. Stanley Hall and John Dewey.

As founder of the child study movement, G. Stanley Hall believed that modern civilization placed too much emphasis on book learning, giving insufficient attention to the "nature and needs of childhood." Finding much to praise in primitive societies where youths' impulse for natural growth and physical activity were given their legitimate due, the renowned psychologist found the current approach to Indian education especially cruel. In one of two addresses to Indian educators at the National Education Association, Hall urged teachers to build on an Indian child's natural capacities and background rather than obliterate them. Hall asked, "Why not make him a good Indian rather than a cheap imitation of the white man?" John Dewey, educational progressivism's chief theorist, may also have given Indian educators cause to doubt the practice of abruptly separating a child from his native roots. Although Dewey never addressed the question of Indian education directly, his proposition that education must begin with "psychological insight into the child's capacities, interests, and habits" as well as his belief that the school should build upon "activities with which the child is already familiar in the home," if taken to heart, were hardly compatible with the Indian Office's time-honored reliance on boarding schools.[19]

It is important to emphasize, however, that neither Hall nor Dewey were willing to acknowledge the equality of native culture. Hall's view in this regard stemmed from two interconnected beliefs. First, Hall believed there was a direct correspondence between stages in an individual's physical-psychological development and stages in the evolution of human society. Just as children were less than psychologically mature at their present level of development, so Indian cultures were less than completely civilized. This devastating evaluation of Indian culture was followed by a second belief that mental traits were unevenly distributed across the races. Because Indians were a "lower race," Hall doubted their capacity to move much beyond their present cultural condition. Indians, therefore, were noble savages and were genetically programmed to largely remain so. Dewey, on the other hand, although rejecting Hall's attribution of mental traits to race, fully subscribed to the idea of social evolution, including the distinction between savagism and civilization. Thus, even though educators were urged to give proper pedagogical attention to a child's background, however primitive, in the final analysis all humankind should ultimately be encouraged to join the march of scientific and social progress.[20]

Whether Commissioner Leupp was acquainted firsthand with the theories of either Hall or Dewey is not clear, but the progressive idea of utilizing a child's background as a point of pedagogical departure was clearly consistent with his overall belief that educators should seek to modify rather than obliterate, to develop rather than transform, Indian nature. Taking a page from the handbook of the horticulturalist,

> We do not let the soil in our gardens alone because we can not turn clay into sand: we simply sow melon seed in the one and plant plum trees in the other. It does not follow that we must metamorphose whatever we wish to improve. Our aim should be to get out of everything the best it is capable of producing, and in improving the product it is no part of our duty to destroy the source. What would be thought of a horticulturist who should uproot a tree which offers a first-rate sturdy stock simply because its natural fruit is not of the highest excellence?[21]

In the final analysis, the campaign against the off-reservation school drew from strains of thought that were at various points racist, progressive, pluralistic, and humanistic. Taken together, they offered a compelling case for reassessing the ideological underpinnings of Indian education, particularly when one considers the larger context in which the discussion took place: the fact that the previous twenty-year effort of rapid assimilation had proven—at least measured by expectations—a miserable failure. Ironically, Indians themselves were a contributing factor to the new pessimism. Continued student resistance, the tendency of returned students to revert back to old tribal habits, the bitter rhetoric of a Zitkala-Sa, all served to reinforce critics' disenchantment with the boarding school.

NEW DEVELOPMENTS

Criticisms of the existing system translated into several new policy developments. The first was a growing emphasis on vocational training. In 1901, Commissioner Jones announced that "the ground work of all instruction in Indian schools is the systematic inculcation of the principles of work." That same year Superintendent of Indian Schools Estelle Reel unveiled a new course of study consistent with the new emphasis. Whereas before the curriculum had attempted to strike a balance between academic and industrial content, the new curriculum, although maintaining the half-day division between the two types of class work, made a concerted effort to infuse academic coursework with practical, job-related applications. Subsequent revisions in later years pursued this path, to the point that by 1916 all but a few select schools followed a curriculum divided into four levels—primary, prevocational, junior vocational, and senior vocational—with students at the last tier taking such courses as shop mathematics, agricultural botany, and rural economics.[22]

Leupp enthusiastically supported the new emphasis. Convinced that the vast majority of Indian students could eventually earn their living as common laborers on the fringes of a frontier economy, he was impatient with the idea that schooling the race in the higher branches of knowledge should be a high priority. "Now, if anyone can show me what advantage will come to this large body of manual workers from being able to reel off the names of the mountains in Asia, or extract the cube root of 123456789, I shall be deeply grateful," Leupp quipped in an early report. Indians' scholastic needs were more rudimentary: enough English to read the local newspaper or the terms of a simple contract; enough mathematics to prevent being cheated by a dishonest trader or to calculate earnings from a healthy wheat crop. Beyond this, time was better spent in the shop learning how to shoe a horse or repair a section of harness. Certainly talented children should not be denied the best academic education possible, but the plain truth was that the great majority, "like the corresponding mass of white children, are not prepared for conveyance beyond the elementary studies."[23]

Although vocational training marked a definite shift in emphasis, it would be wrong to assume that these changes significantly altered the aims of Indian schooling. The simple truth is that industrial training had always constituted a large segment of the school program. It was not Francis Leupp but Thomas Jefferson Morgan who approvingly observed in 1892 that "the whole underlying thought of the industrial school, . . . is that intelligent, systematic labor by both men and women lies at the basis of civilization, and that if Indians are ever to be lifted on a higher plane it must be through the training of boys and girls alike to the performance of whatever manual labor may be essential for their welfare." It was not Leupp but William Hailmann who declared in 1897 that literary training must always remain subservient to the "fundamental aim of securing industrial fervor and efficiency on the part of the children." In the main, the shift toward vocationalism was not so radical a departure from the past as it might first appear.[24]

A second area of reform was the movement to incorporate elements of Indian culture into the school program. Actually, this first gesture toward pluralism came in 1897 with Superintendent Hailmann's announcement that teachers should seek to better understand the positive attributes of their students' native heritage. Such familiarization would lead them to the conviction that Indian societies were, at least in some instances, not so much a "lower civilization" as a "different civilization." In a direct reference to Pratt's philosophy, educators in the field were urged to disregard the idea that it was necessary "to kill the Indian in order to save the man." As an early American interpreter and advocate of the German kindergarten, Hailmann searched for higher ground. The more the teacher could discover in Indian character and culture that which was "high and noble and good," Hailmann pleaded, "the more successful will he be in fostering these seeds of high character in the children intrusted to his care, in leading them to vigorous germination and development into the light of the new civilization."[25]

A decade later, Commissioner Leupp explicitly stated his support for incorporating Indian material into the curriculum. "I have none of the prejudice which exists in many minds against the perpetuation of Indian music and other arts, customs and traditions," Leupp announced in an office circular in late 1907. "Although I would use every means to encourage the children to learn English, . . . I do not consider that their singing their little songs in their native tongue does anybody any harm, and it helps to make easier the perilous and difficult bridge which they are crossing at this stage of their race development." Leupp also lent his official support to a composition experiment, apparently pioneered by Haskell Institute, whereby students polished their written English by retelling tribal legends or describing some aspect of home life. Beyond the opportunity to draw upon familiar subject matter, an additional incentive was the knowledge that the best compositions would be published in the school's newspaper, *The Indian Leader.* Over the years, Haskell allotted numerous columns to such creations as "An Indian Burial Custom," "Why Frogs

Cannot Walk," "Why the Turtle Has a Checkered Back," and "The Papago Legend of the Formation of the Earth." With Leupp's blessing, this sensible innovation, one fully consistent with the spirit of educational progressivism, rapidly spread to other off-reservation schools.[26]

Another manifestation of the new attitude was the encouragement of Indian arts and crafts. "I have no sympathy with the sentiment which would throw the squaw's bead bag into the rubbish heap and set her to making lace," Leupp declared in his first annual report. Certainly Indian girls should be taught new skills, "but don't set down her beaded moccasins as merely barbarous, while holding up her lace handkerchief as a symbol of advanced civilization." Having observed firsthand the attempts of young Navajo girls to use chair legs as makeshift looms for weaving small rugs in the dormitory at Albuquerque Indian School, Leupp had no doubts about the desire of students to work in native art forms. Superintendents were instructed to build their programs around their students' particular heritage. Navajos should be encouraged at rug weaving and silversmithing, Papagos at basketry, Pueblos at pottery, and Cheyennes at beadwork. Literally in a matter of months, Carlisle, Albuquerque, Santa Fe, Phoenix, Chilocco, and many other schools as well instituted some kind of native arts program. At Leupp's direction, several schools employed native artists to direct students' work.[27]

Leupp justified these changes in a couple of ways. For one thing, preserving and building upon the Indians' artistic heritage in no way contradicted the established aims of Indian schooling. Just as white civilization still cherished simple stories of Cinderella and Sleeping Beauty, products of an earlier stage in its own social evolution, why shouldn't Indians be allowed the same privilege? "As a matter of fact," Leupp opined, "the last thing that ought to be done with youth of any people whom we are trying to indoctrinate with notions of self-respect is to teach them to be ashamed of their ancestry." Also, there was a practical side to the question. Native crafts were an important source of tribal income, particularly in the Southwest, where "authentic" Indian rugs, baskets, and pottery were in high demand by traders and tourists. In 1905 the superintendent at Fort Defiance informed Leupp that during the previous year alone, Navajo rug sales had accounted for about 25 percent of the tribe's income. By encouraging such industries, schools could contribute significantly to the goal of economic self-reliance.[28]

It must be stressed that neither the increased emphasis on vocationalism nor Leupp's fainthearted gesture on behalf of Indian culture did much to alter the overall character of boarding school life. As already discussed, vocational training and chore work had always been important components of Indian schooling. The new appreciation for Indian folklore and crafts, moreover, never entertained the possibility that these accomplishments were anything more than aesthetically pleasing, enchanting renderings of a noble race still in the childhood of civilization ("Like other primitive peoples" introduces a collection of Indian stories published in 1913 by Haskell Institute).[29] In the main, the defining institutional features remained intact—the routine, the iron discipline, the long separations. The fact is that two graduates of Haskell, one from the class of 1890, the other from the class of 1920, would have had little difficulty identifying with the other's experience.

Two other proposals, however, held out the possibility of producing genuine change. The first was the call to shift the emphasis away from the off-reservation school to the reservation boarding school and the day school. A segment of opinion within the Indian Office had always questioned the wisdom of educating Indian children far from home. Writing from the field in 1890, Superintendent of Indian Schools David Dorchester announced that "the time has come to build more at the base and less at the apex." Three years later, he reiterated this theme by proclaiming that reservation schools were the location where the *great mass of the Indian children should be educated.*" It remained for Leupp, however, to suggest that some off-reservation schools actually be shut down. The whole question of Indian education, Leupp wrote in his 1907 annual report, "pivots on the question whether we are to carry civilization to the Indian or carry the Indian to civilization." Favoring the former approach, Leupp was willing to grant that reservation boarding schools would remain a practical necessity in those regions where Indians still lived a nomadic or seminomadic existence. Perhaps, a few off-reservation schools also should be maintained for those seeking "higher" education. But in the main, "the non-reservation schools can be, and ought to be, dropped off one by one or two by two, . . . the beginning of their gradual dissolution ought to be no longer deferred."[30]

The vacuum would be filled by enlarging the day school system. Leupp's faith in day schools is revealed in his experimentation with building open-air schools in the arid Southwest. Called "bird cages" by his detractors, the distinctive architectural feature of these wooden-frame buildings was the top half of the walls, which was constructed of wire screen, complete with mounted rolls of canvas to be lowered in case of sand- or rainstorms. In addition to cutting costs and providing plenty of fresh air as a preventive to tuberculosis, the open-air design was consistent with the commissioner's view that Indian children were "little wild creatures, accustomed to life in the open air, familiar with the voices of nature rather than the voices of men." At one point, Leupp even flirted with a more radical idea: creating "portable schools" for tribes like the seminomadic Navajo. Under this plan, specially constructed buildings and school furniture would be transported from campsite to campsite of migrating tribesmen. The problem, he admitted, would be finding teachers willing to undergo the hardship. For this and other practical considerations, the scheme was soon abandoned. But Leupp held firm to his original conviction: day schools should be the focus of future educational efforts.[31]

Even more significant was the growing support for transferring responsibility for Indian education to the public schools.[32] Late-nineteenth-century reformers had always looked upon the public school as the quintessential American institution, a symbol of freedom and democracy, the ideal forum for transmitting traditional American beliefs of republicanism, capitalism, and protestantism. Now that land allotment and white settlement had thrown the two races into closer association, public schools were now a practical possibility. Actually, the first efforts along these lines began in the early 1890s when the Indian Office offered local districts a financial inducement—$10 per capita per quarter—for accepting Indian pupils. In the beginning, progress was slow, evidenced by the fact that in 1896 only 303 Indian students were officially enrolled in local school systems. The next twenty years, however, would constitute a virtual revolution. In 1917, Commissioner Cato Sells announced that the Indian Office had contracts with some forty-six school districts and that the $20,000 appropriated was inadequate. Intensive pressure from the Indian Office as well as the added incentive of a higher rate of reimbursement—now up to an average of fifteen cents per day—was clearly getting results.[33]

How did the call for day and public schools affect patterns of Indian schooling? One consequence was a steady decline in the number of government schools. Between 1900 and 1925, the total number dropped from 253 (25 off-reservation boarding, 81 reservation boarding, 147 day schools) to 209 (18 off-reservation boarding, 51 reservation boarding, 140 day schools). Particularly significant is the precipitous decline in boarding schools. What the figures do not reveal is the dramatic increase in day schools during the second decade, a rise from 139 in 1905 to 228 in 1915, a direct result of Leupp's and his successor's efforts. The steady decline in subsequent years can be explained by the growing reliance on public schools.[34]

Periodic snapshots on the distribution of student enrollment offer another useful perspective (see Table 10.1). The figures are revealing in three respects. First, one notes the rise and decline in day school enrollments between 1905 and 1920. Second, the overall level of enrollment in government schools, including boarding schools, was actually *higher* in 1925 than in 1900, although a slight decline occurred after 1915. The third and most significant development, however, is the sharp increase in public school enrollment. By 1915, the number was nearly equal to those at-

Table 10.1. Distribution of Indian Students by Institutional Type, 1900–1925

	1900	1905	1910	1915	1920	1925
Government Schools						
Off-reservation boarding	7,430	9,736	8,863	10,791	10,198	8,542
Reservation boarding	9,604	11,402	10,765	9,899	9,433	10,615
Day schools	5,090	4,399	7,152	7,270	5,765	4,604
Subtotal	22,124	25,537	26,780	27,960	25,396	23,761
Public Schools	246	84	2,722	26,438	30,858	34,452
Other Mission, private, and state institutions—contract and noncontract	4,081	4,485	5,150	5,049	5,546	7,280
TOTAL	26,451	30,106	34,652	59,447	61,800	65,493

Source: Annual Report of the Commissioner of Indian Affairs (ARCIA), 1900, 22; ARCIA, 1905, 50; ARCIA, 1910, 56; ARCIA, 1915, 51; ARCIA, 1920, 147; and ARCIA, 1925, 51.

tending government schools, and thereafter, would capture an ever-growing percentage of Indian students.

Still, one is struck by the large number of students still attending boarding schools. Several factors explain this. First, in some regions Indian settlement patterns, terrain, and poor road conditions often dictated the maintenance and even expansion of some institutions. Second, a large number of school-age children still were not enrolled in any school. In 1924, the Indian Bureau admitted that "there are several thousand Navajo children of school age out of school because of lack of school facilities." For this population especially, boarding schools were deemed to be a practical necessity. Third, for those students moving through the system into the higher grades—and there were increasing numbers—the only possibility for future educational advancement in some localities was to attend one of the larger federal institutions. (In 1926, the Indian Office announced that the Albuquerque, Chilocco, and Salem schools would offer grades ten through twelve. Fourth, local communities, which derived considerable economic benefits from federal institutions—either in the form of government contracts, student spending, or cheap labor through outing programs—were frequently loath to give up such facilities. Finally, some policymakers questioned whether the wholesale transfer of pupils to the public realm was in Indian children's best interests. It was claimed that Indian students' poverty, backwardness, and poor language skills, combined with white prejudice and discriminatory school policies, hardly enhanced educational opportunity.[35]

At the same time, the discerning observer of Indian affairs could not miss the fact that unmistakable changes were taking place. In this respect, the closing of Carlisle, as well as the demise of the Indian program at Hampton Institute, spoke volumes.

THE CLOSING OF CARLISLE

In the beginning there had been only Pratt and his Florida prisoners. Pratt, with his faith in Indian capacity. Pratt, the destroyer of all things Indian. Pratt, the benevolent father figure. By the 1890s, as one of the most revered figures in Indian reform, one would think that the indomitable captain—still on leave from his regiment—would have been content to quietly manage his beloved Carlisle until his retirement. But passivity was not in Pratt's character, particularly when principles dear to his heart were at stake. For Pratt, the all-encompassing objective of Indian policy always had been the complete assimilation of the race into American society. Convinced that the government was settling for less, he lashed out at those who questioned his prescriptions for the solution of the Indian problem. Pratt's talent for inspiring reformers was matched only by his penchant for making enemies, a trait that finally brought him down.

By the 1890s Pratt spent as much time criticizing fellow reformers as he did attacking the Indian Office. Although some of this invective can be attributed to sheer jealousy and obstinacy, part can also be explained by his very real differences with mainstream reformers. First, until the early 1890s, reformers favored government support of religious contract schools. Pratt was an ardent critic of this policy, believing that missionaries, in their efforts to build Christian congregations, frequently ignored the larger business at hand—preparing Indians for citizenship in the white man's civilization. Second, Pratt was a vehement critic of extending civil service rules to the Indian school service. Although his opposition can be explained in part by his resentment of any bureaucratic interference in his freedom to select Carlisle's teachers, it originated also from his conviction that the policy was fundamentally flawed. As Pratt complained to Senator Henry Dawes in 1898, "character and force is one thing, and the ability to answer civil service questions quite another." Finally, Pratt was intensely embittered by reform organizations' general neutrality on the issue of the one best institutional model for educating Indians. Until the end of his days, Pratt remained convinced that only off-reservation schools—and even then, only those that were located in white communities far removed from the reservation and frontier environments—would genuinely accomplish Indian assimilation.[36]

Pratt's declining influence is evident in his ever-widening split with Herbert Welsh. In the summer of 1892, when Carlisle's *Red Man* published a brief column intimating opposition to civil service reform, Welsh, in disbelief, immediately wrote Pratt asking if he had properly understood the article's meaning. In an insulting letter, Pratt confirmed Welsh's interpretation of the column and then plainly told him that he and his organization could accomplish much more by actually doing the day-to-day work of uplifting Indians rather than attempting to manage government policy. Shortly thereafter, Welsh, to his later regret, shared a speaker's platform with Carlisle's superintendent. Welsh wrote Charles Painter concerning the event, "Captain Pratt was present and gave us the most extreme illustration of his salient peculiarity,—his fondness for attempting to knife his friends." Welsh's anger stemmed from the fact that he had graciously assented to the captain's request that he be allowed to speak last. As Welsh recounted to Painter: "He did speak after me, and in a most violent and outrageous manner gave the lie to everything that I said; informed the audience, . . . that he spoke as he did in order to disabuse the minds of what the previous speaker had told them."[37]

The complete falling out, however, did not come until the last months of the Cleveland administration, when Pratt broke with Welsh on his efforts to have William Hailmann retained as Superintendent of Indian Schools. Hailmann's retention, Welsh believed, would constitute a major victory over the tradition of spoils in the Indian Office. Pratt, who had had his differences with Hailmann, mainly over the right to select his own teachers, openly made his opposition known. In the fall of 1896, Welsh, convinced that Pratt's criticism of Hailmann bordered on outright insubordination, toyed with the idea of suggesting Pratt's dismissal, but fearing a public brawl among reformers decided instead to recommend to Secretary of the Interior David Francis that Pratt only be disciplined in some way. Leupp, now Washington agent for the association, confirmed the difficulty of actually attaining Pratt's dismissal, "Every Commissioner and Secretary has been terrorized by Pratt, on the theory that to dismiss him would be to call down upon the administration a storm of abuse from well-meaning but misguided champions of Carlisle." In late November, Leupp informed Welsh that Pratt had gotten off with a stiff warning.[38]

But Pratt was not so easily silenced. In January 1897, *Red Man* published a blistering indictment of civil service reform, and in the same issue offered this assessment of the Indian Rights Association:

> In our judgement and knowing its work through all the years, it never had any usefulness, and has only been a hindrance. It was founded on false principles, and has been so conducted throughout. It never removed an atom of dirt from a single Indian, nor did it ever take a single Indian by the hand and lead him from his dirt and vermin surroundings out into the clean atmosphere of civilization where

he can divest himself of these inherited infirmities; nor has it tried in all its years to introduce any Indian to civilization and induce him to locate and feel at home and to make himself useful to his fellow men in that civilization; nor does it in any of its work or plans tend to accomplish these things, but it rather hinders the accomplishment of them.[39]

Welsh immediately defended the association's record but was still unwilling to risk open warfare by calling for Pratt's dismissal. Meanwhile, the Cleveland administration, now in its last days, chose to leave the question of Pratt's future to another administration.[40]

Pratt hung onto his post for several more years.[41] In early 1904, now in his early sixties, the old campaigner was apparently looking for an opportunity to leave the field of battle with cannons roaring and flags fluttering. The opportunity presented itself when he was invited to address the New York Ministers' Conference on May 9, 1904. "I believe that nothing better could happen to the Indians than the complete destruction of the Bureau," Pratt told his audience. "Better for the Indians had there never been a Bureau." Its chief function had been only to segregate Indians on reservations where the light of civilization and citizenship were all but impenetrable. "Theorizing citizenship into a people is a slow operation," Pratt proclaimed. "THEY MUST GET INTO THE SWIM OF AMERICAN CITIZENSHIP. They must feel the touch of it day after day until they become saturated with the spirit of it, and thus become equal to it." It was vintage Pratt. But with the Carlisle philosophy increasingly out of step with the emerging policy of gradualism, and with the number of Pratt's supporters now greatly diminished, on June 15, 1904, Commissioner Jones informed the founder of Carlisle that his services were no longer required. The Pratt years were over.[42]

Under Pratt's successors, William Mercer and Moses Friedman, Carlisle entered a period of general decline.[43] By late 1913, conditions had deteriorated to the point that some 276 students signed a petition requesting an official investigation of conditions at the school. On January 19, 1914, Secretary of the Interior Franklin Lane dispatched Inspector E. B. Linnen to Carlisle to conduct an independent inquiry but also to lay the groundwork for a follow-up investigation by a four-member joint congressional committee. Both Linnen and the committee took extensive testimony from members of the staff and student body. The investigation focused on three issues: Moses Friedman's fitness as superintendent, the role of athletics, and allegations of excessive corporal punishment.[44]

It was immediately clear to Linnen, and later the committee, that Carlisle had suffered greatly under Friedman's rule. The consequences could be seen in the health-threatening decline in dietary standards, a dangerous weakening of the school's moral atmosphere (as evidenced by increased instances of drunkenness and fornication), and perhaps most important of all, a "lack of any human side or fatherly interest in the welfare of this student body." Testimony revealed that the superintendent was regarded with "contempt" by the vast majority of students and employees. According to Linnen, students were nearly in "open rebellion" when he arrived. Friedman was so despised by students that on various occasions he had been hooted and jeered and even made the target of such epithets as "old Jew," "Christ-Killer," and "pork-dodger," perhaps out of resentment to the superintendent's penchant for calling students "savages." Friedman's wife also drew fire in the course of testimony. On one occasion she had been seen on the school lawn performing a "skirt-dance," kicking up her heels "until you could see up to her knees," on another, playing "peek-a-boo" with her husband around porch pillars. And then there was the hypocrisy of the girls not being allowed to use "paint and powder" on their faces even though Mrs. Friedman did and even blackened her eyebrows. The larger issue however was Friedman's incompetency. Carlisle, once the crown jewel in the Indian school service, was gradually being destroyed.[45]

The athletic program was a particular object of criticism. At issue here was the exaggerated status of athletics in the overall school program. In the course of winning glory on the gridiron, the school had lost sight of its priorities. Coach Glen Warner, not Friedman, was the real lord and master of Carlisle. Nonathletic students were resentful of the special treatment accorded to the football players, who were provided with separate quarters and given a superior diet. And then there were all the gifts—the sweaters, the overcoats, the suits of clothing, the watches, and even cash payments—all paid for by the athletic fund. Notwithstanding these special privileges, some of the football players despised Coach Warner. In sworn statements, team members volunteered that Warner, although a brilliant gridiron strategist, possessed a character that made him fundamentally unfit as a leader and role model. Summarizing the affidavit of Gus Welsh, Linnen noted in his report, "He believes Mr. Warner is a good football coach, but a man with no principle; . . . that he has used the worst cursing and swearing that he could use; that Coach Warner would say to football boys he was vexed at: 'You God damn bone head,' or 'You son of a bitch'; that he would use such language most every day on the athletic field." Warner, others testified, once had kicked a player and struck another with a switch. They had seen him in hotel lobbies pocketing the rake-off from selling complimentary tickets and gambling on game outcomes. In short, the Indians had seen enough of this ill-tempered, disrespectful, dishonest white man, in spite of his reputation as the "greatest coach in the world."[46]

The controversy surrounding corporal punishment mainly centered on the whipping of Julia Hardin, an eighteen-year-old Potawatomi student. The episode began when Hardin, who had signed on for an outing assignment, refused to leave on short notice, giving the reason that she had not had the time to acquire the necessary clothes nor trunk. Hardin appealed to Superintendent Friedman but to no avail; she must go to the country. In the last hours before the train's departure, Hardin was ordered to the sewing room, where Hannah Ridenour, the hard-nosed matron, was to supervise her packing and secure the girl's signature on a check for train fare. But Hardin refused to cooperate, whereupon Claude Stauffer, the school bandmaster and sometime disciplinarian, entered the room (earlier in the day Stauffer had told Friedman that the defiant Hardin needed a good "straightening out" and had received permission to spank her). When Hardin repeated her determination not to leave at the stipulated time, Stauffer slapped her across the face and announced, "You are going to sign the check and go to the country tonight at 5 o'clock." At this point, Hardin later testified, Stauffer "jerked a board down from one of the window sills and he punched me down on the floor, and two of the matrons held me; Miss Ridenour was one, and I don't know who the other was. They put down the curtains, so no one could see in, and they locked the door." Stauffer gave Hardin a good beating, striking several blows to the head. Still, it was only after some persuading from one of the teachers that the stubborn Potawatomi relented (Matron Ridenour testified that the girl's punishment "was not half enough").[47]

After receiving Linnen's and the committee's separate reports, Commissioner Cato Sells followed up on their recommendations. Both Friedman and Stauffer were dismissed from the school service and Matron Ridenour was transferred to another institution. The renowned "Pop" Warner, who technically speaking was never a government employee, moved on to greener gridirons. Several other employees received "stiff" reprimands. To restore Carlisle's now tainted reputation, Oscar Lipps, a school service veteran, was brought in to replace Friedman. Lipps did his best to upgrade the program and rekindle the old spirit, at one point writing Pratt, "Carlisle was a very sick child two years ago, and it required drastic measures to bring it back to recovery." At this point, however, the school was living on borrowed time. In 1918, on the pretext that Carlisle's facilities were needed as a hospital for soldiers returning from the war in Europe, Secretary of War Newton Baker requested that the property be returned to the War Department. In the fall of the same year, the school was closed.[48]

For those who once had looked upon Carlisle as the solution to the Indian question, and no doubt for a good many graduates as well, the news must have been received with more than a tinge of sadness. Haskell, perhaps fearing for its own life, responded with:

Carlisle is not dead. Carlisle will never die. The thousands of Carlisle students will transmit its history and its glories to their children and their children's children, and generations hence it will be a matter of pride, not exceeded by that of the descendent of a *Mayflower* passenger, to say that an ancestor was a graduate of the Carlisle Indian school.[49]

INDIANS LEAVE HAMPTON INSTITUTE

In some respects, the death of the Indian program at Hampton Institute was even more tortuous. The crucial moment came in 1912 when Congress eliminated Hampton's annual appropriation of $167 per student. This turn of events can be explained along several lines. Certainly one reason was the fact that Hollis Frissell, Hampton's superintendent after Armstrong's death in 1893, never commanded the public following that his more charismatic predecessor had inspired. The ever-growing dissatisfaction with off-reservation schools, particularly those located a great distance from the students' native environment, was another factor. Also, there was long-standing congressional opposition to funding church-affiliated contract schools. Although technically speaking Hampton was nondenominational and nonsectarian, it was still an anomaly in the Indian school system.[50]

The determining factor in the funding debate, however, was the biracial character of the school, the fact that Hampton educated both blacks and Indians. Ever since the arrival of Pratt's "Florida boys" in 1878, Armstrong had viewed the presence of Indians as an ideal opportunity for illustrating on a grander scale the Hampton philosophy on race and education. Blacks, according to the Hampton philosophy, although not as civilized as whites, were still more advanced than Indians for the simple reason that they had undergone the experience of slavery. Slavery, for all its brutality, had taught Africans two vital aspects of civilization: the importance of work and the Christian religion. Indians, therefore, could benefit immensely through their association with blacks, who might serve as role models for upward advancement. In line with this philosophy, Hampton used blacks as supervisors in the dormitory, on the drill field, and in the shops. Meanwhile, the two races were integrated in some areas of school life and segregated in others. In later years, when Indians arrived fluent in English, the general policy was to place them in classrooms alongside blacks. In other areas of school life the races were largely kept apart. Indians usually lived in a separate dormitory, ate at separate dining tables, and after 1890, drilled in a separate company. Interracial dating was strictly forbidden.[51]

But even this limited association between the races was insufficient to quell a rising chorus of critics who saw in Hampton's biracial experiment a serious breach of the "color line." The importance of the race issue immediately became clear in the course of congressional deliberations. The funding crisis began when the House Committee on Indian Affairs, chaired by Representative John Stephens of Texas, recommended dropping Hampton from the annual appropriation bill. In the subsequent debate, key congressmen made known their objections to Hampton's policy of race mixing. "Why humiliate the Indian boys and girls, our wards and dependents, by educating them in the same schools with Negro children?" Stephens asked. In the opinion of the committee, the federal government ought to "elevate the red race to the level of the white race and not degrade and humiliate him by sinking him to the low plane of the Negro race." Charles Carter, an Indian (Chickasaw) congressman from Oklahoma, fought off the attempt to restore funding by offering the observation that the Indian "has nothing left but his self-respect, and now you come to him with Hampton school and ask him to surrender that self-respect by placing his children on a social equality with an inferior race, a level to which you yourself will not deign to descend." But mostly the opposition to funding came from white southerners. In an era of heightened racism and negrophobia, amid predictions of black degeneracy and fears of racial amalgamation, the Hampton philosophy of race, in spite of its assumptions of white superiority in the racial hierarchy, was clearly out of step with the times.[52]

Behind the scenes, Hampton and its supporters attempted to influence the outcome in its favor. In a letter to members of the House and Senate committees on Indian affairs, Frissell reiterated the school's belief that it was "a distinct advantage to the Indian to be placed at his work in the classroom beside the best element of the Negro race," but went on to emphasize the separation of the races in other spheres of school life. Writing to Representative Carter, he made special note of the fact that

> I sympathize with you strongly in your earnest desire to keep the Indian on the highest possible plane, and am quite as much opposed as you are to anything which looks like amalgamation of the Indian and Negro races. As far as I know, and we keep very careful records of our students, there has never resulted a single marriage from the bringing together here of Negroes and Indians.

Meanwhile, Booker T. Washington took an active role in the campaign, writing several letters to prominent congressmen on behalf of his alma mater, as did Hampton's Indian students, who submitted a lengthy petition to the Senate stressing that "the thrifty, hard-working Negro boys and girls at Hampton have much . . . to give us.''[53] But the fears of race mixing were not easily assuaged. Although Hampton's lobbying did succeed in restoring the school's funding in the Senate version of the bill, ultimate defeat of the provision was sealed when a joint conference committee voted against it by the narrow margin of a single vote.[54]

No doubt Booker Washington was less surprised than most regarding the outcome. As the first dormitory supervisor of the Indians, he had experienced on two occasions the painful incongruence between Hampton's philosophy that placed blacks above Indians on the scale of civilization and prevailing racial attitudes just beyond the school gate where physical features, including skin color, assumed much more importance. Both incidents had occurred when Washington, at Armstrong's request, was accompanying a returning Indian student as far as Washington, D.C. Traveling by steamboat, Washington naively assumed there would be no difficulty with the two eating in the ship's dining room. Waiting until the "greater number of passengers had finished their meal," Washington and his charge made their entrance, only to be informed that the Indian could be served but Washington could not. The same situation repeated itself in the nation's capital when the two travelers sought hotel accommodations. The Indian could stay the night, the clerk informed them, but Washington must seek lodging elsewhere. In *Up from Slavery,* Washington would describe the episode as an interesting illustration of "the curious workings of caste in America."[55]

In any event, the loss of funding in 1912 killed the school's Indian program. The number of Indians dropped from eighty-one in 1912 to forty-five in 1915, and to a mere sixteen in 1919. "The indications are that Hampton's work for the Indians is coming to an end," the school's principal moaned in 1918.[56] The Indian years were nearly over, and by 1923, they were gone.

TOWARD PLURALISM

The decade of the 1920s was an era of contradictions. On one level, little changed in the overall direction of federal Indian policy. In a depressed postwar economic climate, the Indian school service tightened its belt and devoted most of its energies to fine-tuning the existing educational program. On another level, the decade was marked by turmoil and bitter debate as a new breed of reformers ferociously assaulted not only the government's conduct of Indian policy but its ideological underpinnings as well. Although older reform organizations like the Board of Indian Commissioners and especially the Indian Rights Association still continued to wield influence, new organizations made their appearance, notably the

Indian Welfare Committee of the General Federation of Women's Clubs, chaired by Stella Atwood, and more importantly, the American Indian Defense Association, led by the irrepressible John Collier. Initially galvanized into action by the so-called Barsum bill, an attempt to dispossess New Mexican Pueblo Indians of a substantial amount of real estate, but also by renewed attempts by the Indian Office to suppress Indian dances, the new reformers, particularly Collier, drew from an ideological wellspring altogether different from their predecessors—pluralism.[57]

Born in 1884, John Collier spent his youth in Atlanta, Georgia. From his mother, he acquired a deep love of literature and appreciation for nature; from his father, a prominent lawyer and banker, he learned the importance of community service. Still in his teens, Collier was devastated by the death of both parents, his mother's in 1897 after a long and painful illness, his father's three years later by suicide. After these shattering events, Collier, deeply depressed, began a long search for a direction and meaning in his life. Vowing to reject "all desire for worldly or hedonistic success," he was slowly rejuvenated by his reading of Wordsworth and long camping trips in the Appalachians. On one of these camping retreats, Collier, sitting on a mountaintop, experienced a vision when a bird appeared at sunset and uttered a silent but unmistakable appeal for Collier to join his soul in "the immortal effort toward creation in which I, the bird, need you." In 1902, he left for Columbia University, where he pursued studies in literature, biology, and sociology and along the way encountered works by Freud, Jung, Nietzsche, and Lester Frank Ward. During this period a central tenet of Collier's social outlook was emerging: the belief in the capacity of man to willfully shape social institutions toward utopian ends. After visiting Europe, where he familiarized himself with labor and cooperative organizations, Collier returned to the United States and threw himself into the cause of social reform.[58]

In 1907 he accepted a position as civic secretary at the People's Institute, a settlement house serving mainly Jewish and Italian immigrants in New York's bustling Manhattan district. Endeavoring to use the institute as a forum for both cushioning the process of adjustment to urban society and as a force for fostering community consciousness, Collier organized an array of recreational and educational programs consistent with these aims. Using the institute as a base, he was soon developing school community centers and setting up a school for training social workers. But the election of a conservative mayor and the nation's entry into World War I soon reduced Collier's beloved school community centers, which had once blossomed with educational programs devoted to ethnic culture and social reform, to selling war bonds and performing other patriotic activities. Collier had mixed feelings about the war, but when he saw the terms of settlement in 1919, his disillusionment with Western, industrial-capitalist society "was complete." Wanting a change of scenery, he left New York to become director of adult education for the state of California. Assuming the post in the middle of the "red scare," he was soon in trouble with West Coast politicians for his radical views and within the year was again without employment. At this point he did what he always did in periods of frustration, retreated to the wilderness. Or at least that was his intent until a letter arrived from Mabel Dodge Luhan, whom Collier had known in New York, beseeching him to visit her at her newly adopted home in Taos, New Mexico. Knowing of Collier's constant search for examples of "deep community," she wanted him to see the "magical" Indian pueblo at Taos.[59]

The visit to Taos proved to be a turning point in Collier's life. Arriving in late December, he was in time to witness the Taos Indians' performance of the Red Deer Dance, an event that appealed greatly to his communal-mystical being. Pueblo Indian life surely had something to teach modern civilization. As he later wrote in his memoirs:

> The discovery that came to me there, in that tiny group of a few hundred Indians, was of personality-forming institutions, even now unweakened, which had survived repeated and immense historical shocks, and which were going right on in the production of states of mind, attitudes of mind, earth-loyalties and human loyalties, amid a context of beauty which suffused all the life of the group. What I observed and experienced was a power of art—of the life-making art—greater in kind than anything I had known in my own world before. Not tiny, but huge, this little group and its personalities seemed. There were solitary vigils which carried the individual out into the cosmos, and there were communal rituals whose grave, tranquil, yet earth-shaking intensity is not adequately suggested by anything outside the music of Bach.

Visiting Taos "led me to say within myself, with absolute finality about the Indians: *This* effort toward community must not fail; there can be no excuse or pardon if it fails."[60]

And so Collier threw himself into the cause of Indian reform. In the summer of 1923 he founded the American Indian Defense Association, and over the next decade he waged a relentless war against the government's Indian policy, concentrating his fire on two broad themes: the failure of the Indian Office to protect native landholdings (Collier was for abandoning allotment policies) and its determination to destroy Indian culture in the name of assimilation. It was in connection to the latter that he vigorously denounced past educational policies, including the continued reliance on boarding schools. Such schools were fundamentally bankrupt, not only because they severed a child's familial ties but also because they systematically attempted to "proselyte the child and shame him away from his tribal settings, his Indianhood." All and all, boarding schools stood as a glaring symbol of the diabolical character of government Indian policy.[61]

Although other critics were seldom as vehement as Collier, the collective sting of reformers' attacks began to take its toll, eventually convincing Secretary of the Interior Hubert Work that a comprehensive evaluation of Indian policy was in order. In January 1926, at the advice of the Board of Indian Commissioners, Work commissioned the Institute for Government Research, an independent unit of the Brookings Institution, to conduct just such a study in a "thoroughly impartial and scientific spirit." The person selected to direct this investigation was Lewis Meriam, one of the institute's most knowledgeable staff members on government efficiency. Meriam, in turn, selected a panel of eight investigators, all chosen for their expertise in some particular policy area. Carson Ryan, a noted progressive educator, was selected to head up the study of Indian schools. Once assembled, Meriam's team spent seven months in the field including visitations to schools and hospitals. In January 1928, the group presented its findings to Secretary Work in a massive document that was published as *The Problem of Indian Administration,* more commonly known as the Meriam Report.[62]

The Meriam Report began with a simple statement, which if taken to heart was a declaration of the failure of government Indian policy to achieve its historic objective: "An overwhelming majority of the Indians are poor, even extremely poor, and they are not adjusted to the economic and social system of the dominant white civilization." In the areas of economic development, health services, and education, government programs were found to be terribly inadequate. A particular problem was the poor quality of Indian service personnel. Poor salaries and impossible living conditions meant that the Indian Bureau had become the employer of last resort for legions of underqualified teachers, doctors, nurses, and farmers. Moreover, until the Indian Bureau was properly funded, until Indians were protected against the ravages of tuberculosis and trachoma, until the upper levels of Indian administration possessed the technical expertise to modernize reservation economies, and until Indian schools genuinely prepared students for economic self-sufficiency and civic participation, the Indian problem could never be solved.[63]

The report's section on education found much to criticize. Noting that four-fifths of those Indian students educated by the government were still attending boarding schools, the report offered a seething indictment of the conditions observed in these institutions. In many schools poor quality of diet presented a genuine threat to children's health. Forced to feed children at the rate of eleven cents a day, superintendents, except in those schools favored by sizable school farms and dairys, were compelled to deny students the necessary amounts of fruits, vegetables, and milk. Lack of nutrition, combined with the overcrowded dormitories and unsanitary living conditions, was positively health-threatening. Moreover, the terrible "routinization" of school life was squelching all "initiative and independence" in students. The survey team found the use of student labor particularly pernicious. Much of what went under the title of industrial education was in fact nothing more than "production work" performed to maintain the institution. Even instruction in the higher trades was terribly deficient. In some cases the training was simply irrelevant to home conditions; in others, students were mastering "vanishing trades."[64]

The fundamental challenge facing policymakers, however, was not merely that of upgrading the existing system. On the contrary, "the first and foremost need in education is a change in point of view." Whereas past educational efforts had been based on the perceived need "to remove the child as far as possible from his home environment," the "modern point of view" stressed the necessity of connecting children's education to family and community. In short, students should be educated as long as practical in day schools, where educational methods could be "adapted to individual abilities, interests, and needs." In such schools the idea of a standard or uniform curriculum must be abandoned and the teacher allowed "to gather material from the life of the Indians about her, so that the little children may proceed from the known to the unknown and not be plunged at once into a world where all is unknown and unfamiliar." The report fully acknowledged that boarding schools, owing principally to the "nature of Indian country," would continue for many years to be a fact of life for students educated beyond the sixth grade. Recognizing this, it recommended that at the upper levels the course of study be brought into closer alignment with the public schools, thereby encouraging promising scholars to attend college. The report also generally praised the policy of moving Indian students into local public schools. But the overriding theme could not be missed: the community day school, firmly rooted in the pedagogy of progressive education, should constitute the basis for Indian advancement.[65]

But advancement along what lines? On whose terms? On these questions Meriam and his associates were intentionally vague. In the final analysis, future government policy "must give consideration to the desires of the individual Indians." Thus, Indians wishing to enter mainstream white society "should be given all practicable aid and advice in making the necessary adjustments." On the other hand, an Indian "who wants to remain an Indian and live according to his old culture should be aided in doing so." In fact, the survey team, viewing firsthand how the "advancing tide of white civilization" was pressing upon native life, doubted both the practicality and desirability of the second option, at least for the younger generation.[66] Thus, in the final analysis, the Meriam Report was not so much an indictment of the assimilationist ideal as a renewed call for the government to live up to its humanitarian obligations in light of that ideal. Still, for the first time in fifty years, the possibility for a new era in Indian policy—for an Indian "New Deal"—had been suggested. It had been a long time coming.

CONCLUSION

In retrospect it is not surprising that reformers should look to schools as central to the solution of the Indian problem. As an instrument for fostering social cohesion and republicanism, no institution had been more important in the spread of the American system. In the case of Indians, the challenge facing educators was particularly difficult: the eradication of all traces of tribal identity and culture, replacing them with the commonplace knowledge and values of white civilization. Reformers believed that the school's capacity to accomplish this transformation would determine the long-term fate of the Indian race, for if the doctrine of historical progress and the story of westward expansion taught anything, it was the incompatibility of white civilization and Indian savagism. The former must inevitably supplant the latter. Fortunately, Indians need not perish as a race. Once they shed their attachment to tribal ways—that is to say, their Indianness—and joined the march of American progress, their continued existence in the nation's future was assured. Schools would show them the way.

Boarding schools, especially the off-reservation variety, seemed ideally suited for this purpose. As the theory went, Indian children, once removed from the savage surroundings of the Indian camp and placed in the purified environment of an all-encompassing institution, would slowly learn to look, act, and eventually think like their white counterparts. From the daily regimentation and routine Indian children would learn the need for order and self-discipline. In the half-day schedule devoted to academics they would master the fundamentals of English, take to heart the moral maxims of McGuffey, and from their history textbook appreciate the meaning of 1492. Balancing the academic side would be classes in industrial training and domestic science, a rotating system of institutional chores, and outing assignments, all designed to prepare them for the path ahead. Sunday sermons, midweek prayer meetings, holiday ceremonies, patriotic drills, and football contests, all in their own way, would contribute to the students' cultural metamorphosis. When it was all over, the onetime youthful specimens of savagism would be thoroughly Christianized, individualized, and republicanized, fit candidates for American citizenship and ideal agents for uplifting an older generation still stranded in the backwaters of barbarism—"a little child shall lead them."

Judged by the ambitious scope of their assimilationist vision, reformers clearly failed to achieve their objective. Beyond the fact that congressional parsimony never allowed the educational assault to be waged with the intensity that reformers envisioned, the reasons for their failure go much deeper. Underlying the reform program was the presupposition that the acculturation process was a relatively simple matter of exchanging one cultural skin for another. The possibility that Indians, either as students or returnees, once having been exposed to the white man's cultural system would react in any manner other than complete embracement, that the acculturation process itself could involve various forms of selective incorporation, syncretization, and compartmentalization, was beyond their comprehension. As this study has shown, Indian students were anything but passive recipients of the curriculum of civilization. When choosing the path of resistance, they bolted the institution, torched buildings, and engaged in a multitude of schemes to undermine the school program. Even the response of accommodation was frequently little more than a conscious and strategic adaptation to the hard rock of historical circumstance, a pragmatic recognition that one's Indianness would increasingly have to be defended and negotiated in the face of relentless hegemonic forces.

If the boarding school failed to fulfill reformers' expectations, it still had a profound impact on an Indian child's psychological and cultural being. Returning students, whatever their disposition toward their late experience, could not help but be affected by their sustained exposure to white ways of knowing and living during which time they inevitably acquired new attitudes, values, skills, prejudices, desires, and habits of behavior. Like it or not, most returned students were agents of cultural change, and over time white education would constitute one of the major acculturative forces shaping Indian society. On the other hand, one of the chief consequences for students attending an off-reservation facility was an enlarged sense of identity as "Indians." At schools like Carlisle and Haskell, Sioux children were regularly thrown into intimate association with Comanche and Navajo. At Sherman Institute, Hopi slept, ate, drilled, and played alongside Cahuilla and Serrano. At such institutions students learned that the "Great Father" made no allowances for tribal distinctions; Indians were simply Indians. Ironically, the very institution designed to extinguish Indian identity altogether may have in fact contributed to its very persistence in the form of twentieth-century pan-Indian consciousness.

In the final analysis, the boarding school story constitutes yet another deplorable episode in the long and tragic history of Indian-white relations. For tribal elders who had witnessed the catastrophic developments of the nineteenth century—the bloody warfare, the near-extinction of the bison, the scourge of disease and starvation, the shrinking of the tribal land base, the indignities of reservation life, the invasion of missionaries and white settlers—there seemed to be no end to the cruelties perpetrated by whites. And after all this, the schools. After all this, the white man had concluded that the only way to save Indians was to destroy them, that the last great Indian war should be waged against children. They were coming for the children.

NOTES

PROLOGUE

1. All quotations are taken from Herbert Welsh, *Four Weeks Among Some of the Sioux Tribes of Dakota and Nebraska, Together with a Brief Consideration of the Indian Problem* (Philadelphia: Horace F. McMann, 1882), and Henry Pancoast, *Impressions of the Sioux Tribes in 1882 with Some First Principles in the Indian Question* (Philadelphia: Franklin Printing House, 1883).

CHAPTER ONE. REFORM

1. The formative years in federal Indian policy are examined in Francis Paul Prucha, *The Great Father: The United States Government and the American Indians,* 2 vols. (Lincoln: University of Nebraska Press, 1984), esp. vol. 1, chap. 5; Prucha, *American Indian Policy in the Formative Years: The Indian Trade and Intercourse Acts, 1790–1834* (Cambridge: Harvard University Press, 1962); Reginald Horsman, *Expansion and Indian Policy* (Ann Arbor: University of Michigan Press, 1967); and George D. Harmon, *Sixty Years of Indian Affairs: Political, Economic, and Diplomatic, 1789–1850* (Chapel Hill: University of North Carolina

Press, 1941). For brief but perceptive discussions of the land issue see Robert F. Berkhofer, Jr., *The White Man's Indians: Images of the American Indian from Columbus to the Present* (New York: Alfred A. Knopf, 1978), 134–57, and Wilcomb E. Washburn, *Red Man's Land, White Man's Law: A Study of the Past and Present Status of the American Indian* (New York: Charles Scribner's Sons, 1971), chaps. 2–3.

2. For colonial images of the Indians see Alden T. Vaughan, "From White Man to Red Skin: Changing Anglo-American Perceptions of the American Indian," *American Historical Review* 87 (October 1982): 917–53; Francis Jennings, *The Invasion of America: Indians, Colonialism, and the Cant of Conquest* (Chapel Hill: University of North Carolina Press, 1975), esp. chaps. 4–5; James Axtell, *The Invasion Within: The Contest of Cultures in Colonial North America* (New York: Oxford University Press, 1985), chap. 7; Bernard Sheehan, *Savagism and Civility: Indians and Englishmen in Colonial Virginia* (Cambridge: Cambridge University Press, 1980), chaps. 1–3; and Berkhofer, *The White Man's Indians*, 3–31, 34–38, 72–85, 115–34.

3. See Roy Harvey Pearce, *The Savages of America: A Study of the Indian and the Idea of Civilization*, rev. ed. (Baltimore: Johns Hopkins University Press, 1965); Bernard W. Sheehan, *Seeds of Extinction: Jeffersonian Philanthropy and the American Indian* (Chapel Hill: University of North Carolina Press, 1973), pt. 1; and Francis Paul Prucha, "The Image of the Indian in Pre–Civil War America," in Francis Paul Prucha, William T. Hagan, and Alvin M. Josephy, Jr., *American Indian Policy* (Indianapolis: Indiana Historical Society, 1971), 2–19.

4. Berkhofer, *The White Man's Indians*, 134–45. For Jefferson's statement see Paul L. Ford, ed., *The Writings of Thomas Jefferson* (New York: G. P. Putnam's Sons, 1892), vol. 8, 214.

5. The House Committee report is quoted in Alice C. Fletcher, *Indian Education and Civilization,* Senate Exec. Doc. no. 95, 48th Cong., 2nd sess., 1888, serial 2542, 162–63.

6. See Robert B. Berkhofer, Jr., *Salvation and the Savage: An Analysis of Protestant Missions and American Indian Response, 1787–1862* (New York: Atheneum, 1972); Berkhofer, "Model Zions for the American Indian," *American Quarterly* 15 (Summer 1963): 176–90; Sheehan, *Seeds of Extinction,* chap. 5, 123, 146–47; R. Pierce Beaver, *Church, State, and the American Indian: Two and a Half Centuries of Partnership in Missions Between Protestant Churches and Government* (St. Louis: Concordia Publishing House, 1966), chap. 2; Herman Viola, *Thomas L. McKinney: Architect of America's Early Indian Policy: 1816–1830* (Chicago: Sage Books, 1974), 185–99; Viola, "From Civilization to Removal: Early American Indian Policy," in *Indian-White Relations: A Persistent Paradox,* ed. Jane F. Smith and Robert M. Kvasnicka (Washington, D.C.: Howard University Press, 1976), 45–56; William G. McLoughlin, *Cherokees and Missionaries, 1789–1862* (New Haven: Yale University Press, 1984), chaps. 2, 3, and 5–7; Ronald Rayman, "Joseph Lancaster's Monitorial System of Instruction and American Indian Education, 1815–1838," *History of Education Quarterly* 21 (Winter 1981): 395–409; and Lawrence A. Cremin, *American Education: The National Experience, 1783–1876* (New York: Harper and Row, 1980), 239–42.

7. For the growing pessimism see Reginald Horsman, *Race and Manifest Destiny: The Origins of American Racial Anglo-Saxonism* (Cambridge: Harvard University Press, 1981), 189–98; Horsman, "Scientific Racism and the American Indian in the Mid-Nineteenth Century," *American Quarterly* 27 (May 1975): 152–68; Berkhofer, *The White Man's Indians*, 55–59, 86–96; William Scanton, *The Leopard's Spots: Scientific Attitudes Towards Race in America, 1815–1859*

(Chicago: University of Chicago Press, 1960), esp. 24–44; Brian W. Dippie, *The Vanishing American: White Attitudes and U.S. Indian Policy* (Middletown, Conn.: Wesleyan University Press, 1982), esp. chap. 2; Pearce, *The Savages of America,* chaps. 5–7; and Richard Slotkin, *Regeneration Through Violence: The Mythology of the American Frontier, 1600–1860* (Middletown Conn.: Wesleyan University Press, 1973), chaps. 10–13. For Indian removal see Prucha, *The Great Father,* vol. 1, chaps 7–9; Sheehan, *Seeds of Extinction,* chap. 9; Ronald N. Satz, *American Indian Policy in the Jacksonian Era* (Lincoln: University of Nebraska Press, 1975), chaps. 1–4; Berkhofer, *The White Man's Indians,* 157–66; Dippie, *The Vanishing American,* 56–71; Viola, *Thomas L. McKinney,* chap. 11; and Grant Foreman, *Indian Removal: The Emigration of the Five Civilized Tribes of Indians* (Norman: University of Oklahoma Press, 1953).

8. The subjugation of Native Americans during this period is examined in Robert M. Utley, *The Indian Frontier of the American West, 1846–1890* (Albuquerque: University of New Mexico Press, 1984), esp. chaps. 4 and 6; Utley, *Frontiersmen in Blue: The United States Army and the Indian, 1848–1865* (New York: Macmillan, 1967); Utley, *Frontier Regulars: The United States Army and the Indian, 1866–1890* (New York: Macmillan, 1973); and Ralph K. Andrist, *The Long Death: The Last Days of the Plains Indians* (New York: Macmillan, 1964). For the evolution and nature of the reservation system see Robert A. Trennert, Jr., *Alternative to Extinction: Federal Indian Policy and the Beginnings of the Reservation System, 1846–1851* (Philadelphia: Temple University Press, 1975); Prucha, *The Great Father,* vol. 1, chap. 22; Prucha, *American Indian Policy in Crisis: Christian Reformers and the Indian, 1865–1900* (Norman: University of Oklahoma Press, 1976), 103–13; and William T. Hagan, "Indian Policy After the Civil War: The Reservation Experience," in Prucha, Hagan, and Josephy, *American Indian Policy,* 20–36. Particularly fine case studies of the reservation experience are Donald J. Berthrong, *The Cheyenne and Arapaho Ordeal: Reservation and Agency Life in the Indian Territory, 1875–1907* (Norman: University of Oklahoma Press, 1976); and William T. Hagan, *United States-Commanche Relations: The Reservation Years* (New Haven: Yale University Press, 1976).

9. The Peace Policy years are analyzed in Robert H. Keller, Jr., *American Protestantism and United States Indian Policy 1869–1882* (Lincoln: University of Nebraska Press, 1983); Robert Winston Mardock, *The Reformers and the American Indian* (Columbia: University of Missouri Press, 1971), chaps. 4–9; Henry E. Fritz, *The Movement for Indian Assimilation, 1860–1890* (Philadelphia: University of Pennsylvania Press, 1963), chaps. 3–7; Loring Benson Priest, *Uncle Sam's Stepchildren: The Reformation of United States Indian Policy, 1865–1887* (1942; reprint Lincoln: University of Nebraska Press, 1975), chaps. 3–4; Prucha, *The Great Father,* vol. 1, chap. 20; Prucha, *American Indian Policy in Crisis,* chap. 2; Henry G. Waltman, "Circumstantial Reformer: President Grant and the Indian Problem," *Arizona and the West* 21 (Winter 1971): 323–42; and Richard R. Levine, "Indian Fighters and Indian Reformers: Grant's Indian Peace Policy and the Conservative Consensus," *Civil War History* 31 (December 1985): 329–52.

10. Dippie, *The Vanishing American,* chap. 10; Prucha, *American Indian Policy in Crisis,* 113–28; Priest, *Uncle Sam's Stepchildren,* chaps. 5–6; Mardock, *The Reformers and the American Indian,* chap. 10; and Helen Hunt Jackson, *A Century of Dishonor: A Sketch of the United States Government's Dealings with Some of the Indian Tribes* (New York: Harper and Brothers, 1881).

11. Chief Joseph, "An Indian's View of Indian Affairs," *North American Review* 128 (April 1979), 433.

12. Herbert Welsh, "The Indian Question Past and Present," *New England Magazine* 3 (October 1890), 264; and IRA *Report,* 1884, 5.

13. See Indian Rights Association, *Brief Statement of the Aims, Work, and Achievements of the Indian Rights Association* (Philadelphia: Indian Rights Association, 1886); Charles C. Painter, *The Indian Rights Association, Its Aims, Methods, and Work* (Philadelphia: Indian Rights Association, 1890); and Mathew K. Sniffen, *The Record of Thirty Years: A Brief Statement of the Indian Rights Association, Its Objects, Methods and Achievements* (Philadelphia: Indian Rights Association, 1912). Also, William T. Hagan, *The Indian Rights Association: The Herbert Welsh Years, 1882–1904* (Tucson: University of Arizona Press, 1985), and Vine Deloria, Jr., "The Indian Rights Association: An Appraisal," in *Aggressions of Civilization: Federal Indian Policy Since the 1880's,* ed. Sandra L. Cadawalader and Vine Deloria, Jr. (Philadelphia: Temple University Press, 1984), 3–18.

14. Keller, *American Protestantism and United States Indian Policy,* chap. 4; Prucha, *American Indian Policy in Crisis,* 33–46; and Henry E. Fritz, "The Board of Indian Commissioners and Ethnocentric Reform, 1878–1893," in *Indian-White Relations,* ed. Smith and Kvasnicka, 57–78; and Fritz, "The Last Hurrah of Christian Humanitarian Reform: The Board of Indian Commissioners, 1909–1918," *Western Historical Quarterly* 16 (April 1985): 147–62.

15. For background on the Boston Indian Citizenship Association see Mardock, *The Reformers and the American Indian,* 198; Fritz, *The Movement for Indian Assimilation, 1860–1890,* 188–97; and Prucha, *American Indian Policy in Crisis,* 133–34. For Women's National Indian Association see Mary E. Dewey, *Historical Sketch of the Formation and Achievements of the Women's National Indian Association in the United States* (Philadelphia: Women's National Indian Association, 1900); and Amelia Stores Quinton, *A Brief Historical Sketch of the National Indian Association with Suggestions and Facts for Helpers* (Philadelphia: Women's National Association, 1882). Also see Helen M. Wanken, " 'Women's Sphere' and Indian Reform: The Women's National Indian Association, 1879–1901," (Ph.D. dissertation, Marquette University, 1981); Peggy Pascoe, *Relations of Rescue: The Search for Female Moral Authority in the American West, 1874–1939* (New York: Oxford University Press, 1990), 7–10; and Valerie Sherer Mathes, "Nineteenth Century Women and Reform: The Women's National Indian Association," *American Indian Quarterly* 14 (Winter 1990): 1–18.

16. See Larry E. Burgess, "The Lake Mohonk Conferences on the Indian, 1883–1916" (Ph.D. dissertation, Claremont Graduate School, 1972); Burgess, "We'll Discuss It At Mohonk," *Quaker History* 60 (Spring 1971): 14–28; Prucha, *American Indian Policy in Crisis,* 143–47; and Utley, *The Indian Frontier,* 203–10.

17. It would prove especially fateful for Indians that the future of their race was being determined precisely at the moment when the "quest for a Protestant America" was in full swing. See Robert T. Handy, "The Protestant Quest for a Christian America," *Church History* 22 (March 1953): 8–19; Handy, *A Christian America: Protestant Hopes and Christian Realities* (New York: Oxford University Press, 1971), 110–15; and Winthrop S. Hudson, *American Protestantism* (Chicago: University of Chicago Press, 1961), 109–27. The connection between Protestantism and Indian reform has been established by Prucha, *The Great Father,* vol. 2, chap. 24; and Prucha, *American Indian Policy in Crisis,* 147–52.

18. Carl F. Kaestle, "Ideology and American Educational History," *History of Education Quarterly* 22 (Summer 1982): 127–28. Also, John Higham, "Hanging Together: Divergent Unities in American History," *Journal of American History* 61 (June 1974): 12–18.

19. The idea of civilization is examined in Pearce, *The Savages of America,* esp. chaps. 3–4; Sheehan, *Seeds of Extinction,* chaps. 1–3; and Berkhofer, *The White Man's Indians,* 38–49. The relationship of the idea of progress to the idea of civilization is treated in Fred W. Voget, "Progress, Science, History and Evolution in Eighteenth and Nineteenth Century Anthropology," *Journal of the History of the Behavioral Sciences* 3 (April 1967): 132–55; and Voget, "Anthropology in the Age of Enlightenment: Progress and Utopian Functionalism," *Southwestern Journal of Anthropology* 24 (Winter 1968): 321–45. On the American idea of progress and its origins see Rush Welter, *The Mind of America, 1820–1860* (New York: Columbia University Press, 1975), chap. 1; Arthur A. Ekirch, Jr., *The Idea of Progress in America, 1815–1860* (New York: Peter Smith, 1951), chap. 1; and Robert Nisbet, *History of the Idea of Progress* (New York: Basic Books, 1980), 193–206. The idea of progress is a recurrent theme in Ernest Tuveson, *Redeemer Nation: The Idea of America's Millenial Role* (Chicago: University of Chicago Press, 1968).

20. Quoted in Pearce, *The Savages of America,* 155.

21. Ibid., 49.

22. For a discussion of Morgan's ideas and their general context see Carl Resek, *Lewis Henry Morgan: American Scholar* (Chicago: University of Chicago Press, 1960); Bernard J. Stern, *Lewis Henry Morgan: Social Evolutionist* (New York: Russell and Russell, 1931), esp. chap. 6; George W. Stocking, *Race, Culture, and Evolution: Essays in the History of Anthropology* (New York: Free Press, 1968), chap. 6; and Robert E. Bieder, *Science Encounters the Indian, 1820–1880* (Norman: University of Oklahoma Press, 1986), chap. 6. The significance of Morgan's ideas to evolving Indian policy is treated in Dippie, *The Vanishing American,* 102–6, and Frederick E. Hoxie, *A Final Promise: The Campaign to Assimilate the Indians, 1880–1920* (Lincoln: University of Nebraska Press, 1984), 17–21.

23. Lewis Henry Morgan, *Ancient Society: Or Researches in the Lines of Human Progress from Savagery Through Barbarism to Civilization,* ed. Eleanor Burke Leacock (1877; reprint, Cleveland: World Publishing Company, 1963), 6. Although the views of reformers on the idea of progressive evolution closely paralleled Morgan's, as a group they tended to discount a significant point in the line of his argument. Morgan argued that cultural evolution was in fact linked to biological evolution, that there was a corresponding relationship between the level of cultural development and skull size. Although the limited cranial capacity of those at the lower ends of the scale of civilization was not a permanent phenomenon, that is, although primitive intellectual capacity and institutions would eventually mature to the level of civilized men, Morgan was skeptical of policy proposals that attempted to speed up the evolutionary process by assimilating the Indians in a single generation's time. As we shall soon see, this is exactly what reformers proposed to do. See Lewis Henry Morgan, "The Indian Question," *The Nation,* 28 November 1878, 332.

24. See Helen M. Bannan, "The Idea of Civilization and American Indian Policy Reformers in the 1880's," *Journal of American Culture* 1 (Winter 1978): 787–99; and Alexandra Harmon, "When Is an Indian Not an Indian? The 'Friends of the Indian' and the Problems of Indian Identity," *Journal of Ethnic Studies* 18 (Summer 1990): 95–123.

25. LMC, 1895, 36.

26. ARCIA, 1879, 124; and ARCIA, 1884, 182.

27. Carl Schurz, "Present Aspects of the Indian Problem," *North American Review* 133 (July 1881): 7; ARSI, 1886, 4; and ARCIA, 1881, 1–2.

28. ARCIA, 1888, 89, 262; and Schurz, "Present Aspects of the Indian Prob-

lem," 7. See also ARCIA, 1901, 10; and Herbert Welsh, ed., *Addresses Delivered at the Twenty-seventh Annual Meeting of the Indian Rights Association* (Philadelphia: Indian Rights Association, 1909), 40. To the extent that reformers were influenced by Darwin, they subscribed to the optimistic posture of reformed Darwinism, that the course of man's evolution was amenable to human engineering. Still, philanthropists were not entirely untouched by the views of Herbert Spencer and others who saw history as a brutish struggle where only the most fit should survive. For the general impact of Darwin on American social thought see Richard Hofstadter, *Social Darwinism in American Thought* (Philadelphia: University of Pennsylvania Press, 1944), and Robert C. Bannister, *Social Darwinism: Science and Myth in Anglo-American Social Thought* (Philadelphia: Temple University Press, 1979). For a case study of how one prominent philanthropist fused theology with Darwin see Ira V. Brown, *Lyman Abbot: Christian Evolutionist* (Cambridge: Harvard University Press, 1953).

29. Merrill Edward Gates, *Land and Law as Agents in Educating Indians,* ARSI, 1885, 776–84; Herbert Welsh, *Four Weeks Among Some of the Sioux Tribes of Dakota and Nebraska,* (Philadelphia: Horace F. McMann, 1882), 25; and LMC, 1885, 53.

30. Notable treatments of the Dawes Act and its impact on Indian societies are D. S. Otis, *The Dawes Act and the Allotment of Indian Lands,* ed. Francis P. Prucha (Norman: University of Oklahoma Press, 1973); Janet A. McDonnell, *The Dispossession of the American Indian, 1887–1934* (Bloomington: Indiana University Press, 1991); Priest, *Uncle Sam's Stepchildren,* chaps. 17–19; Prucha, *The Great Father,* vol. 2, chaps. 26, 34; Prucha, *American Indian Policy in Crisis,* chap. 8; J. P. Kinney, *A Continent Lost, A Civilization Won: Indian Land Tenure in America* (Baltimore: John Hopkins University Press, 1937); Hoxie, *A Final Promise,* 42–53, 70–81; Wilcomb E. Washburn, *The Assault on Indian Tribalism: The General Allotment Law (Dawes Act) of 1887* (Philadelphia: J. B. Lippincott, 1975); and William T. Hagan, "Private Property, the Indian's Door to Civilization," *Ethnohistory* 3 (Spring 1956): 126–37. Although the Dawes Act did not turn out to be the panacea envisioned by reformers, it did succeed in divesting Indians of much of their land. Possessing over 138 million acres in 1881, Indian landholdings were reduced to 52 million acres by 1934. See McDonnell, *The Dispossession,* 121.

31. Gates, *Land and Law as Agents in Educating Indians,* 779. For background on efforts to extend federal law over Indians see William T. Hagan, *Indian Police and Judges* (New Haven: Yale University Press, 1966); Hagan, "Indian Policy After the Civil War: The Reservation Experience," in *American Indian Policy,* ed. Prucha, Hagan, and Josephy, 31–33; and Prucha, *American Indian Policy in Crisis,* chap. 11.

32. For the role of education in the reform campaign see Hoxie, *A Final Promise,* chap. 6; Prucha, *The Great Father,* vol. 2, chap. 27; Prucha, *American Indian Policy in Crisis,* chaps. 9–10; Priest, *Uncle Sam's Stepchildren,* chap. 11; Wilbert H. Ahern, "Assimilationist Racism: The Case of the 'Friends of the Indian,' " *Journal of Ethnic Studies* 4 (Summer 1976): 23–32; and David Wallace Adams, "Fundamental Considerations: The Deep Meaning of Native American Schooling, 1880–1900," *Harvard Educational Review* 58 (February 1988): 1–28.

33. The literature on the American faith in education generally and the common school movement specifically for the first half of the nineteenth century is especially rich. I have benefited in particular from Cremin, *American Education: The National Experience;* David Tyack and Elizabeth Hansot, *Managers of Virtue: Public School Leadership in America, 1820–1980* (New York: Basic Books,

1982), pt. 1; Carl F. Kaestle, *Pillars of the Republic: Common Schools and American Society, 1780–1860* (New York: Hill and Wang, 1983); and Welter, *The Mind of America,* chap. 11. A strong case can be made for the argument that the movement to assimilate Indians through education was part of a larger turn-of-the-century movement to achieve national unity in the wake of increased immigration and urbanization. This and related themes are treated in David Tyack, *The One Best System: A History of American Urban Education* (Cambridge: Harvard University Press, 1975); and Charles Burgess, "The Goddess, the School Book, and Compulsion," *Harvard Educational Review* 46 (May 1976): 199–216.

34. ARBIC, 1880, reprinted in Francis Paul Prucha, ed., *Americanizing the American Indians: Writings by the "Friends of the Indian" 1880–1900* (Cambridge: Harvard University Press, 1973), 196.

35. ARCIA, 1880, 163; ARCIA, 1885, 438; ARCIA, 1905, 2; and ARCIA, 1886, 447.

36. LMC, 1895, 36–37; and ARCIA, 1891, 5. It should be noted that there was not universal agreement among philanthropists that Indians were capable of being uplifted to the level of whites in a single generation. J. B. Harrison and Merrill Gates even raised the possibility that Indians might be inherently inferior to whites in intellectual capability, but such views were in the minority. J. B. Harrison, *The Latest Studies on Indian Reservations* (Philadelphia: Indian Rights Association, 1887), 168, and LMC, 1896, 10.

37. ARSI, 1882, 14–15; and ARSI, 1883, 8–9.

38. Carl Schurz, "Present Aspects of the Indian Problem," 16–17; and ARSI, 1882, 16.

39. Thomas J. Morgan, "A Plea for the Papoose," in Prucha, *Americanizing the American Indians,* 249.

40. LMC, 1887, in ARCIA, 1887, 959; LMC, 1888, 11; and LMC, 1885, in ARSI, 1885, 848. See also Agent Reports of V. T. McGillycuddy at Pine Ridge Agency and John D. Miles at Cheyenne and Arapaho Agency, ARCIA, 1880, 162–63, 191.

41. ARCIA, 1903, 2.

42. George Wilson, "How Shall the American Savage Be Civilized?" *Atlantic Monthly,* November 1882, 604.

43. ARCIA, 1887, 761, 21.

44. ARCIA, 1885, 108; and ARCIA, 1890, cxlvi.

45. Gates, *Land and Law as Agents in Educating Indians,* 777.

46. Teaching the work ethic and industrial skills were educational objectives not limited to Indian schooling alone, and they became important curricular components of most schools attended by minority populations, including southeastern European immigrants. On the significance and role of work in late nineteenth-century America see Daniel T. Rodgers, *The Work Ethic in Industrial America 1850–1920* (Chicago: University of Chicago Press, 1974), and James Gilbert, *Work Without Salvation: America's Intellectuals and Industrial Alienation, 1880–1910* (Baltimore: Johns Hopkins University Press, 1977). General treatments of the industrial education movement include Marvin Lazerson, *Origins of the Urban School: Public Education in Massachusetts, 1870–1915* (Cambridge: Harvard University Press, 1971), chaps. 3–7; Paul Violas, *The Training of the Urban Working Class: A History of Twentieth Century American Education* (Chicago: Rand McNally, 1978), chaps. 6–8; Harvey Kantor and David B. Tyack, eds., *Work, Youth, and Schooling: Historical Perspectives on Vocationalism in American Education* (Stanford: Stanford University Press, 1982); and Marvin Lazerson and W. Norton Grubb, eds., *American Education and Vocationalism: A Documentary History, 1870–1970* (New York: Teachers College Press, 1974).

47. ARCIA, 1885, 108; and ARCIA, 1886, 221–22. See also ARCIA, 1881, 3; AR-CIA, 1888, 89; and ARCIA, 1895, 344.

48. Possessive individualism and related themes are treated in John G. Cawelti, *Apostles of the Self-Made Man: Changing Concepts of Success in America* (Chicago: University of Chicago Press, 1965); Irvin G. Wyllie, *The Self-Made Man in America* (New Brunswick, N.J.: Rutgers University Press, 1954); and Rex Burn, *Success in America: The Yeoman Dream and the Industrial Revolution* (Amherst: University of Massachusetts Press, 1976).

49. ARCIA, 1888, 89; LMC, 1896, 11–12; and *Journal of the Thirteenth Annual Conference with Representatives of the Missionary Boards,* in ARCIA, 1883, 731–32.

50. *Journal of Proceedings and Addresses of the National Education Association,* 1903, 1048; and LMC, 1895, 37.

51. ARCIA, 1890, cxlvi.

52. LMC, 1885, in ARSI, 1885, 850.

53. Quoted in Pearce, *The Savages of America,* 57.

54. The text is reprinted in Wilcomb E. Washburn, ed., *The Indian and the White Man* (New York: Anchor Books, 1964), 128–30. For the cultural meaning of Columbia as a national symbol see Thomas J. Schlereth, "Columbia, Columbus, and Columbianism," *Journal of American History* 79 (December 1992): 939–43.

55. ARCIA, 1913, 183; ARBIC, 1900, in ARCIA, 1900, 643; ARCIA, 1884, 19; ARBIC, 1890, in ARCIA, 1890, 782; and Laurence F. Schmeckebier, *The Office of Indian Affairs* (Baltimore: John Hopkins University Press, 1927), 209.

56. LMC, 1891, in ARCIA, 1891, 1144.

57. George E. Ellis, *The Red Man and the White Man in North America* (Boston: Little, Brown, 1882), 600.

CHAPTER TWO. MODELS

1. ARCIA, 1890, cliv–clv.

2. ARCIA, 1878, 649; and ARCIA, 1879, 112.

3. ARCIA, 1882, 152; and ARCIA, 1880, 159.

4. ARSI, 1979, 10.

5. ARCIA, 1890, clii. For the reservation boarding-school story see Jacqueline Mary Fear, "American Indian Education: The Reservation Schools, 1870–1900" (Ph.D. dissertation, University College, London, 1978).

6. ARCIA, 1885, 111–12; and ARCIA, 1886, 137. For the views of Indian agents, see ARCIA, 1883, 221; ARCIA, 1880, 137; ARCIA, 1878, 508; ARCIA, 1880, 148; and ARCIA, 1886, 285.

7. See, for example, Josiah Butler, "Pioneer School Teaching at the Comanche-Kiowa Agency School 1870–1873, *Chronicles of Oklahoma* 6 (December 1928): 508, and ARCIA, 1887, 143.

8. ARCIA, 1885, 113.

9. ARCIA, 1879, 174; ARCIA, 1881, 144; ARCIA, 1886, 418; and ARCIA, 1899, 237.

10. ARCIA, 1885, 407–8; ARCIA, 1884, 50–51.

11. ARCIA, 1891, 292; and ARCIA, 1893, 211–12.

12. Francis La Flesche, *The Middle Five: Indian School-boys of the Omaha Tribe* (1900; reprint, Madison: University of Wisconsin Press, 1963), 84–85.

13. ARCIA, 1888, 153.

14. J. B. Harrison, *The Latest Studies on Indian Reservations* (Philadelphia: Indian Rights Association, 1887), 125–28. See also ARCIA, 1885, 305, and *Southern Workman,* January 1882, 4.

15. *Red Man,* March 1980, 3; and Jim Whitewolf, *The Life of a Kiowa-Apache Indian,* ed. Charles S. Grant (New York: Dover Publications, 1969), 87. After 1890, the slaughter and distribution of beef were strictly regulated by a directive from Commissioner of Indian Affairs Thomas J. Morgan: "The killing is to be done in a pen, in as private a manner as possible, and by a man who understands the duty, who uses the most speedy and painless method practicable; and during the killing, children and women are especially prohibited from being present." Morgan's restrictions are reprinted in Francis Paul Prucha, ed., *Americanizing the American Indians: Writings by the 'Friends of the Indian' 1880–1900* (Cambridge: Harvard University Press, 1973), 306–8.

16. ARCIA, 1879, 174; ARCIA, 1899, 237; and ARCIA, 1896, 257.

17. ARCIA, 1888, 77, 153.

18. ARCIA, 1887, 219; and ARCIA, 1879, 111.

19. ARCIA, 1883, 67.

20. Richard Henry Pratt, *Battlefield and Classroom: Four Decades with the American Indian, 1867–1904,* ed. Robert M. Utley (New Haven: Yale University Press, 1964), 107–8.

21. Ibid., 109; and Student Records (James Bear's Heart), Indian Collection, HA.

22. Actually, sixty-nine of the prisoners were charged with crimes related to the Red River War. The two Arapaho and the Caddo were added to the group for crimes unrelated to the Red River conflict. For some unexplained reason Black Horse, a prominent Comanche, was allowed to take his wife and daughter. In all, seventy-four Indians would be taken to Fort Marion. Pratt, *Battlefield and Classroom,* 138–44.

23. Robert M. Utley, *Frontier Regulars: The United States Army and the Indian, 1866–1890* (New York:Macmillan, 1973), chap. 13; Wilbur Sturtevant Nye, *Plains Indian Raiders: The Final Phases of Warfare From the Arkansas to the Red River* (Norman: University of Oklahoma Press, 1968), chap. 17.

24. For the removal and exile of the prisoners including their Fort Marion experience see Pratt, *Battlefield and Classroom,* chaps. 10–17; Pratt, "American Indians: Chained and Unchained: Being an Account of How the Carlisle Indian School was Born and Grew in the First 25 Years," *Red Man,* June 1914, 395–98. Pamela Holco Oestreicher, "On the White Man's Road? Acculturation and the Fort Marion Southern Plains Prisoners" (Ph.D. dissertation, Michigan State University, 1981), chaps. 2–3; and Louis Morton, "How the Indians Came to Carlisle," *Pennsylvania History* 29 (January 1962): 53–63.

25. For an uncritical account of Pratt's life and career see Elaine Goodale Eastman, *Pratt: The Red Man's Moses* (Norman: University of Oklahoma Press, 1935). More useful are Everett Arthur Gilcreast, "Richard Henry Pratt and American Indian Policy, 1877–1906: A Study of the Assimilation Movement" (Ph.D. dissertation, Yale University, 1967); Pearl Lee Walker-McNeil, "The Carlisle Indian School: A Study of Acculturation" (Ph.D. dissertation, American University, 1979), chap. 3; and Frederick J. Stefon, "Richard Henry Pratt and His Indians," *Journal of Ethnic Studies* 15 (Summer 1987): 88–112. The humanitarian theme is emphasized in Richard N. Ellis, "The Humanitarian Soldiers" *Journal of Arizona History* 10 (Summer 1969): 53–66; Ellis, "The Humanitarian Generals," *Western Historical Quarterly* 3 (April 1972): 169–78; and Robert M. Utley, "The Frontier Army: John Ford or Arthur Penn?" in *Indian-White Relations: A Persistent Paradox,* ed. Jane

F. Smith and Robert M. Kvasnicka (Washington, D.C.: Howard University Press, 1976), 140. The complexity and range of soldier attitudes is treated in Thomas C. Leonard, "Red, White and the Army Blue: Empathy and Anger in the American West," *American Quarterly* 26 (May 1974): 176–90.

26. Pratt, *Battlefield and Classroom,* 112–15. Once at Fort Marion, Lean Bear went on a prolonged hunger strike. Finally, in a seriously weakened state, he was moved to a nearby army hospital where he eventually died.

27. Ibid., 117–18.

28. Ibid., 118–120; and Pratt, "American Indians," 397. In the spring of 1876, a group of Kiowa planned an escape from the prison, but once the plot was discovered by Pratt, it was quickly aborted. Pratt, *Battlefield and Classroom,* chap. 14.

29. Ibid., 120, 124–27, 131–32.

30. Ibid., 119–20, 126, 128–30, 174; Pratt, "American Indians," 397–98; Oestreicher, "On the White Man's Road?" 59–60, 70; and Morton, "How the Indians Came to Carlisle," 60.

31. Pratt, *Battlefield and Classroom,* 121, 175; Pratt, "American Indians," 397.

32. Pratt, *Battlefield and Classroom,* 158, and *Southern Workman,* May 1878, 36.

33. Henry B. Whipple, *Lights and Shadows of a Long Episcopate* (New York: Macmillan, 1899), 34. Whipple described his visits to the prison in a letter published in the *New York Daily Tribune,* 1 April 1876, reprinted in Pratt, *Battlefield and Classroom,* 162–64.

34. Quoted in Oestreicher, "On the White Man's Road?" 64–65. See also Lawrie Tatum, *Our Red Brothers and the Peace Policy of President Ulysses S. Grant* (Philadelphia: John C. Winston and Company, 1899), 196.

35. Pratt, *Battlefield and Classroom,* 156–62; *Harper's Weekly,* 11 May 1978, 375; and Morton, "How the Indians Came to Carlisle," 63.

36. Pratt, *Battlefield and Classroom,* chap. 16.

37. Ibid., 187–90; Pratt, "Violated Principles the Cause of Failure in Indian Civilization," *Journal of the Military Service Institution of the United States* 7 (March 1886): 58; Pratt, "American Indians," 398–400; LMC, 1913, 200–201; *Southern Workman,* May 1878, 36; and Morton, "How the Indians Came to Carlisle," 63–64.

38. For accounts of Armstrong's life see Suzanne C. Carson, "Samuel Chapman Armstrong: Missionary to the South," (Ph.D. dissertation, Johns Hopkins University, 1952), and Edith Armstrong Talbot, *Samuel Chapman Armstrong: A Biographical Study* (New York: Doubleday, Page, and Company, 1904). Hampton's ideology and program are examined in James D. Anderson, *The Education of Blacks in the South, 1860–1935* (Chapel Hill: University of North Carolina Press, 1988), chap. 2; Robert Francis Engs, *Freedom's First Generation: Black Hampton, Virginia, 1861–1890* (Philadelphia: University of Pennsylvania Press, 1979), chap. 8; and Francis Greenwood Peabody, *Education for Life: The Story of Hampton Institute* (New York: Doubleday, Page, 1918).

39. Hampton's Indian program is examined in David Wallace Adams, "Education in Hues: Red and Black at Hampton Institute, 1878–1893," *South Atlantic Quarterly* 76 (Spring 1977): 159–76; Linda K. Kerber, "The Abolitionist Perception of the Indian," *Journal of American History* 62 (September 1975): 271–95; Joseph Willard Tingey, "Indians and Blacks Together: An Experiment in Biracial

Education at Hampton Institute, 1878–1923" (Ed.D. dissertation, Columbia University Teachers College, 1978); and Donal Fred Lindsey, "Indian Education at Hampton Institute, 1877–1923" (Ph.D. dissertation, Kent State University, 1989).

40. Cora Folsom, "Memories of Old Hampton," unpublished manuscript, 2–3, Cora M. Folsom Papers, Indian Collection, HA.

41. Samuel C. Armstrong to Richard H. Pratt, 26 January 1878, Pratt Papers, BRBML; and Samuel C. Armstong to Robert C. Ogden, 8 March 1878, Ogden Papers.

42. Tsait-Kope-ta to Richard H. Pratt, April 1878, Pratt Papers, HA.

43. *Southern Workman,* May 1878, 36.

44. In late May, Armstrong agreed to accept fifty Nez Percé, who along with their leader, Chief Joseph, were being held as prisoners of war at Fort Leavenworth, but the plan fell through when Joseph refused to agree to it. See Samuel C. Armstrong to General E. R. Townsend, 20 May 1878, Armstrong Papers, HA; Pratt, *Battlefield and Classroom,* 195–96; and Pratt, "American Indians," 400.

45. Samuel C. Armstrong to Richard H. Pratt, 1 August 1878, Pratt Papers, BRBML; Samuel C. Armstrong to Richard H. Pratt, 18 August 1878, Pratt Papers, BRBML; Secretary of War to Richard H. Pratt, 19 August 1878, Pratt Papers, BRBML; and Samuel C. Armstrong to Richard H. Pratt, 26 August 1878, Pratt Papers, BRBML.

46. Samuel C. Armstrong to Richard H. Pratt, 26 August 1878, Pratt Papers, BRBML; Richard H. Pratt to Samuel C. Armstrong, 7 September 1878, Armstrong Papers, HA; and Richard H. Pratt to Samuel C. Armstrong, 13 October 1878, Armstrong Papers, HA.

47. Pratt, *Battlefield and Classroom,* 213–14; Walker-McNeil, "The Carlisle Indian School," 107–8; Gilcreast, "Richard Henry Pratt and American Indian Policy," 32–37; O. B. Super, "Indian Education at Carlisle," *New England Magazine* 18 (April 1895), 226–27; and Morton, "How the Indians Came to Carlisle," 64–65.

48. Secretary of War to Richard H. Pratt, 19 March 1879, Pratt Papers, BRBML; Richard H. Pratt to Secretary of War, 22 March 1879, Pratt Papers, BRBML; Commissioner of Indian Affairs to Richard H. Pratt, 6 September 1879, Pratt Papers, BRBML; Pratt, *Battlefield and Classroom,* 215–20; Robert L. Brunhouse, "The Founding of the Carlisle Indian School," *Pennsylvania History* 6 (April 1969): 76–78; and Morton, "How the Indians Came to Carlisle," 65–68.

49. Pratt, *Battlefield and Classroom,* 219–32; Morton, "How the Indians Came to Carlisle," 68–73; and Brunhouse, "The Founding of the Carlisle Indian School," 78–81. The best institutional histories of Carlisle are Walker-McNeil, "The Carlisle Indian School," and Carmelita S. Ryan, "The Carlisle Indian Industrial School" (Ph.D. dissertation, Georgetown University, 1962).

50. Quoted in Brunhouse, "The Founding of the Carlisle Indian School," 85.

51. ARCIA, 1880, 303–4; and Ryan, "The Carlisle Indian Industrial School," 79–80, 96.

52. *Eadle Keatah Toh,* November 1880, 1.

53. For Pratt's personality and character, see Helen Ludlow and Elaine Goodale, *Captain Pratt and His Work for Indian Education* (Philadelphia: Indian Rights Association, 1886), 6; Gilcreast, "Richard Henry Pratt and American Indian Policy," 21–24; and Ryan, "The Carlisle Indian Industrial School," 22–24.

54. Richard H. Pratt, "The Advantages of Mingling Indians with Whites," *Proceedings of the National Conference of Charities and Correction,* 1892, 46; and *Proceedings and Addresses of the National Education Association,* 1895, 761–62.

55. Pratt, "The Advantages of Mingling Indians with Whites," 56. Also, *Proceedings and Addresses of the National Educational Association,* 1895, 2, 5, and LMC, 1889, 876.

56. *Journal of the Twentieth Annual Conference with Representatives of Missionary Boards and Indian Rights Associations,* 1890, in ARCIA, 1890, 945–46.

57. *ARCIA,* 1885, 447; Richard H. Pratt, "A Way Out," LMC, 1891, reprinted in *Red Man,* October-November 1891, 5; *Proceedings and Addresses of the National Education Association,* 1895, 760–62; LMC, 1913, 199; Pratt, "The Advantages of Mingling Indians with Whites," 56–57; and ARCIA, 1884, 231. Pratt was particularly critical of the Indian Office, missionaries, and ethnologists—the Indian Office because it administered the reservation system, missionaries because they placed a greater importance on conversion to a particular faith than on assimilation, and ethnologists because they perpetuated the public image of Indians as a savages. See Pratt, *Battlefield and Classroom,* 270–72, 283, 293; Pratt, "The Advantages of Mingling Indians with Whites," 54–56; ARCIA, 1899, 426; LMC, 1903, 136; and LMC, 1913, 199. Pratt also was convinced that the forced segregation of the reservation system had placed a greater burden on Indians than that faced by either blacks or immigrants. See Richard H. Pratt to D. A. Sanford, 8 October 1902, Pratt Papers, BRBML; Pratt, "The Advantages of Mingling Indians with Whites," 50–51, 56; LMC, 1913, 198–99; Pratt, "Violated Principles the Cause of Failure in Indian Civilization," 48; ARCIA, 1886, 237; ARCIA, 1885, 447; *Journal of the Fifteenth Annual Conference with Representatives of Missionary Boards,* in ARCIA, 1885, 884; and *Journal of the Twentieth Annual Conference with Representatives of Missionary Boards and Indian Rights Associations,* in ARCIA, 1890, 947.

58. Quoted in Gilcreast, "Richard Henry Pratt and American Indian Policy," 247. Also Richard H. Pratt to Evastus Brainerd, January 1881, Pratt Papers, BRBML; and Pratt, "The Advantage of Mingling Indians with Whites," 52–53.

59. LMC, 1891, 67. Denying Indians even the right to an allotment was one of Pratt's heated overstatements. On another occasion he remarked at Mohonk that he was not opposed to allotment, just to the notion that Indians should be congregated in communities. Pratt favored a proposal suggested by U.S. Senator Henry Teller that Indians and whites be allotted alternate tracks of land, thereby forcing Indian homesteaders into closer relationships with their more civilized neighbors. See LMC, 1889, 877; Pratt, "The Advantages of Mingling Indians with Whites," 58, and Pratt, "A Way Out," 5. For an extended discussion of Pratt's views on the allotment question see Gilcreast, "Richard Henry Pratt and American Indian Policy," 245–52.

60. Pratt, "The Advantages of Mingling Indians with Whites," 54, 58; LMC, 1893, 83; and *Proceedings and Addresses of the National Education Association,* 1895, 761.

61. ARCIA, 1899, 422; and ARCIA, 1884, 230–31. Carlisle's outing system will be explored in depth in Chapter 5.

62. LMC, 1889, in ARCIA, 1889, 876; LMC, 1913, 201; and *Native American,* 6 April 1912, 185.

63. Richard H. Pratt to Henry Dawes, 4 April 1881, Pratt Papers, BRBML; and LMC, 1893, 83.

64. Quoted in Gilcreast, "Richard Henry Pratt and American Indian Policy," 99. Pratt always encouraged his students to pursue higher courses of study after leaving Carlisle. See ARCIA, 1898, 390; and ARCIA, 1897, 373.

65. Pratt, *Battlefield and Classroom,* 283.

66. Richard H. Pratt to Rutherford B. Hayes, 9 March 1880, Pratt Papers, BRBML.

67. ARSI, 1879, 10–11. See also ARSI, 1880, 7–8; and Carl Schurz, "Present Aspects of the Indian Problem," 16–17.

68. ARCIA, 1881, 88. For other agent reports in support of off-reservation schools see ARCIA, 1880, 181; ARCIA, 1881, 140; ARCIA, 1882, 190; ARCIA, 1884, 50–51, 183; ARCIA, 1885, 312, 428, 407–8; and ARCIA, 1889, 118.

69. See chap. 10.

70. LMC, 1886, 11; and Merrill Edward Gates, *Land and Law as Agents in Educating Indians,* ARSI, 1885, 783.

71. As Everett Gilcreast has shown, although this argument made sense on the surface, Pratt clearly demonstrated that his per capita cost was lower than that of many western schools. The major reason for this was twofold: Carlisle's extensive outing system, which released some of the burden for supporting students; and the dependence of western schools on eastern goods, the cost of shipment often being more than the transportation of students. See Gilcreast, "Richard Henry Pratt and American Indian Policy," 114–15.

72. Quoted in Lillie G. McKinney, "History of the Albuquerque Indian School," *New Mexico Historical Review* 20 (April 1945): 116.

73. Quoted in Robert A. Trennert, *The Phoenix Indian School: Forced Assimilation in Arizona, 1891–1935* (Norman: University of Oklahoma Press, 1988), 21.

74. Laurence F. Schmeckebier, *The Office of Indian Affairs* (Baltimore: Johns Hopkins University Press, 1927), 216.

CHAPTER THREE. SYSTEM

1. LMC, 1885, in ARSI, 1885, 848; and J. B. Harrison, *The Latest Studies on Indian Reservations* (Philadelphia: Indian Rights Association, 1887), 139.

2. For the bureaucratization of the Indian system see Paul Henry Stuart, "The U.S. Office of Indian Affairs, 1865–1900: The Institutionalization of a Formal Organization" (Ph.D. dissertation, University of Wisconsin, 1978); Stuart, "Administrative Reform in Indian Affairs," *Western Historical Quarterly* 16 (April 1985): 133–46; and Francis Paul Prucha, *The Great Father: The United States Government and the American Indians,* 2 vols. (Lincoln: University of Nebraska Press, 1984), vol. 2, chap. 28. The search for system in Indian education was mirrored by the similar efforts in urban education. The rise of the "one best system" in urban America is told in David Tyack, *The One Best System: A History of American Urban Education* (Cambridge: Harvard University Press, 1975), 126–98; Tyack and Elizabeth Hansot, *Managers of Virtue: Public School Leadership in America, 1820–1980* (New York: Basic Books, 1982), 94–114; and Raymond E. Callahan, *Education and the Cult of Efficiency: A Study of the Social Forces That Have Shaped the Administration of the Public Schools* (Chicago: University of Chicago Press, 1962).

3. Francis Paul Prucha, "Thomas Jefferson Morgan," in Robert M. Kvasnicka and Herman J. Viola, eds., *The Commissioners of Indian Affairs, 1824–1977* (Lincoln: University of Nebraska Press, 1979), 193–203; Thomas J. Morgan, *The New Indian School Policy* (Philadelphia: Indian Rights Association, 1889); ARCIA, 1889, 93–114; Morgan, "A Plea for the Papoose," in Francis Paul Prucha, ed.

Americanizing the American Indians: Writings by the "Friends of the Indian" 1880–1900 (Cambridge: Harvard University Press, 1973), 242–43; Commissioner of Indian Affairs to Herbert Welsh, 5 February 1892, IRA; and Commissioner of Indian Affairs to Herbert Welsh, 10 July 1891, IRA.

4. ARCIA, 1889, 97–104.

5. Morgan was not the first to call for greater standardization of curriculum. See ARCIA, 1885, 122; LMC, reprinted in ARSI, 1885, 851; and ARCIA, 1887, 761.

6. ARCIA, 1890, clviii; and ARCIA, 1891, 65.

7. Revisions would be issued in 1901, 1916, 1922, and 1926. See Prucha, *The Great Father,* 2: 826–35.

8. ARCIA, 1913, 22; William N. Hailmann, *Education of the Indian,* Monographs on Education in the United States, no. 19 (St. Louis: Department of Education, Universal Exposition, 1904), 18, 20; ARCIA, 1925, 6; and ARCIA, 1926, 7.

9. Everest Arthur Gilcreast, "Richard Henry Pratt and American Indian Policy, 1877–1906: A Study of the Assimilation Movement" (Ph.D. dissertation, Yale University, 1967), 310.

10. During the treaty-making era (1857–1891), a number of treaties called for the establishment of schools and even contained compulsory attendance clauses but rarely provided for the means of enforcement. See Robert Laurence, "Indian Education: Federal Compulsory School Attendance Law Applicable to American Indians: The Treaty-Making Period: 1857–1891, *American Indian Law Review* 6 (Winter, 1977): 393–413.

11. ARCIA, 1885, 113; and LMC, 1892, in ARCIA, 1892, 1323.

12. *The Statutes at Large of the United States of America,* vol. 26, 1014; and Ibid., vol. 27, 635. This policy was reaffirmed in Education Circular no. 130, 15 January 1906, OIA.

13. For this reason supporters of compulsory education kept the issue before policymakers. See for example ARCIA, 1899, 441; H. B. Peairs, "The Need of Compulsory Education for Indians," *Southern Workman,* November 1901, 394–98; ARCIA, 1901, 18; and IRA *Report,* 1908, 25–26.

14. The movement for compulsory Indian education parallels in some respects the compulsory education movement at large. By 1890 twenty-seven states had compulsory attendance laws in place, although as David Tyack points out, in many communities these statutes were "dead letters" until civic groups were able to erect the bureaucratic apparatus necessary to compel attendance. See David B. Tyack, "Ways of Seeing: An Essay on the History of Compulsory Schooling." *Harvard Educational Review* 46 (August 1976): 355–96, and Tyack, *The One Best System,* 66–71.

15. ARCIA, 1881, 132; ARCIA, 1884, 69; ARCIA, 1887, 773–78; ARCIA, 1893, 10, 167–68; and ARCIA, 1890, 300.

16. ARCIA, 1887, 778; ARCIA, 1892, 176; and ARCIA, 1893, 369; ARCIA, 1902, 397; and ARCIA, 1909, 17.

17. ARCIA, 1896, 20; and ARCIA, 1908, 19.

18. ARCIA, 1886, 144; ARCIA, 1892, 176; and ARCIA, 1893, 9–10.

19. ARCIA, 1893, 10–11; and *The Statutes at Large of the United States of America,* vol. 28, 313–14.

20. ARCIA, 1886, 136–37.

21. But this victory for Protestant reformers only applied to congressional appropriations. Still to be resolved was the question whether treaty and trust funds, at the request of Indians, could be granted to sectarian schools. When the Indian Rights Association failed to gain legislation in Congress forbidding the use of trust and treaty funds in this manner, it took the issue to the Supreme Court. In *Quick*

Bear v. Leupp the Court ruled that strictly speaking treaty and trust funds were not public funds but Indian funds held in trust for them by the government and thereby upon the request of Indians could be used for sectarian schooling. For an excellent discussion of the contract question including the Quick Bear ruling see Francis Paul Prucha, *The Churches and the Indian Schools, 1888–1912* (Lincoln: University of Nebraska Press, 1979), chap. 1–11. Also, Prucha, *The Great Father,* 2: 707–11, and Theodore Fischbacher, *A Study of the Role of the Federal Government in the Education of the American Indian* (San Francisco: R and E Research Associates, 1974), 133–38.

22. IRA *Report,* 1888, 33; Francis Paul Prucha, *American Indian Policy in Crisis: Christian Reformers and the Indian, 1865–1900 (Norman: University of Oklahoma Press, 1976), chap. 12; and Prucha, The Great Father,* 2: 723–36.

23. For the role and authority of the Indian agent in education see "Rules for Indian Schools," ARCIA, 1890, cxlvii; ARCIA, 1885, 109, 120; and Stuart, "The U.S. Office of Indian Affairs, 1865–1900," chap. 4. For reformers views see Herbert Welsh, *Four Weeks Among Some of the Sioux Tribes of Dakota and Nebraska* (Philadelphia: Horace F. McMann, 1882), 27–28; Welsh, "The Meaning of the Dakota Outbreak," *Scribner's Magazine* 9 (April 1891), 448–50, 452; IRA *Report,* 1891, 9; *Journal of the Thirteenth Annual Conference of the Board of Indian Commissioners with Representatives of the Missionary Boards,* in ARCIA, 1883, 730; and ARCIA, 1891, 540.

24. ARCIA, 1889, 336.

25. ARCIA, 1888, lxxxiv. Because of Oberly's support for the merit system, Welsh's Indian Rights Association campaigned for the commissioner's retention by the Harrison administration. Failing in this objective, Welsh quickly established a close relationship with Morgan and came to view him as the primary force for reform under Harrison. See Commissioner of Indian Affairs to Herbert Welsh, 7 March 1889, IRA; Thomas J. Morgan to Herbert Welsh, 14 March 1889, IRA; IRA *Report,* 1889, 9; and IRA *Report,* 1891, 6.

26. ARCIA, 1891, 65; *Ninth Annual Report of the U.S. Civil Service Commission,* 1892, 43, 70; and ARCIA, 1896, 3.

27. Prucha, *The Great Father,* 2: 733–36; William T. Hagan, "Civil Service Commissioner Theodore Roosevelt and the Indian Rights Association," *Pacific Historical Review* 44 (May 1975): 187–200; and Richard E. Jensen, ed., "Commissioner Theodore Roosevelt Visits Indian Reservations, 1892," *Nebraska History* 62 (Spring 1981): 85–106.

28. See for example U.S. Office of Indian Affairs, *Rules for the Indian School Service* (Washington, D.C.: Government Printing Office, 1894, 1898, 1900).

29. *Journal of the Thirteenth Annual Conference of the Board of Indian Commissioners with Representatives of the Missionary Boards,* 730; ARCIA, 1888, xxi–xxiv; ARCIA, 1889, 313–15; and ARCIA, 1890, cxlvi. See also Stuart, "The U.S. Office of Indian Affairs, 1865–1900," 283–84, 289–90, 293–302; and Fischbacher, *A Study of the Role of the Federal Government in the Education of the American Indian,* 89–92. Occasionally congressional critics made moves to abolish the position altogether. When the House Committee on Indian Affairs suggested this possibility in 1894, reformers countered with Herbert Welsh, *The Position of Superintendent of Indian Schools Threatened—A Serious Danger to be Averted* (Philadelphia: Indian Rights Association, 1894); Welsh, *Indian School Welfare* (Philadelphia: Indian Rights Association, 1894), 1; and Executive Committee, Indian Rights Association to House Committee on Indian Affairs, 19 April 1894, IRA.

30. See C.C. Painter to Herbert Welsh, 2 October 1886, IRA; Richard H. Pratt to

Henry Dawes, 5 February 1888, Pratt Papers, BRBML; Herbert Welsh to Secretary of the Interior, 9 November 1894, IRA; and IRA *Report,* 1915, 72.

31. LMC, 1897, 34; and Superintendent of Indian Schools to Herbert Welsh, 6 March 1898, IRA. As late as 1910 there were only six supervisors. ARCIA, 1910, 13.

32. Stuart, "The U.S. Office of Indian Affairs, 1865–1900," chaps. 7–8.

33. Prucha, *The Great Father,* 1: 592.

34. ARCIA, 1897, 189–91; ARCIA, 1898, 204–5; ARCIA, 1899, 241–43; and ARCIA, 1900, 283. For background on these two Indian groups see two articles in Warren L. d'Azevedo, ed., *Handbook of North American Indians,* vol. 2, *Great Basin* (Washington D.C.: Smithsonian Institution, 1986), (1) David H. Thomas, Lorann S. A. Pendleton, and Stephen C. Cappannari, "Western Shoshone," 262–83, and (2) Catherine S. Fowler and Sven Liljeblad, "Northern Paiute," 435–65. Also see Catherine S. and Don D. Fowler, "Notes on the History of the Southern Paiutes and Western Shoshonis," *Utah Historical Quarterly* 39 (Spring 1971): 95–113, and Omer C. Stewart, "The Western Shoshone of Nevada and the U.S. Government, 1863–1950," in *Selected Papers from the 14th Great Basin Anthropological Conference,* ed. Donald R. Tuohy (Socorro, N.Mex.: Ballena Press, 1978), 77–114.

35. Unless indicated otherwise the material on the episode at Duck Valley is based on documents contained in Inspection Report no. 4439 (Western Shoshone), 12 June 1899, OSI.

36. ARCIA, 1899, 242.

37. John S. Mayhugh to Commissioner of Indian Affairs, 30 January 1899, LR, no. 6459, OIA.

38. Commissioner of Indian Affairs to John S. Mayhugh, 16 February 1899, Letters Sent, vol. 105, Letterbook 315, OIA.

39. The readiness of the council to call for the removal of Valley and Blaine may be explained in part by the fact that both had come to the school from a railroad settlement some distance away and were thus outside the community structure of the reservation. Frank Smith, one of the judges, for instance, told Duncan, "Both Essie Valley and Kitty Blaine belong to the railroads, and the court decided they should be sent off the reservation—they both being bad women." Charlie Wines also made note of the fact that the two women did not "belong" to the reservation.

40. Egan also stated that Wines gave her the names of several boys in her school who he claimed had testified against the two girls. "I at once went to the boys Wines mentioned as making the charges and every boy in Miss Rodger's presence, denied . . . any such statements as Wines credited them with."

41. Mayhugh maintained that the second shot was intended for him. "Doctor A. P. Merriweather deliberately looked me in the face and fired a shot at me exceedingly close to my temple which stunned me, the bullet whizzing so close I was stunned and became sick at my stomach."

42. IRA *Report,* 1899, 74.

43. U.S. Office of Indian Affairs, *Rules for the Indian School Service, 1898,* 9.

44. It is interesting that historians have been rather exhaustive in their treatment of teachers who went south to uplift freedmen in the Reconstruction Era. See for example Henry L. Swint, *The Northern Teacher in the South, 1862–1870* (Nashville: Vanderbilt University Press, 1941); Jacqueline Jones, *Soldiers of Light and Love: Northern Teachers and Georgia Blacks, 1865–1873* (Chapel Hill: University of North Carolina Press, 1980); Ronald E. Butchart, *Northern Schools, Southern Blacks, and Reconstruction: Freedmen's Education, 1862–1875* (West-

port, Conn.: Greenwood Press, 1980), chap. 7; and Robert C. Morris, *Reading, 'Riting, and Reconstruction: The Education of Freedmen in the South, 1861–1870* (Chicago: University of Chicago Press, 1981), chaps. 1–2. On the other hand, they have totally ignored the subject of women who went west to teach Indians.

45. *Ninth Annual Report of the U.S. Civil Service Commission,* 1892, 118–19; *Twelfth Annual Report of the U.S. Civil Service Commission,* 1895, 40; *Seventeenth Annual Report of the U.S. Civil Service Commission,* 1900, 535.

46. For examinations of "women's sphere" in nineteenth-century America, see Barbara Welter, "The Cult of True Womanhood: 1820–1860," *American Quarterly* 18 (Summer 1966): 151–74; Nancy F. Cott, *The Bonds of Womanhood: "Woman's Sphere" in New England, 1780–1835* (New Haven: Yale University Press, 1977); Carl N. Degler, *At Odds: Women and the Family in America from the Revolution to the Present* (New York: Oxford University Press, 1980), esp. chaps. 2–5; and Linda K. Kerber, "Separate Spheres, Female Worlds, Woman's Place: The Rhetoric of Women's History," *Journal of American History* 75 (June 1988): 9–39. For the relationship of women to the teaching profession see John L. Rury, "Who Became Teachers? The Social Characteristics of Teachers in American History," in *American Teachers: Histories of a Profession at Work,* ed. Donald Warren (New York: Macmillan, 1989): 9–48; Keith E. Melder, "Woman's High Calling: The Teaching Profession in America, 1830–1860," *American Studies* 13 (Fall 1972): 19–32; and Redding S. Sugg, Jr., *Mother-Teacher: The Feminization of American Education* (Charlottesville: University Press of Virginia, 1978), chaps. 2–5.

47. ARCIA, 1892, 837–73. For the story of women teachers on the frontier see Polly Welts Kaufman, *Women Teachers on the Frontier* (New Haven: Yale University Press, 1984); Mary Hurlbut Cordier, *Schoolwomen of the Prairies and Plains* (Albuquerque: University of New Mexico Press, 1992); and Wayne E. Fuller, *The Old Country School: The Story of Rural Education in the Middle West* (Chicago: University of Chicago Press, 1982); chaps. 9–10.

48. Reprinted in Prucha, *Americanizing the American Indians,* 244.

49. As Cindy Sondik Aron has demonstrated, as the number of civil service positions expanded with the growth of the federal bureaucracy in the last two decades of the nineteenth century, women, and especially single women, turned to the government as a source of employment, primarily in the role of government clerks. "Traditionally," Aron observes, "school teaching had been the occupation to which middle-class women in need of economic assistance had turned, but numerous genteel yet impoverished ladies found the profession wanting in several aspects." Although this truism may explain why many women might choose a government clerkship over school teaching, it should be noted that by signing on with the Indian school service, women were given the opportunity both to secure a government post and to pursue a line of work which many were predisposed to follow, in part because it lay within the realm of "woman's sphere." See Aron, *Ladies and Gentlemen of the Civil Service: Middle-Class Workers in Victorian America* (New York: Oxford University Press, 1987), 45, and Aron, " 'To Barter Their Souls for Gold': Female Clerks in Federal Government Offices, 1862–1890," *Journal of American History* 67 (March 1981): 835–53.

50. Estelle Aubrey Brown, *Stubborn Fool: A Narrative* (Caldwell, Idaho: Caxton Printers, 1952), 16–21.

51. Ibid., 15–16. Minnie Jenkins joined the Indian school service in the wake

of the College of William and Mary's refusal to admit her on the basis of her sex. See Minnie Braithwaite Jenkins, *Girl from Williamsburg* (Richmond Va.: The Dietz Press, 1951).

52. Flora Gregg Iliff, *People of the Blue Water: My Adventures Among the Walapai and Havasupai Indians* (New York: Harper and Brothers, 1954), 3–6.

53. The historical literature has produced a plethora of "images" of frontier women including such depictions as the gentle tamer, the victim, the sun-bonneted helpmate, and the strong-willed frontierswoman. Most teachers, however, who came west to teach Indians do not fit neatly into such categories. For instance, it appears that self-sufficient and strong-willed teachers also usually went west imbued with the idea that it was their duty to "tame" the Indian. For varying interpretations of women on the frontier see Sandra L. Myers, *Westering Women and the Frontier Experience, 1800–1915* (Albuquerque: University of New Mexico Press, 1982), chap. 1; Joan M. Jensen and Darlis A. Miller, "The Gentle Tamers Revisited: New Approaches to the History of Women in the American West," *Pacific Historical Review* 49 (May 1980): 173–213; and Glenda Riley, *The Female Frontier: A Comparative View of Women on the Prairie and the Plains* (Lawrence: University Press of Kansas, 1988).

54. Gertrude Golden, *Red Moon Called Me: Memoirs of a School Teacher in the Government Indian Service* (San Antonio: Naylor, 1954), xi.

55. ARCIA, 1897, 322. A high turnover in teachers was typical of most public schools during this period. See Fuller, *The Old Country School,* 120, 215–17; and Cordier, *Schoolwomen of the Prairies and Plains,* 35–36.

56. Golden, *Red Moon Called Me,* 125.

57. Jenkins, *Girl from Williamsburg,* 28–29; Harriet Patrick Gilstrap, "Memoirs of a Pioneer Teacher," *Chronicles of Oklahoma* 38 (Spring 1960): 22; Harrison, *The Latest Studies on Indian Reservations,* 152–53; and *The Native American* 17 (March 1917): 84.

58. U.S. Office of Indian Affairs, *Rules for the Indian School Service,* 1898, 18; and Jenkins, *Girl from Williamsburg,* 32, 128, 133–34, 210. Also see Golden, *Red Moon Called Me,* 90; and Brown, *Stubborn Fool,* chap. 10.

59. Jenkins, *Girl from Williamsburg,* 88, 93–94, 110, 185; and Brown, *Stubborn Fool,* 67. Also see Golden, *Red Moon Called Me,* 44.

60. Golden, *Red Moon Called Me,* 12–13.

61. Ibid., 50–51.

62. *Journal of the Nineteenth Annual Conference with Representatives of Missionary Boards and Indian Rights Associations,* in ARCIA, 1889, 933; and Report of Supervisors' Conference, Washington, D.C., June 22 to July 10, 1911, Records of the Board of Indian Commissioners, Reference Material, 1875–1933, Tray no. 112, OIA.

63. Jenkins, *Girl from Williamsburg,* 69; Golden, *Red Moon Called Me,* 93; and Brown, *Stubborn Fool,* 148.

64. For Victorian attitudes toward courtship and sex see Degler, *At Odds,* 20–25, chap. 11. For a splendid overview of nineteenth-century bourgeois attitudes toward love and sex see Peter Gay, *The Bourgeois Experience Victoria to Freud,* vol. 1: *Education of the Senses* (New York: Oxford University Press, 1984), vol. 2, *The Tender Passion* (New York: Oxford University Press, 1986).

65. Aron, *Ladies and Gentlemen of the Civil Service,* 162–63, 165.

66. Brown, *Stubborn Fool,* 202–3, 68, 147.

67. Maud Mosher to Herbert Welsh, 27 January 1895, IRA; and Henry Heidenreich to Herbert Welsh, 12 November 1893, (enclosure), IRA. Also see Jenkins, *Girl from Williamsburg,* 70–71.

68. Brown, *Stubborn Fool,* 250–51.
69. Ibid., 251–53.
70. *Proceedings and Addresses of the National Education Association,* 1905, 949; and Brown, *Stubborn Fool,* 257–58. Several historians have suggested that frontierswomen altered their perceptions of Indians as savages after having contact with them. See Glenda Riley, *Women and Indians on the Frontier, 1825–1915* (Albuquerque: University of New Mexico Press, 1984), esp. 167–68, 202–3, 249–51; Riley, "Frontierswomen's Changing Views of Indians in the Trans-Mississippi West," *Montana the Magazine of Western History* 34 (Winter 1984): 20–35; Myers, *Westering Women,* chap. 3; and Helen M. Bannan, "Newcomers to Navajoland: Transculturation in the Memoirs of Anglo Women, 1900–1945," *New Mexico Historical Review* 59 (April 1984): 165–85. All three memoirs are written by women teachers and reflect a growing sensitivity and respect for Indian ways, but only Brown goes so far as to condemn the Indian Bureau for its aggressive assimilation policies.
71. *The Native American,* 7 July 1906, 221. Also, *The Indian Leader,* 27 July 1906, 4.

CHAPTER FOUR. INSTITUTION

1. Luther Standing Bear, *My People, the Sioux* (1928; reprint, Lincoln: University of Nebraska Press, 1975), 123.
2. Standing Bear, *Land of the Spotted Eagle* (Boston: Houghton Mifflin Company, 1933), 68–69, 230–31. Also, Standing Bear, *My People, the Sioux,* 124, 128.
3. Standing Bear, *My People, the Sioux,* 187.
4. Ibid., 128–29.
5. Standing Bear, *Land of the Spotted Eagle,* 231–32, and Standing Bear, *My People, the Sioux,* 129–30.
6. Standing Bear, *My People, the Sioux,* 130–32.
7. Ibid., 133.
8. "Hoke Denetsosie" in *Stories of Traditional Navaho Life and Culture,* ed. Broderick H. Johnson (Tsaile, Ariz.: Navajo Community College Press, 1977), 81. For other accounts see "Max Hanley," in ibid., 36–37; Frank Mitchell, *Navajo Blessingway Singer: The Autobiography of Frank Mitchell, 1881–1967,* ed. Charlotte J. Frisbie and David A. McAllester (Tucson: University of Arizona Press, 1978), 57–61; Albert Yava, *Big Falling Snow: A Tewa-Hopi Indian's Life and Times and the History and Traditions of His People,* ed. Harold Courlander (Albuquerque: University of New Mexico Press, 1978), 14–18; Richard Henry Pratt, *Battlefield and Classroom: Four Decades with the American Indian, 1867–1904,* ed. Robert M. Utley (New Haven: Yale University Press, 1964), 203–4; Clark Wissler, *Indian Cavalcade or Life on the Old-time Indian Reservations* (New York: Sheridan, 1938), 183–84; and *Southern Workman,* August 1881, 85. For an excellent analysis of autobiographical accounts of leaving for school see Michael C. Coleman, *American Indian Children at School, 1850–1930* (Jackson: University Press of Mississippi, 1993), chap. 4.
9. According to Erving Goffman total institutions include the following characteristics. "First, all aspects of life (eating, sleeping, playing, working, learning) are conducted in the same place and under the same single authority. Second, each phase of a member's daily activity is carried out in the immediate company of a large batch of others, all of whom are treated alike and required to do the same

thing together. Third, all phases of the day's activities are tightly scheduled, with one activity leading at a prearranged time into the next, the whole circle of activities being composed from above through a system of explicit, formal rules and a body of officials. Finally, the contents of the various enforced activities are brought together as parts of a single, overall, rational plan purportedly designed to fulfill the official aims of the institution." By Goffman's definition, examples of total institutions include concentration camps, mental hospitals, army barracks, prisons, and work camps. See Erving Goffman, "The Characteristics of Total Institutions," in *Complex Organizations: A Sociological Reader,* ed. Amitai Etzioni (New York: Holt, Rinehart, and Winston, 1961), 313–14; also see Goffman, *Asylums: Essays on the Social Situation of Mental Patients and Other Inmates* (Chicago: Aldine Publishing, 1961), 3–124, and C. A. McEwen, "Continuities in the Study of Total and Nontotal Institutions," *Annual Review of Sociology* 6 (1980): 143–85. Historians have applied the concept with varying degrees of accuracy and insight. One of the most important results of this discussion has been the recognition that there are great differences between total institutions—for instance, concentration camps and prisons—in their capacity to shape and control behavior. Slavery historians, for instance, have argued that the concept is of limited use in understanding the "peculiar institution." See, for instance, John W. Blassingame, *The Slave Community: Plantation Life in the Antebellum South* (New York: Oxford University Press, 1972), appendix. Other applications include David Rothman, *The Discovery of the Asylum* (Boston: Little, Brown, 1971); George Harwood Phillips, "Indians and the Breakdown of the Spanish Mission System in California," *Ethnohistory* 21 (Fall 1974): 291–302; and Thomas James, *Exile Within: The Schooling of Japanese Americans, 1942–1945* (Cambridge: Harvard University Press, 1987), 92. Were Indian boarding schools total institutions? They clearly fulfill the requirements of Hoffman's definition and even appear to go beyond it when he states that "total institutions do not substitute their own unique culture for something already formed. We do not deal with acculturation as assimilation but with something more restricted than these. In a sense, total institutions do not look for cultural victory" (Goffman, "The Characteristics of Total Institutions," 317). Boarding schools, of course, existed for the express purpose of achieving "cultural victory." It is also suggestive that in 1891 Commissioner Morgan compared boarding schools to juvenile asylums and houses of correction. ARCIA, 1891, 62–63. Still, as this book later shows, the boarding school's control over Indian students was not absolute (see Chapter 7).

10. Standing Bear, *My People, the Sioux,* 140–41.

11. Mitchell, *Navajo Blessingway Singer,* 62.

12. Standing Bear, *Land of the Spotted Eagle,* 189. McCowan is quoted in Lorraine M. Scherer, "Great Chieftains of the Mohave Indians," *Southern California Quarterly* 48 (March 1966): 18.

13. ARCIA, 1892, 615.

14. Julia B. McGillycuddy, *McGillycuddy, Agent: A Biography of Dr. Valentine T. McGillycuddy* (Stanford: Stanford University Press, 1941), 205–6.

15. Standing Bear, *My People, the Sioux,* 140.

16. Pratt, *Battlefield and Classroom,* 232.

17. ARCIA, 1890, cli; and U.S. Office of Indian Affairs, *Rules for the Indian School Service* (Washington, D.C.: Government Printing Office, 1898), 31.

18. Carnelita S. Ryan, "The Carlisle Indian Industrial School" (Ph.D. dissertation, Georgetown University, 1962), 42; and ARCIA, 1893, 429.

19. ARCIA, 1897, 161; and Helen Sekaquaptewa (as told to Louise Udall), *Me and Mine: The Life Story of Helen Sekaquaptewa* (Tucson: University of Arizona Press, 1969), 32.

20. Frederick Riggs, "Peculiarities of Indian Education," *Southern Workman,* February 1901, 69; and Standing Bear, *My People, the Sioux,* 142.

21. ARCIA, 1904, 424; ARCIA, 1890, clx; and U.S. Office of Indian Affairs, *Rules for the Indian School Service,* 1898, 26.

22. ARCIA, 1890, clx. See Daniel F. Littlefield, Jr., and Lonnie E. Underhill, "Renaming the American Indian: 1890–1913," *American Studies* 12 (Fall 1971): 33–45.

23. ARCIA, 1890, clx-xlxi, and ARCIA, 1904, 424.

24. ARCIA, 1904, 426.

25. ARCIA, 1890, clxi; and Harriet Patrick Gilstrap, "Memories of a Pioneer Teacher," *Chronicles of Oklahoma* 38 (Spring 1960): 23.

26. *Southern Workman,* May 1889, 55.

27. George A. Pettit, *Primitive Education in North America* (Berkeley: University of California Press, 1946), 59–74.

28. Standing Bear, *My People, the Sioux,* 137.

29. Quoted in Pratt, *Battlefield and Classroom,* 293.

30. Jason Betzinez, *I Fought with Geronimo,* ed. Wilber S. Nye (Harrisburg, Pa.: Stackpole Company, 1959), 154.

31. ARCIA, 1882, p. 30. Agents continually complained of conditions. See ARCIA, 1886, 222, 230; ARCIA, 1887, 148; ARCIA, 1888, 77; ARCIA, 1889, 343–44; ARCIA, 1900, 266.

32. ARCIA, 1892, 605; LMC, 1897, 36; and ARCIA, 1898, 18.

33. For contrasting definitions of Indian and white concepts of space see Bernard L. Fontana, "The Melting Pot that Wouldn't: Ethnic Groups in the American Southwest Since 1846," *American Indian Culture and Research Journal* 1 (1974): 21; Jamake Highwater, *The Primal Mind: Vision and Reality in Indian America* (1981; reprint, New York: New American Library, 1982), chap. 5; Peter Nabokov and Robert Easton, *Native American Architecture* (New York: Oxford University Press, 1989); and Joseph Epes Brown, *The Spiritual Legacy of the American Indian* (New York: Crosswood Publishing, 1982), 50–52.

34. Raymond J. DeMallie, ed., *The Sixth Grandfather: Black Elk's Teachings Given to John G. Neihardt* (Lincoln: University of Nebraska Press, 1984), 290–91. Also see George W. Linden, "Dakota Philosophy," *American Studies* 18 (Fall 1977): 33, and John (Fire) Lame Deer and Richard Erdoes, *Lame Deer Seeker of Visions* (1972; reprint, New York: Washington Square Press, 1976), 96–97, 100–101.

35. Highwater, *The Primal Mind,* 119; ARCIA, 1898, 20; and U.S. Office of Indian Affairs, *Rules for the Indian School Service, 1898,* 25.

36. ARCIA, 1890, cli; and Mitchell, *Navajo Blessingway Singer,* 62.

37. Quoted in Theodore Stern, *The Klamath Tribe: A People and Their Reservation* (Seattle: University of Washington Press, 1965), 107; Don Talayesva, *Sun Chief: The Autobiography of a Hopi Indian,* ed. Leo Simmons (New Haven: Yale University Press, 1942), 95–96; and Sekaquaptewa, *Me and Mine,* 94–95. Also see Edmund Nequatewa, *Born a Chief: The Nineteenth Century Hopi Boyhood of Edmund Nequatewa, as told to Alfred F. Whiting,* ed. P. David Seaman (Tucson: University of Arizona Press, 1993), 87–89.

38. Pratt, *Battlefield and Classroom,* 233, and Estelle Aubrey Brown, *Stubborn Fool: A Narrative* (Caldwell, Idaho: Caxton Printers, 1952), 60, 185.

39. K. Tsianina Lomawaima, *They Called It Prairie Light: The Story of Chilocco Indian School* (Lincoln: University of Nebraska Press, 1994), 59, 133, 135–

38; Sally Hyer, *One House, One Voice, One Heart: Native American Education at the Santa Fe Indian School* (Santa Fe: Museum of New Mexico Press, 1990), 25; Jim Whitewolf, *The Life of a Kiowa Apache Indian,* ed. Charles S. Brant (New York: Dover Publications, 1969), 96; Fred Kabotie (as told to Bill Belknap), *Fred Kabotie: Hopi Indian Artist* (Flagstaff: Museum of Northern Arizona and Northland Press, 1977), 18; Nequatewa, *Born a Chief,* 93; and Marla N. Powers, *Ogalala Women: Myth, Ritual, and Reality* (Chicago: University of Chicago Press, 1986), 109–10.

40. ARCIA, 1890, cli; ARCIA, 1892, 604–5; and Mitchell, *Navajo Blessingway Singer,* 63.

41. ARCIA, 1887, 348, and Whitewolf, *The Life of a Kiowa Apache Indian,* 84.

42. Hopi hearings, July 15–30, 1955, BIA, Phoenix Area Office, Hopi Agency, Keams Canyon, Arizona, 33; Alexander H. Leighton and Dorothea C. Leighton, *The Navajo Door: An Introduction to Navajo Life* (Cambridge: Harvard University Press, 1945), 125–26; and K. Tsianina Lomawaima, "Oral Histories From Chilocco Indian Agricultural School, 1920–1940," *American Indian Quarterly* 11 (Summer 1987): 250. Also Peter Blaine, Sr. (as told to Michael S. Adams), *Papagos and Politics* (Tucson: Arizona Historical Society, 1981), 23–25; Kabotie, *Fred Kabotie,* 17–18; Jerry Suazo, Interview no. 868, Doris Duke Collection, University of New Mexico; Lomawaima, *They Called It Prairie Light,* 101–5; Hyer, *One House, One Voice, One Heart,* 11; Robert A. Trennert, *The Phoenix Indian School: Forced Assimilation in Arizona, 1891–1935* (Norman: University of Oklahoma Press, 1988), 115–18; and Coleman, *American Indian Children at School,* 86–88.

43. Anna Moore Shaw, *A Pima Past* (Tucson: University of Arizona Press, 1974), 133.

44. ARCIA, 1898, 357; E. P. Grinstead, "Value of Military Drills," *Native American,* 21 March 1914, 151–52; and ARCIA, 1886, 224.

45. ARCIA, 1892, 616; Fontana, "The Melting Pot that Wouldn't," 20; and Althea Bass, *The Arapaho Way: A Memoir of an Indian Boyhood* (New York: Clarkson N. Potter, 1966), 6.

46. *Sherman Bulletin,* 21 December 1910, 1; and Grinstead, "Value of Military Drills," 153.

47. *Native American,* 23 October 1909, 342; and *Sherman Bulletin,* 21 December 1910, 1.

48. ARCIA, 1890, clii.

49. ARCIA, 1891, 541; ARCIA, 1892, 617; ARCIA, 1896, 343; LMC, 1895, 28; and U.S. Office of Indian Affairs, *Rules for the Indian School Service,* 1898, 31.

50. Sekaquaptewa, *Me and Mine,* 136–37; "Myrtle Begay" in *Stories of Traditional Navajo Life and Culture,* ed. Johnson, 63, and quoted in Sally J. McBeth, *Ethnic Identity and the Boarding School Experience of West-Central Oklahoma American Indians* (Washington, D.C.: University Press of America, 1983), 106. For other examples see Talayesva, *Sun Chief,* 130; "Paul Blatchford," in *Stories of Traditional Navajo Life and Culture,* ed. Johnson, 175; Mitchell, *Navajo Blessingway Singer,* 67; Stern, *The Klamath Tribe,* 107; Lame Deer and Erdoes, *Lame Deer Seeker of Visions,* 25; and Ray Yazzi, Interview no. 281, Doris Duke Collection, University of New Mexico.

51. IRA *Report,* 1903, 52; and IRA *Report,* 1904, 69.

52. IRA *Report,* 1912, 57; and IRA *Report,* 1914, 34. Also see Robert A. Trennert, "Corporal Punishment and the Politics of Indian Reform, *History of Education Quarterly* 29 (Winter 1989): 595–617.

53. An investigation of the jail at Chilocco in 1907 included the statement of one eyewitness: "It was about the dirtiest and most unsanitary place I ever

saw. . . . It has since been partly renovated and clean bedding put in, but the last time it was inspected I found one young man there with below freezing weather and of course exposed to all the winds, and no heat. . . . The whole scheme reminded me very forcibly of George Kennon's [*sic*] stories of Siberian prison life." Charles L. Davis to Commissioner of Indian Affairs, 2 February 1907, encl. in Chilocco Indian School—Incoming Correspondence, Reports and Related Documents Concerning the Investigation of Chilocco Indian School, Oklahoma, 1907, Box 5, Special Series A, OIA.

54. Sekaquaptewa, *Me and Mine,* 137; Mitchell, *Navajo Blessingway Singer,* 67; Leighton and Leighton, *The Navajo Door,* 126; Lame Deer and Erdoes, *Lame Deer Seeker of Visions,* 23, Jean O. Barnd, "Some Day School Methods," *Native American,* 14 October 1916, 278; Stern, *The Klamath Tribe* 107; "Jeanette Blake" and "Ernest Nelson," in *Stories of Traditional Navajo Life and Culture,* ed. Johnson, 204, 241; and Whitewolf, *The Life of a Kiowa Apache Indian,* 89.

55. Quoted in McBeth, *Ethnic Identity and the Boarding School Experience,* 105; and Jo Ann Ruckman, ed. "Indian Schooling in New Mexico in the 1890s: Letters of a Teacher in the Indian Services," *New Mexico Historical Review* 56 (January 1981), 45. See also Lomawaima, *They Called It Prairie Light,* 106–12, and Coleman, *American Indian Children at School,* 89–90.

56. ARCIA, 1886, 413; and ARCIA, 1895, 249.

57. ARCIA, 1881, 240; and Albert H. Kneale, *Indian Agent* (Caldwell, Idaho: Caxton Printers, 1950), 85–86. Also see ARCIA, 1892, 224.

58. ARCIA, 1916, 5. For an excellent survey of the Indian health policy during this period see Diane Putney, "Fighting the Scourge: American Morbidity and Federal Policy, 1897–1928" (Ph.D. dissertation, Marquette University, 1980). Also see Francis Paul Prucha, *The Great Father: The United States Government and American Indians,* 2 vols. (Lincoln: University of Nebraska Press, 1984), vol. 2, chap. 33.

59. ARCIA, 1880, 301.

60. Pratt, *Battlefield and Classroom,* 224.

61. White Thunder to Ernest White Thunder, reprinted in *Eadle Keahtah Toh,* April 1880, 2. Also see White Thunder to Ernest White Thunder, 25 March 1880, and White Thunder to Ernest White Thunder, 17 April 1880, LRIS, HA.

62. *Eadle Keahtah Toh,* April 1880, 3.

63. Pratt, *Battlefield and Classroom,* 239.

64. Richard H. Pratt to Secretary of the Interior, 6 December 1880, Pratt Papers, BRBML, and Richard H. Pratt to White Thunder, 14 December 1880, Pratt Papers, BRBML.

65. Richard H. Pratt to White Thunder, 15 December 1880, Pratt Papers, BRBML.

66. Ibid.

67. Richard H. Pratt to Swift Bear, 15 December 1880, Pratt Papers, BRBML and Richard H. Pratt to Swift Bear, 15 December 1880, Pratt Papers, BRBML.

68. White Thunder to Richard H. Pratt, 16 January 1881, Pratt Papers, BRBML. According to Luther Standing Bear, White Thunder was angry with Pratt for not bothering to notify him sooner that his son was ill and later for not placing a headstone on his grave. Standing Bear, *My People, the Sioux,* 159.

69. Richard H. Pratt to Swift Bear, 14 December 1880, Pratt Papers, BRBML; and Standing Bear, *My People, the Sioux,* 159.

70. ARCIA, 1881, 253. In 1899 the Reverend J. Roberts calculated that of the

seventy-three Indians sent from the Wind River Agency to off-reservation schools between 1881 and 1894, forty-seven died either while at school or shortly after their return. Putney, "Fighting the Scourge," 10.

71. Putney, "Fighting the Scourge," 23–28.

72. ARCIA, 1897, 268.

73. Brown, *Stubborn Fool,* 50.

74. ARCIA, 1904, 34–37; Education Circular No. 10, 23 March 1904. Ales Hrdlicka, *Tuberculosis Among Certain Indian Tribes of the United States,* Bureau of American Ethnology Bulletin, No. 42 (Washington, D.C.: Government Printing Office, 1909), 25, 32; ARCIA, 1908, 796; and Joseph Murphy, "Health Problems of the Indians, *Annals of the Academy of Political and Social Science* 37 (March 1911): 106–7.

75. "Contagious and Infectious Diseases Among the Indians," Senate Doc. no. 1038, 62nd Cong., 3rd sess., 1913, serial 6365, 16–19, and Putney, "Fighting the Scourge," 141–43.

76. Whitewolf, *The Life of a Kiowa Apache Indian,* 92.

77. "Contagious and Infectious Diseases Among the Indians," 19–32.

78. ARCIA, 1882, 120; ARCIA, 1886, 230; ARCIA, 1898, 184–85; and ARCIA, 1901, 179, 307. Also Putney, "Fighting the Scourge," 20–21, 67–71, and Virginia R. Allen, "Agency Physicians to the Southern Plains Indians, 1868–1900," *Bulletin of the History of Medicine* 49 (Fall 1975): 323–24.

79. Hrdlicka, *Tuberculosis Among Certain Indian Tribes of the United States,* 12–14.

80. Joseph Murphy, "The Prevention of Tuberculosis in the Indian Schools, *Proceedings and Addresses of the National Education Association,* 1909, 920; Murphy, "Health Problems of the Indians," 104; ARCIA, 1882, 20; ARCIA, 1887, 258; ARCIA, 1901, 179, 307; and Narrative and Statistical Reports, Moqui [Hopi], 1912, 15–16, OIA.

81. ARCIA, 1883, 232; ARCIA, 1885, 470; Martha Waldron, "The Indian Health Question," in *Twenty-Two Years' Work of the Hampton Normal and Agricultural Institute at Hampton, Virginia* (Hampton, Va.: Hampton Normal School Press, 1893), 496; Hrdlicka, *Tuberculosis Among Certain Indian Tribes of the United States,* 32; and Irene Stewart, *A Voice in Her Tribe: A Navajo Woman's Own Story,* ed. Doris Ostrander Dawdy (Socorro, N.Mex.: Ballena Press, 1980), 21.

82. ARCIA, 1881, 131; ARCIA, 1882, 120; ARCIA, 1886, 222, 230; ARCIA, 1887, 774, 776; ARCIA, 1889, 237, 332, 343–344; ARCIA 1898, 18; ARCIA, 1901, 179; ARCIA, 1903, 231; ARCIA, 1904, 34; and ARCIA, 1905, 198; Hrdlicka, *Tuberculosis Among Certain Indian Tribes of the United States,* 22–24, 32, and Cora M. Folsom, "Memories of Old Hampton," 52–53, Folsom Papers, HA.

83. ARCIA, 1904, 37; ARCIA, 1908, 796–97; ARCIA, 1913, 23; ARCIA, 1916, 4–9; Education Circular no. 106, 23 March 1904; Education Circular no. 602, 15 February 1912; Education Circular no. 613, 1 April 1912; Education Circular no. 825, 13 February 1914; and Education Circular no. 1028, 1 October 1915. Also Putney, "Fighting the Scourge," 155–65, 234–44, 249–54, and Robert A. Trennert, "Indian Sore Eyes: The Federal Campaign to Control Trachoma in the Southwest, 1910–1940," *Journal of the Southwest* 32 (Summer 1990): 121–49.

84. Education Circular no. 595, 28 December 1911; Education Circular no. 602, 15 February 1912; W. H. Harrison, *Trachoma: Its Cause, Prevention, and Treatment* (Washington, D.C.: Government Printing Office, 1915); and John McMullen, *Trachoma: Its Nature and Prevention,* Supplement no. 8 to the Public

Health Reports, (Washington, D.C.: Government Printing Office, 1915). For examples of "health talks" see *Native American,* 28 December 1912, 619–21; *Native American,* 1 May 1915, 203–5.

85. *Native American,* 12 May 1917, 159.

86. Prucha, *The Great Father,* 2: 852–55, and Putney, "Fighting the Scourge," chaps. 8 and 10.

87. "A Study of the Need for Public-Health Nursing on Indian Reservations," in *Survey of Conditions of the Indian in the United States,* hearings before a Subcommittee of the Committee on Indian Affairs, U.S. Senate, 70th Cong., 2nd sess., 1929, pt. 3, 960, 970, 974–75, 976.

CHAPTER FIVE. CLASSROOM

1. ARCIA, 1884, p. 241.

2. See for example ARCIA, 1880, 301, 305; ARCIA, 1881, 243; ARCIA, 1882, 241; ARCIA, 1883, 225; ARCIA, 1884, 241; and ARCIA, 1905, 397.

3. ARCIA, 1884, 241.

4. ARCIA, 1887, 334; and ARCIA, 1883, 226.

5. ARCIA, 1884, 241–42.

6. Jason Betzinez, *I Fought with Geronimo,* ed. Wilber S. Nye (Harrisburg, Pa.: Stackpole Company, 1959), 154; Anonymous, Interview no. 662, Doris Duke Collection, University of New Mexico; and Charles A. Eastman, *From the Deep Woods to Civilization* (Boston: Little, Brown, 1923), 45–46.

7. Standing Bear, *Land of the Spotted Eagle* (Boston: Houghton Mifflin Company, 1933), 16–18.

8. For an introduction to the subject see Robert F. Spencer, Jesse D. Jennings, et al., *The Native Americans: Ethnology and Backgrounds of the North American Indians* (New York: Harper and Row, 1977), chap. 2.

9. William H. Vanderburg, *The Growth of Minds and Cultures: A Unified Theory of the Structure of Human Experience* (Toronto: University of Toronto Press, 1985), chap. 5; Clyde Kluckhohn, *Mirror for Man* (New York: McGraw-Hill, 1949), chap. 6; and Benjamin Lee Whorf, *Language, Thought, and Reality,* ed. John B. Carroll (New York: John Wiley and Sons, 1956).

10. Clyde Kluckhohn and Dorothea Leighton, *The Navaho* (1946; reprint, Garden City: Doubleday, 1962), 271–73.

11. Frederick B. Riggs, "What Does the Child Bring to the School Intellectually?" *Southern Workman,* October 1895, 174. Also Riggs, "Peculiarities of Indian Education," *Southern Workman,* February 1901, 66–71.

12. ARCIA, 1890, cli; ARCIA, 1882, 239; ARCIA, 1888, 281; ARCIA, 1881, 130; and Minnie Braithwaite Jenkins, *Girl from Williamsburg* (Richmond, Va.: Dietz Press, 1951), 320–21.

13. *Eadle Keatah Toh,* January 1881, 4.

14. Robert L. Brunhouse, "A History of the Carlisle School: A Phase of Government Indian Policy, 1879–1918" (Thesis, University of Pennsylvania, 1935), 26–27; ARCIA, 1888, 281; and ARCIA, 1883, 226.

15. ARCIA, 1898, 132; Lame Deer and Richard Erdoes, *Lame Deer: Seeker of Visions* (1972; reprint, New York: Washington Square Press, 1976), 23; and Frank Mitchell, *Navajo Blessingway Singer: The Autobiography of Frank Mitchell, 1881–1967,* ed. Charlotte J. Frisbie and David A. McAllester (Tucson: University of Arizona Press, 1978), 67.

16. Brunhouse, "A History of the Carlisle School," 26–27.

17. *Indian Leader,* 13 November 1908, 4.

18. *Proceedings and Addresses of the National Education Association,* 1901, 897–98.

19. ARCIA, 1890, clvi-clix.

20. ARCIA, 1887, 351, and ARCIA, 1882, 242.

21. Eastman, *From the Deep Woods to Civilization,* 47; Eve Ball, ed., *Indeh: An Apache Odyssey* (Provo, Utah: Brigham Young University Press, 1980), 145; and Edmund Nequatewa, *Born a Chief: The Nineteenth Century Hopi Boyhood of Edmund Nequatewa, as told to Alfred F. Whiting,* ed. P. David Seaman (Tucson: University of Arizona Press, 1993), 127–28.

22. Luther Standing Bear, *My People, the Sioux* (1928; reprint, Lincoln: University of Nebraska Press, 1975), 155.

23. ARCIA, 1884, 242, and *Southern Workman,* February 1887, 20.

24. ARCIA, 1890, clviii-clx.

25. Joseph Epes Brown, *The Spiritual Legacy of the American Indian* (New York: Crosswood Publishing, 1982), chap. 2; Jamake Highwater, *The Primal Mind: Vision and Reality in Indian America* (1981; reprint, New York: New American Library, 1982), chap. 5; N. Scott Momaday, "Native American Attitudes to the Environment," in *Seeing with a Native Eye: Essays on Native American Religion,* ed. Walter Holden Capps (New York: Harper and Row, 1976), chap. 6; Clara Sue Kidwell, "Science and Ethnoscience," *Indian Historian* 6 (Fall 1973): 43–54; and Calvin Martin, ed., *The American Indian and the Problem of History* (New York: Oxford University Press, 1987), Introduction.

26. Richard Henry Pratt, *Battlefield and Classroom: Four Decades with the American Indian, 1867–1904,* ed. Robert M. Utley (New Haven: Yale University Press, 1964), 241.

27. See in Francis Paul Prucha, *American Indian Policy in Crisis: Christian Reformers and the Indian, 1865–1900* (Norman: University of Oklahoma Press, 1976), chap. 26; Prucha, *The Great Father: The United States Government and the American Indians,* 2 vols. (Lincoln: University of Nebraska Press, 1984), 2:875–79; and Frederick E. Hoxie, *A Final Promise: The Campaign to Assimilate the Indians, 1880–1920* (Lincoln: University of Nebraska Press, 1984), chaps 5 and 7. Also see Michael T. Smith, "The History of Indian Citizenship," *Great Plains Journal* 10 (Fall 1970): 25–35.

28. Prucha, *The Great Father,* 2:882–83; Brian W. Dippie, *The Vanishing American: White Attitudes and U.S. Indian Policy* (Middletown, Conn.: Wesleyan University Press, 1982), 194–95; and Gary C. Stein, "The Indian Citizenship Act of 1924," *New Mexico Historical Review* 47 (July 1972): 257–74. In some respects this was a hollow victory. See Hoxie, *A Final Promise,* 231–34.

29. Horace E. Scudder, *A History of the United States of America* (Philadelphia: J. W. Butler, 1884), iv. For the interpretive perspective of school texts on historic themes during this period see Ruth M. Elson, *Guardians of Tradition: American Schoolbooks of the Nineteenth Century* (Lincoln: University of Nebraska Press, 1964), 71–81, 166–85; Lawrence M. Hauptman, "Mythologizing Westward Expansion: Schoolbooks and the Image of the American Frontier Before Turner," *Western Historical Quarterly* 8 (July 1977): 269–82; and Hauptman, "Westward the Course of Empire: Geography Schoolbooks and Manifest Destiny," *Historian,* 40 (May 1978): 423–40.

30. Scudder, *A History of the United States of America,* 18, 21, 93, 94, 95, 418.

31. ARCIA, 1882, 243; and ARCIA, 1887, 352.

32. Office of Indian Affairs, *Course of Study for the Indian Schools* (Washing-

ton, D.C.: Government Printing Office, 1901), 1901, 143; and "Instructions to Indian Agents in Regard to Inculcation of Patriotism in Indian Schools," ARCIA, 1891, clxvii.

33. *Southern Workman,* February 1885, 20.

34. *Red Man,* March-April 1893, 4. See also William T. Harris's remarks to Carlisle students at the 1899 graduating ceremonies, *Red Man,* February-March 1899, 5.

35. ARCIA, 1890, clii.

36. ARCIA, 1881, 27; and ARCIA, 1890, 296. Also ARCIA, 1888, 258; and ARCIA, 1890, 298. For the nature and role of industrial education in two schools, see Robert A. Trennert, *The Phoenix Indian School: Forced Assimilation in Arizona, 1891–1935* (Norman: University of Oklahoma Press, 1988), 46–47, 68–70, 123–24; and K. Tsianina Lomawaima, *They Called It Prairie Light: The Story of Chilocco Indian School* (Lincoln: University of Nebraska Press, 1994), 68–79.

37. ARCIA, 1890, 296, 299; and ARCIA, 1882, 240. See Robert A. Trennert, "Educating Indian Girls at Nonreservation Boarding Schools, 1878–1920," *Western Historical Quarterly* 13 (July 1982): 275, 277–83, and Lomawaima, *They Called It Prairie Light,* 82–90.

38. ARCIA, 1886, 220.

39. ARCIA, 1895, 344; Estelle Aubrey Brown, *Stubborn Fool: A Narrative* (Caldwell, Idaho: Caxton Printers, 1952), 45–46, and Clark Wissler, *Indian Cavalcade or Life on the Old-Time Indian Reservations* (New York: Sheridan, 1938), 179–80.

40. LMC, 1914, 86; and Helen Sekaquaptewa (as told to Louise Udall), *Me and Mine: The Life Story of Helen Sekaquaptewa* (Tucson: University of Arizona Press, 1969), 122.

41. Anna Moore Shaw, *A Pima Past* (Tucson: University of Arizona Press, 1974), 135–36, and Irene Stewart, *A Voice in Her Tribe: A Navajo Woman's Own Story,* ed. Doris Ostrander Dawdy (Socorro, N.Mex.: Ballena Press, 1980), 17.

42. ARCIA, 1895, 344; ARCIA, 1897, 334; and *Course of Study for the Indian Schools,* 1901, 230.

43. Estelle Reel to Commissioner of Indian Affairs, 28 December 1906, Incoming Correspondence from Estelle Reel, 1904–1907, Box 8, Special Series A, OIA; and Estelle Reel to Commissioner of Indian Affairs, 20 August 1904, Incoming Correspondence from Estelle Reel, 1904–1907, Box 8, Special Series A, OIA.

44. The sharing and cooperative tradition of most Indian societies is richly documented in ethnographic literature. See, for instance, Raymond J. DeMallie, "Pine Ridge Economy: Cultural and Historical Perspectives," in *American Indian Economic Development,* ed. Sam Stanley (The Hague: Monton Publishers, 1978), 250; Royal B. Hassrick, *The Sioux* (Norman: University of Oklahoma Press, 1964), 36–37, 296; Edward P. Dozier, *Hano: A Tewa Indian Community in Arizona* (New York: Holt, Rinehart and Winston, 1966), 88–89; Malcolm McFee, *Modern Blackfeet: Montanans on a Reservation* (New York: Holt, Rinehart and Winston, 1972), 46; and E. Adamson Hoebel, *The Cheyennes: Indians of the Great Plains* (New York: Holt, Rinehart & Winston, 1962), 94.

45. *Native American,* 19 October 1907, 338. For other poetic expressions of this theme see "Opportunity," *Indian Leader,* 20 January 1911, 1; "Winning," *Native American,* 24 September 1910, 395; "The Boy Who Succeeds," *Indian Leader,* 2 May 1902, 4; "There's Always a Way," *Native American,* 13 September 1902, 1; "Ben's Bank," *Indian Leader,* 19 April 1907, 1; "A Junior Partner Wanted," *Indian Leader,* 12 October 1900, 1; and "The Hard Work Plan," *Indian Leader,* 17 February 1911, 1.

46. *Red Man,* May 1982, 5; and *Native American,* 19 October 1907, 331.

47. ARCIA, 1881, 246; ARCIA, 1893, 451; ARCIA, 1895, 351; and ARCIA, 1897, 324–25. Also see Everett Arthur Gilcreast, "Richard Henry Pratt and American Indian Policy, 1877–1906: A Study of the Assimilation Movement" (Ph.D. dissertation, Yale University, 1967), 83–85.

48. *Native American,* 10 April 1915, n.p.

49. For discussions of the outing system see Robert A. Trennert, "From Carlisle to Phoenix: The Rise and Fall of the Indian Outing System, 1878–1930," *Pacific Historical Review* 52 (August 1983): 267–91; Robert L. Brunhouse, "Apprenticeship for Civilization: The Outing System at the Carlisle Indian School," *Educational Outlook* 13 (May 1939): 30–38; Pearl Lee Walker-McNeil, "The Carlisle Indian School: A Study of Acculturation" (Ph.D. dissertation, American University, 1979), chap. 5; Beulah Fitz, "The History of the Carlisle Indian School," (M.S. thesis, University of New Mexico, 1935), chap. 2; and Pratt, *Battlefield and Classroom,* chap. 24.

50. Richard Henry Pratt, "The True Origin of the Indian Outing System at Hampton (Va.) Institute," *Red Man,* September-October 1985, 2, and Pratt, *Battlefield and Classroom,* 194.

51. Walker-McNeil, "The Carlisle Indian School," 198; Gilcreast, "Richard Henry Pratt and American Indian Policy," 320; and Brunhouse, "Apprenticeship for Civilization," 33.

52. Richard Henry Pratt, "A Way Out," LMC, 1891, reprinted in *Red Man,* October-November 1891, 4–5; ARCIA, 1882, 238; ARCIA, 1893, 451; Gilcreast, "Richard Henry Pratt and American Indian Policy," 315–16; and *Red Man,* September 1898, 2.

53. Walker-McNeil, "The Carlisle Indian School," 172–73.

54. Ibid., 175–77.

55. Standing Bear, *My People, the Sioux,* 178–79.

56. *Red Man,* September-October, 1896, 6; *Red Man,* June 1895, 4; Brunhouse, "Apprenticeship for Civilization," 35; and Pratt, *Battlefield and Classroom,* 275.

57. *Red Man,* September 1891, 2, and *Red Man,* November-December 1892, 5.

58. *Red Man,* June 1895, 2; *Red Man,* September 1891, 2; and *Red Man,* September-October 1896, 6.

59. *Red Man,* September 1891, 2–3.

60. *Red Man,* June 1895, 4.

61. *Red Man,* September 1891, 3, and *Red Man,* June 1895, 3–4.

62. ARCIA, 1892, 588, and Gilcreast, "Richard Henry Pratt and American Indian Policy," 326.

63. ARCIA, 1894, 370–71. For a richly detailed account of the Phoenix outing program see Trennert, "From Carlisle to Phoenix," 277–91; Trennert, "Victorian Morality and the Supervision of Indian Women Working in Phoenix, 1906–1930," *Journal of Social History* 22 (Fall 1988): 113–28; and Trennert, *The Phoenix Indian School,* 51–54, 70–73, 87–92, 100–101, 136–38, 167–68.

64. ARCIA, 1901, 537; ARCIA, 1903, 209; and ARCIA, 1904, 437.

65. The initial effort at Genoa to release Indian boys to work in Nebraska thinning beets for the Oxnard Beet Company sparked opposition from local whites, who saw the arrangement as inimical to the interests of labor. Morgan, however, urged Genoa's superintendent to press ahead with the program, which he did. For the correspondence on the issue see ARCIA, 1891, 151–55. Interestingly enough, although Pratt viewed Genoa's agreement with Oxnard as a major deviation from

his concept of outing, and stated so to Morgan, he supported the commissioner's position in the belief that the government should make the point that it would not, in the face of community opposition, retreat from its determination to integrate Indians into the economic life of the nation. *Red Man,* July-August, 1891, 6.

66. Dan Talayesva, *Sun Chief: The Autobiography of a Hopi Indian,* ed. Leo Simmons (New Haven: Yale University Press, 1942), 109, 129.

CHAPTER SIX. RITUALS

1. Sally F. Moore and Barbara G. Myerhoff, eds., *Secular Ritual* (Amsterdam: Gorcum, 1977), 3–5.

2. *Proceedings and Addresses of the National Education Association,* 1903, 1,048; and Herbert Welsh, "The Meaning of the Dakota Outbreak," *Scribner's Magazine* 9 (April 1891): 452.

3. *Southern Workman,* January 1897, 7.

4. For an introduction to this aspect of Indian societies, see Joseph Epes Brown, *The Spiritual Legacy of the American Indian* (New York: Crossword Publishing, 1982); Ake Hultkrantz, *Belief and Worship in Native North America* (Syracuse, N.Y.: Syracuse University Press, 1981); Hultkrantz, *The Religions of the American Indians* (Berkeley: University of California Press, 1979); Hartley Burr Alexander, *The World's Rim: Great Mysteries of the North American Indians* (Lincoln: University of Nebraska Press, 1953); and Sam D. Gill, ed., *Native American Religions: An Introduction* (Belmont, Calif.: Wadsworth Publishing, 1982).

5. See Brown, *Spiritual Legacy of the American Indian,* x, 69.

6. Ibid., 38–40, 53–54, 71–72, 124; Christopher Vecsey, "American Indian Environmental Religions," in *American Indian Environments: Ecological Issues in Native American History,* ed. Christopher Vecsey and Robert W. Venables (Syracuse, N.Y.: Syracuse University Press, 1980), 1–37; Hultkrantz, *Belief and Worship in Native North America,* chap. 7; N. Scott Momaday, "Native American Attitudes to the Environment," in *Seeing with a Native Eye: Essays on Native American Religion,* ed. Walter Holden Capps (New York: Harper and Row, 1976), chap. 6.

7. See works cited in note 4.

8. Henry Warner Bowden, *American Indians and Christian Missions: Studies in Cultural Conflict* (Chicago: University of Chicago Press, 1981), 121.

9. Homer G. Barnett, *Indian Shakers: A Messianic Cult of the Pacific Northwest* (Carbondale: Southern Illinois University Press, 1957); James S. Slotkin, *The Peyote Religion: A Study in Indian-White Relations* (Glencoe, Ill.: Free Press, 1956); Weston LaBarre, *The Peyote Cult* (New York: Schocken Books, 1969); Omer C. Stewart, *Peyote Religion: A History* (Norman: University of Oklahoma Press, 1987); James Mooney, *The Ghost-Dance Religion and the Sioux Outbreak of 1890,* Fourteenth Annual Report of the Bureau of American Ethnology, 1892–1893, pt. 2 (Washington, D.C.: Government Printing Office, 1896); and Robert M. Utley, *The Last Days of the Sioux Nation* (New Haven: Yale University Press, 1963), chap. 5.

10. Brown, *Spiritual Legacy of the American Indian,* 27.

11. U.S. Office of Indian Affairs, *Rules for the Indian School Service, 1898* (Washington, D.C.: Government Printing Office, 1898), 25; ARCIA, 1880, 302–3; ARCIA 1881, 132–33; ARCIA, 1882, 120; ARCIA, 1886, 225; ARCIA, 1887, 350; ARCIA, 1891, 542; and LMC, 1903, 86–87. Hailmann quoted in Indian Rights Association, *Answers to Charges Made Against William N. Hailmann, Superin-*

tendent of Indian Schools, Submitting Quotations from His Writings, etc. (Philadelphia: Indian Rights Association, 1898), 5.

12. ARCIA, 1887, 350; and ARCIA, 1883, 231.

13. ARCIA, 1884, 68.

14. Harry Raven to Richard H. Pratt, 7 November 1887, Pratt Papers, BRBML.

15. *Indian Leader,* March 1915, 4. Also *Indian Leader,* 8 May 1915, 2–3, and *Indian Leader,* October 1915, 14.

16. "Hoke Denetsosie," in *Stories of Traditional Navajo Life and Culture,* ed. Broderick H. Johnson (Tsaile, Ariz.: Navajo Community College Press, 1977), 93; and Frank Mitchell, *Navajo Blessingway Singer: The Autobiography of Frank Mitchell, 1881–1967,* ed. Charlotte J. Frisbie and David A. McAllester (Tucson: University of Arizona Press, 1978), 65–66.

17. Jason Betzinez, *I Fought with Geronimo,* ed. Wilber S. Nye (Harrisburg, Pa.: Stackpole Company, 1959), 257; Thomas Wildcat Alford (as told to Florence Drake), *Civilization, and the Story of the Absentee Shawnees* (Norman: University of Oklahoma Press, 1936), 105–6; and Don Talayesva, *Sun Chief: The Autobiography of a Hopi Indian,* ed. Leo Simmons (New Haven: Yale University Press, 1942), 116–17. Also Charley Joseph Atsye, Interview no. 522, Doris Duke Collection, University of New Mexico; and Edmund Nequatewa, *Born a Chief: The Nineteenth Century Hopi Boyhood of Edmund Nequatewa, as told to Alfred F. Whiting,* ed. P. David Seaman (Tucson: University of Arizona Press, 1993), 111–12, 121–22.

18. Helen Sekaquaptewa (as told to Louise Udall), *Me and Mine: The Life Story of Helen Sekaquaptewa* (Tucson: University of Arizona Press, 1969), 129.

19. Ibid., and *Iapi Oaye: The Word Carrier,* February 1882, 15.

20. Talayesva, *Sun Chief,* 119–28.

21. Morris E. Opler, *Apache Odyssey: A Journey Between Two Worlds* (New York: Holt, Rinehart and Winston, 1969), 126–27.

22. Ibid., 123.

23. Ibid., 123–24.

24. Schurz, "Present Aspects of the Indian Problem," *North American Review* 133 (July 1881): 16; and ARCIA, 1888, lxxxix.

25. ARCIA, 1897, 259; and ARCIA, 1887, 352. Also see *Southern Workman,* March 1879, 31; ARCIA, 1881, 87; ARCIA, 1883, 413; and ARCIA, 1900, 193.

26. Christine Bolt, *American Indian Policy and Indian Reform* (Boston: Allen and Unwin, 1987), 269. In addition to Bolt, see Nancy Bonvillain, "Gender Relations in Native North America," *American Indian Culture and Research Journal* 13 (1989): 1–28; Rayna Green, "The Pocahontas Perplex: The Image of Indian Women in American Culture," *Massachusetts Review* 16 (Winter 1975): 698–714; Green, "Native American Women," *Signs* 6 (1980): 248–67; Clara Sue Kidwell, "The Power of Women in Three American Indian Societies," *Journal of Ethnic Studies* 6 (Fall 1978): 113–21; Katherine M. Weist, "Plains Indian Women: An Assessment," in *Anthropology of the Plains,* ed. W. Raymond Wood and Margot Liberty (Lincoln: University of Nebraska Press, 1980): 255–71; Valerie Shirer Mathes, "A New Look at the Role of Women in Indian Society," *American Indian Quarterly* 2 (Summer 1975): 131–39; David D. Smits, "The 'Squaw Drudge': A Prime Index of Savagism," *Ethnohistory* 29 (1982): 281–306; and Jordan Paper, "The Post-contact Origin of an American Indian High God: The Suppression of Feminine Spirituality," *American Indian Quarterly* 7 (Fall 1983): 1–24.

27. *Southern Workman,* March 1898, 52.

28. ARCIA, 1903, 972.

29. Estelle Aubrey Brown, *Stubborn Fool: A Narrative* (Caldwell, Idaho: Caxton Printers, 1952), 60–62.

30. ARCIA, 1887, 349, and *Eadle Keatah Toh,* March 1882, 2.

31. ARCIA, 1890, cli; ARCIA, 1886, 231, 244; ARCIA, 1887, 349; ARCIA, 1889, 343; ARCIA, 1899, 454; *Southern Workman,* June 1893, 104; *Southern Workman,* September 1900, 530; and Minnie Braithwaite Jenkins, *Girl from Williamsburg* (Richmond, Va.: Dietz Press, 1951), 261. See also K. Tsianina Lomawaima, *They Called It Prairie Light: The Story of Chilocco Indian School* (Lincoln: University of Nebraska Press, 1994), 51, 90–94.

32. Jim Whitewolf, *The Life of a Kiowa Apache Indian,* ed. Charles S. Brant (New York: Dover Publications, 1969), 91–92.

33. ARCIA, 1903, 9. In fact, many Native American cultures placed a premium on chastity. See, for example, Morris E. Opler, *Childhood and Youth in Jicarilla Apache Society* (Los Angeles: Southwest Museum, 1946), 158; E. Adamson Hoebel, *The Cheyennes: Indians of the Great Plains* (New York: Holt, Rinehart and Winston, 1966), 95; and John C. Ewers, *The Blackfeet: Raiders of the Northwestern Plains* (Norman: University of Oklahoma Press, 1958), 99.

34. U.S. Office of Indian Affairs, *Rules for the Indian School Service, 1898,* 30, 13, and ARCIA, 1884, 50–51.

35. Helen W. Ludlow, "Indian Education at Hampton and Carlisle," *Harper's Magazine* 62 (April 1881): 667–68, and Anna Moore Shaw, *A Pima Past* (Tucson: University of Arizona Press, 1974), 137. Also Nequatewa, *Born a Chief,* 118–20.

36. Talayesva, *Sun Chief,* 103, 107.

37. Nequatewa, *Born a Chief,* 92, and Talayesva, *Sun Chief,* 111, 117–18.

38. Everett Arthur Gilcreast, "Richard Henry Pratt and American Indian Policy, 1877–1906: A Study of the Assimilation Movement" (Ph.D. dissertation, Yale University, 1967), 321.

39. Gertrude Golden, *Red Moon Called Me: Memoirs of a School Teacher in the Government Indian Service* (San Antonio: Naylor, 1954), 155.

40. Ibid., 155–56.

41. Brown, *Stubborn Fool,* 224–26.

42. Ibid., 225.

43. Richard Henry Pratt, *Battlefield and Classroom: Four Decades with the American Indian, 1867–1904,* ed. Robert M. Utley (New Haven: Yale University Press, 1964), 317–18, and Richard H. Pratt to *Boston Herald,* 5 November 1896, Pratt Papers, BRBML. Particularly good on the Carlisle football story are John S. Steckbeck, *The Fabulous Redmen: The Carlisle Indians and Their Famous Football Teams* (Harrisburg, Pa.: Jack Horace McFarland, 1951); and J. Newcombe, *The Best of the Athletic Boys: The White Man's Impact on Jim Thorpe* (Garden City, N.Y.: Doubleday, 1975). By 1920, Haskell, Albuquerque, Phoenix, and Sherman were sending teams onto the gridiron to contest nearby high schools and colleges. The best of these was probably Haskell, which as early as 1900 was making a name for itself as a regional pigskin power. But until Carlisle closed its doors in 1918, no one questioned that it fielded the best Indian football team in America. If Haskell had any misconceptions about this, they were put to rest in 1904 when it challenged Carlisle "for the Indian championship of the world," a game to be played at the St. Louis World's Fair. Haskell, which had defeated Texas, Nebraska, and Kansas during the season, had high hopes for the outcome. The result, however, was a stern lesson in humility, as Haskell went down to the tune of 38 to 4. Steckbeck, *Fabulous Redmen,* 140.

44. On the evolution of football including its place in American college life see

Allison Danzig, *The History of American Football: Its Great Teams, Players, and Coaches* (Englewood Cliffs, N.J.: Prentice-Hall, 1956), chaps. 9–10; Ronald Smith, *Sports and Freedom: The Rise of Big-Time College Athletics* (New York: Oxford University Press, 1988), chaps. 6–7; Frederick Rudolph, *The American College and University: A History* (New York: Vintage Books, 1962), chap. 18; David Riesman and Reuel Denny, "Football in America: A Study of Cultural Diffusion," *American Quarterly* 3 (Winter 1951): 309–25; and John Hammond Moore, "Football's Ugly Decades, 1893–1913," *Smithsonian Journal of History* 2 (Fall 1957): 49–68.

45. Quoted in *Red Man,* September-October 1895, 6.

46. For Warner's career see F. J. Powers, *The Life Story of Glen S. (Pop) Warner: Gridiron's Greatest Strategist* (Chicago: Athletic Institute, 1969); Edwin Pope, *Football's Greatest Coaches* (Atlanta: Tuffer and Love, 1955), chap. 25; and Reet A. Howell and Maxwell L. Howell, "The Myth of 'Pop Warner': Carlisle Revisited," *Quest* 30 (Summer 1978): 19–27. Warner's approach to football is explained in his *Football for Players and Coaches* (Carlisle: N.p., 1912), published at the height of his Carlisle fame.

47. Warner, "The Indian Massacres," *Collier's* 88 (17 October 1931): 61; Warner, "The Difference Between Red and White Football Material," *Literary Digest* 67 (11 May 1920): 79; and Joseph B. Oxendine, *American Indian Sports Heritage* (Champaign, Ill.: Human Kinetics Books, 1988), 189–90.

48. Warner, "The Indian Massacres," 62, and Oxendine, *American Indian Sports Heritage,* 188, 191–92.

49. Johan Huizinga, *Homo Ludens: A Study of the Play Element in Culture* (1938; reprint, New York: Harper and Row, 1970), 19. For the classic essay on "deep play" see Clifford Geertz, "Deep Play: Notes on the Balinese Cockfight," in his *The Interpretation of Cultures* (New York: Basic Books, 1973), chap. 15. For the social meaning of play and sport generally, in addition to Huizinga, see Allen Guttman, *From Ritual to Record: The Nature of Modern Sports* (New York: Columbia University Press, 1978); and Brian Sutton-Smith and John M. Roberts, "Play, Games, and Sports," in *Handbook of Cross-Cultural Psychology: Developmental Psychology,* vol. 4, ed. Harry C. Triandis and Alastair Heron (Boston: Allyn and Bacon, 1981), 425–71. For the social meaning of turn-of-the-century football see Smith, *Sports and Freedom,* 84, 95–98; Donald J. Mrozek, *Sports and the American Mentality, 1880–1910* (Knoxville: University of Tennessee Press, 1983), 166–71; and Patrick Miller, "College Sports and American Culture, 1850–1920" (Ph.D. dissertation, University of California, Berkeley, 1987), 237–38, 353–54.

50. LMC, 1896, 35–36; Richard H. Pratt to C. E. Patterson, 23 November 1896, Pratt Papers BRBML; Richard H. Pratt to Gen. John Eaton, 25 November 1896, Pratt Papers, BRBML; and Richard H. Pratt to Abram R. Vail, 10 December 1896, Pratt Papers, BRBML.

51. Quoted in Newcombe, *The Best of the Athletic Boys,* 64.

52. Richard H. Pratt to Kelly Lay, 8 August 1900, Pratt Papers, BRBML; Richard H. Pratt to Frank Beaver, 23 August 1901, Pratt Papers, BRBML; and Richard H. Pratt to Glen S. Warner, 23 August 1901, Pratt Papers, BRBML.

53. *Red Man and Helper,* 12 December 1902, 1–2; *Red Man,* March 1910, reprinted in *Red Man,* vol. 2, *1909–1910* (New York: Johnson Reprint Corporation, 1971), 44; A. R. Kennedy, "Haskell Reputed for Clean Sports," *Indian Leader,* 2 January 1914, 3–4; and C. E. Birch, "Effect of Football on Scholarship," *Indian Leader,* 2 January 1914, 7–8.

54. Quoted in Warner, "Heap Big Run—Most Fast," *Collier's* 88 (24 October 1931): 46.

55. *Red Man and Helper,* 24 October 1902, 1.

56. James Oliver Robertson, *American Myth, American Reality* (New York: Hill and Wang, 1980), 256.

57. Reprinted in *Red Man,* November 1896, 6.

58. Reprinted in *Red Man,* December 1898, 5; and reprinted in *Red Man,* September-October, 1896, 8.

59. Huizinga, *Homo Ludens,* 27, 32–33.

60. Reprinted in *Red Man,* November 1896, 6.

61. Ibid., 4.

62. Ibid., 5.

63. Warner, "The Difference Between Red and White Football Material," 78–79, and Warner, "The Indian Massacres," 7, 61.

64. *Red Man,* September-October 1895, 6; and Warner, "Heap Big Run—Most Fast," 19.

65. Reprinted in *Indian Leader,* 9 October 1914, 3, and Warner, "Heap Big Run—Most Fast," 46.

66. Richard S. Gruneau, "Freedom and Constraint: The Paradoxes of Play, Games, and Sports," *Journal of Sport History* 7 (Winter 1980): 74; and Sutton-Smith and Roberts, "Play, Games, and Sports," 454.

67. *Red Man,* January 1898, 4.

68. Ibid., 4, 6.

69. Ibid., 5.

70. Huizinga, *Homo Ludens,* 33, 40.

71. For the symbolic significance of holiday myths and rituals in American life see Wilber Zelinsky, *Nation into State: The Shifting Symbolic Foundations of American Nationalism* (Chapel Hill: University of North Carolina Press, 1988), 69–75, and Robertson, *American Myth, American Reality,* esp. 9–18. For background on the various holidays see George William Douglas, *American Book of Days* (New York: Wilson, 1937); Trevor Nevitt Dupuy, ed., *Holidays: Days of Significance for All Americans* (New York: Franklin Watts, 1965); and Jane M. Hatch, ed., *The American Book of Days* (New York: H. W. Wilson, 1978).

72. ARCIA, 1892, 62.

73. ARCIA, 1893, 452–53, and *Red Man,* November-December 1982, 2–4.

74. Reprinted in *Red Man,* November-December 1892, 3.

75. Jenkins, *Girl from Williamsburg,* 184–85.

76. Sekaquaptewa, *Me and Mine,* 102. For another account of Christmas at Keam's Canyon see Nequatewa, *Born a Chief,* 97–99.

77. Whitewolf, *The Life of a Kiowa Apache Indian,* 93.

78. This and subsequent paragraphs are drawn from Flora Gregg Iliff, *People of the Blue Water: My Adventures Among the Walapai and Havasupai Indians* (New York: Harper and Brothers, 1954), chap. 28.

79. "Instructions to Indian Agents in Regard to Inculcation of Patriotism in Indian Schools," ARCIA, 1890, clxvii.

80. Quoted in Cora Folsom, "Memories of Old Hampton," Cora Folsom Papers, HA, 107.

81. The complete script for "Columbia's Roll Call" appears in the *Southern Workman,* March 1892, 42–44.

82. Ibid., March 1889, 33.

83. *Red Man,* March 1890, 5.

84. *Talks and Thoughts,* February 1898, 3.

85. See Daniel J. Boorstin, *The Americans: The National Experience* (New York: Random House, 1965), chap. 39; Garry Wills, *Cincinnatus: George Washington and the Enlightenment* (Garden City, N.Y.: Doubleday, 1984); Robertson, *American Myth, American Reality,* 10–15; Lawrence J. Friedman, *Inventors of the Promised Land* (New York: Knopf, 1975), chap. 2; and Howard N. Rabinowitz, "George Washington as Icon: 1865–1900," in Ray B. Browne and Marshall Fishwick, eds., *Icons of America* (Bowling Green, Ohio: Popular Press, 1978), chap. 6.

86. Reprinted in *Indian Leader,* 17 March 1911, 1.

87. ARCIA, 1901, 524.

88. Shaw, *A Pima Past,* 134.

89. James Fenimore Cooper, *The Prairie* (1827; reprint, New York: New American Library, 1964), 78.

90. Robertson, *American Myth, American Reality,* 12–13.

91. Quoted in Wills, *Cincinnatus,* 53.

92. ARCIA, 1890, clii.

93. U.S. Department of Agriculture, *Arbor Day: Its Purpose and Observance,* Farmers Bulletin no. 1492 (Washington D.C.: U.S. Government Printing Office, 1926), 7.

94. *Indian Leader,* 15 June 1906, 1.

95. *Indian Leader,* 5 June 1914, 1.

96. ARCIA, 1893, 243; ARCIA, 1900, 267; and ARCIA, 1901, 343.

97. E. Jane Gay, *With the Nez Perces: Alice Fletcher in the Field, 1889–92,* ed. Frederick E. Hoxie and Joan T. Mark (Lincoln: University of Nebraska Press, 1981), 90.

98. Talayesva, *Sun Chief,* 99.

99. ARCIA, 1901, 342–43.

CHAPTER SEVEN. RESISTANCE

1. Eugene E. White, *Experiences of a Special Indian Agent* (Norman: University of Oklahoma Press, 1965), 168–69.

2. Ibid., 169–70.

3. Ibid., 170–72.

4. Ibid., 172.

5. For discussions of student response, including resistance, see David Wallace Adams, "From Bullets to Boarding Schools: The Educational Assault on the American Indian Identity," in *The American Indian Experience: A Profile,* ed. Philip Weeks (Arlington Heights, Ill.: Forum Press, 1988), 230–37. Michael C. Coleman, *American Indian Children at School, 1850–1930* (Jackson: University Press of Mississippi, 1993), esp. chaps. 4 and 8–9; Coleman, "Motivations of Indian Children at Missionary and U.S. Government Schools," *Montana the Magazine of Western History* 40 (Winter 1990): 30–45; Coleman, "The Responses of American Indian Children to Presbyterian Schooling in the Nineteenth Century: An Analysis Through Missionary Sources," *History of Education Quarterly* 27 (Winter 1987): 473–97; Coleman, "The Mission Education of Francis La Flesche: An Indian Response to the Presbyterian Boarding School in the 1860's," *American Studies in Scandinavia* 18 (1986): 67–82; K. Tsianina Lomawaima, *They Called It Prairie Light: The Story of Chilocco Indian School* (Lincoln: University of Nebraska Press, 1994), 94–99, 115–26, chap. 6; Sally J. McBeth, *Ethnic Identity and the Boarding*

School Experience of West-Central Oklahoma American Indians (Washington, D.C.: University Press of America, 1983), esp. 127–34; and Alice Littlefield, "The B.I.A. Boarding School: Theories of Resistance and Social Reproduction," *Humanity and Society* 13 (1989): 428–41.

6. ARCIA, 1882, 152; ARCIA, 1890, 307; ARCIA, 1897, 164; and ARCIA, 1900, 220. Also see ARCIA, 1881, 188; ARCIA, 1884, 100; ARCIA, 1895, 278; ARCIA, 1899, 168, 202; and ARCIA, 1906, 237.

7. ARCIA, 1886, 318, and ARCIA, 1887, 226–27.

8. ARCIA, 1886, 417.

9. Frank Mitchell, *Navajo Blessingway Singer: The Autobiography of Frank Mitchell, 1881–1967,* ed. Charlotte J. Frisbie and David A. McAllester (Tucson: University of Arizona Press, 1978), 57.

10. Edward Dozier, "Forced and Permissive Acculturation," *The American Indian* 7 (Spring 1955): 38.

11. On the role of factionalism see Richard P. Metcalf, "Who Should Rule at Home? Native American Politics and Indian-White Relations," *Journal of American History* 61 (December 1974): 651–65, and Robert B. Berkhofer, Jr., *Salvation and the Savage: An Analysis of Protestant Missions and American Indian Response, 1787–1862* (New York: Atheneum, 1972), chap. 7.

12. Hamlin Garland, "The Red Man's Present Needs," *North American Review* 174 (April 1902): 479.

13. Quoted, LMC, 1901, 76.

14. See for example ARCIA, 1882, 223–24; Thomas Wildcat Alford (as told to Florence Drake), *Civilization, and the Story of the Absentee Shawnees* (Norman: University of Oklahoma Press, 1936), 90; ARCIA, 1879, 124; ARCIA, 1887, 321; ARCIA, 1888, 253; and LMC, 1893, 1025.

15. For an account of Spotted Tail's visit to Carlisle see George E. Hyde, *A Sioux Chronicle* (Norman: University of Oklahoma Press, 1956), 51–57, and Richard Henry Pratt, *Battlefield and Classroom: Four Decades with the American Indian, 1867–1904,* ed. Robert M. Utley (New Haven: Yale University Press, 1964), 236–40.

16. Inspection Report no. 9020 (Navajo), 23 December 1892, OSI.

17. Ibid. For a fuller firsthand account of Navajo opposition to the school at Fort Defiance see Council of the Chief Men of the Navajo Tribe, 25 November 1892, encl., David L. Shipley to Commissioner of Indian Affairs, 13 December 1892, LR, no. 45001, OIA; and Open Council of the Chiefs and Head Men of the Navajo Tribe, 25 November 1892, encl., Commissioner of Indian Affairs to Secretary of the Interior, 6 December 1892, LR, no. 43345, OSI.

18. ARCIA, 1901, 382.

19. ARCIA, 1890, 35; ARCIA, 1884, 89; ARCIA, 1891, 214–15; ARCIA, 1883, 195–96; and ARCIA, 1889, 259.

20. Quoted in Robert H. Ruby and John A. Brown, *The Spokane Indians: Children of the Sun* (Norman: University of Oklahoma Press, 1970), 216–18.

21. ARCIA, 1883, 195–96, and ARCIA, 1884, 89.

22. Proceedings of Council Held at Navajo School, 20 April 1891, LR, no. 15559, OIA.

23. Robert F. Murphy and Yolanda Murphy, "Northern Shoshone and Bannock," in Warren L. d'Azevedo, ed., *Handbook of North American Indians,* vol. 2, *Great Basin* (Washington, D.C.: Smithsonian Institution, 1986), pp. 284–307; Brigham D. Madsen, *The Northern Shoshone* (Caldwell, Idaho: Caxton Printers,

1980); Madsen, *The Bannock of Idaho* (Caldwell, Idaho: Caxton Printers, 1958); and Sven Liljeblad, "Epilogue: Indian Policy and the Fort Hall Reservation," *Idaho Yesterdays* 2 (Summer 1958): 14–19.

24. ARCIA, 1885, 290; Inspection Report no. 7322 (Fort Hall), 11 December 1889, OSI, and Inspection Report no. 2357 (Fort Hall), 17 March 1891, OSI.

25. ARCIA, 1881, 121; ARCIA, 1892, 662; Inspection Report no. 9007 (Fort Hall), 30 November 1891, OSI; and ARCIA, 1892, 661.

26. Inspection Report no. 9077 (Fort Hall), 30 November 1891, OSI; William T. Lecke to Commissioner of Indian Affairs, 9 January 1892, LR, no. 1809, OIA; and Superintendent of Indian Schools to Commissioner of Indian Affairs, 16 December 1892, LR, no. 45179, OIA.

27. ARCIA, 1892, 150.

28. ARCIA, 1891, 229, and ARCIA, 1895, 143.

29. Joseph G. Jorgensen, "Ghost Dance, Bear Dance, and Sun Dance," in d'Azevedo, ed., *Handbook of North American Indians:* vol. 2, *Great Basin,* 660–62.

30. ARCIA, 1890, 286.

31. ARCIA, 1892, 151.

32. George P. Gregory to Commissioner of Indian Affairs, 21 September 1892, LR, no. 34774, OIA; ARCIA, 1891, 559; Superintendent of Indian Schools to Commissioner of Indian Affairs, 16 December 1892, LR, no. 45179, OIA; and ARCIA, 1892, 233, 235.

33. Jim Ballard and Tom Gibson to President of the United States, 7 October 1895, encl. in Captain Daniel T. Wells to Secretary of the Interior, 28 October 1895, LR, no. 46605, OIA; ARCIA, 1892, 175. For a discussion of treaty and boundary issues at Fort Hall see Madsen, *The Northern Shoshone,* chap. 7.

34. ARCIA, 1885, 291; and ARCIA, 1888, 80–81.

35. Inspection Report no. 9007 (Fort Hall), 30 November 1891, OSI; ARCIA, 1891, 559; and John Y. Williams to Commissioner of Indian Affairs, 29 April 1892, LR, no. 16463, OIA.

36. Superintendent of Indian Schools to Commissioner of Indian Affairs, 16 December 1892, LR, no. 45179, OIA.

37. Lena M. Tife to Commissioner of Indian Affairs, 27 October 1892, LR, no. 39324, OIA.

38. Ibid.

39. For a period, Morgan flirted with the possibility of recruiting students from Western Shoshone Agency where the school was overcrowded, but the Indians there strenuously protested the idea saying, "We do not want to take any steps backward by sending our children among the wild Indians at Fort Hall." W. O. Vore to Commissioner of Indian Affairs, 10 May 1892, encl. in William I. Plumb to Commissioner of Indian Affairs, 10 May 1892, LR, no. 18651, OIA, and Chiefs and Headmen of Shoshone and Paiute Tribes to Commissioner of Indian Affairs, 11 May 1892, enclosed in William I. Plumb to Commissioner of Indian Affairs, 11 May 1892, LR, no. 18652, OIA.

40. ARCIA, 1892, 152.

41. Ibid., 170.

42. Ibid., 174. For background on Navajo and Hopi resistance see Ruth M. Underhill, *The Navajos* (Norman: University of Oklahoma Press, 1956), 205–6; Left-Handed Mexican Clansman et al., *The Trouble at Round Rock,* U.S. Indian Service, Navajo Historical Series, no. 2 (Phoenix: Phoenix Indian School, 1952);

Harry C. James, *Pages from Hopi History* (Tucson: University of Arizona Press, 1988), 76–83; and David Wallace Adams, "Schooling the Hopi: Federal Indian Policy Writ Small, 1887–1917," *Pacific Historical Review* 48 (August 1979): 335–56.

43. LMC, 1892, in ARCIA, 1892, 1323–1324. Also *Journal of the Twenty-Second Annual Conference of the U.S. Board of Indian Commissioners with Representatives of Missionary Boards and Indian Rights Associations,* 1893, in ARCIA, 1892, 1399–1401.

44. ARCIA, 1892, 174–75.

45. See Inspection Report no. 4033 (Fort Hall), 16 May 1893, OSI; Inspection Report no. 8839 (Fort Hall), 24 November 1893, OSI; J. L. Baker to Commissioner of Indian Affairs, 11 September 1893, LR, no. 34895, OIA; ARCIA, 1895, 142; and 1st Quarter Statement of Arrival and Departure of Pupils (Fort Hall Industrial School), 2 October 1895, LR no. 42073, OIA. In the petition sent to Washington on October 7, 1895 (see note 33, first reference), Shoshone and Bannock headmen spelled out a number of complaints with conditions at the agency. With respect to the school, "When they (the children) are sick we cannot go to see them the distance is so far we are not allowed to stay at the school and some of our children died without us seeing them."

46. *Pocatello Tribune,* 29 September 1897, 1.

47. Ibid.; and ARCIA, 1898, 144.

48. For the nature of cultural conflict as well as its connection to education see Dozier, "Forced and Permissive Acculturation"; John W. Berry, "Social and Cultural Change," in *Handbook of Cross-Cultural Psychology,* vol. 5, *Social Psychology,* ed. Harry C. Triandis and Richard W. Brislin (Boston: Allyn and Bacon, 1980), 250–65; Reed D. Riner, "American Indian Education: A Rite That Fails," *Anthropology and Education Quarterly* 10 (Winter 1979): 236–53; John Ogbu, "Cultural Discontinuities and Schooling," *Anthropology and Education Quarterly* 8 (December 1982): 290–307; and Harry F. Wolcott, "The Teacher as an Enemy," in *Education and Cultural Process: Toward an Anthropology of Education,* ed. George D. Spindler (New York: Holt, Rinehart and Winston, 1974), 411–25.

49. George D. Spindler, "Psychocultural Adaption," in *The Study of Personality: An Interdisciplinary Appraisal,* ed. Edward Norbeck, Douglas Price-Williams, and William M. McCord (New York: Holt, Rinehart and Winston, 1968), 337–43.

50. ARCIA, 1886, 222, and ARCIA, 1887, 319. Also ARCIA, 1899, 206; ARCIA, 1903, 185, 300; and ARCIA, 1905, 250.

51. ARCIA, 1891, 292; and ARCIA, 1895, 201. Not surprisingly, the "Messiah Craze" had a destabilizing effect on school enrollments. Its connection to the Bannocks' opposition to the school at Fort Hall has already been mentioned. But the superintendent at a Cheyenne school also listed "the rumor coming of the Messiah" as one of the factors keeping children out of school. The situation was much the same with the Arapaho. See ARCIA, 1890, 183; and ARCIA, 1891, 183.

52. Lomawaima, *They Called It Prairie Light,* 121; and Minnie Braithwaite Jenkins, *Girl from Williamsburg* (Richmond, Va.: Dietz Press, 1951), 283.

53. Peter Blaine, Sr. (as told to Michael S. Adams), *Papagos and Politics* (Tucson: Arizona Historical Society, 1981), 25; Edmund Nequatewa, *Born a Chief: The Nineteenth Century Hopi Boyhood of Edmund Nequatewa, as told to Alfred F. Whiting,* ed. P. David Seaman (Tucson: University of Arizona Press, 1993), chaps. 10–11; and Robert A. Trennert, *The Phoenix Indian School: Forced Assimilation in Arizona, 1891–1935* (Norman: University of Oklahoma Press, 1988), 125–26.

54. ARCIA, 1901, 562.

55. Helen Sekaquaptewa (as told to Louise Udall), *Me and Mine: The Life Story of Helen Sekaquaptewa* (Tucson: University of Arizona Press, 1969), 130–31.

56. Jim Whitewolf, *The Life of a Kiowa-Apache Indian,* ed. Charles S. Grant (New York: Dover Publications, 1969), 87–89.

57. Ibid., 89–90.

58. John S. Collins to T. F. McCormick, 8 November 1926, Southern Pueblo Agency, Decimal File 1911–1935, 802.0–806, Box 124, OIA—Denver Branch.

59. Mildred P. Mayhall, *The Kiowas* (Norman: University of Oklahoma Press, 1962), 313, and ARCIA, 1903, 300.

60. ARCIA, 1892, 657.

61. Gertrude Golden, *Red Moon Called Me: Memoirs of a School Teacher in the Government Indian Service* (San Antonio: Naylor, 1954), 77.

62. ARCIA, 1886, 220; ARCIA, 1895, 205; and ARCIA, 1899, 159. For other examples of arson see ARCIA, 1892, 310; ARCIA, 1883, 76; and ARCIA, 1899, 26.

63. Francis E. Leupp, *The Indian and His Problem* (New York: Charles Scribner's Sons, 1910), 239–40.

64. *Red Man,* February 1898, 1.

65. U.S. Office of Indian Affairs, *Rules for the Indian School Service, 1898* (Washington, D.C.: Government Printing Office, 1898), 24, 27, and ARCIA, 1899, 27.

66. *Indian Leader,* 27 July 1906, 4.

67. Ibid., 17 January 1908, 3, and Leupp, *The Indian and His Problem,* 241. Leupp clearly states that he went out of his way to aggressively prosecute an arson case and, after conviction of the guilty party, widely publicized the stiff sentence handed out. The case of the two Menomini girls appears to be that case, although Leupp mentions three, not two, conspirators in his recollection, perhaps confusing this case with the one involving the three Potawatomie girls. In any event he claims that the primary guilty party was "condemned to imprisonment for life, narrowly escaping the death sentence," but goes on to say that by prearrangement with the president, the girl's sentence was quietly commuted to a lesser one in a reformatory. If the life sentence of Lizzie Cardish was in fact Leupp's showcase, the three Potawatomie girls seem not to have gotten the message.

68. Harry F. Wolcott, *A Kwakiutle Village and School* (1967; reprint, Prospect Heights, Ill.: Waveland Press, 1984), 95–108; Wolcott, "Teacher as an Enemy," 411–25; Murray L. Wax, Rosalie H. Wax, and Robert V. Dumont, Jr., *Formal Education in an American Indian Community: Peer Society and the Failure of Minority Education* (1964; reprint, Prospect Heights, Ill.: Waveland Press, 1989), 90–101; Gordon MacGregor, *Warriors Without Weapons: A Study of the Society and Personality Development of the Pine Ridge Sioux* (Chicago: University of Chicago Press, 1946), 135–37; Paul E. Greenbaum and Susan D. Greenbaum, "Cultural Differences, Nonverbal Regulation, and Classroom Interaction: Sociolinguistic Interference in American Indian Education," *Peabody Journal of Education* 61 (Fall 1983): 16–33; and Reed D. Riner, "American Indian Education: A Rite That Fails," 248.

69. Brown, *Stubborn Fool,* 42. Also, ARCIA, 1900, 251; and ARCIA, 1890, 307.

70. Rose Brandt, ed., *The Colored Land: A Navajo Indian Book* (New York: Charles Scribner's Sons, 1937), 80.

71. Thisba Huston Morgan, "Reminiscences of My Days in the Land of the Ogalalla Sioux," *Report and Historical Collections* (South Dakota State Historical Society) 19 (1958): 26–28; Don Talayesva, *Sun Chief: The Autobiography of a*

Hopi Indian, ed. Leo Simmons (New Haven: Yale University Press, 1942), 102; Whitewolf, *The Life of a Kiowa Apache,* 964; Mitchell, *Navajo Blessingway Singer,* 65; and Francis La Flesche, *The Middle Five: Indian School-boys of the Omaha Tribe* (1900; reprint, Madison: University of Wisconsin Press, 1963), 67–68.

72. Nequatewa, *Born a Chief,* 91–92.

73. Mitchell, *Navajo Blessingway Singer,* 66, and Anna Moore Shaw, *A Pima Past* (Tucson: University of Arizona Press, 1974), 135.

74. Albert H. Kneale, *Indian Agent* (Caldwell, Idaho: Caxton Printers, 1950), 124–25.

75. La Flesche, *The Middle Five,* 29–31, 57–60, and chap. 13; Irene Stewart, *A Voice in Her Tribe: A Navajo Woman's Own Story,* ed. Doris Ostrander Dawdy (Socorro, N.Mex.: Ballena Press, 1980), 18; Morris E. Opler, *Apache Odyssey: A Journey Between Two Worlds* (New York: Holt, Rinehart and Winston, 1969), 87; and Lomawaima, *They Called It Prairie Light,* chap. 6.

76. Morgan, "Reminiscences of My Days in the Land of the Ogalalla Sioux," 28–29.

77. ARCIA, 1892, 667; ARCIA, 1893, 11; and James McCarthy, *A Papago Traveler* (Tucson: University of Arizona Press, 1985), 26–67.

78. ARCIA, 1916, 24–25.

79. Flora Gregg Iliff, *People of the Blue Water: My Adventures Among the Walapai and Havasupai Indians* (New York: Harper and Brothers, 1954), 215–16.

80. Ibid., 217–18.

81. Ibid. Also see ARCIA, 1901, 209.

82. Encl., E. H. Plummer to Commissioner of Indian Affairs, 8 June 1894, LR, no. 22506, OIA. Punctuation has been added and misspelling corrected to make this and the following letter more readable.

83. Ibid.

84. Ibid.

CHAPTER EIGHT. ACCOMMODATION

1. Hampton Institute, *Twenty-Two Years' Work of the Hampton Normal and Agricultural Institute at Hampton, Virginia* (Hampton, Va.: Hampton Normal School Press, 1893), 418.

2. Charles A. Eastman, *From the Deep Woods to Civilization* (Boston: Little, Brown, 1923), 24–28, 46–47.

3. This is a central theme in Michael Coleman, *American Indian Children at School, 1854–1930* (Jackson: University Press of Mississippi, 1993), 84–85.

4. For the nature and varieties of acculturation see Edward E. Spicer, *Perspectives in American Indian Culture Change* (Chicago: University of Chicago Press, 1961); Ralph Linton, ed., *Acculturation in Seven American Indian Tribes* (New York: D. Appleton-Century, 1940), chaps. 8–10; Robert L. Bee, *Patterns and Processes: An Introduction to Anthropological Strategies for the Study of Sociocultural Change* (New York: Free Press, 1974); John W. Berry, "Social and Cultural Change," in *Handbook of Cross-Cultural Psychology,* vol. 5, *Social Psychology,* ed. Harry C. Triandis and Richard W. Brislin (Boston: Allyn and Bacon, 1980); Berry, "Acculturation as Varieties of Adaption," in *Acculturation: Theory, Models and Some More Findings,* ed. Amado M. Padilla (Boulder, Colo.: Westview Press, 1980), 9–25; and J. Milton Yinger and George

Eaton Simpson, "The Integration of Americans of Indian Descent," *Annals of the American Academy of Political and Social Science* 436 (March 1978): 137–51.

5. The discussion of "Chief Strong Arm's Change of Heart" is based on descriptions and selections of the play printed in *Indian Leader,* 19 May 1916, 4; *Indian Leader,* 2 July 1909, 1, 5; and *Indian Leader,* June 1916, 24–25. Also see the description of another original play, "Wa-ya-wa-ble," performed at Haskell in 1908, *Indian Leader,* 26 June 1908, 4.

6. *Southern Workman,* October 1905, 555–64.

7. Minnie Braithwaite Jenkins, *Girl from Williamsburg* (Richmond, Va.: Dietz Press, 1951), 57. See also Josiah Butler, "Pioneer School Teaching at the Comманche-Kiowa Agency School 1870–1873," *Chronicles of Oklahoma* 6 (December 1928): 508, and Thisba Huston Morgan, "Reminiscences of My Days in the Land of the Ogalalla Sioux," *Report and Historical Collections* (South Dakota State Historical Society) 19 (1958): 31–32.

8. ARCIA, 1893, 245. Also ARCIA, 1883, 163–64; ARCIA, 1884, 163; and ARCIA, 1893, 243–45.

9. In 1890, several Hopi headmen were brought to Washington specifically to discuss Hopi opposition to schools. Conference with Moqui Pueblos, June 27, 1890, LR no. 19797, OIA. For background, see Harry C. James, *Pages from Hopi History* (Tucson: University of Arizona Press, 1988), 106–45; Scott Rushforth and Steadman Upham, *A Hopi Social History: Anthropological Perspectives on Sociocultural Persistence and Change* (Austin: University of Texas Press, 1992), 123–29; and David Wallace Adams, "Schooling the Hopi: Federal Indian Policy Writ Small, 1887–1917," *Pacific Historical Review* 48 (August 1979): 340–41.

10. Lt. Edwin Plummer to Commissioner of Indian Affairs, 5 June 1893, LR, no. 21159, OIA, and Left-Handed Mexican Clansman et al., *The Trouble at Round Rock,* U.S. Indian Service, Navajo Historical Series, no. 2 (Phoenix: Phoenix Indian School, 1952), 19–20.

11. Clansman, *The Trouble at Round Rock,* 20.

12. Particularly good on the Chicago World's Columbian Exposition are Robert W. Rydell, *All the World's a Fair: Visions of Empire at American International Expositions, 1876–1916* (Chicago: University of Chicago Press, 1984), chap. 2; C. H. Edson, "Chicago: 1893," *Educational Studies* 19 (Spring 1988): 1–29; Robert A. Trennert, "Selling Indian Education at World's Fairs and Expositions, 1893–1904, "*American Indian Quarterly* 11 (Summer 1987): 203–12; and Trennert, "Fairs, Expositions, and the Changing Image of Southwestern Indians, 1876–1904," *New Mexico Historical Review* 62 (April 1987): 133–40.

13. ARCIA, 1894, 1044–45.

14. ARBIC, 1894, 1034–35; Edwin Plummer to Herbert Welsh, 22 January 1894, IRA; Edwin Plummer to Herbert Welsh, 23 February 1894, IRA; and Darwin James to Herbert Welsh, 7 June 1894, IRA.

15. Jenkins, *Girl from Williamsburg,* 58–59.

16. ARCIA, 1880, 9; ARCIA, 1882, 190; and C. E. Vandever to Herbert Welsh, 10 January 1890, IRA.

17. *Southern Workman,* August 1880, 85, and *Southern Workman,* March 1891, 166–67.

18. *Southern Workman,* February 1883, 19; *Indian Craftsman,* September 1909, 37; and quoted in Jesse H. Meyer, "Development of Technical-Vocational Education of the Carlisle Indian Industrial School," (Thesis: Oregon State College, 1954), 39.

19. ARCIA, 1880, 307. See also Lone Bear to Daughter, 8 March 1880, LRIS, HA; and Hampton Institute, *Twenty-Two Year's Work of the Hampton Normal and Agricultural Institute,* 398.

20. Swift Bear to Rainwater and White Woman, 17 April 1880, LRIS, HA; AR-CIA, 1880, 306; Bobtail to Son, 15 December 1879, LRIS, HA. Also see Standing Bear to William Snake, and Yellow Horse to William Snake, reprinted in *Eadle Keatah Toh,* June 1881, 4; Spotted Tail to Son, 19 March 1880, LRIS, HA; and Bull Bear to Davis and Oscar Bull Bear, 13 January 1880, LRIS, HA; Bull Bear to Oscar Bull Bear, 3 March 1880, LRIS, HA.

21. Black Crow to Daughter, 10 December 1879, LRIS, HA; and Black Crow to Daughter, 27 February 1880, LRIS, HA.

22. Cloud Bull to Son, 22 November 1879, LRIS, HA; Long Face to Red Rose, 4 March 1880, LRIS, HA; and Brave Bull to Daughter, 4 January 1880, reprinted in Helen W. Ludlow, "Indian Education at Hampton and Carlisle," *Harper's Magazine* 62 (April 1881): 675. Also, Stranger Horse to Hole-in-the-Ground, 1 March 1880, LRIS, HA, and Big Head to Daughter, 19 April 1880, LRIS, HA.

23. Cloud Shield to Son, 15 April 1880 and Brave Bull to Daughter, 4 January 1880, reprinted in Ludlow, "Indian Education at Hampton and Carlisle," 675.

24. *Southern Workman,* May 1881, 55.

25. Erving Goffman notes that "conversion" is one of the possible responses to life in the total institution. In this instance "the inmate appears to take over the official or staff view of himself and tries to act out the role of the perfect inmate." See Erving Goffman, *Asylums: Essays on the Social Situation of Mental Patients and Other Inmates* (Chicago: Aldine Publishing, 1961): 43–44.

26. *Talks and Thoughts,* February 1892, 1; and *Southern Workman,* April 1887, 43. For other examples see the speeches of Haskell's 1902 graduation class, *Indian Leader,* 4 July 1902; John M. Lolorias, "As an Indian Sees It," *Southern Workman,* September 1902, 476–80; *Journal of the Sixteenth Annual Conference with Representatives of Missionary Boards and Indian Rights Associations,* in ARCIA, 1886, 1028; and Carlisle students' remarks in Richard Henry Pratt, "Violated Principles the Cause of Failure in Indian Civilization," *Journal of the Military Service Institution of the United States* 7 (March 1886): 52–57.

27. *Talks and Thoughts,* February 1904, 4.

28. *Indian Leader,* 4 July 1902, 6.

29. Ibid., 7 July 1905, 1.

30. *Talks and Thoughts,* March 1907, 4.

31. *Morning Star,* July 1886, 4.

32. For both the process and facts of evolving Indian dependency see Richard White, *The Roots of Dependency: Subsistence, Environment, and Social Change Among the Choctaws, Pawnees, and Navajos* (Lincoln: University of Nebraska Press, 1983).

33. ARCIA, 1881, 172–73. Also, ARCIA, 1896, 176, and ARCIA, 1897, 177.

34. Reprinted in *Native American,* 29 November 1913, 503.

35. LMC, 1913, 202.

36. Luther Standing Bear, *My People, the Sioux* (1928; reprint, Lincoln: University of Nebraska Press, 1975), 151–52; Standing Bear, *Land of the Spotted Eagle* (Boston: Houghton Mifflin Company, 1933), 234–35; and *Southern Workman,* January 1895, 11.

37. Jean O. Barnd, "Some Day School Methods," *Native American,* 28 October 1916, 295–96.

38. *Southern Workman,* March 1891, 167; and *Southern Workman,* March 1894, 44–45. Also, *Southern Workman,* January 1882, 5; and *Native American,* 25 October 1913, 453–54.

39. ARCIA, 1884, 19; ARCIA, 1887, 343; and ARCIA, 1903, 216.

40. Morris E. Opler, *Apache Odyssey: A Journey Between Two Worlds* (New York:

Holt, Rinehart and Winston, 1969), 83; Don Talayesva, *Sun Chief: The Autobiography of a Hopi Indian,* ed. Leo Simmons (New Haven: Yale University Press, 1942), 100; and Frank Mitchell, *Blessingway Singer: The Autobiography of Frank Mitchell, 1881–1967,* ed. Charlotte J. Frisbie and David A. McAllester (Tucson: University of Arizona Press, 1978), 40, 62. Also, "Mrs. Bob Martin," in *Stories of Traditional Navajo Life and Culture,* ed. Broderick H. Johnson (Tsaile, Ariz.: Navajo Community College Press, 1977), 131.

41. Helen Sekaquaptewa (as told to Louise Udall), *Me and Mine: The Life Story of Helen Sekaquaptewa* (Tucson: University of Arizona Press, 1969), 125, 138.

42. Albert Yava, *Big Falling Snow: A Tewa-Hopi Indian's Life and Times and the History and Traditions of His People,* ed. Harold Courlander (Albuquerque: University of New Mexico Press, 1978), 12–20.

43. George E. Balenti to Richard H. Pratt, Pratt Papers, BRBML; Jason Betzinez, *I Fought with Geronimo,* ed. Wilber S. Nye (Harrisburg, Pa.: Stackpole Company, 1959), 150–51; and Helen Ludlow and Elaine Goodale, *Captain Pratt and His Work for Indian Education* (Philadelphia: Indian Rights Association, 1886), 6. Also see Robert Agosa's comments on Haskell's superintendent, Charles Meserve, LMC, 1909, 58.

44. *Indian Leader,* 12 January 1906, 2; *Indian Leader,* 17 February 1905, 4; and Gertrude Golden, *Red Moon Called Me: Memoirs of a School Teacher in the Government Indian Service* (San Antonio: Naylor, 1954), 196.

45. *Sherman Bulletin,* 21 December 1910, 1.

46. Lucille Winnie, *Sah-gan-de-oh: The Chief's Daughter* (New York: Vantage Press, 1969), 44.

47. The material on Irene Stewart is based on her autobiography, *A Voice in Her Tribe: A Navajo Woman's Own Story,* ed. Doris Ostrander Dawdy (Socorro, N.Mex.: Ballena Press, 1980). A growing acceptance of school is a prominent theme in several autobiographical accounts, including Standing Bear, *My People, the Sioux,* Talayesva, *Sun Chief,* Betzinez, *I Fought with Geronimo,* Eastman, *From the Deep Woods to Civilization,* and Belle Highwalking, *Belle Highwalking: The Narrative of a Northern Cheyenne Woman,* ed. Katherine Weist (Billings: Montana Council for Indian Education, 1979).

48. Flora Gregg Illif, *People of the Blue Water: My Adventures Among the Walapai and Havasupai Indians* (New York: Harper and Brothers, 1954), 236–37.

49. Ibid., 238.

50. Ibid., 239–41.

51. Ibid., 242.

52. Ibid., 241.

53. For brief accounts of Wohaw's life see Karen Daniels Peterson, *Plains Indian Art from Fort Marion* (Norman: University of Oklahoma Press, 1971), 207–14, and Pamela Holco Oestreicher, "On the White Man's Road? Acculturation and the Fort Marion Southern Plains Prisoners" (Ph.D. dissertation, Michigan State University, 1981), 287–88.

CHAPTER NINE. HOME

1. *Indian Leader,* 4 July 1902, 3–4.

2. Ibid., 3.

3. *Red Man,* March 1898, 7. For other examples, see *Red Man,* February-March, 1899, 1, 4–5, 11–12, and *Red Man,* March-April, 1893, 4.

4. *Red Man,* June 1891, 8, and *Red Man,* 25 July 1902, 1. Also, *Native American,* 21 May 1910, 262–63, and *Indian Craftsman,* May 1909, 8–10.

5. *Eadle Keatah Toh,* February 1882, 6, and *Red Man,* January-February 1894, 3.

6. Clark Wissler, *Indian Cavalcade or Life on the Old-Time Indian Reservations* (New York: Sheridan, 1938), 183–84.

7. For other discussions of the subject of returned students, see Wilbert H. Ahern, "The Returned Indians: Hampton Institute and Its Indian Alumni, 1879–1893," *Journal of Ethnic Studies* 10 (Winter 1983): 101–24; Michael C. Coleman, *American Indian Children at School, 1850–1930* (Jackson: University Press of Mississippi, 1993), chap. 10; and David Wallace Adams, "Schooling the Hopi: Federal Indian Policy Writ Small, 1887–1917," *Pacific Historical Review* 48 (August 1979): 350–56.

8. ARCIA, 1884, 246–47.

9. Ibid.

10. *Red Man,* January-February 1890, 4, and Returned Student Survey, Bulletin no. 24, 79, BIC, Reference Material, 1875–1933, Tray 121.

11. Albert H. Kneale, *Indian Agent* (Caldwell, Idaho: Caxton Printers, 1950), 171.

12. Polingaysi Qoyawayma (Elizabeth White), as told to Vada F. Carlson, *No Turning Back: A Hopi Indian's Struggle to Live in Two Worlds* (Albuquerque: University of New Mexico Press, 1964), chap. 5.

13. Quoted in Samuel Chapman Armstrong, *The Indian Question* (Hampton, Va.: Hampton Normal School Steam Press, 1883), 30, and Thomas Wildcat Alfort to Armstrong, 6 February 1888, reprinted in Helen Ludlow, *Ten Years' Work for Indians at Hampton Institute, Virginia* (Hampton, Va.: Hampton Institute, 1888), 49–50. Also *Red Man,* March 1912 (reprint; New York: Johnson Reprint Corporation, 1971), 271.

14. *Southern Workman,* January 1897, 11, and *Red Man,* April 1910 (reprint; New York: Johnson Reprint Corporation, 1971), 25.

15. Hampton Institute, *Twenty-Two Years' Work of the Hampton Normal and Agricultural Institute at Hampton, Virginia* (Hampton, Va.: Hampton Normal School Press, 1893), 427–28, and Student Records (Frank Black Hawk), Indian Collection, HA. Black Hawk was one of Hampton's "bad boys" and eventually died in prison awaiting trial for murder.

16. ARCIA, 1892, 556–57; *Southern Workman,* June 1900, 338–43; and Don Talayesva, *Sun Chief: The Autobiography of a Hopi Indian,* ed. Leo Simmons (New Haven: Yale University Press, 1942), 155, 157, 178.

17. ARCIA, 1887, 168, and Jason Betzinez, *I Fought with Geronimo,* ed. Wilber S. Nye (Harrisburg, Pa.: Stackpole Company, 1959), 176–77.

18. LMC, 1904, 25–26; Harrison, *The Latest Studies on Indian Reservations* (Philadelphia: Indian Rights Association, 1887), 149–50; Returned Student Survey, Bulletin no. 24, 18, BIC, Reference Material, 1875–1933, Tray 121; and Thomas Wildcat Alford to Samuel C. Armstrong, 6 February 1888, reprinted in Ludlow, *Ten Years' Work for Indians at Hampton Institute,* 49–50.

19. *Red Man,* July-August 1893, 1, and Quoyonah to Richard H. Pratt, 29 April 1879, reprinted in *Southern Workman,* June 1879, 68.

20. ARCIA, 1897, 319.

21. Cora Folsom, "Record of Returned Indian Students: Introduction," in Hampton Institute, *Twenty-Two Years' Work,* 322, and Richard H. Pratt to Chief Killer, 5 July 1887, Pratt Papers, BRBML.

22. ARCIA, 1918, 31, and *Southern Workman,* September 1902, 505. Also, AR-

CIA, 1884, 244; ARCIA, 1887, 262; Folsom, "Report on Returned Indian Students," in *Ten Years' Work for Indians at Hampton Institute,* 44; Returned Student Survey, Bulletin no. 24, 218–19, BIC, Reference Material, Tray 121; and *Red Man,* January-February 1894, 2.

23. The Spindlers also go on to note that beyond the traditional female role of being wife and mother, Menomini women have always had considerable role flexibility, something that may help explain their ability to "adapt to new expectations without much disturbance and without deep psychological reformulation." The Spindlers also credit women with being the primary transmitters of traditional Menomini values. See Louise Spindler and George Spindler, "Male and Female Adaptations in Cultural Change," *American Anthropologist* 60 (April 1958): 229–31. Also Louise S. Spindler, *Menomini Women and Cultural Change,* American Anthropological Association Memoir 91, vol. 64 (Menasha, Wis.: Banta and Sons, 1962), 97–98.

24. *Southern Workman,* September 1902, 505, and ARCIA, 1885, 478.

25. *Southern Workman,* May 1881, 55.

26. Student Records (James Bear's Heart), Indian Collection, HA.

27. Ibid.

28. Ibid.

29. See Armstrong's and Pratt's early school reports for optimistic accounts of returned students.

30. *Congressional Record,* 49th Cong., 1st sess., 1886, 17, pt. 3, 2275.

31. Richard H. Pratt to B. M. Cutcheon, 17 March 1886, Pratt Papers, BRBML; Herbert Welsh, *Are the Eastern Industrial Training Schools for Indian Children a Failure?* (Philadelphia: Indian Rights Association, 1886). Also see Everett Arthur Gilcreast, "Richard Henry Pratt and American Indian Policy, 1877–1906: A Study of the Assimilation Movement" (Ph.D. dissertation, Yale University, 1967), 146–50.

32. Quoted in Charles C. Painter, *Extravagance, Waste, and Failure of Indian Education* (Philadelphia: Indian Rights Association, 1892), 7.

33. Frank Blackmar, "Indian Education," *Annals of the American Academy of Political and Social Science* 2 (May 1892): 831.

34. Painter, *Extravagance, Waste, and Failure of Indian Education,* 9; Welsh, *Are the Eastern Industrial Training Schools for Indian Children a Failure?* and Samuel Chapman Armstrong, *Hampton Normal and Agricultural Institute: Its Reply to a New Attack on Eastern Schools* (Hampton, Va.: Hampton Institute, 1890).

35. *Southern Workman,* July 1895, 115. This is an underlying theme in Welsh, *Are the Eastern Industrial Training Schools for Indian Children a Failure?* Also, Folsom, "Report on Returned Indian Students," in *Ten Years' Work for Indians at Hampton Institute,* 44.

36. A particularly useful study on Hampton's efforts to document returned students' records is Ahern's "The Returned Indians." See individual student records for the list of questions asked returned students, HA.

37. Category descriptions are taken from Folsom, "Report on Returned Indian Students," in *Ten Years' Work for Indians at Hampton Institute,* 42–44, and Folsom, "Summary," in *Twenty-Two Years' Work,* 487–88. Also, ARCIA, 1887, 352–53.

38. "Notes on the Returned Indian Students of the Hampton Normal and Agricultural Institute," *Senate Exec. Doc.* no. 31, 52nd Cong., 1st sess., serial 2892, 1892.

39. For Carlisle's record see LMC, 1899, 49; *Red Man and Helper,* 1 February, 1901, 1, and ARCIA, 1901, 40–41, 537. Jones's remarks are reprinted in *Red Man,*

February-March 1899, 12. For other schools' claims see ARCIA, 1899, 399; LMC, 1900, 51–52; LMC, 1909, 53–54; *Indian Leader,* December 1913, 11–14; and Robert A. Trennert, *The Phoenix Indian School: Forced Assimilation in Arizona, 1891–1935* (Norman: University of Oklahoma Press, 1988), 141–44.

40. Folsom, "Summary," in *Twenty-Two Years' Work,* 487–88; ARCIA, 1899, 399; ARCIA, 1908, 138–39.

41. Some reports of student success were clearly exaggerated. Consider the report submitted by the agent for the Pueblo community, Acoma, New Mexico, region. By 1932, some 138 students had returned from off-reservation schools, almost all from Albuquerque or Santa Fe. Using evaluation categories of "good" and "poor," the agent rated all former students on two factors, their "standing in the "community" and their financial status. Incredibly, with the exception of a single student, who was classified as "unknown," all individuals received the classification of "good." As for occupation, all males were reportedly employed, most as farmers but a number as laborers and tradesmen. Females, not surprisingly, were almost all classified as housewives or housekeepers. See "Acomita Pueblo—Returned Students," Records of Southern Pueblo Agency, 1911–193535, DF 820.10–829, Box 146, OIA—Denver Branch.

42. Ahern, "The Returned Indians," 108; Gilcreast, "Richard Henry Pratt and American Indian Policy," 310; *Red Man,* March 1912 (reprint; New York: Johnson Reprint Corporation, 1971): 282–83; and LMC, 1909, 53–54.

43. IRA *Report,* 1890, 42–43. Also see Returned Student Survey, Bulletin no. 59, 29 April 1918, BIC, Reference Material, 1875–1933, Tray 121.

44. LMC, 1885, in ARSI, 1885, 851; and LMC, 1892, 45. Also see T. L. Riggs to Samuel Chapman Armstrong, 2 January 1883, reprinted in Armstrong, *The Indian Question,* 26–27; ARCIA, 1889, 334; ARCIA, 1892, 586; and Francis E. Leupp, "The Failure of the Educated American Indian," *Appelton's Magazine* 7 (May 1906): 595.

45. LMC, 1885, 852.

46. ARCIA, 1888, 262; Charles C. Painter, *A Plea for Enlarged School Work* (Philadelphia: Indian Rights Association, 1890), 4.

47. ARCIA, 1886, 101; ARCIA, 1889, 335; and *Proceedings and Addresses of the National Education Association,* 1885, 178. The issuance of certificates of competency in 1917 to students over twenty-one completing the full course of instruction was an attempt to link allotment with education. See ARCIA, 1917, 3–4, and ARCIA, 1918, 30–32.

48. ARSI, 1883, xi–xii; ARCIA, 1892, 28–31; and ARCIA, 1889, 337.

49. ARCIA, 1902, 13–15.

50. Ibid., and LMC, 1903, 118.

51. Harrison, *Latest Studies on Indian Reservations,* 149; Proceedings and Addresses of the National Education Association, 1903, 1047; and *Proceedings and Addresses of the National Education Association,* 1895, 84.

52. ARCIA, 1895, 6–7; ARCIA, 1896, 3–5, 351; ARCIA, 1888, xx–xxi; ARCIA, 1896, 351; ARCIA, 1897, 321–22; and LMC, 1897, 37. The movement to employ returned students in the school service was not welcomed in all quarters. See IRA *Report,* 1896, 71; Commissioner of Indian Affairs to Herbert Welsh, 16 February 1891, IRA; and Leupp, *The Indian and His Problem,* (New York: Charles Scribner's Sons, 1910), 111.

53. ARCIA, 1903, 377–78; ARCIA, 1905, 5; Trennert, *The Phoenix Indian School,* 141–42; and Robert A. Trennert, "Educating Indian Girls at Non-reservation Boarding Schools, 1878–1920," *Western Historical Quarterly* 13 (July 1982): 287–88.

54. ARCIA, 1886, 101; Valerie Sherer Mathes, "Nineteenth Century Women and Reform: The Women's National Indian Association," *American Indian Quarterly* 14 (Winter 1990): 11; and ARSI, 1885, 758.

55. Armstrong, *The Indian Question,* 30; *Southern Workman,* April 1897, 72; and Benjamin Brave to Cora Folsom, 10 June 1887, Student Records (Benjamin Brave), Indian Collection, HA.

56. ARCIA, 1897, 321; U.S. Office of Indian Affairs, *Rules for the Indian School Service, 1898* (Washington, D.C.: Government Printing Office, 1898), 33; and *Southern Workman,* December 1901, 704.

57. Benjamin Brave to Cora Folsom, 28 February 1893, Student Records (Benjamin Brave), Indian Collection, HA, and George Balenti to Richard H. Pratt, 1 December 1920, Pratt Papers, BRBML. The Pratt papers and student records at Hampton contain many such letters.

58. *Native American,* 18 April 1914, 211; *Native American,* 8 June 1912, 338; *Native American,* 31 May 1913, 329; *Native American,* 1 April 1916.

59. LMC, 1892, 44–51; ARCIA, 1892, 587–88; ARCIA, 1889, 335; and Returned Student Survey Bulletin, no. 57, 13 March 1918, 9–14, BIC, Reference Material, 1875–1933, Tray 121.

60. Harrison, *Latest Studies on Indian Reservations,* 150; and Richard H. Pratt to Fred Big Horse, 9 May 1893, Pratt Papers, BRBML. This is also a strong theme in the writings of Indian reformer Francis Campbell Sparhawk. See *Onoqua* (Boston: Lee and Shepard Publishers, 1892); "Home Again," *Red Man,* August 1889, 1–2; "After School Days," *Red Man,* November 1890, 5; and "The Indian's Yoke," *North American Review* 182 (January 1906): 50–61.

61. Returned Student Survey, 30 January 1917, 1–2, BIC, Reference Material, 1875–1933, Tray 121.

62. Ibid. and Returned Student Survey, Bulletin no. 57, 13 March 1918, 1, 8, BIC, Reference Material, 1875–1933, Tray 121.

63. Ahern, "The Returned Indians," 105.

64. Althea Bass, *The Arapaho Way: A Memoir of an Indian Boyhood* (New York: Clarkson N. Potter, 1966), 66, and Talayesva, *Sun Chief,* 134.

65. Returned Student Survey, 1916–1917, Bulletin no. 24, BIC, Reference Material, 1875–1933, Tray 121.

66. Ibid.

67. Ibid.

68. Ibid.

69. Ralph Linton, ed., *Acculturation in Seven American Indian Tribes* (New York: D. Appleton-Century, 1940), 468.

70. For the concept of cultural broker and the role of educated Indians in this regard, consult Margaret Connell Szasz, ed., *Between Indian and White Worlds: The Cultural Broker* (Norman: University of Oklahoma Press, 1994). In addition to the introduction and conclusion, see especially those articles by Szasz, Michael C. Coleman, and Donald J. Berthrong. Also Nancy L. Hagedorn, " 'A Friend to Go Between Them': The Interpreter as Cultural Broker During the Anglo-Iroquois Councils, 1740–1770," *Ethnohistory* 35 (Winter 1988): 60–80; Berthrong, "Struggle for Power: The Impact of Southern Cheyenne and Arapaho 'Schoolboys' on Tribal Politics," *American Indian Quarterly* 16 (Winter 1992): 1–24; and Coleman, *American Indian Children at School,* chap. 7.

71. See Frederick E. Hoxie, "Exploring a Cultural Borderland: Native American Journeys of Discovery in the Early Twentieth Century," *Journal of American History* 79 (December 1992): 987–90.

72. Robert L. Bee, *Patterns and Processes: An Introduction to Anthropologi-*

cal Strategies for the Study of Sociocultural Change (New York: Free Press, 1974), 105–6; Malcolm McFee, "The 150% Man, a Product of Blackfeet Acculturation," *American Anthropologist* 70 (December 1968): 1096–1107; J. Milton Yinger and George Eaton Simpson, "The Integration of Americans of Indian Descent," *Annals of American Academy of Political and Social Science* 436 (March 1978): 137–51; and James A. Clifton, "Alternate Identities and Cultural Frontiers," in Clifton, *Being and Becoming Indian: Biographical Studies of North American Frontiers* (Chicago: Dorsey Press, 1989), 29–30.

73. Albert Yava, *Big Falling Snow: A Tewa-Hopi Indian's Life and Times and the History and Traditions of His People,* ed. Harold Courlander (Albuquerque: University of New Mexico Press, 1978), 133.

74. Hensley wrote two brief autobiographies, and as H. David Brumble III has pointed out, each in a distinct mode: one in the tradition of the "Peyote Conversion Narrative," the other as a "Carlisle Success Story," suggesting that Hensley's identity was actually a compilation of the two selves. The reconstruction of Hensley's life above is based on both autobiographies, which are reprinted in full in Brumble, *American Indian Autobiography* (Berkeley: University of California Press, 1988), chap. 7. Also see Brumble, "Albert Hensley's Two Autobiographies and the History of American Indian Autobiography," *American Quarterly* 37 (Winter 1985): 702–18.

75. Omer C. Stewart, *Peyote Religion: A History* (Norman: University of Oklahoma Press, 1987), esp. 91–92, 150–54, and Weston LaBarre, *The Peyote Cult* (New York: Schocken Books, 1969), 57–92, Appendix 8.

76. For Hensley's leadership among the Winnebago peyotists and his remarks in defense of peyote see Stewart, *Peyote Religion,* 152–57. Also Paul Radin, *The Winnebago Tribe* (1923; reprint, Lincoln: University of Nebraska Press, 1970), 373.

77. House Subcommittee of the Committee on Indian Affairs, *Peyote,* Hearings on H.R. 2614, pt. 1, 21–25 February, and pt. 2, 23 March, 67th Cong., 2nd sess., 1918. For background on the effort to outlaw peyote, see Stewart, *Peyote Religion,* chap. 8.

78. House Subcommittee of the Committee on Indian Affairs, *Peyote,* 68.

CHAPTER TEN. POLICY

1. ARCIA, 1901, 3–4.

2. Ibid., 2–3, 5.

3. Apparently Herbert Welsh appointed Leupp as Washington agent for the Indian Rights Association partly at the urging of Roosevelt. See Theodore Roosevelt to Herbert Welsh, 23 January 1895, IRA. For background material on Leupp see Donald L. Parman, "Francis Ellington Leupp," in *The Commissioners of Indian Affairs, 1824–1977,* ed. Robert M. Kvasnicka and Herman J. Viola (Lincoln: University of Nebraska Press, 1979), 221–32, and Necah Furman, "Seedtime for Indian Reform: An Evaluation of the Administration of Commissioner Francis Ellington Leupp," *Red River Valley Historical Review* 2 (Winter 1975): 495–517.

4. ARCIA, 1905, 2.

5. Francis Paul Prucha, *The Great Father: The United States Government and the American Indians,* 2 vols. (Lincoln: University of Nebraska Press, 1984), 2:764–66, 772–74; Frederick E. Hoxie, *A Final Promise: The Campaign to Assim-*

ilate the Indians, 1880–1920 (Lincoln: University of Nebraska Press, 1984), chaps. 4–8.

6. ARCIA, 1903, 4.

7. Francis E. Leupp, "The Failure of the Educated American Indian," *Appelton's Magazine* 7 (May 1906): 597; Leupp, *Notes of a Summer Tour Among the Indians of the Southwest* (Philadelphia: Indian Rights Association, 1897), 24; ARCIA, 1905, 6–8; and ARCIA, 1907, 21. Also see Leupp, "Outlines of an Indian Policy," *Outlook* 79 (15 April 1905): 949; Leupp, "Put Yourself in His Place," *Southern Workman,* November 1900, 620; and Leupp, *The Indian and His Problem* (New York: Charles Scribner's Sons, 1910), 135.

8. *Proceedings and Addresses of the National Education Association,* 1902, 861–62; *Proceedings and Addresses of the National Education Association,* 1904, 984. Also Returned Student Survey, 1916–1917, 187, Bulletin no. 24, BIC, Reference Material, 1875–1933, Tray 121; ARCIA, 1899, 240; and ARCIA, 1905, 249.

9. See Hoxie, *A Final Promise,* chap. 4; Robert F. Berkhofer, Jr., *The White Man's Indians: Images of the American Indian from Columbus to the Present* (New York: Alfred A. Knopf, 1978), 59–60; and George W. Stocking, *Race, Culture, and Evolution: Essays in the History of Anthropology* (New York: Free Press, 1968), chap. 6.

10. *Proceedings and Addresses of the National Education Association,* 1909, 932. Also E. C. Rowe, "Five Hundred Forty-Seven White and Two Hundred Sixty-Eight Indian Children Tested by the Binet-Simon Tests," *Pedagogical Seminary* 21 (September 1914): 454–68.

11. Returned Student Survey, 1916–1917, 72, Bulletin no. 24, BIC, Reference Material, 1875–1933, Tray 121. The Indian Bureau's summary of field opinions includes these comments: "Heredity plays a most important part on the lapses of returned students according to a large group of superintendents but it is noticeable that heredity is offered as an excuse for failures rather than a cause. Many writers cite the centuries of evolution required to produce the white man of today and pertinently inquire if it is fair to insist that the Indian in thirty years should reach the stage of development which it took over fifteen hundred years for the white men to attain." Returned Student Survey, 30 January 1917, 9, BIC, Reference Material, 1875–1933, Tray 121. Also see Estelle Reel's comments on Indian inferiority as quoted in K. Bianina Lomawaima, *They Called It Prairie Light: The Story of Chilocco Indian School* (Lincoln: University of Nebraska Press, 1994), 93.

12. ARCIA, 1901, 2; Leupp, *The Indian and His Problem,* 137; and Returned Student Survey, Bulletin no. 57, 13 March 1918, 5–7, BIC, Reference Material, 1875–1933, Tray 121.

13. Hamlin Garland, "The Red Man's Present Needs," *North American Review* 174 (April 1902): 483–84, and Charles F. Lummis, "A New Indian Policy," *Land of Sunshine* 15 (December 1901): 463. Lummis was an ardent critic of boarding schools. See "My Brother's Keeper," *Land of Sunshine* 11 (August 1899): 139–47; (September 1899): 207–13; (October 1899): 263–67; (November 1899): 333–35; 12 (December 1899): 28–30; (January 1900): 90–94; and (February 1900): 178–80. See also Lummis, *Bullying the Moqui,* ed. Robert Easton and MacKenzie Brown (Prescott, Ariz.: Prescott College Press, 1968).

14. See Dexter Fisher, "Zitkala-Sa: The Evolution of a Writer," *American Indian Quarterly* 5 (August 1979): 229–38.

15. Zitkala-Sa (Gertrude Bonnin), "Impressions of an Indian Childhood," *Atlantic Monthly* 85 (January 1900): 37–47.

16. *Atlantic Monthly* 85 (February 1900): 185–93.

17. Ibid.

18. *Atlantic Monthly* 85 (March 1900): 381–86.

19. *Proceedings and Addresses of the National Education Association,* 1908, 1163; John Dewey, "My Pedagogic Creed," (1897), reprinted in *Dewey on Education,* ed. Martin S. Dworkin (New York: Teachers College Press, 1959), 22–23; and Dewey, *The School and Society* (1899), reprinted in *Dewey on Education,* 42–43.

20. *Proceedings and Addresses of the National Education Association,* 1904, 443–44; *Proceedings and Addresses of the National Education Association,* 1903, 1056; and Dewey, *Democracy and Education* (1916; reprint, New York: Free Press, 1966), 36–37.

21. ARCIA, 1905, 8. Also Leupp, "Back to Nature for the Indian," *Charities and the Commons* 20 (6 June 1908): 340.

22. ARCIA, 1901, 13, and Laurence F. Schmeckebier, *The Office of Indian Affairs* (Baltimore: Johns Hopkins University Press, 1927), 217–22.

23. ARCIA, 1905, 3; Leupp, "Outlines of an Indian Policy," 949; and Leupp, "The Failure of the Educated American Indian," 601–2.

24. ARCIA, 1892, 617; and ARCIA, 1897, 334. For a different interpretation see Hoxie, *A Final Promise,* chap. 6, and Hoxie, "Redefining Indian Education: Thomas J. Morgan's Program in Disarray," *Arizona and the West* 24 (Spring 1982): 5–18.

25. ARCIA, 1897, 329.

26. Education Circular no. 175, 3 December 1907, OIA. and ARCIA, 1905, 12–13. For Indian stories cited see *Indian Leader,* October 1914, 7–10; *Indian Leader,* March 1915, 16; *Indian Leader,* April 1915, 8; and *Indian Leader,* May 1915, 6–7, 15. Also see *Indian Legends and Superstitions, as Told by Pupils of Haskell Institute* (Lawrence, Kans.: Haskell Institute, 1913).

27. ARCIA, 1905, 12, 395–97. Also, Robert A. Trennert, *The Phoenix Indian School: Forced Assimilation in Arizona, 1891–1935* (Norman: University of Oklahoma Press, 1988), 109–10, and Carmelita S. Ryan, "The Carlisle Indian Industrial School" (Ph.D. dissertation, Georgetown University, 1962), 137–38.

28. ARCIA, 1905, 10–13, 395–97; Leupp, "The Failure of the Educated American Indian," 599; Leupp, "Back to Nature for the Indian," 339; and Leupp, "The Story of Four Strenuous Years," *Outlook* 92 (5 June 1909): 331.

29. *Indian Legends and Superstitions,* 5.

30. ARCIA, 1907, 17–20; Leupp, *The Indian and His Problem,* 135, 147–48; and Leupp, "The Story of Four Strenuous Years," 330. Also see ARSI, 1905, 23.

31. ARCIA, 1907, 22–24, and ARCIA, 1908, 23–25. Support for the day school began building during the Jones administration. At a summer conference of Indian educators sponsored by the Indian Office, the following resolution drew wide support from participants: "Resolved, that the reservation day school should be made the prime factor in Indian education." See ARCIA, 1901, 467–68, and ARCIA, 1903, 5.

32. See Irving G. Hendrick, "The Federal Campaign for the Admission of Indian Children into Public Schools, 1890–1934," *American Indian Culture and Research Journal* 5 (1981): 13–32; Hoxie, *A Final Promise,* 66–67, 203–9; and Prucha, *The Great Father,* 2: 823–25.

33. ARCIA, 1897, 5–6, and ARCIA, 1916, 24.

34. ARCIA, 1900, 23; ARCIA, 1905, 50; ARCIA, 1910, 164; ARCIA, 1915, 169; ARCIA, 1920, 156; and ARCIA, 1925, 51.

35. ARCIA, 1925, 6, 51; ARCIA, 1924, 6; ARCIA, 1926, 7; and ARCIA, 1921, 13.

For a discussion of white opposition to integrating Indians in public schools as well as discriminatory school policies, see Hoxie, *The Final Promise*, 208–9, 234–35.

36. Richard H. Pratt to Henry L. Dawes, 29 March 1898, Pratt Papers, BRBML. For an excellent overview of Pratt's differences with reformers see Everett Arthur Gilcreast, "Richard Henry Pratt and American Indian Policy, 1877–1906: A Study of the Assimilation Movement" (Ph.D. dissertation, Yale University, 1967), chapter 6.

37. *Red Man,* June-July 1892, 1; Herbert Welsh to Editor of the *Red Man,* 2 July 1892, IRA; Richard H. Pratt to Herbert Welsh, 13 July 1892, IRA; and Herbert Welsh to Charles Painter, 18 July 1892, IRA.

38. Francis E. Leupp to Herbert Welsh, 30 October 1896, IRA; Herbert Welsh to Francis E. Leupp, 31 October 1896, IRA; Francis E. Leupp to Herbert Welsh, 9 November 1896, IRA; Herbert Welsh to Francis E. Leupp, 16 November 1896, IRA; and Francis E. Leupp to Herbert Welsh, 25 November 1896, IRA.

39. *Red Man,* January 1897, 2, 1.

40. Francis E. Leupp, *Indian School Management* (Philadelphia: Indian Rights Association, 1897); and N. Dubois Miller, Charles E. Pancoast, and Charles F. Jenkins, *The Importance of Retaining Dr. Hailmann, Superintendent of Indian Schools, and the Attack Made Upon Him and the Indian Rights Association by Captain Pratt* (Philadelphia: Indian Rights Association, 1897). For the correspondence surrounding these developments see William Hailmann to Herbert Welsh, 28 January 1897, IRA; Francis E. Leupp to Herbert Welsh, 28 January 1897, IRA; Herbert Welsh to William Hailmann, 29 January 1897, IRA; Herbert Welsh to William Hailmann, 4 February 1897, IRA; William Hailmann to Herbert Welsh, 6 February 1897, IRA; Francis E. Leupp to Herbert Welsh, 8 February 1897, IRA; and William Hailmann to Herbert Welsh, 9 February 1897, IRA.

41. In early 1903, when Pratt was informed by the War Department that he was being retired from the military, he immediately resigned as superintendent. Urged by Commissioner William Jones to stay on, apparently after some pressure from Pratt's friends, he resumed the superintendency. See Merrill E. Gates to Richard H. Pratt, 26 February 1903, Pratt Papers, BRBML; Merrill E. Gates to Richard H. Pratt, 11 March 1903, Pratt Papers, BRBML; and Merrill E. Gates to Richard H. Pratt, 5 March 1903, Pratt Papers, BRBML.

42. *Red Man and Helper,* 13 May 1904, 1, 4. Before departing, Pratt launched yet another attack on the Indian Bureau in *Red Man and Helper,* 24 June and 1 July, 1904, 47, 48.

43. Ryan, "The Carlisle Indian Industrial School," 211–21.

44. Hearings before the Joint Commission of the Congress of the United States to Investigate Indian Affairs, *Carlisle Indian School,* 63 Cong., 2nd sess., 1914. Linnen's report is reprinted in the commission report.

45. Ibid., 1027–28, 1335–36, 1376–78, 1388.

46. On 21 March 1914, approximately a month after Linnen's investigation, fifty-five boys of the Athletic Association sent a letter to Commissioner Sells requesting that Warner be removed. At the top of the nine reasons given was that Warner "possesses a weak moral character." Hearings, *Carlisle Indian School,* 1335, 1340–43, 1386. Also Reet A. Howell and Maxwell L. Howell, "The Myth of 'Pop Warner': Carlisle Revisited," *Quest* 30 (Summer 1978): 19–27.

47. Hearings, *Carlisle Indian School,* 1101–2, 1195–98, 1243–46, 1334–35, 1349–50, 1377, 1385, 1389.

48. Ibid., 1379–80, 1388–90; Oscar Lipps to Richard Pratt, 13 January 1916, Pratt Papers, BRBML; and ARCIA, 1918, 32–33.

49. *Indian Leader,* 27 September 1918, 3. Also IRA *Report,* 1918, 8.

50. Joseph Willard Tingey, "Indians and Blacks Together: An Experiment in Biracial Education at Hampton Institute, 1878–1923" (Ed.D. dissertation, Columbia University Teachers College, 1978), chap. 12, and Donal Fred Lindsey, "Indian Education at Hampton Institute, 1877–1923" (Ph.D. dissertation, Kent State University, 1989), chap. 8.

51. David Wallace Adams, "Education in Hues: Red and Black at Hampton Institute, 1878–1893," *South Atlantic Quarterly* 76 (Spring 1977): 161–72; Tingey, "Indians and Blacks Together," chaps. 5 and 7; Lindsey, "Indian Education at Hampton Institute," chaps. 3–6; and Robert Francis Engs, "Red, Black, and White: A Study of Intellectual Inequality," in *Region, Race, and Reconstruction: Essays in Honor of C. Vann Woodward,* ed. James M. McPherson and J. Morgan Kouss (New York: Oxford University Press, 1982), 241–65.

52. *Congressional Record,* 62nd Cong., 2nd sess., 1912, 48, pt. 5: 4456–59. The heightened racism of the era is examined in C. Vann Woodward, *The Strange Career of Jim Crow* (New York: Oxford University Press, 1955), chap. 3; George M. Fredrickson, *The Black Image in the White Mind: The Debate on Afro-American Character and Destiny, 1817–1914* (New York: Harper and Row, 1971), esp. chap. 9; and Joel Williamson, *The Crucible of Race: Black-White Relations in the American South Since Emancipation* (New York: Oxford University Press, 1984), pt. 2.

53. Hollis Frissell to Members of the Senate and House Committee on Indian Affairs, 8 February 1912, Frissell Papers, HA; Hollis Frissell to Charles Carter, 10 May 1912, Frissell Papers, HA; Booker T. Washington to Hollis Frissell, 4 May 1912, Frissell Papers, HA; Booker T. Washington to Hollis Frissell, 18 May 1912, Frissell Papers; and Student petition to U.S. Senate, 23 April 1912, correspondence regarding appropriations for Indian students at Hampton, HA.

54. Daniel Stephens to Booker T. Washington, 4 May 1912, correspondence regarding appropriations for Indian Students at Hampton, HA; J. D. Post to Booker T. Washington, 1 May 1912, enclosed in Booker T. Washington to Hollis Frissell, 4 May 1912, Frissell Papers, HA; and Charles Carter to Hollis Frissell, 11 May 1912, correspondence regarding appropriations for Indian students at Hampton, HA.

55. Booker T. Washington, *Up from Slavery* (1901; reprint, New York: Doubleday, 1928), 102.

56. *Southern Workman,* June 1918, 186.

57. For an overview of Indian policy during this period see Prucha, *The Great Father,* vol. 2, chap. 21; and Randolph C. Downes, "A Crusade for Indian Reform, 1922–1934," *Mississippi Valley Historical Review* 32 (December 1945): 331–54.

58. A key source for Collier's early life and social outlook is his memoirs, *From Every Zenith* (Denver: Sage Books, 1963), chaps. 1–5. Also see Lawrence C. Kelly, *The Assault on Assimilation: John Collier and the Origins of Indian Policy Reform* (Albuquerque: University of New Mexico Press, 1983), chap. 1; Kenneth R. Philp, *John Collier's Crusade for Indian Reform, 1920–1954* (Tucson: University of Arizona Press, 1977), 9–10; and Frederick J. Stefon, "The Indians' Zarathustra: An Investigation into the Philosophical Roots of John Collier's New Deal Educational and Administrative Policies," *Journal of Ethnic Studies* 11 (Fall 1983): 1–28, (Winter 1984): 28–45.

59. Collier, *From Every Zenith,* chaps. 6–9; Kelly, *The Assault on Assimilation,* chaps. 2–3; Philp, *John Collier's Crusade for Indian Reform,* 10–25.

60. Collier, *From Every Zenith,* 126, 123.

61. For Collier's reform activities during this period see Collier, *From Every Zenith,* chaps. 10–13; Kelly, *The Assault on Assimilation,* chaps. 7–10; and Philp,

John Collier's Crusade for Indian Reform, chaps. 2–4. For Collier's criticism of Indian educational policies see "The Red Atlantis," *Survey* 48 (October 1922): 19; "Our Indian Policy," *Sunset Magazine* 50 (March 1923): 89–90; and "America's Treatment of Her Indians," *Current History* 18 (August 1923): 773–80.

62. For background on the Meriam Report see Prucha, *The Great Father,* 2: 806–13; Donald T. Critchlow, "Lewis Meriam, Expertise, and Indian Reform," *Historian* 43 (May 1981): 325–44; Margaret Szasz, *Education and the American Indian: The Road to Self-Determination, 1928–1973* (Albuquerque: University of New Mexico Press, 1974), 16–24; and Institute for Government Research, *The Problem of Indian Administration* (Baltimore: Johns Hopkins University Press, 1928), chap. 3.

63. Institute for Government Research, *The Problem of Indian Administration,* chap. 1.

64. Ibid., 11–14, 33–34, 314–40, 351, 370–74.

65. Ibid., 32–33, 35, 346–47, 411–16.

66. Ibid., 87–88.

INDEX